THE
EDUCATIONAL
IMAGINATION

THE
EDUCATIONAL
IMAGINATION

On the Design and Evaluation of School Programs

THIRD EDITION

ELLIOT W. EISNER

Stanford University

Merrill
Prentice Hall

Upper Saddle River, New Jersey
Columbus, Ohio

KH

Library of Congress Cataloging in Publication Data
Eisner, Elliot W.
 The educational imagination : on the design and evaluation of school programs / Elliot W. Eisner.—3rd ed.
  p. cm.
 Includes bibliographical references and index.
 ISBN 0-13-094287-1 (pbk.)
  1. Curriculum planning—United States. 2. Education—Aims and objectives—United States. 3. Curriculum evaluation. 4. Curriculum change—United States. I. Title.
LB1570.E4254 2002
375'.001—dc21

                2001042749

Vice President and Publisher: Jeffery W. Johnston
Executive Editor: Debra A. Stollenwerk
Production Editor: Linda Hillis Bayma
Design Coordinator: Diane C. Lorenzo
Cover Designer: Thomas Borah
Cover Photos: Corbis
Production Manager: Pamela D. Bennett
Director of Marketing: Kevin Flanagan
Marketing Manager: Amy June
Marketing Coordinator: Barbara Koontz

This book was set in New Baskerville by Prentice Hall. It was printed and bound by R. R. Donnelley & Sons Company. The cover was printed by Phoenix Color Corp.

Pearson Education Ltd., *London*
Pearson Education Australia Pty. Limited, *Sydney*
Pearson Education Singapore Pte. Ltd.
Pearson Education North Asia Ltd., *Hong Kong*
Pearson Education Canada, Ltd., *Toronto*
Pearson Educación de Mexico, S. A. de C. V., *Mexico*
Pearson Education–Japan, Inc., *Tokyo*
Pearson Education Malaysia Pte. Ltd.
Pearson Education, *Upper Saddle River, New Jersey*

Merrill
Prentice Hall

10 9 8 7 6 5 4 3
ISBN: 0-13-027153-5

10/25/04

PREFACE

The third edition of *The Educational Imagination* emerges in the midst of a fresh new national effort at educational reform. Past efforts have been less than successful. Will the current effort with its emphasis on national goals and measured achievement, on national standards and public report cards, on national curriculum frameworks and national teacher certification standards do the trick or will this reform effort echo the failed efforts of the past?

The Educational Imagination explores the current state of American education and provides a historical view of earlier efforts to reform our schools. It describes the ideological positions of those who wish to shape the aims and content of school programs in ways that reflect their values. It examines an array of important concepts used in the process of curriculum development and it often questions the premises on which these concepts rest. The major aim of this book is to make problematic what is often taken for granted either because of tradition or because of the attractiveness of new bandwagons rolling down the educational road. Educators, I believe, have a special responsibility to critique prevailing assumptions and proposed practices. To do this well requires a healthy intellectual skepticism, a propensity for critique, and an instructional memory. We need to be able to put new proposals for school improvement into a historical context if we are not to become new Columbuses rediscovering an old world that doesn't work. *The Educational Imagination* provides some of this context.

If there is one idea that permeates these pages, it is the belief that no single educational program is appropriate for all children, everywhere, forever. Which educational values are appropriate for children and adolescents depends on the characteristics of those the program is designed to serve, the features of the context in which they live, and the values that they and the community embrace. Further, these values and this context itself is likely to change over time. Looked at this way, the practice of education is a dynamic one, subject to change over time. This means that educators cannot rest with fixed solutions to educational problems or with "breakthroughs" that once and for all define or prescribe how and what should be done. Ours is a practical enterprise, and practical enterprises elude fixed solutions.

A word about some of the new features of the third edition of *The Educational Imagination*. A new first chapter addresses the current climate and prevailing policy impacting American schools. These policies rest on premises that deserve careful scrutiny by thoughtful educators. You will find serious questions raised about these policies in Chapter 1. The third edition also includes a major replacement of the second edition's chapter on orientations to curriculum. The new chapter, "Curriculum Ideologies," is a modified version of a chapter that was prepared for *The Handbook of Research on Curriculum*. I have included this chapter because I believe it addresses the issues more broadly, more deeply, and more adequately.

A new chapter on assessment has been added to the third edition. The concept of assessment is new in American educational discourse. It represents an effort to develop fresh ways of thinking about what has been historically regarded as "evaluation." The historical background of this development and its implications for practice are examined in this new chapter. In addition to the foregoing, a new example of an educational criticism written by Mary Burchenal has been added to the collection included in the previous edition. This new addition addresses the teaching of English and provides a fine illustration of the kind of writing that can shed light on the subtleties and dilemmas of teaching at the high school level.

Finally, numerous small changes were made in virtually all of the chapters, some of fact, others to clarify what was written.

ACKNOWLEDGMENTS

I wish to express my thanks to the five individuals who gave me permission to include their work in this volume. Lorna Catford, Barbara Porro, and Mary Burchenal were graduate students at Stanford who worked with me. Tom Barone, who also worked with me at Stanford, is now an Associate Professor of Education at Arizona State University. Stuart Cohen is Professor of Educational Psychology at Purdue University. All of these individuals have added much to the current edition. I am grateful to them.

I also want to express my appreciation to Valerie J. Janesick, University of Kansas, and Edmund C. Short, The Pennsylvania State University, for their insightful reviews of the text.

I also wish to thank Debbie Stollenwerk, my supportive and patient editor at Merrill. And, as always, I want to acknowledge the contributions of my wife, Ellie, who never fails to provide the love and the conditions that make it possible for me to get my work done.

Elliot W. Eisner
Stanford University

CONTENTS

1

Schooling in America: Where Are We Heading?

"The road to hell is paved with good intentions."

Those of us professionally engaged in education live in interesting times. Never during this century has concern about the quality of our schools been so acute or the proposals for reform so strident. We are told almost daily that American public education is a disaster area. Students graduate from our high schools barely able to read; they are said to lack the rudimentary skills needed to be productively employable; they do not possess the habits and attitudes that America needs to regain its competitive edge in a world economy. In fact, a national report—*A Nation at Risk,* published in 1983 by the National Commission on Excellence in Education—claimed that an invading army could not do more damage to our country than our schools have already done. *America 2000* (U.S. Department of Education, 1991), another major reform document, says things have not improved. From almost every quarter, the verdict is clear: American students fail to meet even minimal standards of academic achievement, and so too have our schools.

Are things as bad as portrayed? How can we find out? What evidence counts? Are all our schools failing, or only some? And what does failing mean? What really counts in education and are there ways to determine if what really counts is being achieved? Indeed, how should we think about the functions of our schools, their practices, the kinds of programs they ought to provide, and how might we determine if they are educationally effective? Students of education must move beyond the rhetoric of reform

1

and the use of alarmist language about the state of schooling to penetrate more deeply, more analytically, into the factors that influence the state of our schools. The mass media seldom address complexity, make fine-grained distinctions, or deal with nuance. The media function more like meat cleavers; they deliver short, sharp blows, separating one part of the bone from another—a kind of either/or on the butcher's block.

Such sharp, quick separations will not do justice either to our children or to the teachers and school administrators who work with them. They certainly will fall short of the kind of careful reflection and analysis needed to understand schools as complex social institutions influenced by and influencing the socioeconomic environment in which they function. This book is intended to lead to a deeper conversation about education, not only about schools, but also about the processes of education in general. It is designed to provide a perspective on the development of schooling in America, on its shifting aims, on the kind of programs that can be created for them, and on the ways in which such programs can be assessed.

The Educational Imagination provides no formulas for effective teaching, nor does it offer recipes for producing programs. You will not find on its pages a list describing "what works," as if what works works for everyone in all places, forever. The process of education always occurs within a context and decisions about educational practices need to be sensitive to that context. What *The Educational Imagination* does provide are tools for thinking about the issues that beset schools; it describes options that can be considered, the ways in which, for example, the practice of educational evaluation can be undertaken. In short, *The Educational Imagination* is a book that provides food for thought about the means and ends of education so that the analysis of schooling and the issues that practitioners and policymakers confront can be probed more deeply. Put more simply, *The Educational Imagination* attempts to deepen the discourse and provide some ways of doing sophisticated analytical work on the aims, structure, and process of schooling.

Just what are the charges leveled against American schools? And what solutions are being proposed? One of the major charges is that American schools are not doing as well as they once were. Many believe we are in a state of decline. Students, many say, are not meeting expected levels of academic achievement and, as a result, our competitive position in an economic arms race is being weakened. Critics claim that the quality of our schools is intimately related to the strength of our economy.

Critics also charge that American schools have failed to keep students from dropping out of school. The dropout rate—about 25% overall—is regarded as prima facie evidence that schools are ineffective, boring, and unable to engage students in meaningful learning. Students, they claim, are voting with their feet and, given the exodus, our schools have lost the election.

Critics claim further that American schools are too expensive (Berliner, 1992). They say that money will not solve educational problems. Other solutions (which I will identify later) are needed. According to some critics, we are paying for more but getting less.

The evidence that is used to support these claims comes from a wide variety of sources: business people who complain that high school graduates—even some college students—lack basic skills. They cannot write a simple sentence without making errors in spelling, grammar, and punctuation. Others point to the decline in scores on the Scholastic Aptitude Test, a decline of 36 points in the verbal section for college bound seniors from 1966 to 1986 and 28 points in the math section for the same period (College Entrance Examination Board, 1989). Other critics point to the low national ranking of American students among the students of other nations on international comparisons of academic achievement in mathematics. The evidence, critics say, abounds and the failed reform efforts of the recent past require more drastic action today. In the words of one critic, "We must take charge" (Finn, 1991).

The "we" that Chester Finn refers to are not members of the education profession. The profession, according to Finn, has failed. The general public has to take charge. Given our dismal educational history, it's time to turn over the reins to others.

And what about solutions? If the problems are as real and as severe as critics claim, how do they propose to solve them? What are the cures for our educational ills?

One array of solutions is found in *America 2000* (U.S. Department of Education, 1991), the 1990 federally initiated educational reform package. According to then President Bush, America needs an educational renaissance or, as *Time* magazine puts it, "Schools need a revolution in search of a miracle." *America 2000* provides an agenda for change that has several major "parts." Its introduction states, *"America 2000* is a long-term strategy to help make this land all that it should be—a nine year crusade to move us toward the six ambitious national goals that the President and the governors adopted in 1990 to close our skills-and-knowledge gap."

One part of the plan is to provide a set of goals for American schools, destinations we must reach by the year 2000. According to the critics, one reason schools have failed is that until now we didn't have national goals for education. Once we have them, the argument goes, we will know where we are headed and, what's even more important, we will be able to determine if the goals are being achieved. Its six major goals are intended to guide the educational destinies of 110,000 schools serving a student population of 46 million students. Interestingly, how one can have a renaissance without the fine arts is something that is not altogether clear, but the fine arts are nowhere to be found in the "ambitious national goals" for American schools proposed in *America 2000*. It was only after major lobbying by those who think that the arts are an important addition to students' educational lives that the arts were included; in some ways, as a reluctant afterthought.

Once goals are formulated and, in general terms, *America 2000* provides them, the next task is to create an assessment system to determine if the goals have been achieved. Without assessment, goals remain, it is claimed, empty aspirations. And once having an assessment system in place, there needs to be standards for each domain being assessed so that it is possible to determine if levels of student performance are adequate. The measures provide the information and the standards provide the bases for determining the adequacy of student performance.

Although the measurement of student performance through something called "The American Achievement Test" is necessary for getting information, and standards are necessary for judging the adequacy of the performance, neither ensure that the American public will know the results of student performance. To address this need, *America 2000* proposes the use of a national report card that displays the achievement scores of students, presumably by school, district, and state. The plan proposed is quite rational. First, goals are defined, then subgoals for each subject field are formulated, then an assessment system is constructed that is related to those goals and subgoals. Following this, standards for each subject are created so the scores can be interpreted and appraised. Finally, a display system is put into place—the public report card—so that information about the effectiveness of schools can be made available to the American public.

There is, of course, a major dimension of schooling absent from the approach to reform I have just described; so far, no mention has been made of the curriculum. It makes little sense to develop an assessment system and define standards through which comparisons among students can be made if one does not have a common program for students. If students are given differing amounts of time in school to study particular subjects, or if the content and aims of a particular subject—say social studies—differ among schools, or if a school district promotes curricular innovation, say, it encourages teachers to develop integrated curricula, the meaningfulness of comparisons among students in different programs becomes problematic. How does one make valid comparisons among students in programs that differ in content and in aims?

Yet, there is no single, legitimate version of social studies education or even mathematics education. There is no one right version of the sciences. There are not only many ways to teach and learn in these fields, there are also different educational aims that can be legitimately employed for each. What does such diversity mean for assessment and for accountability? Will meaningful comparisons be possible without some significant degree of uniformity in content, aims, and time for instruction? Is a common standardized curriculum appropriate for a nation with 45 million students attending

110,000 schools in which 2½ million teachers work? And what about local control? We have 16,000 school districts in America and a tradition that puts a premium on community decision making regarding many, if not all, aspects of schooling. Is a one-size-fits-all curriculum desirable in a nation as diverse as ours? Is it reasonable within a framework that encourages teachers to become genuine stakeholders in the schools, to reflect and to innovate, to take educational risks in pursuit of better teaching methods and new forms of learning, to impose a uniform set of standards and assessment practices? Put another way, how does one reconcile an image of a teaching profession committed to the promotion of creativity in teaching with an image of accountability so closely tied to standardized outcomes?

But these are not the only complications. We know that children come to school with very different backgrounds. Is it reasonable to expect students whose prior experience differs significantly from the forms of life and the sorts of values that schools typically embrace to be compared with children whose backgrounds give them a huge head start? In a race, equity requires that all of the runners have a place on the same start line. Can we claim that all our children begin the race at the same place?

But even if all children started at the same place (which they do not), the schools they attend may differ significantly with respect to the resources available to teachers and children. Jonathan Kozol (1991) describes these inequities this way:

> If the New York City schools were funded, for example, at the level of the highest-spending suburbs of Long Island, a fourth grade class of 36 children such as those I visited in District 10 would have had $200,000 more invested in their education during 1987. Although a portion of this extra money would have gone to administrative costs, the remainder would have been enough to hire two extraordinary teachers at enticing salaries of $50,000 each, divide the class into *two* classes of some 18 children each, provide them with computers, carpets, air conditioning, new texts and reference books and learning games—indeed, with everything available today in the most affluent school districts—and also pay the costs of extra counseling to help those children cope with the dilemmas that they face at home. Even the most skeptical detractor of "the worth of spending further money in the public schools" would hesitate, I think, to face a grade-school principal in the South Bronx and try to tell her this "wouldn't make much difference." (pp. 123–124)

Kozol reminds us that those whose backgrounds are least congruent with the tasks that schools expect children to address and the values the school holds dear also tend to go to schools most depleted in the resources teachers need to teach well and students need to achieve well. Is it fair to hold teachers and students accountable for achieving common outcomes in the face of such "savage inequities"? What will such inequities mean for the children?

Making meaningful comparisons among students or holding teachers accountable for the achievement of nationally prescribed educational goals defined with respect to standards to be attained runs into several difficulties, regardless of how rational the original plan appeared. First, the plan is predicated on the belief that it is possible *and* desirable to develop a national program for American schools; local values and regional differences are apparently not regarded as important. Second, it supposes that meaningful comparisons can be made among children coming from very different communities and having very different backgrounds. This supposition disregards the experiential advantages that well-to-do parents provide their children that children of the poor never receive. Third, it supposes that schools as institutions are comparable. Yet, we know that there are vast differences in resources between an Andover Academy or a New Trier Township High School and schools in rural areas of the country or those serving poor children of color within the inner-cities. Might we not be better served talking about standards for schools rather than standards for the academic performance of children? I wonder.

My aim in focusing on *America 2000* is not only to call into question the premises and prescriptions of the major educational reform effort of the 1990s but, even more, to illustrate the importance of examining assumptions behind educational policy. My aim is to provide a brief critique of a program that has been widely disseminated and broadly accepted by an American public concerned about its schools. If those of us in education have neither the skill nor the appetite to examine such programs, who will? Some trains are better left unboarded. Put another way, I believe it is imperative for students of education—teachers, school administrators, those who teach at the university level, and those who make or implement educational policy—to have both the historical perspective and the conceptual and analytic skills to do what laypeople cannot do as well. My aim in this book is to contribute to the development of those skills.

One might well ask why smart people in high places would fail to appreciate the complexity of meaningful educational reform. Why are they so attracted to superficial "solutions" that turn out to be nonsolutions? One reason, I think, is that complexity is difficult to sell politically. Simple solutions are more appealing. To acknowledge the complexity of competing values, regional differences, inequities among school resources, cognitive and stylistic differences among children, and the like is to create an untidy picture. Untidy pictures do not lend themselves to simple solutions.

Second, there is a feeling of desperation among some regarding the state of American education. It's almost as though some have given up on those working within the field of education. So many reform efforts have failed; it must be due to the incompetence of teachers or the inertia of school administrators. The solution: We must take charge.

A third reason is endemic to the policymakers themselves who do not see and therefore do not know the people their policies affect. For those who occupy the statehouse or the White House, or who sit in state and federal legislatures, fourth-graders are fourth-graders, a middle school is a middle school: If you've seen one redwood, you've seem them all. Distance breeds generalizations, and generalizations yield broad categories that provide little place for particulars. Thus, the unique needs of particular individuals, constituencies, and circumstances are unnoticed and because they are unnoticed, they are neglected in educational policy. Policies, by definition are general, not particular. Indeed, a policy that made it possible for each particular to be addressed on its own terms would be no policy at all.

There is a fourth reason as well. When a public loses confidence in a group to get a job done, it reduces the group's discretionary space and prescribes solutions it believes will work. It then monitors the performance of those who are to implement policy and measures the outcomes of the work that they do. By prescribing goals and methods and measuring student performance, the profession becomes *accountable*. Standardization is thought to reduce ambiguity and uncertainty. The aim is to create an efficient and effective system that will produce the results desired. At last, as the saying goes, the public will get what it paid for.

There is no doubt that technicist approaches to the management of complex systems have great appeal. In some situations, especially those in which the raw materials with which one works harbor no intentions, have no aspirations, do not daydream—the leather or steel used in the production of shoes or jet engines, for example—such methods can bring about a systematically efficient system. Because the material on which workers labor is also standardized, the worker on the assembly line or behind a teller's window requires little in the way of discretionary space. Complex judgments are not usually called for. Operations are prescribed and policies are fixed and the function of the worker is largely to perform as specified. Although this model of performance is, as I indicate, useful in some settings, its application to schools is treacherous. Children, as all of us know, do not come in standard sizes. A visit to any fifth grade classroom will make plain at the outset differences in temperament, the rates with which children process different types of information, the backgrounds they bring with them to the classroom, their level of self-confidence—one could go on and on. This means that those who work with them will always need the discretionary space and the educational imagination to invent practices that are appropriate for not only the individual child, but also suitable for the particular time and situation in which something is to occur. Standardized teaching, from an educational perspective, is an oxymoron.

The same could be said for the school as a whole. The community it serves, the talents of the faculty it employs, the children who attend, the resources it has available to it, significantly affect the kinds of decisions, policies, and practices that are appropriate. To assume that schools are like factories is either to reduce schools to factories, in which case education flies out the window, or to misunderstand the demands of teaching and the meaning of the concept "education."

Those familiar with the history of education know that the aspiration to standardize educational practice is not a newcomer to the educational scene. It made its debut after the turn of the century in what has come to be called the efficiency movement in education (Callahan, 1962). Because I believe that historical understanding is so important for educators to possess, I turn now to that particular period in our history in order to illustrate some of the similarities between the assumptions and prescriptions emanating from the reform movement today and those reform efforts that occurred from roughly 1913 to about the end of the 1920s. Santayana once said "Those who are ignorant of the past are condemned to repeat it." There may be more truth there than meets the eye. To revisit that part we return to the 19th century.

It was in the second half of the 19th century that the scientific study of human behavior first emerged. In Germany, scholars such as Wilhelm Wundt and Gustav Fechner developed laboratories that would provide the empirical data that supported their theories of psyche. In England, Francis Galton developed statistical methods through which mental performance could be described. The invention and use of procedures that would transform philosophical speculation into rigorous methods of measurement and inference provided the conditions for the separation of psychology from philosophy, the field of which historically it had been a part. Philosophy now has a kind of competitor: psychology as an emerging science became a field in its own right.

The ideas and procedures advanced by Wundt, Fechner, and Galton provided the groundwork for the development of psychology in America. G. Stanley Hall, the father of American psychology and the first person to receive a Ph.D. in psychology from Harvard University (Cremin, 1970), went to Europe to study with Wundt. A little over a decade later, Edward L. Thorndike, a student of William James, one of America's leading 19th century psychologists, became a major force in American educational psychology. Indeed, the psychological legacy that Thorndike left is still with us. Just what is that legacy and how does it relate to the current situation in American education?

Edward L. Thorndike, the psychologist who invented what is often called "connectionism" (Thorndike, 1921) was primarily interested in learning and in understanding the conditions that would bring it about. He believed that it would be possible to ensure that learning would occur if the responses made to a stimulus were reinforced by rewards. These rewards would, in turn, ensure learning by strengthening the connections among the synapses within the brain. The pedagogical problem for the teacher was to define the appropriate unit to be learned and to employ a reinforcer appropriate to it. When student responses were reinforced with sufficient recency, frequency, and intensity, the law of effect would take place. The organism would indeed learn.

For educators seeking a way to give scientific rigor to what otherwise would be a theoretically uninformed field of practice, Thorndike's ideas had great appeal. Thorndike himself was extremely optimistic about the potential of psychology to bring about the behaviors desired by educators. In 1910, as editor of the *Journal of Educational Psychology*, he authored its lead article, titled "The Contribution of Psychology to Education." In this piece, he states with great confidence his conception of the promise of psychology in the development of the science of education.

> A complete science of psychology would tell every fact about everyone's intellect and character and behavior, would tell the cause of every change in human nature, would tell the result which every educational force—every act of every person that changed any other or the agent himself—would have. It would aid us to use human beings for the world's welfare with the same surety of the result that we now have when we use falling bodies or chemical elements. In proportion as we get such a science we shall become masters of our own souls as we now are masters of heat and light. Progress toward such a science is being made. (p. 6)

I refer to Thorndike because his work represented a vision of what he believed a science of human behavior could do for the realization of social ambitions. The belief that behavior was controllable, that it could be shaped by method, that, in a sense, free will could be harnessed by a technology of reinforcing procedures, is philosophically compatible with the scientific management of human behavior. It is this new "science" that is related to our current efforts pertaining to school reform.

One of the important aims of the reform efforts of the 1990s is the creation of a system that defines an array of educational goals and a framework through which each segment of the whole can be aligned with its goals: first, goals must be formulated; then assessment tasks related to those goals are to be designed; following the design of assessment tasks, standards are to be set for the content of each curriculum domain for specified age levels; finally after assessment, tasks are used to measure student performance. Public report cards make the results available for all to inspect. This last phase is critical because the public display of student performance is intended not only to inform parents and other taxpayers, but also to motivate educators. All of the foregoing aspects of reform are predicated on the presence of programs in schools that are comparable with respect to aims and similar with respect to content. In all, the intent is to improve student performance by a process grounded in standardization.

A similar approach to the improvement of schools—more radical and less well-informed to be sure, but nevertheless similar in spirit—was reflected in the efficiency movement in education near the turn of the century. Frederick Taylor, an industrial troubleshooter and the creator of scientific management, had developed a method of time and motion study through which what he called excess motion could be eliminated from the actions of workers on an assembly line. By observing and measuring the worker's behavior on the job, wasted motion could be eliminated, the worker's productivity could be increased, the worker would be less tired, and increased profits could be reflected in higher returns to both shareholders and workers. The key, however, was that all parts of the system had to be scientifically managed. There were a number of steps that the managers of such a system needed to take.

> First. They develop a science for each element of a man's work, which replaces the old rule-of-thumb method.
>
> Second. They scientifically select and then train, teach, and develop the workman, whereas in the past he chose his own work and trained himself as best he could.
>
> Third. They heartily cooperate with the men so as to insure all of the work being done in accordance with the principles of the science which has been developed.
>
> Fourth. There is an almost equal division of the work and the responsibility between the management and the workmen. The management take over all work for which they are better fitted than the workmen, while in the past almost all of the work and the greater part of the responsibility were thrown upon the men. (Callahan, 1962, p. 27)

What one sees here is a highly rationalized managerial approach to the production process. The worker's job is to follow the procedures prescribed. These procedures were detailed, discrete, and mandatory. The aim of scientific managers was to increase levels of productivity, and this could, they believed, be achieved if scientific methods were used to study the system and then employed to provide precise prescriptions for performance. Once the goals or objectives for each worker were specified and the means for achieving them given, the worker and the plant became more productive, profits grew, shareholders profited, and workers received larger paychecks.

In this system, individual initiative and inventiveness by workers were regarded as sources of error; like sand in a motor, they impeded the operation of a smooth running machine that depended on adherence to formula. What was wanted was a scientifically based system that would leave no room for worker discretion.

This utopian approach to school reform did not work. Instead, it infected schools with industrial values that diluted educational aspirations and converted curricula to training programs. Decisions about "investments in schools" were made in ways that resembled those made in industrial settings. Raymond Callahan (1962), one of the leading students of the efficiency movement, reports on one superintendent's recommendation for school improvement:

> One may easily trace an analogy between these fundamentals of the science of industrial management and the organization of a public school system. For example: (1) The state as employer must cooperate with the teacher as employee, for the latter does not always understand the science of education; (2) the state provides experts who supervise the teacher, and suggest the processes that are most efficacious and economical; (3) the task system obtains in the school as well as in the shop, each grade being a measured quantity of work to be accomplished in a given term; (4) every teacher who accomplishes the task receives a bonus, not in money, but in the form of a rating which may have money value; (5) those who are unable to do the work are eliminated, either through the device of a temporary license or of a temporary employment; (6) the differential rate is applied to the teacher, quantity and quality of service being considered in the rating; (7) the result ought to be a maximum output at a low relative cost, since every repeater costs as much as a new pupil; (8) the teacher thus receives better wages, but only after demonstrated fitness for high position; (9) hence we ought to have the most desirable combination of a educational system—relative cheapness of operation and high salaries. (pp. 103–104)

Why, one might ask, would such an approach to school reform be embraced so warmly by educators responsible for shaping the lives of children? Why would school administrators be so eager to become "scientific managers"? Callahan offers an explanation that could well be applied to the uncritical acceptance of today's reform proposals. He calls it the *vulnerability thesis*.

Then as now, schools were under fire for failing to educate. According to critics at the turn of the century, too many students were repeating grade levels they had failed to pass. Students' test scores were low. There simply was too much waste in education. One critic (Callahan, 1962) saw salvation by looking abroad:

> In a group of great industrial nations, there has come forward in recent years one that has taken place in the very front rank among industrial competitors. That nation is Germany. . . . I have had a somewhat unusual opportunity to study the underlying causes of the economic success of Germany, and I am firmly convinced that the explanation of that progress can be encompassed in a single word—schoolmaster. He is the great corner-stone of Germany's remarkable commercial and industrial success. From the economic point of view, the school system of Germany stands unparalleled. (p. 12)

Does the "solution" seem familiar? Just what does a vulnerable school administrator do when his schools are found wanting? One of the things he does is try to improve them and, at the same time, to look for cover. In their efforts to improve their schools and to avoid public criticism, practices clothed in the mantle of scientifically proved method have enormous appeal. Scientific management, something that could turn a profit in the industrial plant, was seen as a solution to problems in American schools. What better way to increase a school's productivity than by implementing what had worked so well on the factory floor. Besides, it made sense. It was not only scientific, it was also rational. By adopting scientific management, scientific principles rather than craft judgment could be employed. Craft depends on an individual's expertise and sensitivity to the context and materials with which the individual works. Craft knowledge is "merely" local. Science is universal. It provides a much less context sensitive conception of procedure. The point of the scientific enterprise is to discover those natural conditions that one can manipulate or use to make accurate predictions without the need for idiosyncratic interpretation. Science—in this view—is much more dependable.

If one is under fire, the appeal of scientifically "proved" methods for increasing productivity is great. By wrapping themselves in the mantle of science, school administrators could protect themselves from criticism and, at the same time, appear "up to date."

As I indicated earlier, these tactics eventually backfired: teacher-proofing methods of instruction did not—nor does not—work. The context always matters. The anemic conception of science advanced by school administrators in the name of professional salvation was not science, but scientism. It was a parody of the scientific enterprise that they barely understood.

The similarities that I see between the efficiency movement from 1913 to the end of the 1920s and the reform movement in education in the 1990s is that they are both built on a belief that practices can be directed by "scientifically" derived rules and that these practices can be standardized across situations. Although the educational reform movement of the 1990s goes nowhere near the extremes reached during the teens and twenties of this century, the theories behind each movement are related.

I believe that the motivation for educational reform around the turn of the century and the motivations today emanate from much the same sources: a discontent with existing practices and a desire to find a solution that once and for all can be more or less uniformly applied. Furthermore, the uniformity of outcomes that current reform efforts advocate facilitates the comparison of performance among schools, districts, and individual students. When one lives in a culture such as ours that has strong meritocratic values, the attractiveness of being able to make such comparisons is obvious. Knowing where you stand is a part of social competence. Knowing where you stand makes it possible to get ahead and to know that you have. Yet, it is also the case that comparisons among students who start at different places and who go to schools that have different resources to provide is not necessarily a way to create an equitable society: those already advantaged relative to schooling are likely to win. Furthermore, there remains a tension between a professional orientation that places high value on both local control and individual initiative and an orientation that sees knowledge acquisition as a process of acquiring a standardized body of information—a cultural dictionary (Hirsch, 1988)—for which students can be tested, compared, and assigned to different tracks. I believe it is the responsibility of the educator to reveal the values embedded in prescriptions that others take for granted and to provide alternative visions that others can consider concerning what education might be for the young.

As important as the scientific study of psychology was in shaping a view of what was needed in schools, it was not the only important perspective influencing our vision of education. John Dewey (1916) provided another. Dewey, with Thorndike, can be regarded as one of the two major pillars of American education in the 20th century. Thorndike, a scientific psychologist whose research touched on just about everything, was primarily interested in understanding learning. His work appealed to educators because it provided a way of bringing about the kind of learning teachers and administrators wanted. His method was systematic and offered a kind of technology of practice that would take chance out of teaching and learning. As I indicated earlier, his work made it possible to hope that there would eventually be a science of teaching, something that would be both efficient and effective.

Dewey was of another mind. His view was substantially influenced by Darwin's conception of the biological nature of the human organism. Dewey's conception of humans was also biological. He regarded the human as a live creature seeking both equilibrium within the environment and the stimulation that comes from its loss. Disequilibrium—a feeling of having a problem or being upset—was a potentially productive condition for the growth of mind. It was through a temporary sense of disequilibrium that people began to create means that would restore the organism's also temporary state of equilibrium. This shift or oscillation between equilibrium and disequilibrium was, like the systole and diastole of the beating heart, at the center of the educational process.

Dewey believed that much of what was being taught in traditional schools paid too little attention to the needs and to the experience of the growing child. The child in the standard classroom of turn of the century America was much too passive: the child was essentially to receive the information provided by the teacher; from the big jug into the little mug. The result, Dewey believed, was temporary learning that never became a useful part of the child's behavioral repertoire. Although it left a residue, the residue did not conduce to the student's growth. For growth to occur—and Dewey meant by the term *growth* the increase of a child's ability to frame and pursue his or her own purposes—the child needed a stake in the learning activity. The teacher's task was to create the classroom conditions that would generate in the child a sense of disequilibrium so that the situation could be made problematic by the child and therefore resolved through inquiry. It was a feeling of disequilibrium that provided the child with a motive for inquiry and it was the process of restoring equilibrium through inquiry that provided the satisfaction of the journey.

For Dewey, growth was not the result of a set of externally reinforcing agents that Thorndike had described, but rather the outcome of an effort by the child to convert what Dewey called an indeterminate situation into a determinate one. Growth occurred because intelligence grew; the child became increasingly able to form purposes and to plan strategies for pursuing them. In a sense, the child adapted the environment to his or her own aims. When such a process became a general model of how students learned, the curriculum became problem-centered. The teacher became someone who knew how to structure the environment so that the problems the child was able to form were within his or her capacity to resolve. This meant that the teacher not only had to understand the subject matter in which ideas having intellectual substance could be acquired; the teacher also needed to know the backgrounds and capacities of the child in order for the classroom conditions to be made appropriate, that is, within the child's abilities.

This model of teaching and learning is formidable. Recipes are much easier and much more comforting to those who require direction regarding what to do. If students were uniform in background, desires, and aptitudes, recipes might be useful. Children are not uniform, hence recipes simply will not do. Contexts within which teachers work differ, children differ, schools have different levels of resources, and, equally as important, teachers differ with respect to their aptitudes and backgrounds. There is no one best method. Dewey's ideas, as he once paradoxically put it, make teaching more complex precisely because his views of learning and of human nature are simpler than the ones they were intended to replace.

The major point I wish you to carry away from this discussion pertains to the idea that there are competing visions for our schools. The current federal reform effort provides one such vision. Its language and allusions about regaining our competitive edge and meeting national standards for student performance are more closely aligned with the ideas of Thorndike than those of Dewey.

One might think, given a view as persuasive as Dewey's, that it would have swept the educational world. Progressive education was fathered by Dewey and he was named a life member in the Progressive Education Association (Cremin, 1970). Yet, the ideas promoted by progressive education, even at its height in the 1930s, was only a small part of the American educational scene. Their presence was to be found much more frequently on the pages of educational journals than it was in classrooms.

There never was, and there is not today, despite efforts to standardize, a single view of educational practice. At the very time that Dewey's ideas were most popular, there was another orientation competing successfully for attention. This orientation is considerably closer to the scientific tradition within which Thorndike worked than Dewey's. It was a tradition that was given particular force by the man who is sometimes thought of as the founder of the field of curriculum: Franklin Bobbitt (1924).

Bobbitt was a professor of school administration at the University of Chicago who worked at a time at which the appetite among scholars to create a scientifically based approach to education was at its height. The years were 1910 through the 1930s. Bobbitt formulated an approach to education that in some ways reflected the values and visions of the efficiency movement that was built on the work of Frederick Taylor. Bobbitt describes his conception of curriculum planning this way:

> The central theory [of curriculum] is simple. Human life, however varied, consists in the performance of specific activities. Education that prepares for life is one that prepares definitely and adequately for these specific activities. However numerous and diverse they may be for any social class they can be discovered. This requires only that one go out into the world of affairs and discover the particulars of which these affairs consist. These will show the abilities, attitudes, habits, appreciations and forms of knowledge that men need. These will be the objectives of the curriculum. They will be numerous, definite and particularized. The curriculum will then be that series of experiences which children and youth must have by way of attaining these objectives. (Bobbit, 1918, p. 14)

One can easily get a sense from the foregoing of the systematic, linear approach to planning that Thorndike advocated. It all appeared quite rational. Define your goals, identify the tasks, organize the tasks from simple to complex so that as the child proceeds along the way, progress toward the ultimate goal is assured. In a certain sense, Bobbitt's work provides what we now consider to be a naive view of rational planning. Yet, when one works in a field that yearns for academic respectability and that seeks uniform procedures that would assure professional effectiveness, the attractiveness of a framework that promises to provide for the achievement of such ambitions is enormous. In addition, the American culture in general is characterized by a kind of pragmatism: the cash value of an idea, as William James said prior to the turn of the century, is what counts. Getting the job done is what really matters and philosophical speculation that could not be lined up with specific steps to be taken have been historically less attractive to Americans than to their European counterparts. In this sense, both Thorndike and Bobbitt may, perhaps, be closer to America's conceptual mainstream than the more complex and I believe subtle aspects of Dewey's thinking. Bobbitt's work provided a major foundation for a long following of educators who came after him.

As I recount the orientations to education and, more specifically, to curriculum that are reflected in the ideas of the individuals whose work I have just described, I hope you will not believe that this is, as they say, "ancient history." The ideas that I have examined (and I will be examining further in a moment) are alive and well in contemporary educational thought. Unless students of education have at least a general understanding of the historical conditions that have animated schools, we are likely to regard each new bandwagon as an intellectual innovation that had never before appeared. This is seldom the case. Learning some lessons from the past is the best way I know of to avoid some of the pitfalls that virtually any approach to education possesses. And that goes for Dewey's ideas and the scholars and practitioners that followed his lead, as well as those of Thorndike. In short, all approaches to education have both strengths and weaknesses, all have their own specific limitations.

In 1932 the curriculum field saw the publication of *The Technique of Curriculum Making* by Henry Harap. This work, too, like Bobbitt's, has a technological flavor. Harap viewed the technique of curriculum making as a linear systematic activity. One first defines the aims of education and then the term *objective*. From these one identifies the major activities of life, con-sults subject matter specialists, analyzes the activities of children, deter-mines the child's social needs, and eventually formulates those activities that are instrumental to the achievement of the objectives one has formu-lated at the outset.

What is clear from Harap's work, as well as from that of his predecessors in the curriculum field, is the desire to create a systematic technology of curriculum development. In 1932, when his book appeared, Harap was able to write, "The process of systematic curriculum making is still in its infancy—it is hardly ten years old." What I think we see in the work of these early curricularists is the desire to continue in the scientific tradition advanced by men as prestigious as Thorndike and Dewey. I do not believe that they anticipated that the tradition they embraced and used in their work would set such an important precedent not only for those in the field of curriculum, but for those in psychology, as well. Indeed, B. F. Skinner (Joncich, 1968) himself has said that he regards his work as a footnote to what Thorndike started.

One cannot give an account of where the curriculum field has been with-out attention to the work of Ralph Tyler (1950). Tyler's *Basic Principles of Curriculum and Instruction* was first published in 1949 and since that time has undergone over 40 printings. One would be hard pressed to identify a more influential piece of writing in the field. In 128 brief pages, Tyler lays out the basic questions he believes must be answered by anyone interested in creating a curriculum for any subject matter field or level of schooling. Tyler's work follows the lead first laid down by Thorndike and Dewey and articulated for the field of curriculum by Bobbitt and Harap. From Thorndike, Tyler's curriculum rationale draws on the need for observable behavior as evidence of learning. He also shares both Thorndike's and Judd's faith in the educational utility of the social sciences, particularly in psychology, as a source through which curriculum decisions can be "screened."

From Dewey's work Tyler extracts a belief in the importance of experience as the basic condition influencing what children learn. Tyler's curriculum work also shares a family resemblance to that of his predecessors in the curriculum field, notably to Bobbitt and Harap. Bobbitt's emphasis on the importance of objectives is echoed in Tyler's observation that objectives are the single most important consideration in curriculum planning because, in Tyler's words, "they are the most critical criterion for guiding all the other activities of the curriculum maker." Tyler's attention to the various data sources for objectives we find described 20 years earlier by Harap; the style is different, but the intent is essentially the same.

What Tyler (1950) has given the field of curriculum through his monograph is a powerful, although in my view oversimplified, conception of what curriculum planning entails. Once learned, Tyler's four questions are hard to forget. These questions are:

1. What educational purposes should the school seek to attain?
2. What educational experiences can be provided that are likely to attain these purposes?
3. How can these educational experiences be effectively organized?
4. How can we determine whether these purposes are being attained?

Once having learned about the need for objectives and the form they should take, one is hard pressed to neglect them, at least in theory. The Tyler monograph on curriculum is a model of a systematic approach to curriculum planning. Although it embraces no particular explicit view of education, the technical procedures it prescribes are bound to have consequences for what individuals trained to use this rationale will come to consider professionally adequate decision making in curriculum. Ends, for example, are always to precede means, objectives come before activities; not a hint is given in the monograph that in complex organizations ends can be constructed out of action and that only a textbook rendering of educational planning would provide such a pristine view of rational thinking. Nothing is said in the monograph about the student's role in curriculum planning or about the idea that different views of education conceive of curriculum planning in different ways. Although Tyler emphatically says that the monograph deals with the principles rather than with specific steps in curriculum building, the tone of the work, like the tone of so much that preceded it in the field, is a no-nonsense, straightforward, systematic conception of what in practice is a complex, fluid, and often halting and adventitious task.

Tyler's work on curriculum planning was and is influential not only because of the straightforward character of his writing—particularly his monograph on curriculum—but also because of the people in the field of education who had the opportunity to work with him. Robert Anderson,

Benjamin Bloom, Lee Cronbach, John Goodlad, Ole Sand, Hilda Taba, and others constituted a generation of influential educators who devoted much, if not all, of their attention to curriculum matters. Like Tyler, these authorities can be characterized as basically scientific in their assumptions, systematic in their procedures, and means-ends oriented in their view of educational planning.

Since the 1950s, American education has gone through a series of essentially failed efforts at school reform. One of these efforts was motivated by people dissatisfied with what they regarded as misguided progressivism. For Arthur Bestor and Admiral Hyman Rickover, two vocal critics of American education, American schools were far too laissez-faire; they had little in the way of standards; they were preoccupied with the psychological needs of the child and paid inadequate attention to the substance of the curriculum. Educational wastelands, Arthur Bestor (1953) called them in his book of the same title. Arid institutions unable to flower. American schools needed a major overhaul. Indeed, our nation needed to restore the educational substance of the past to the educationally feckless institutions that American schools had become.

Admiral Hyman Rickover (1962) wrote a book comparing Swiss schools to those in America. The title was *Swiss Schools and Ours: Why Theirs Are Better*. With the demise of the Progressive Education Association in the early 1950s, critics of progressive education had something of a field day. Many of their concerns were those Dewey himself alerted progressive educators to in the late 1930s. The message that he conveyed then simply did not get across to those who believed that the child was the beginning, middle, and end of the educational enterprise. For the most romantic of the progressives, teaching itself was almost an invasion of privacy.

What gave a major boost to school reform efforts, however, was the assent of Sputnik—a Soviet-flown spacecraft—on October 4, 1957. America does not like to come in second—particularly when the stakes are political. Seeing the rise of Sputnik, the Congress of the United States allocated millions of dollars for curriculum reform, first in math and science and then later in the social studies. Subjects concerned with aesthetic or literary aspects of life were simply neglected. Through the creation of new curricula, hope was generated that schools would become more rigorous and that America would catch up. The idea was to start from the top down: secondary schools first and then elementary schools. This top-down view of school reform did not bring about the kind of change that was wanted. All of the curricula were, for example, designed to fit into existing school structures. No curricula made any new demands on the ways in which schools were organized and, therefore, on the constraints placed on teachers with respect to planning time, collaboration with colleagues, or the ways evaluation could occur. Shortly after the rise of Sputnik, in 1960, Jerome Bruner wrote his extremely influential book, *The Process of Education*. Bruner provided a forceful and lucid theoretical conception of the basis for substantive curricula. The idea that students should grasp the "structure of the disciplines," that is, that they should learn to understand how ideas within a discipline are related, made sense to most educators at the time. In addition, Bruner claimed that children of any age could learn in an intellectually respectable way ideas that mattered. Indeed, he argued that the more the curriculum engaged students in the kind of thinking that was done by adults working in the disciplines, the better. Summer institutes for teachers and curriculum development efforts in chemistry, physics, math, and the social studies were undertaken. Bruner himself had a major hand in shaping a most imaginative curriculum in the social studies called *Man: A Course of Study*.

Despite these efforts, schools remained essentially the same. Ironically, fewer students rather than more students enrolled in physics and chemistry subsequent to the development of these curriculum resources.

The late 1960s saw the introduction in a formal way of both the behavioral objectives movement and educational accountability. The problem as others saw it was that teachers did not have clearly specified measurable objectives. Once objectives were formulated in measurable terms at relatively high levels of specificity, it would be possible to determine without ambiguity whether or not curricular goals were being achieved and, by implication, the extent to which teachers and others responsible for the school were successful. In this way, educational accountability for faculty as well as for students could be secured.

The development of specific accountability procedures was no more effective than earlier efforts to reform school. Another approach had to be found. What followed was the back-to-basics movement. Echoing the earlier work of Arthur Bestor, schools were urged to return to older, more halcyon days. These efforts were followed by the effective schools movement and later still, in the early 1980s, by a federally initiated reform effort called *A Nation at Risk*. In view of the current state of schooling in America, one might conclude with some justification that efforts at school reform have not been a rousing success. Will the current effort be more successful?

The Current State of American Education and the Forces Affecting It

You will recall that I began this chapter with a portrait of some of the major features of the federal reform effort in American education called *America 2000*. In that portrait, I identified some of the charges that have been leveled against American schools, although I did not in the pages you have read address the evidence for such charges. I will do so here.

It should be recognized that the claims that American schools cost too much and provide too little, that American students are not doing as well as they once did, that our position educationally among the nations lags far behind, that American education is essentially a disaster area that is undermining our economy and the viability of our nation are beliefs that are not only widely promulgated, but also widely shared. What evidence supports these beliefs? Let's examine three of these beliefs, one at a time.

1. American education costs too much. We spend more on our schools than any other country.

The belief that America is a spendthrift when it comes to education is widely held. Politicians make the claim and the media pick it up without critical examination. The fact of the matter is that, according to UNESCO data, America is tied with Canada and the Netherlands with respect to school expenditures. All four of these countries fall far behind Sweden in the amount spent per pupil for education in grades K–12 *and* higher education (Berliner, 1992). One of the reasons for our elevated position in the distribution of dollars to education across the nations is the fact that our ranking includes allocations to higher education. The United States has a much higher percentage of students attending colleges and universities than almost any other country and, as a result, our expenditures tend to match the higher percentage of the college-age cohort that continues in higher education. However, if we examine only expenditures for pre-primary, primary, and secondary education, we discover that we spend much less than the average industrialized nation. Among the 16 industrialized nations in the UNESCO report, the United States ranked 14th out of the 16 when expenditures for K–12 education are calculated as a percentage of per capita income. In other words, although we have more, we spend less, indeed much less, than Sweden, Austria, Switzerland, Norway, Belgium, Denmark, Japan, Canada, West Germany, France, the Netherlands, the United Kingdom, and Italy. In fact, Sweden, Austria, and Switzerland spend over 3 times the amount that we spend to support K–12 education as a percent of per capita income. Thus, the claim that we spend more than other countries is simply not true when one examines expenditures at the pre-primary, primary, and secondary school level.

2. American students are not doing as well as they once did in school; in fact, they know far less than their parents did at the same age.

One of the major sources of evidence that critics of American schools use to "document" the decline in educational quality is the decrease in mean SAT scores over the previous 25-year period. They regard this decline as prima facie evidence that schools are not as good as they once were, that students are not as bright as they once were, and that standards for American schools have fallen. One of the reasons for the gross misinterpretation of test score data is that newspapers are not inclined to provide much in the way of interpretation or context when it comes to the reporting of scores. Blaring headlines sell more papers than careful analysis. Although SAT scores have declined, the decline is nowhere near the magnitude that people believe exists. In fact, the decline has only been 3.3% of the raw total score, which amounts to eight fewer test items answered correctly over a 25-year period. When one considers that the SAT is a multiple choice test having 80 items in each of its two sections, the number of items missed—3.3%, or less than eight items for both sections of the test—this decline is not what one might call an educational disaster (Berliner, 1992). When one considers further that the population taking the test is far larger now than it was 25 years ago and therefore far less selective than it was then, the decline could be regarded as just the opposite; an indication that student performance would have actually increased *if* the same population parameters were being compared. When one considers further that the expansion of the population taking the SATs include a much larger percentage of African Americans, Asian Americans, Native American, Mexican Americans, and Puerto Rican students, populations that for the most part have been economically and socially marginalized in America, the fact that only 8 more items would be missed by test takers over a 25-year period can be regarded as a genuine educational achievement rather than an educational disaster. In short, the claim that students are not as well prepared as they once were on the basis of the data provided by SATs simply cannot be sustained.

3. Our educational position among nations lags far behind our economic competitors.

America is a nation that likes to come in first. When we lost the space race to the Soviets in October, 1957, a massive influx of funds came to American schools to produce more scientists and mathematicians who were to restore our nation to first place. We don't like to come in second.

If we compare academic achievement in mathematics, American students rank not second, but near the bottom of the distribution. There are a host of considerations that ought to be taken into account when attempting to interpret such cross-national comparisons of school achievement. Some of these considerations include the comparability of the populations taking the test. First, it is not particularly meaningful to compare populations that differ significantly in their exposure to what is tested and then to claim that one nation has a more effective educational system than the other. The cohorts must be alike in characteristics other than the variables being measured in order to make the process of comparison interpretable.

Second, in making interpretations of academic achievement, it is important to understand the relationship between the tests that are administered to students and the congruence of test items with the curriculum that was actually provided to the students. If a test's questions are in line with the curriculum that was provided in one country but out of line with the curriculum provided in anther country, the conclusion that students in the first country did better on the test than the students in the second is a rather obvious one to draw. However, whether students in the second country are actually doing well or better than those in the first would depend on what the tests assessed in relation to what teachers taught. Put more simply, unless one knows something about the program that was provided in the first place, the ability to draw conclusions about school effectiveness is simply not possible. Schools may very well be effective in doing the things they set out to do. If students are measured on forms of learning that have not been developed, their low performance may not at all be a function of school ineffectiveness, but rather the results of a different program.

Third, the amount of instructional time that is provided to students has a direct bearing on what they have the opportunity to learn. In making comparisons of student performance across nations, it is important to know the amount of instructional time that was provided, not only in school, but outside of school as well. For example, it is well known that in Japan, students who have academic ambitions attend special schools outside of the normal school day for additional instruction. If mathematics is emphasized both in school and out of schools, it should not be surprising that compared with students who do not have as much instructional time, Japanese students do better on tests that were aligned to the curricula to which they were exposed.

When one decides to emphasize a particular subject by devoting more attention to it in the school curriculum, one also, in effect, decides to diminish the amount of attention that can be devoted to other subjects. In other words, there is an opportunity cost paid for additional time devoted to any particular subject. Thus, the entire question of the kind of general education one wants students to receive enters the picture. It is simplistic to look at a single measured variable and to draw widespread generalizations about the effectiveness of schools on the basis of international comparisons of student performance. The differences have to be interpreted not only with respect to the alignment of the curriculum to the assessment device, and to the amount of time devoted inside and outside of school, but also to the conception of education that a people believe appropriate for their children. These considerations are seldom raised by critics of American schools. They need to be.

If the appetite for efficiency leads to a constricted view of education and if international comparisons of student performance miss the point of the purposes of education, how should we think about these matters? More specifically, how should we think about the curriculum we provide and how it should be taught?

It is tempting to think about the improvement of schools as being essentially related to the improvement of curriculum and teaching. Although I believe that these two functions are to schooling like the systole and diastole are to the beating heart, I also know that the heart is influenced by the body that contains it and that the health of the body is influenced by the environment in which it lives. To carry the analogy further, the improvement of schooling needs attention not only to the heart, but also to the school that envelops it and the environment that affects the school. Although such considerations may seem so daunting that one feels one's self slipping slowly into a pit of pessimism, what is truly pessimistic is a failure to recognize the complexity of educational reform and the need to pay attention to a wide variety of factors that affect what teachers and school administrators are able to do. What is optimistic is a willingness to address this complexity and to take it into account in one's planning.

Planning for the future also requires attention to the future. Attention to the future as a way of planning for the present is always riddled with uncertainties. The fact of the matter is that we cannot make very good predictions about what the future will consist of, although we do feel we need to take into account what it might require. For example, it seems almost certain that our nation will become increasingly multicultural. The old image of America as a melting pot that dissipates the distinctiveness of each group arriving on its shores will no longer do. What does such a shift in perspective mean for the content and goals of the school curriculum or, for that matter, for the ways in which we organize time and pace? And what about the kind of sexism that has long been tolerated in our culture? How does that issue get addressed in our schools? What do we do about the fact that individuals will be changing jobs more often? Does the kind of flexibility implied by such shifts in vocation have implications for what and how we teach in schools? Matters of health maintenance, the quality of the environment, the individual's responsibility in an increasingly dangerous world are not irrelevant to educational planning. Just what they mean and what priority they should have will depend on the values we bring to the planning process and the conceptions we hold of the nature of human nature.

It is true that American schools were initially organized to reflect the needs of an agrarian society. We no longer have those needs to the degree to which they once existed. What schools must now become may, in fact, differ not only from the common structural features they now possess into new structures suited not only for the demands of tomorrow, but also to the local contexts in which they are to function. In fact, there may not be a single model of scholastic virtue that suits all children in all places forever. What schools need to be may be significantly influenced by what the community wants, what the students need, and what visions of education animate the planning enterprise. What follows in Chapter 2 is an array of conceptual tools that students of education might find useful in thinking about curriculum matters. These issues are not the only vital ones that need to be addressed, but they are of central importance. As you proceed through this book, additional considerations will become a part of your repertoire so that near the end you ought to have a much finer-grained framework for thinking about the means and ends of education. In this sense, paradoxically, this book is designed to complicate rather than simplify your life. It aims to bring an appropriate uncertainty to mind as you think deeply about the functions of education and the forms that schools can take.

References

Berliner, D. (1992). *Educational reform in an era of disinformation.* Paper presented at the meetings of the American Association of Colleges of Teacher Education, San Antonio, Texas.

Bestor, A. (1953). *Educational wastelands: The retreat from learning in our public schools.* Urbana: University of Illinois Press.

Bobbitt, F. (1918). *The curriculum.* Boston: Houghton Mifflin.

Bobbitt, F. (1924). *How to make a curriculum.* Boston: Houghton Mifflin.

Callahan, R. (1962). *Education and the cult of efficiency.* Chicago: University of Chicago Press.

College Entrance Examination Board. (1989). *National report on college-bound seniors.* New York: Author.

Cremin, L. (1970). *The transformation of the school.* New York: Knopf.

Dewey, J. (1916). *Democracy in education.* New York: Macmillan.

Eisner, E. (1967). "Franklin Bobbitt and the 'Science' of Curriculum Making," *School Review, 75*(1), 29–47.

Finn, C. (1991). *We must take charge.* New York: Maxwell Macmillan International.

Harap, H. (1932). *The technique of curriculum making.* New York: Macmillan.

Hirsch, E. D. (1988). *Dictionary of cultural literacy.* Boston: Houghton Mifflin.

Joncich, G. (1968). *The sane positivist.* Middletown, CT: Wesleyan University Press.

Kozol, J. (1991). *Savage inequalities.* New York: Crown.

National Commission on Excellence in Education. (1983). *A Nation at Risk.* Washington, DC: Author.

Rickover, H. (1962). *Swiss schools and ours: Why theirs are better.* Boston: Little, Brown.

Thorndike, E. (1921). *Educational psychology.* New York: Teachers College.

Tyler, R. (1950). *Basic principles of curriculum and instruction.* Chicago: University of Chicago Press.

U.S. Department of Education. (1991). *America 2000.* No. 1. Week of September 1, 1991. Washington, DC.

2

Some Concepts, Distinctions, and Definitions

It is the creative image, vital and burgeoning, that we see before us in the work of these artists, and the new reality that takes shape is not the inhuman world of the machine but the passionate world of the imagination.

HERBERT READ

In the previous chapter I have described ways in which conceptions of schools and the field of curriculum have developed over the past 80 years. But what I have not done is to provide an analysis of the term *curriculum*. It is to that task that we now turn.

The Meanings of Curriculum

Curriculum as "The Course to Be Run"

As a term in educational discourse, *curriculum* is used in a wide variety of ways. It has a commonsense meaning as broad as "what schools teach" to as narrow as "a specific educational activity planned for a particular student at a particular point in time." Initially, the word came from the Latin *currere*, which means "the course to be run." This notion implies a track, a set of obstacles or tasks that an individual is to overcome, something that has a beginning and an end, something that one intends to complete. This metaphor of a racetrack is not altogether inappropriate. Schools have historically established "courses" of study through which a student is to pass. Successful completion of the course warrants a diploma or degree certifying competence. In other ways, too, the idea of a curriculum as a course filled with increasingly difficult obstacles is an appropriate metaphor. Schools have functioned historically as institutions that serve as a type of educational sieve, selecting the more from the less able at each level of schooling by giving increasingly difficult examinations to pass that open or close the doors to further schooling. This is still true today. The concept of the curriculum as the course to be run is one that fits one of the school's historical functions.

Curriculum as School Experiences

Curriculum has also been conceived of and defined as "all of the experiences the child has under the aegis of the school." This conception of curriculum was created by progressive educators during the 1920s to emphasize several beliefs that they considered central to any adequate conception of education. First, they wished to remind other educators that the reality of a curriculum for a child was determined by the quality of the experience that the child had in the school and was not simply a piece of paper on which lesson plans were prepared. Although some degree of planning was considered appropriate and important, the real curriculum for the child, the one that made a difference in his or her life, was the curriculum that he or she experienced. Second, because children differ from one another in background, aptitudes, interests, and the like, the curriculum was never identical for different children. In a sense, one could have a curriculum only *after* it was experienced by a child. The curriculum was, one might say, to be discovered by looking backward. To their credit, these same progressive educators recognized that what children learn in school is wider than what goes on in classrooms and more varied than what teachers intend to teach. The experiences secured in the hallways and the playgrounds of the school were also influential aspects of educational life and should not, in their view, be separated from the responsibility educators should assume for guiding the child's experience in other aspects of school life. It was educational folly to care about the child's experience in the classroom but to disregard it in the playing fields. Indeed, progressive educators felt so strongly about the need to focus on the kind of experience the child had under the aegis of the school that they made a formal distinction between the curriculum, which was that experience (and hence each child had a different curriculum because his or her experience was never the same as another's), and the course of study, which was a written document that outlined the content, topics, and goals that a teacher was to use in planning the curriculum for a class or a child.

Whatever the conception of *curriculum*—and each of the two conceptions described has important consequences for the way in which one thinks about educational planning—it is clear that a school cannot function without some kind of program that it offers to its students. Whether that program is conceived as a preplanned series of educational hurdles over which the student must jump or the entire range of experiences a child has within the school, the school as an institution has some mission, some set of general aims or direction, and must provide some activities, programs, or means that engage those who work and study there. The design and evaluation of these activities and programs are what we are attempting to understand.

In considering such a plan or program, there are some distinctions we can make regarding the scale or scope of our attention and the location of our planning over time. In Figure 1 two continua are outlined, one dealing with *scale* and *scope*, the other dealing with *time*.

Levels of Curriculum Decision Making

The design of an educational program is influence by a wide variety of decisions that range from the broadest types of educational policy bearing on the aims or content of educational programs to those decisions that have to do with very specific, highly focused aspects of a particular program. Take, as an example, decisions about what the schools of a state should be

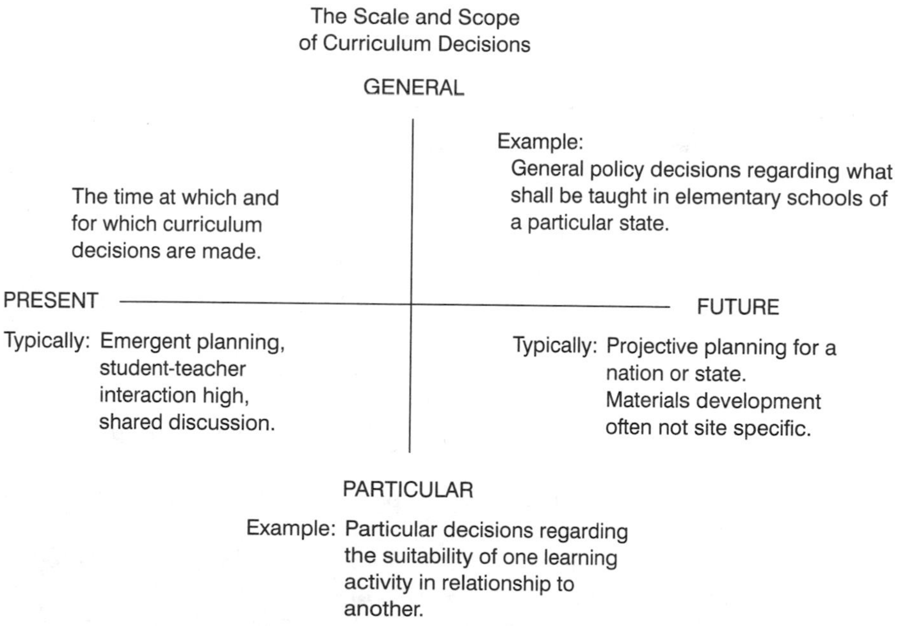

The Scale and Scope
of Curriculum Decisions

GENERAL

The time at which and
for which curriculum
decisions are made.

Example:
General policy decisions regarding what
shall be taught in elementary schools of
a particular state.

PRESENT ———————————————————— FUTURE

Typically: Emergent planning,
student-teacher
interaction high,
shared discussion.

Typically: Projective planning for a
nation or state.
Materials development
often not site specific.

PARTICULAR

Example: Particular decisions regarding
the suitability of one learning
activity in relationship to
another.

Figure 1

required to teach. Virtually all states have in their education code a section that prescribes the content of instruction. In California, for example, it is required that schools teach reading, writing, arithmetic, social studies, art, music, physical education, and science at various grade levels (Department of General Services, Documents Section, 1976). The decisions that led to these policies were curriculum decisions. Some group (in this case the state board of education) decided that schools should devote their attention, energy, time, and resources to a particular array of subject matters. In New York, books or the resources to purchase books to ensure adequate attention to these fields are also provided. This type of decision, like other large-scale decisions bearing directly on the program that the schools provide, exemplifies large-scale, general curriculum decisions. The creation of a Computer Education Program, the decision to emphasize the so-called basic skills, and the formulation of policy bearing on the development of new approaches to the teaching of science all represent molar types of curriculum decision making. The point here is that when one talks about curriculum planning or about the design of educational programs, one might be referring to planning at this level: the planning of curriculum policy or curriculum priorities. Obviously, such policies do not exhaust the decisions that need to be made, nor are they adequate for operating programs within schools, but they do establish the directions and boundaries for other decisions.

At the other end of the continuum are highly specific decisions bearing on a particular educational situation or a specific set of curriculum materials. Does *this* particular curriculum activity build on what has preceded it? Are *these* examples likely to be meaningful to *this* group of students? Does *this* content adequately exemplify the generalization the students are expected to learn? Does the visual quality of the material stimulate interest or is it dull and unimaginative? Questions such as these are asked by anyone or any group concerned with the creation of curriculum materials. Obviously, such decisions are almost always made after more general curriculum decisions have been made, after one decides, for example, that a social studies program dealing with sex-role socialization is to be created.

The point here is that when one asks what kinds of problems curriculum decision makers encounter or curriculum scholars study, one can point to a range dealing with the most broadly based types of policy that bear on the shape and character of educational programs to the specific, particular decisions that must inevitably be made within particular educational contexts.

In some countries, there is a formal separation between those who make the large-scale molar decisions about the content and aims of the curriculum and those who work within the parameters set by those decisions to create specific learning activities and teaching materials. In Norway, for example, a national board appoints a national educational committee made up of prominent lay persons and scholars from various disciplines to outline the basic topics, content, and aims of the curriculum for children in primary and secondary schools. This committee, representing the views of the polity and the specialized scholarly competence of the school-related subject-matter disciplines, is responsible for formulating directions and priorities in school programs. By using laypeople, the broad interests of the public are believed to be served, and by using scholars from school-related subject fields, the most up-to-date and important ideas within the subject-matter fields are likely to be identified. Once these molar decisions have been made, it is up to others to translate them into specific programs suitable for the interests and abilities of, say, 10-year-olds. The curriculum work here is to translate "new subject matter" into materials that will become useful for creating educational events in the classroom, something for which neither a university scholar, nor a lay person has any particular preparation.

What we see here is not only a division of labor but also a political separation based on perceived areas of competence. Educators responsible for curriculum development perform an essentially technical role in attempting to actualize the collective decisions of selected laypeople and scholars. Educational expertise in such an arrangement is aimed at the translation and implementation of educational policy.

The horizontal axis in Figure 1 extends from decisions made in the present for the present to those that are made to serve as a kind of blueprint or guideline to be followed in the future. Following are some useful examples. Much curriculum work consists of the creation of curriculum materials that are intended to be used by teachers to help students acquire more sophisticated skills or ideas. Typically, such materials are developed for use over one or more academic years. *Man: A Course of Study,* the Physical Science Study Committee's materials, and *Science: A Process Approach* are curriculum materials designed to improve the quality of teaching and learning in elementary and secondary schools. These materials have been developed largely through federal funds by curriculum development groups and are intended for students and schools throughout the country. The general assumption underlying the work of these groups is that teachers would welcome such materials, that national groups having funds and access to nationally known scholars would be able to provide teachers with a higher quality of materials than teachers could create on their own, and that use of such materials over extended periods would result in a higher quality of learning in the fields represented by those materials.

The creation of such materials represents an effort to influence the educational futures of students and teachers for a substantial period of time. Content and sequence are determined; the roles of the teacher and students are defined well in advance of the particular context in which the materials are to be used. Like the minister of education in France who was said once to have boasted that at 11:00 on any morning he knew what all the children in French schools were studying, nationally developed materials often tend to formulate long-term educational plans that are intended to become the course to be run.

At the other end of the continuum is another image of curriculum planning, one that is not so well defined or so long-term in character. That model is perhaps best exemplified by the kind of curriculum planning that goes on in some progressive schools. This model conceives of planning as a joint effort between teacher and student, one that cultivates shared responsibility and that exploits emerging educational opportunities when they occur. At this end of the continuum, the teacher is likely to see his or her role as providing the kind of environment where new, unexpected interests can emerge and where "flexible purposing," to use Dewey's phrase, is both possible and desirable (Dewey, 1938).

The point here is simply that curriculum planning does not need to be long-term and preplanned weeks or months before engagement with students is to occur. The teacher who decides that in the next hour his other class might find a discussion about the effects of robotics or space stations on our lives is engaged in curriculum planning, even though such decisions do not result in the creation of written plans, elaborate visual illustrations, or well-designed boxes of self-instructional materials.

In making this observation I am not writing a brief either for no planning or for elaborate materials. I am attempting to point out that the planning of curricula is something that everyone does who provides an educational program for students. Such planning may be short term or long term, shoddy or careful, tasteful or ugly, appropriate for students or inappropriate. Whatever the quality of the planning, we all decide what we will do or allow to occur. The extent and scope of such planning depend on the context in which one works and on the view of curriculum and teaching that one holds.

Let me review the major points I have tried to make thus far. First, I have tried to show how curriculum planning spans a range that extends from the broadest types of decisions about the content, scope, and aims of programs serving millions of students to highly specific, particular decisions made by curriculum development specialists wrestling with problems of sequence in a particular mathematics curriculum or by a teacher deciding on a particular project for a class or a student. Curriculum planning is not limited to a single level of specificity along the continuum.

Second, I have tried to show that the planning of curriculum is an inevitable aspect of schooling; it *must* occur. The significant question is how well it is done. One need not have long-range plans or printed materials to have an educational program. Teachers can use the present situation to develop short-term plans with or for their students. Time is a variable that varies in relation to the context or the view one holds about what constitutes an appropriate teaching role.

Thus, if someone asks what curriculum specialists do, given these distinctions, it is possible to respond by saying that their responsibilities extend from the shaping of educational policy bearing on the aims and content of educational programs to work dealing with the design of specific elements within particular educational programs. Where and when are such decisions made? They are made by groups developing materials or creating educational policy intended to serve a large educational constituency as well as by teachers deciding on the value and appropriateness of a specific project or task for a particular group of students.

A Definition of Curriculum

Let's return for the moment to the concept *curriculum* and redefine it. *The curriculum of a school, or a course, or a classroom can be conceived of as a series of planned events that are intended to have educational consequences for one or more students.* In formulating this conception, or definition, of curriculum, I am not claiming to formulate a "real" definition. Curricula are not natural entities whose necessary and sufficient properties are capable of being discovered once and for all. What I am doing is formulating a concept of curriculum that I believe is useful. Let's examine this concept more closely. A curriculum is a series of planned events. This implies that there will be more than one event planned, and this is typically the case, although theoretically one could have a single event constituting curriculum (but that likelihood is small). A second feature of the conception is that curricula are planned; someone must do something that has some aim, some purpose, some goal or objective, even though it might be highly diffuse or general. A third feature is that the intention be educational in character. Now this qualification, I readily admit, need not be a part of the definition of curriculum; one could formulate a curriculum designed to train bigots, burglars, or murderers, but within the context of this book and my purposes the qualification that the consequences are intended to be educational is important, if for no other reason than to highlight the fact that schools are supposed to be educational institutions. A fourth feature of this concept deals with the term *consequences*. Educational events or activities do much more than what is intended; they influence people in a wide variety of ways. Furthermore, I want to leave room for the teacher or curriculum developer to plan activities or events that do not have specific, highly predictable goals or objectives. I want to leave room for planning of events that appear to be educationally fruitful but whose specific consequences for different students might not be known in advance. The term *consequences* is sufficiently wide to allow for such planning. In other words, a curriculum is a program that is intentionally designed to engage students in activities or events that will have educational benefits for them. Some of these benefits might be delineated or specified in advance in operational terms; others will be general, broad, and diffuse, but in part capable of being recognized subsequent to the activity. Like other issues in this book, this issue—the character of educational goals—is discussed in greater detail later.

When one is engaged in long-term planning and has formulated an array of goals or objectives, designed materials of various sorts, created learning activities to be used in the classroom, and prepared visual and auditory resources, it is possible to inspect the curriculum to see what its contents are and how they have been related. The curriculum in this context has a physical existence; it is embodied in a set of materials. These materials can be the subject of analysis and criticism in a measure similar to the criticism applied to books, paintings, symphonies, architecture, and the like. To be sure, the criteria will differ, but the principle of being able to criticize what has been created is the same.

The physical existence of such materials also means that they can be transported; the same curriculum can be used in different classrooms and in different schools. School administrators can discuss the strengths and weaknesses of the curriculum. Parents can inspect it and students can use it.

Curriculum planning need not result in the creation of physical materials. The teacher whose plans are in his or her mind alone might have planned a curriculum of an excellent sort, but because the plans are not public, they can neither be shifted about, inspected, nor shared with others. The only way to appraise the quality of the curriculum is to watch the teacher and the students in the class. One must attend to the attributes as they unfold, make judgments about the significance of the content as it is revealed, and appraise the quality of the resources as they are used. One must make one's judgment by observing the curriculum in use. For the teacher who does not make extensive or long-term plans, even of a mental sort, the curriculum may in fact be planned in process. In this situation, it is not simply that plans have been made but have not been written down; in this situation, the teacher plans in process. What the teacher uses are initiating activities, but such activities are employed simply to get the ball rolling, to begin a process whose course is shaped in the conduct of teaching.

The Intended and Operational Curriculum

The differences between what is planned in the way of aims, content, activities, and sequence and what actually transpires in the classroom can be formalized into a distinction between *the intended* and *the operational* curriculum. The intended curriculum is like the course of study; it is that which is planned. Such plans can, as I have already indicated, be inspected, critiqued, revised, and transported to a multitude of locations. The operational curriculum is the unique set of events that transpire within a classroom. It is what occurs between teachers and students and between students and students. To critique or appraise the operational curriculum requires one to be in a position to observe what classroom activities actually unfold. Inspection of plans or of the intended curriculum is not assurance that those plans are actualized.

In a variety of ways, it is useful to distinguish between the intended and the operational curriculum. If in a school or classroom there is an educational problem concerning what students are or are not learning, one can ask whether the source of the problem resides in the curriculum as it is intended or as it is operationalized. It might be the case that the intended curriculum is so rigidly structured that it negatively influences the teacher's operational curriculum. Alternatively, though the intended curriculum might be judged excellent on relevant criteria, the operational curriculum may not resemble what was intended. Because the examinations that a school district employs purportedly reflect the intended, rather than the operational, curriculum the students do poorly. What one does, therefore, is either reduce the discrepancy between what was intended and what was operationalized or one creates an examination system that more adequately reflects what was actually taught.

It is interesting to note that in efforts to upgrade the educational quality of the schools, "solutions" are often provided that take the form of "new courses in subject X or Y," or more instructional time in courses already being taught. Yet it is clear that more of something that is badly handled will be educationally counterproductive. If both the intended and operational curriculum are poor in quality, more of such quality will cause impoverishment rather than enrichment of education. Although one wants to know about the quality and character of what is intended, one also wants to know—and this is extremely important—what the operational curriculum is in the classroom. This is a complex, arduous, and demanding task that requires one to be in a position to see and understand what actually goes on in classrooms. Yet this method is of extreme importance for improving the quality of education. I will have more to say about how such observations might be made in Chapter 13. At this point it is important to understand the distinction between the intended and the operational curriculum and to appreciate the implications of this distinction for improving curriculum and teaching.

Although curriculum and teaching are regarded as separate aspects of educational practice, the distinctions between them are often difficult to make when one examines each carefully. Nevertheless, the general distinction between curriculum and teaching is useful, as I will discuss later in this book, even though there are cases in which the distinction between the two is not clear.

It might be noted that the planning of a curriculum on a long-term basis with clear specifications regarding its use can be compared to the creation of a score written by a composer or the plans prepared by an architect. Although these two examples are much more specific and detailed than what most curricula provide, the relationship between the composer and the pianist or the architect and the builder has similarities to that between the curriculum planner and the teacher. In each case the planner designs, and the performance is executed within the constraints of the design. And in each case the performers have degrees of freedom with which to interpret the plans that have been made. One can inspect the score, the architectural specifications, and the curriculum as planned and assess the ways in which those plans have been executed.

For those using a more emergent model of curriculum planning—the model in which plans are created in process—activities are much closer to the work of the painter or poet. In this model, decisions to do one thing rather than another are decisions that can be made only by considering options as they develop, by "reading" the situation, by exploiting the adventitious, and by allowing intention to grow out of action rather than requiring them to precede it. This is the way a great many artists as well as teachers work. To work this way is not necessarily a mark of incompetence but could be the result of a preference for a particular role, or a sign of commitment to a particular image of education. In such a model of curriculum planning one must place a good deal of faith in the ability of the teacher. To work this way requires, I believe, a great deal of experience, competence, and confidence as a teacher. Although the availability of a curriculum that has been well planned and accompanied by interesting and attractive resources for in-classroom use breeds confidence that what will be offered will be worth the student's time and effort, curriculum materials and particularly that species of materials called curriculum guides are often disregarded by teachers. The existence of a well-planned body of curriculum material is no guarantee that they will be used effectively or with enthusiasm in the classroom. To know that, there is no substitute for direct observation in the classroom.

Thus, when we talk about "the curriculum," we can mean that body of material that is planned in advance of classroom use and that is designed to help students learn some content, acquire some skills, develop some beliefs, or have some valued type of experience. We call this curriculum the *intended curriculum*. We also mean by the term *curriculum* those activities that occur in the classroom, taking into consideration the materials, content, and events in which students are engaged. We refer to this curriculum as the *operational curriculum*. Approaches to the former can be made by inspecting the materials and plans that have been formulated. Approaches to the latter can be made only by directly observing the classroom itself.

Normative and Descriptive Curriculum Theory

When we speak of theory we can distinguish between two types. Normative theory is concerned with the articulation and justification of a set of values. Its aim is to provide a persuasive case for the value of a particular end or state of being. In education, normative theory argues the case for certain educational goals on the basis that the goals themselves are intrinsically valuable. Thus, a theory of education that argues that education should aim at fostering the growth of the individual and that defines growth as the development of those modes of intelligence that enable individuals to secure meaning from experience is normative in character. Such a statement or position becomes theoretical as it presents to the world a coherent set of reasons and concepts that justifies its claims. Although one could ask for further justifications for the claim that education should be conceived of as a process concerned with fostering growth, once having received such justification, further justification leads either to an infinite regress or to a circular argument. Eventually, one arrives at value assumptions that are made rather than justified.

Normative Theory in Education

In educational theory in general, and in curriculum theory in particular, normative ideas are central. Education itself is a normative enterprise—that is, it is concerned with the realization of aims that are considered worthwhile. Thus, educational activities are not simply concerned with learning, because what a person learns might have negative consequences for his or her development. What makes experience educational is its participation in a set of values. To the extent to which those experiences participate in those values, they are educational. To the extent to which they contradict those values, they are miseducational.

For the planning of curricula, normative commitments are also crucial. Such commitments, or images of educational virtue, influence what is regarded as relevant in planning and what data are considered important in making curriculum decisions. Without such values, neither education nor curriculum has a rudder. It should be noted that "theoretical" in the context of normative theory is not the same as a bald statement of values or belief; it is the coherent articulation of a view and a presentation of the grounds for holding it. Such theory is not necessarily predictive and need not employ scientifically verified facts to sustain it. What one looks for is coherence. The curricular ideologies that are presented in the next chapter are examples of such theoretical views.

In saying that normative theory is not simply a bald statement of what someone values, I am not implying that there are necessary and sufficient conditions that can be used as criteria for determining whether a statement is theoretical. Normative theory extends from general statements and beliefs to highly elaborate efforts to justify a view of what is good or beautiful. Thus, the roots of such theory begin as humans speculate on what is good in life and worth achieving. Commonsensically, we call such speculation philosophies of life, and although few philosophers would consider such commonsense speculation philosophical in the technical or professional sense, the difference is one of degree rather than of kind.

To say this is not to equate the commonsense theorizing that all of us do with the heady work of a Paul Tillich, Plato, Boyde Bode, or John Dewey. It is to recognize that the theoretical construction of value is not the sole province of those who are professional philosophers but is a part of the intellectual activity of ordinary men and women. The differences between the two reside in consistency, subtlety, scope, and coherence. These are differences that distinguish levels of quality rather than differences in kind.

Education Not the Same as Schooling

I said earlier that normative theory is critical for education, and this point is worth emphasizing. Education is not the same as schooling, nor is it the same as learning. One can learn many things that are personally and socially dysfunctional: to become neurotic, fearful of people, a torturer, a racist, and the like. In each case, learning has taken place, but whether one considers such learning an instance of education depends on a normative theory of education. The claim that some groups or individuals do or would regard such learning as educational is not in dispute. This might be true, but to make such a claim is not to make a value statement but to describe a social fact. The question is whether one ought to regard such forms of learning as educational. Would you, given your normative theory of education, regard becoming neurotic or becoming a torturer an instance of education? I would not.

Without some view of what counts as education, one is in no position whatsoever to make judgments about the educational quality of the processes of schooling or their consequences. One cannot know whether research conclusions have any relevance to educational practice. One has no basis for appraising the educational merits of teaching. John Dewey (1938) makes this point very well, when he says the following:

> That a man may grow in efficiency as a burglar, as a gangster, or as a corrupt politician, cannot be doubted. But from the standpoint of growth as education and education as growth, the question is whether growth in this direction promotes or retards growth in general. Does this form of growth create conditions for further growth, or does it set up conditions that shut off the person who has grown in this particular direction from the occasions, stimuli, and opportunities for continuing growth in new directions? What is the effect of

growth in a special direction upon the attitudes and habits which alone open up avenues for development in other lines? I shall leave you to answer these questions, saying simply that when and only when development in a particular line conduces to continuing growth does it answer to the criterion of education as growing. For the conception is one that must find universal and not specialized limited application. (pp. 28–29)

Education, Noneducation, and Miseducation

Dewey goes on to distinguish between three types of experience: those that are *educational, noneducational,* and *miseducational.* Education experiences are those, as I have suggested earlier, that contribute to the individual's growth. Growth, for Dewey, represents the extension of human intelligence, the increase in the organism's ability to secure meaning from experience and to act in ways that are instrumental to the achievement of inherently worthwhile ends. Noneducational experiences are those that are simply undergone and have no significant effect on the individual one way or the other. There are many such experiences undergone each day—the activities of habit—that punctuate our lives. Such experiences are had but without significant effect one way or another on our growth. We tie our shoes, walk across the room, drive our car without contributing to or detracting from our growth.

Miseducational experiences are those that thwart or hamper our ability to have further experiences or to cope intelligently with problems in a particular arena of activity. In schooling, many students develop disinclinations to encounter certain fields of study. Their experience, say in mathematics, has been so unfortunate and uncomfortable that they avoid that field of study whenever it is their option to do so. For such students, mathematics was miseducational. It closed rather than opened them up to the intellectual and aesthetic possibilities of that field.

More radical examples of miseducational experience are found in the acquisition of phobias that children are prone to because of the anxieties of their parents. Such phobias might deal with animals, airplanes, failure, and sex. Children learn to become fearful and become incompetent in the areas in which these phobias function. Their experience constrains rather than expands the possibilities that life makes available. In these areas, miseducational experience results in a deep sense of personal discomfort.

Dewey's writings are a prime example of normative theory. He conceptualizes a value, namely growth, and then justifies its significance in argument. He locates the sources of growth in experience and then indicates the relevance of different types of experience for education. The position is thought through, well argued, and has practical consequences for teaching and curriculum planning. Such theory, rooted as it is in a metaphor of a growing organism, shapes our view of what is appropriate and inappropriate in educational practice. The appeal of Dewey's theory has been extraordinary for educators throughout the world, but it is not only the normative theory that appeals, and in the following chapter other conceptions of educational value are presented.

Descriptive Theory

Thus far, I have spoken of normative theory in education and curriculum, but what of descriptive theory, those statements or concepts that attempt to explain, usually through their power to predict, the events of the world? Descriptive theory with respect to the sciences is perhaps best exemplified in the natural sciences: they have provided the model that the social scientists have attempted to emulate. In the natural sciences, the task has been both to give an account of and to account for a set of phenomena. "What has occurred and how?" are major questions theorists ask. With a theory that is useful, one can anticipate the future; one knows what to expect given some set of conditions or circumstances. In some cases, such theory has made it possible not only to predict, but also to control—although this is not always achieved. Although scientists are able to land a spacecraft on Mars, astronomical theory is not yet able to control the path of stars. In the field of curriculum, theory in no way approaches that level of power, and for good reasons. Educational matters are value laden in ways that physics is not. In education, what one seeks is not the explanation of what is, but the achievement of what ought to be. Nuclei, as far as anyone knows, do not form purposes or have intentions: people do. Increasingly, social scientists are coming to appreciate the distinctive characteristics of theory in dealing with the human as a social creature and the institutions humans create. Lee Cronbach (1975), a social scientist who recognizes this difference, writes the following:

> Social scientists are rightly proud of the discipline we draw from the natural science side of our ancestry. Scientific discipline is what we uniquely add to the time-honored ways of studying man. Too narrow an identification with science, however, has fixed our eyes upon an inappropriate goal. The goal of our work, I have argued here, is not to amass generalizations atop which a theoretical tower can someday be erected. The special task of the social scientist in each generation is to pin down the contemporary facts. Beyond that, he shares with the humanistic scholar and the artist in an effort to gain insight into contemporary relationships and to realign the culture's view of man with present realities. To know man as he is is no mean aspiration. (p. 126)

What I believe descriptive theory in curriculum has to provide primarily are concepts that enable us to make more subtle and powerful distinctions. At times, such theory might lead to empirical generalizations that can be considered in making particular decisions for specific circumstances, but such generalizations always need to be applied and interpreted with caution, not as rules but as considerations. No set of generalizations will adequately treat the particular characteristics of specific situations.

In the field of curriculum, descriptive theory has largely been borrowed from psychology. Theories of reinforcement, cognition, perception, learning, sequence, problem solving, and the like have influenced the ways in which curriculum theorists have conceptualized curriculum. Indeed, Dewey himself was greatly influenced by the descriptive theoretical work of Darwin. Dewey's conception of man is biological, as is Piaget's, whereas Bobbitt, particularly in his early work, attempted to apply the theories of scientific management to curriculum and teaching in order to increase the efficiency of schools. What we see both in Dewey and in Bobbitt is the influence descriptive theory has had on their normative theory of education. Once norms are formed, these norms in turn influence the kinds of descriptive data one uses to support one's norms. In short, a dialectic between the normative and the descriptive occurs.

To talk about the differences between normative and descriptive theory implies that the two are wholly distinctive. This is not the case. Normative theory is buttressed by descriptive claims emanating from descriptive theory: Dewey's theory of education is a case in point, as I have indicated. The way in which we understand the world to be influences our conception of its possibilities and therefore shapes our aspirations.

Descriptive theory is in a subtle but important sense pervaded by normative theory because the methods of inquiry we choose and the criteria we choose to apply to test truth; claims reflect beliefs about the nature of knowledge. These beliefs are basically value judgments. Those embracing a different conception of knowledge will employ different methods of inquiry and may therefore come to different conclusions about the world. In short, epistemological commitments reflect a set of values. Theory in curriculum is therefore of two types, each of which penetrates the other: normative and descriptive. Normative theory articulates the values to which the educational program is directed. Descriptive theory provides the concepts and generalizations that are taken into account in planning the school program.

Theory, however, is ideational and problems of curriculum development practical. It is important to distinguish between the ideas one works with and the practical act of constructing an educational program. Curriculum development is the process through which those ideas are transformed by an act of educational imagination. I say imagination because no theory—either normative or descriptive—prescribes what is appropriate for different students. Ideas are guides; they are not recipes. One works with them; one does not follow them. To engage in curriculum development, one must put together much more than any of the theories can provide either individually or collectively. Schwab (1969) makes this point well when he writes:

> A curriculum grounded in but one or a few subsubjects of the social sciences is indefensible; contributions from all are required. There is no foreseeable

hope of a unified theory in the immediate or middle future, nor of a meta-theory which will tell us how to put those subsubjects together or order them in a fixed hierarchy of importance to the problems of curriculum. (p. 10)

It should also be noted that the competencies needed to design curriculum are not identical with those needed to create sophisticated and useful curriculum theory. Aptitude differences exist among individuals, and the kind of experience one needs in each realm of activity differs. Theoretical training requires intensive study of relevant disciplines within philosophy and the social sciences and the critical analysis of one's written work by competent critics. The skills of curriculum development are acquired in the act of designing curricula and in experiencing firsthand the problems of transforming ideas into educational materials and events. Those skills include the ability to work with others, the ability to deal with the complexities of practical deliberation, the ability to establish distance between one's work and oneself in order to see it more clearly, and the ability to envisage the way in which activities might function within a classroom. It requires the ability to appreciate the demands that a task makes on teachers and students and to be able to judge how much guidance they might need to engage in that task. Such skills are not trivial, nor are they nonintellectual. They are demanding, requiring a sense of taste and style and the ability to deal with frustration.

What would a comprehensive, scientifically descriptive theory of curriculum look like if we had one? Such a theory would identify relevant phenomena in the planning of a curriculum. It would provide guidelines for relating these phenomena to each other so that they are maximally effective within a group of students, given a description of the student's characteristics. It would provide a credible explanation of why the relationships between the curriculum and the student were effective for realizing particular ends. Such a theory would, in short, enable the curriculum developer to design curricula that were optimally suited to particular students, given some view of what was educationally desirable. In addition, such theory, if it were necessary for its efficacy, would specify the context conditions that would need to be obtained if the theory were to operate. If the theory were entirely comprehensive, it would provide such guidance for different subject matters, disciplines, or fields of study, and it would be able to accommodate the developmental levels and other relevant personal characteristics of students.

One does not have to exhaust the literature in curriculum to recognize that such theory is nowhere to be found. Instead, we have concepts, rules of thumb, perspectives, and frames of reference. We have theoretical ideas that are to be used flexibly rather than the equivalent of Boyle's Law or Bohr's atom. I believe people's ingenuity and need for forming their own purposes, their curiosity, and their irascibility foreclose on the possibility of developing a theory of curriculum comparable to that of atomic particles.

We are "condemned" to a life of exciting uncertainty in which the flexible use of intelligence is our most potent tool.

Curriculum Diffusion

The task of developing curriculum materials and disseminating them to schools does not ensure that such materials will be used. The problem of creating ways in which such resources will be used is a problem concerned with curriculum diffusion. The concept of diffusion suggests that ideas and materials affecting school programs need in some way to enter the mainstream of schooling, that the process has something of an organic character to it, and that it is not likely to occur if it is treated as a mechanical or bureaucratic task or something that will occur automatically simply because good materials are available. I mention the connotative implication of the term *diffusion* because for many years the term that was employed to describe this process was *curriculum installation. Installation* suggests something akin to changing a muffler or air cleaner on an automobile: one first designs and produces some artifact and one then installs it onto some ongoing enterprise. Curriculum change does not occur in such ways. Teachers have their own priorities, the school possesses its own equilibrium, and the organization has numerous ways of providing superficial accommodations to foreign intruders without making any significant alteration in what it has been doing. To regard educational change—and particularly curriculum change—as something analogous to installing a mechanical device onto another mechanical device is to reveal a profound naivete about how schools operate. Hence, *diffusion,* a softer word, is much more appropriate than *installation.* But it is not simply the word that is at issue, but rather the idea behind the word: the improvement of educational practice is a process that is adaptive in character. In this adaptive process, both the classrooms *and* the materials undergo change. To appreciate the mutually adaptive character of curriculum change is also to recognize that the one widely held aspiration of psychologists and curriculum developers to produce what was called "teacherproof" curriculum is, like the concept of installation, similarly faulty. The idea that it is both possible and desirable to develop curriculum materials that will withstand the most incompetent teachers, or that it is desirable to develop methods that do not require the use of the teacher's judgment, is to demean teachers and to expect them to function as automatons rather than as professionals who have a stake in what they are doing in classrooms.

Earlier in this chapter, I identified a continuum describing the scope and scale of curriculum decision making. I pointed out that at one end of the continuum curriculum decisions are made at very general levels of abstraction that are intended to shape educational policies. At the other end of the continuum, decisions are made about specific curriculum tasks such as the suitability of a particular idea or skill within a sequence of other ideas or skills that are being defined within a body of curriculum materials. Curriculum diffusion can take place at virtually every level, from the most general to the most specific, at which curriculum decision making occurs. For example, assume that the state of New York wants to encourage school districts to develop programs that teach students to use computers. There is much in the way of curriculum diffusion that the state could do to increase the probability that school districts would consider this area. First, high-ranking officials could use the mass media to announce publicly the importance of computers to the school curriculum. Second, the state could sponsor conferences and workshops to discuss the uses of the computer in the schools and to sensitize educators further to its importance. Third, it could encourage local computer industries to provide computers to schools, to offer workshops to teachers, and to provide funds for summer study. Incentives and stimulation would be generated within the state as a result of a general policy position on an important curriculum issue. Such activities heighten consciousness, they stimulate the public, and, in the process, they diffuse the idea that in this electronic age students who will spend most of their future in the twenty-first century should become literate in the tools that will be used.

The Use of State Curriculum Frameworks

There are other ways in which curricula are diffused in the schools. One of these is through state and now national curriculum frameworks within each of the subject areas of the school curriculum. In California, a new state framework for curriculum development within a particular field is produced every 5 years. This framework is generally the product of a committee appointed by the state superintendent of public instruction. The committee usually includes school administrators, teachers, university professors, and subject specialists from the schools. It meets on a regular basis during a 3- to 4-year period to develop a framework designed to encourage local school administrators and teacher-training institutions to revise the program currently in effect so that it is consistent with the ideas and general philosophy of the new framework. For example, the social studies framework for the schools in California places emphasis on using the humanities as both a means and as a content for teaching the subject. The framework provides a theoretical rationale for this new approach to social studies education. It identifies leading concepts and generalizations from fields in the humanities that are relevant to social studies education. It also provides examples that illustrate how these ideas can be used in classrooms. It does not—and frameworks typically do not—constitute a curriculum that school districts can adopt. It provides a structure, a rationale, a set of examples and, perhaps most of all, an orientation to the teaching of a particular field or collection of fields. It is intended to infuse new ideas within existing curricula. It does this by serving as a centerpiece for conferences sponsored by the state, by the fact that it enjoys the endorsement of the state board of education and the superintendent of public instruction, and because school administrators often wish to comply with the expectations of their superordinates.

Use of Textbooks and Curricular Materials

Still another way in which new ideas enter the curriculum of schools is when states adopt or endorse textbooks and other educational materials.

About every 5 years, many states review for the purposes of adoption or endorsement the textbooks that it provides to local school districts. The state reviews, for example, such texts to identify and proscribe bias in race, sex, ethnicity, and religion. It also reviews such texts to ensure that their content in other ways is not objectionable, that reading levels are appropriate, and that the content includes a balanced political point of view. The adoption or endorsement of a book is an extremely important decision for textbook publishers. The amount spent on textbooks for elementary and secondary schools and for colleges in the United States in 1980 was estimated at $2 billion. Even a small share of the market is significant. But it is also significant for teachers and students. Because textbooks are frequently the hub around which school programs revolve, the choice of a textbook and the endorsement of the state in facilitating its use is a significant factor in the diffusion of new ideas in the curriculum.

School districts also diffuse ideas into school programs by adopting existing commercial curriculum materials. Such decisions influence rather directly the ideas students encounter at school. The adoption of a reading series by the Los Angeles School District can have an impact on 300,000 students. In New York, it can influence 500,000 students. Thus, to choose a new program to be used in mathematics, reading, or even in the arts is to influence what teachers are likely to do and to define to some degree what students will study. When the new math was adopted by school districts across the country, elementary and secondary school students had access to mathematics curricula that stressed understanding of mathematical principles more than they stressed skill in computation. What became educationally important was not so much whether students got the right answer to mathematical problems, but rather whether they understood the operations and the assumptions on which those operations were built. Grasping the meaning of set theory was more significant than knowing the number facts.

Yet, the power of such programs is mediated by a teacher. The teacher's comprehension of the materials, the teacher's commitment to the program, and the teacher's sensitivity and support of the spirit of the curriculum is extremely important in affecting the extent to which materials will have educational efficacy.

Because commercial publishers recognize that the teacher is such an important agent in mediating their programs, many of the large publishing houses employ former teachers to "in-service" classroom teachers in those school districts that adopt their materials. These commercial publishers employ dozens of such people to travel across the nation to conduct work-shops for teachers and to maintain rapport with school administrators. Their general aim is to maintain their psychological presence within the schools and to provide the kind of guidance regarding their materials that many school districts could not otherwise provide. In the end both educa-tion and profits are to be enhanced.

Another means for curriculum diffusion emanates from the district itself. A school district may engage teachers in developing its own materials and in designing its own curricula for purposes that are especially relevant to the educational values of the district. For example, in a district that serves an educationally diverse population, teachers were employed to develop a body of curriculum materials that presented to students the history of eth-nic immigration in that particular community. Oral histories from the eldest of community residents were taken; old photograph albums, news-papers, and magazines were secured and reproduced; and letters and other paraphernalia that would enhance children's understanding of the history of the area were secured. The materials were then used as resources that students could study. Students were encouraged to take their own oral his-tories of their own family and to put together reports describing the immi-gration of people from other areas to the area in which they now live. In short, the district, largely motivated by the work of its multicultural commit-tee, made the resources available to teachers to prepare curricula that had special relevance for the district. In most large school districts, some cur-riculum development is currently underway.

There are other factors as well that serve to diffuse curriculum to the schools. One of these is the policy that some districts have of sending teach-ers, and particularly curriculum consultants, to conventions and confer-ences to find out what is current within their particular specialty. In all of the large state and national conferences, publishers display their ware: new curricula, new textbooks, new instructional devices. Symposia are presented on new approaches to teaching X, Y, or Z. Speeches are given advocating the virtues of a new approach to science or to the fine arts. Workshops are held that introduce teachers to new teaching techniques. Historically school boards and school administrators have recognized the importance of such conferences for motivating their staff and for keeping in touch with what is educationally current.

Curriculum diffusion, more broadly curriculum change, occurs in still other ways. When the state university system alters entrance requirements, curriculum change at the local high school is likely to occur. This in turn brings about change at the middle school level and at the elementary school level as well. School districts are particularly sensitive to the requirements set by universities and colleges. Hence, when the state university says that 3 rather than 2 years of mathematics are required for admission, in most states the school district has a legal obligation to offer programs that allow students to meet the entrance requirements of the state university. But even if the requirement were not a legal one, the fact that it is a requirement would be reason enough for most districts to provide such courses within their programs. Furthermore, such new university entrance requirements would, de facto, be required courses of study for college-bound students.

Another source of curriculum change in the schools is related to the timetable. Because of fiscal constraints, some school districts are reducing the number of periods per day that they can offer to students. The reduction may be from a seven-period day to a six-period day. What this reduction does is effectively eliminate courses in the fine arts and in other areas that are regarded as desirable but not essential. The effect is, of course, to reduce the student's access to educational opportunity, a loss that is particularly severe for those students whose aptitudes and interests are in the areas that are cut from the program. When such areas are eliminated, the need for teachers in these areas is similarly diminished, as is the need for curriculum consultants or supervisors in those areas. In very little time, the presence of the areas within the district is virtually eliminated: the so-called nonessential curricula gradually come to be regarded as being the responsibility of other agencies.

In the last analysis, it is what teachers do in classrooms and what students experience that define the educational process. The character of this process might initiate with a vague image of a new way of teaching biology or art or the study of American political behavior. That image might eventually get transformed into a body of handsome resources, well-written prose, and imaginatively conceived opportunities for learning. But such materials, like a brilliantly composed musical score, need skillful and sensitive interpretation and a group of people who can interact meaningfully with what has been created. If any of these components is missing, the process fails. If the score is poor, it is not worth playing. If the performance is poor, it will be poorly received. If the audience is ill-prepared to deal with it, it will fall on deaf ears. Composers need competent performers and performers need an appreciative audience. In education, similar relationships hold. The teacher might be, in some models of education, his or her own composer, but the need for competent performance, if not an artistic one, still exists. And the fit between the teacher's "score" and the students remains as critical in the classroom as it is in the concert hall—probably even more so.

References

Cronbach, L. (1975, February). Beyond the two disciplines of scientific psychology. *The American Psychologist, 30*(2).

Department of General Services, Documents Section. (1976). *California education code: Statutes.* Sacramento, CA: Author.

Dewey, J. (1938). *Experience and education.* New York: Macmillan.

Schwab, J. (1969, November). The practical: A language for curriculum. *School Review, 78*(5).

3

Curriculum Ideologies

"There are as many worlds as there are ways to describe them."
NELSON GOODMAN

Because educational practice is concerned with the achievement of certain desired end-states, it relies on a larger value matrix to identify and justify the directions in which it moves. That values matrix is the subject of this chapter: the ideologies that give direction to one of the school's major means for addressing the aims it values. We call that means *the curriculum*.

The term *ideologies*, rather than *ideology*, is used here to indicate that there is no single ideology that directs education. Values, particularly in America, proliferate, and these values find their educational expression in the ways in which schooling, curriculum, teaching, and evaluation are to occur. Curriculum ideologies are defined as beliefs about what schools should teach, for what ends, and for what reasons. Insofar as an ideology can be tacit rather than explicit, it is fair to say that all schools have at least one ideology—and usually more than one—that provides direction to their functions.

The Significance of Ideologies in Education

Ideologies in general are belief systems that provide the value premises from which decisions about practical educational matters are made. For example, a conception of the aims of education rooted in the desire to help

This is a revised version of an essay originally published in *Handbook of Research on Curriculum*, Philip W. Jackson, Editor, pp. 302-326. Copyright © 1992 by American Educational Research Association. Used by permission of The Gale Group.

students secure Christian salvation will emphasize the importance of developing in the young the ability to read, for without such literacy the scriptures are inaccessible and if inaccessible, salvation is unlikely. A Christian ideology of the kind reflected in the laws of 1642 and 1647 (Cremin, 1961) in the Massachusetts Bay Colonies provided the value premises for both educational policy—schools were legally mandated in towns with over 50 inhabitants—and for curricular goals; biblical literacy, achieved through the ability to read, was of paramount importance.

In some ways, curricular ideologies derive from what might be regarded as *Weltanschauungen*—world views. Although religious ideologies, as they are played out in schooling, often provide the most visible forms of ideological influence, there are many important nonreligious ideologies that have long functioned in schooling. My aim in this chapter is to explore some of the most important and to describe their implications for curriculum practice.

Ideologies in education also influence what is considered problematic and nonproblematic in the curriculum. The term *problematic* can be regarded in two ways. First, what is considered to be a given or believed to be axiomatic in education enjoys a kind of security that is seldom threatened by marginalization: there are few people today for whom the development of literacy is a questionable aim of schooling. In this sense, the attainment of literacy is nonproblematic. By contrast, whether subjects like the arts or courses in sex education should be an important part of the curriculum is another question. Given some educational ideologies, these latter areas of study are problematic in much the same way that for some, federal support to the National Endowment for the Arts is problematic. For some the government has no business supporting the arts, and for others the school has no business teaching adolescents about sex.

Identifying what is problematic in the curriculum by its importance within an ideology is one way to look at the issue. A second way is to recognize that where a curriculum ideology emphasizes the importance of a particular subject, that subject ineluctably becomes problematic. By "problematic" here I mean that because decisions about the best ways of achieving the aims of fields considered important are almost always less than optimal, levels of student performance in the subject is typically a source of discontent and, in this sense, problematic. The problematic character of the most valued subjects makes them continuous objects of attention while those subjects that are marginalized or neglected altogether never achieve, in this latter sense, a problematic status. Anthropology, for example, is simply not a problem in the school's curriculum because it is seldom considered important enough to care about. The same holds true for the arts and a variety of other fields.

I suggested earlier that curricular ideologies emerge in religious-like views of the world. Any orthodoxy attempts to make the world into its own image, especially the educational world. Walker (1978) has pointed out that curriculum policies are like political platforms; they present a public position on some array of curricular options. Beliefs about the importance of the neighborhood school or the self-contained classroom or a multicultural curriculum have similarities to the planks in a political platform. Ideologies also function in much subtler ways. Often they do not announce their positions on important educational matters; rather, they manifest themselves in the kinds of language that imply or suggest rather than state explicitly what is educationally important and what the schools' curricula should address. For example, when the language of industrial competition is used to make a case for particular educational aims—"regaining our competitive edge in a world economy"—our conception of the mission of schools is gradually shaped in industrial terms. The school becomes viewed as an organization that turns out a product—a student—whose knowledge and skills are subject to the same kinds of standards and quality control criteria that are applied to other industrial products. By contrast, when the child is viewed as a biological organism subject to natural laws of growth and atrophy, the kindergarten become a more appropriate model for thinking about the ends worth pursuing and the kind of environment that is most suitable. Getzels (1974) has described how models of the learner influence images of the classroom. When children are regarded as passive receptacles to be filled rather than active, stimulus-seeking organisms, bolting down desks in orderly rows makes sense. If they are thought of as stimulus-seeking organisms, then the classroom is likely to have a very different look.

What is important about such educational practices is that they emanate from ideologies no less powerful than those directed by publicly expressed orthodox religious beliefs. Indeed, because the former practices may obscure their ideological sources, they may be especially difficult to change. Looked at this way, it becomes clear that at the broadest social level, acculturation itself can be regarded as a form of ideological induction. When one ideology becomes ubiquitous it renders those acculturated insensitive to the ways in which their own beliefs have been shaped; they are too close to the scene to recognize its features.

Another impediment to recognition emanates from the incorporation into our language of conceptions that so shape our view of curriculum, or the aims of schooling, or human aptitude that we do not notice them as having this effect. For example, when we define intelligence as the ability to deal with abstraction and identify abstraction solely with the ability to use words and number, we impose on schools standards that reflect those conceptions and, thereby, limit other possibilities.

The foregoing conception of an ideology is neither fundamentally different from a constructivist perspective pertaining to the function of theory in cognition, nor from one that Gruber (1981) calls "images of wide scope." The purported difference is that ideologies are typically regarded as value-

laden commitments, while theories in the social sciences are frequently idealized as merely descriptions of the world rather than an expression of what
is to be valued. Such a distinction will not stand analysis. Language is constitutive of experience; it is not simply descriptive, and the way in which the
world is parsed has significant value consequences for matters of educational practice. Gardner (1983) points out that Piaget's theory of cognitive
structure is essentially an ascension from lower to higher forms of thought
that has as its apotheosis a scientific model of mind. For Piaget (1973) the
pinnacle of cognitive achievement is found in the scientist. For Piaget, the
human as scientist, rather than as artist, is the end-state of cognitive growth.
Gardner writes:

> According to Piaget, a final stage of development comes into being during
> early adolescence. Now capable of *formal operations,* the youth is able to reason
> about the world not only through actions or single symbols, but rather by fig-
> uring out the implications that obtain among a set of related propositions.
> The adolescent becomes able to think in a completely logical fashion: now
> resembling a working scientist, he can express hypotheses in propositions, test
> them, and revise the propositions in the light of the results of such experi-
> mentation. These abilities in hand (or in head), the youth has achieved the
> end-state of adult human cognition. He is now capable of that form of logical-
> rational thought which is prized in the West and epitomized by mathemati-
> cians and scientists. (p. 19)

It takes no huge imagination to recognize how a view as influential as
Piaget's can reinforce a certain conception of knowledge and intelligence
and how, in the process, it can limit other options. If we believe that
Piaget's cognitive structures correctly define a hierarchy of human cognitive
attainment, the works of a Mozart, a Matisse, or a Balanchine are likely to
be diminished. If, however, we regarded artistic thought as the paramount
cognitive achievement, the content of our curriculum and who receives
rewards for success might look very different from the what we provide
today.

Recognition of the constitutive functions of language and the power of
theory to shape perception has been fostered from several sources. First,
that branch of psychology rooted in psycholinguistics and represented early
in the work of Edward Sapir (1962) and Benjamin Lee Whorf (1956), and
more recently in the cognitively oriented work of Bruner (1964), Case
(1984), Cole (1974), and Olsen (1988), has emphasized the complex social
nature of cognition in general and the functions of what Bruner has called
structure in the creation of understanding. To these researchers, the mind is
a cultural achievement influenced by biological predisposition, but nevertheless, shaped by the features of a culture. Second, there is that branch of
philosophy that historically has emphasized the importance of symbol systems in creating different forms of consciousness. Ernst Cassirer (1961),

Nelson Goodman (1978), and Susanne Langer (1942) are scholars whose theories of knowledge are directly related to the ways in which the world is represented. Different symbol systems, they claim, perform different epistemic functions. Third, there are the critical theorists and deconstructivists (Cullen, 1982) who pay special attention to the impact of language on cognition and on the values tacit in the language that is used. Their aim has been to raise consciousness to the covert values residing deeply in the language we use by revealing these values through the techniques of deconstruction—substituting, for example, key terms with other terms representing opposing meanings. Their efforts are not only epistemologically motivated, they are often motivated by particular political commitments (Eagleton, 1983). "Emancipation" from the linguistic and cognitive fetters of the culture is for them an important political aim.

The extension of the concept of ideology into the general sphere of cognitive theory, linguistics, philosophy, and deconstruction is advanced here because it is an arguable case that the most influential ideologies are not those formally acknowledged and publicly articulated, but rather those that are subliminally ingested as a part of general or professional socialization. We may be very much more ideological, given this broadened view, than we realize. Thus, understanding the covert ways in which ideologies operate becomes crucial if they are to be the subject of reflective examination. As long as we remain oblivious to the values that animate our intellectual life, we will be in no position to modify them.

Thus far I have described ideologies largely as a function of acculturation and as an inherent part of the psychological structures—language and theory—that we acquire as members of a culture. Although in some societies ideological commitments can be both uniform and powerful, it is not the case that in pluralistic societies uniformity among ideologies is the norm. More often than not, ideological positions pertaining to curriculum and to other aspects of education exist in a state of tension or conflict. In pluralistic societies, a part of the pluralism emerges in competing views of what schools should teach and for what ends. These competing views prevail or succumb in a political marketplace. For example, the admonitions of evangelical Christians to exclude Darwinist theory in the teaching of biology and to replace it, or at least to complement a Darwinian view with a creationist revelation, encountered sufficient resistance in California to make it possible for a scientific, Darwinian perspective to prevail. In this particular battle for ideological supremacy, evangelical fundamentalism lost.

My point here is that regardless of how powerful an ideological view may be in any individual's or even group's orientation to the world, it is seldom adequate to determine what the school curriculum shall be. There is a political process that inevitably must be employed to move from ideological commitment to practical action. When a society is characterized by value plurality and when the political strength of groups is comparable, the process almost always leads to certain compromises. As a result, the public school curriculum seldom reflects a pure form of any single ideological position. Indeed, the more public the school and the more heterogeneous the community, the less likely there will be ideological uniformity in schooling.

Where schools are private, and Christian fundamentalist schools are examples, it is much more likely that not only the curriculum of the school, but also that other aspects of school life will reflect the values of the group. Peshkin (1986) points out that in the Christian fundamentalist school he studied virtually every aspect of the school—from the hiring of maintenance workers to the extracurricular life students led outside of school—was governed by religious values that went virtually unquestioned. Is such uniformity a virtue or a vice? Is the need to compromise values a necessary evil or something that represents a form of corporate wisdom? Answers to these questions depend, I think, on one's own degree of commitment to an ideological position. If one believes that the truth resides in a particular conception of the human being, compromising that conception for political expediency is not necessarily an asset. Perhaps the major virtue of a democracy is the instantiation of a process that allows individuals to exercise choice, even if at times out of ignorance.

In the foregoing section I described curriculum ideologies as a set of beliefs about what should be taught, for what ends, and for what reasons. I pointed out that although such ideologies are most clearly visible in orthodox views of schooling, whether secular or sectarian, ideological commitments are expressed and developed through the processes of acculturation and professional socialization and are reflected in the tacit as well as the explicit assumptions we make about the nature of reality, knowledge, mind, and education. These ideological commitments reveal themselves in the kind of language we use to describe schools, teaching, and learning; metaphors count in creating a value valence in our attitudes and beliefs about curriculum. Hence, curriculum ideologies can be said to reside on a continuum from the most explicit forms—for example, in positions about education presented, for examples, in manifestos about what should be taught—to the most implicit, delicate shadings of language about education, including language that is intended to be purely descriptive. Indeed, the less visible an ideology is, the more insidious it can be, for in that form it often eludes scrutiny.

It should not be inferred from my remarks that ideologies are, somehow, a kind of infection in education that is to be cured by taking the proper medicine. Nor should it be inferred that ideologies somehow interfere with the exercise of "pure rationality." Because education is a normative enterprise, it cannot be approached value free. Such a position would leave educators with neither rudder nor compass. Any normative enterprise is, by definition, guided by certain beliefs about what counts. These beliefs, in one form or another, constitute an ideological view. Finally, schools or school systems seldom develop their programs through the straightforward application of political decisions deduced from a codified array of value assumptions. The political process in democratic and pluralistic societies requires deliberation, debate, adjustment, and compromise. As a result, examples of "pure" ideologies in action in schools are rare.

One other point. Schools are not objects that once modified in a particular way remain so. Because schools and school districts are subject to the vicissitudes of local and national expectations, changes in schools based on the prevalence of a particular ideological view may last for a short time. As the social and economic conditions of a community change, as its political climate alters, as staff come and go, it becomes necessary for schools to make adjustments and to accommodate to these newly emerging conditions. What this means at the level of practice is the continual readjustment of programs and priorities, even if one wishes to maintain the direction the school has taken prior to those changed conditions. Educational practices and priorities reflecting ideological commitments need modification in order to survive, just as a tightrope walker must correct for movement in the wire if he or she is to remain on it. Put another way, sustaining a direction in schooling or maintaining a set of priorities in the curriculum is much more like nurturing a friendship than installing a refrigerator in the kitchen. The latter requires virtually no attention after installation. The same cannot be said of friendship.

A Comment on the Current State of Curricular Ideologies

Although in the foregoing section I pointed out that ideologies in education can be located on a continuum from the most obvious, public, and articulate statement of purpose, content, and rationale, to the most subtle, private, and latent view, there is a tendency among writers on particular topics—in this case curricular ideologies—to succumb to the temptation to see the world in terms of the topic about which they write. As important as curricular or, more broadly, educational ideologies are for schools, curricular ideologies are rarely presented in a public and articulate form. This is not to say that values do not direct the enterprise. They do. It is to say that American schools are driven by a complex of values and traditions, and by fairly uniform expectations for a shared way of life that is both long-standing and widespread, rather than by a manifesto-like, publicly available ideological doctrine. There are, to be sure, statements of philosophy that school districts dutifully formulate; they are seldom read and what they have to do with the actual operations of schools is less than clear. In this sense most (nonmagnet) public schools in the United States, once one goes beyond general statements of philosophy, do not "stand" for anything. That is, they do not display a uniform articulate ideological position that allows citizens to say this educational view is for me, that isn't.

What most citizens want are good schools. "Good schools" for most parents means teaching children basic skills, preparing them for the world of work or for college, helping them avoid the evil of drugs, and paying attention to those less central topics and issues that arise from time-to-time and from place-to-place in schools across the country (Gallup & Clark, 1987). The major mission, however, of schooling remains largely the same. So, too, does the structure and practice of schooling. Its use of time and space, what it offers, and what it requires of students are remarkably constant. If these features constitute what might be called the operational ideology of schooling, ideological uniformity more than ideological diversity prevails.

If we examine the schools from an operational perspective, as Dreeben (1968) and others have done, that is, from the way in which their day-to-day operations inculcate and tacitly express beliefs and values, and if we regard these beliefs and values as ideological, the following picture appears.

Schools teach children to be punctual. At the middle and secondary school levels where departmentalization prevails, students must arrive and leave class on time, 16 times each day (Eisner, 1985b). Most of these arrivals and departures occur within 5-minute intervals between classes. Schools also teach children to be alone in a crowd (Jackson, 1968) and to delay those gratifications that issue from providing the teacher with the correct answer in order to allow classmates to have a chance to do so. To be in school is to acquire a worldview that appears in the form of largely disconnected subject matters. Children learn to separate ways of knowing that reflect the different subjects they study because of the way those subjects are organized in the curriculum (Eisner, 1985b). Being in school means learning how to complete assignments on time and how to accept such assignments from others rather than generating them for one's self (Apple, 1982). It means regarding rationality as the need to have clear-cut goals in mind at the outset of any intellectual enterprise and to regard means related to those goals as a kind of experimental treatment; rationality is tacitly modeled after a scientist or technological form rather than, for example, an intuitive one.

Schools also convey to students a need to compete. Resources—particularly rewards—are limited and the garlands go to the swiftest. Swiftness, in turn, is defined mainly through achievement in particular forms of cognition. Verbal and mathematical aptitudes are the most useful, given the tasks in which students compete, and the emphasis on these particular aptitudes teaches the young that intellectual ability is defined largely in terms of verbal and mathematical performance.

Because of the ways in which schools organize and sort children, opportunities to learn from other students, younger or older, is diminished. Schools organize children by "litter"—children of the same age are assigned to the same grade and progression through the school keeps constant this form of age-grading (Goodlad & Anderson, 1959). This form of school organization reinforces the idea that the task of being a successful student is to learn the content of the grade, a condition that results in promotion to the next. It also reinforces the idea that knowledge is fixed and tidy, that smart people possess it, that textbooks contain it, and that the aim of schooling is its orderly transmission (Jackson, 1986).

The kind of curricular tasks and subjects emphasized in the early grades are also instructive in ways well beyond their original intent. Reading, writing, and arithmetic at the early levels of schooling are subjects that are highly rule-governed in character. By rule-governed I mean that these so-called skill subjects emphasize the correct application or use of social conventions. Spelling and arithmetic are two examples of rule-governed tasks. Such tasks convey to children that their most important activities in school have single, correct answers, that those answers are known by the teacher, and that their primary responsibility as students is to learn the correct ones. The school creates an environment that does not put much premium on imagination, on personal spirit, or on creative thinking. It emphasizes a form of rationality that seeks convergence on the known more than exploration of the unknown. It emphasizes the virtues of hard work. It limits the degree to which personal goal setting can occur and it rewards conformity to correct outcome more than it rewards productive idiosyncrasy.

Can such practices be regarded collectively as a curricular ideology? The answer to this question is, at base, arbitrary. If an ideology is defined as a *public* statement of a value position regarding curriculum, then the absence of such a statement would disqualify it as an ideology. If, however, an ideology also refers to a shared way of life that teaches a certain worldview or set of values through action, then schools everywhere employ and convey an ideology because they all possess, in practice, a shared way of life or what may be called an operational ideology.

It needs to be said that the ideologies that make a difference for those in school—teachers and students—are those that permeate their activities on a daily basis. A written manifesto of educational beliefs that never infuses the day-to-day operations of schools has no practical import for either teachers or students; such beliefs are window dressing.

The view presented in this chapter is that it is useful to conceive a curriculum ideology, or even more broadly an educational ideology, in two ways. That is, it is useful in comprehending educational practice to understand how beliefs about what is valued influence what is taught, for what ends, and for what reasons. Shifts in those beliefs can have substantial consequences for how schools function. At the same time, it is the way in which schools actually function that, de facto, help shape the way students come to view the world of schooling and the values they secure about it. It is also useful to examine schools to uncover their tacit ideologies, their subtexts, as well as what they publicly espouse. Such inquiries have been undertaken by Dreeben (1968), Eisner (1985b), Jackson (1968), Smith and Geoffrey (1968), Waller (1932), and many others.

It is important to note that in the United States in recent years there has been a movement toward the creation of schools that *do* reflect particular educational ideologies. Magnet schools (Metz, 1986) have been developed throughout the country that provide special programs, emphasizing particular kinds of educational values. For example, there are magnet schools that advertise an emphasis on traditional educational values: homework each day, achievement testing each week, and an emphasis on the three R's. There are other schools that advertise an experientially based program: individualization of the curriculum, hands-on activities, field trips, group projects, and cooperative learning. Such schools provide very different educational environments. Each is guided by a different image of its mission and what students ought to learn in the course of their education. Given their distinctive mission, they do what the typical public school does not do; they hoist an ideological flag that tells the community what they stand for and therefore give the public a choice.

Six Curriculum Ideologies

Thus far I have provided a general description of some of the ways in which ideologies function in the schools. In this section I will identify six curriculum ideologies and describe their core values and views about curriculum, including their views of the mission of the school. Although these six ideological positions do not exhaust those that influence schools, they are among the most prominent. It should also be said that ideologies are never as definite or clear in practice as they are on paper. In addition, interpretations of any particular ideology differ, even among their adherents; hence, what follows are, of necessity, general characterizations of ideological positions rather than unassailable descriptions of the particular views of individual adherents. The six ideologies are refereed to as Religious Orthodoxy, Rational Humanism, Progressivism, Critical Theory, Reconceptualism, and Cognitive Pluralism.

Religious Orthodoxy

One feature that all religious orthodox ideologies share is their belief in the existence of God and the importance of God's message in defining the content, aims, and conditions of educational practice. In America, about 90 percent of all private or independent elementary and secondary schools are Roman Catholic. The major aim of the Roman Catholic schools is to induct the young into the Roman Catholic Church, and through the Church, to Christ. American Evangelical Christians have similar aims, though clearly not "the same" God. Orthodox Jews, whose schools serve less than 1 percent of the American school-age population, are similarly engaged. At the heart of the religious enterprise is a conception of how life ought to be lived and a conception of the kinds of habits and beliefs that will lead to its realization. How do religiously constituted groups with relative clear opinions about the constituents of educational virtue go about realizing their educational aims in schools? How do their beliefs affect the experience of the young? Certain religious groups, the Jesuits for example, have had a long-standing interest in social justice (Kuntz, 1986). This interest is displayed in their educational priorities and in their attention to this aspect of religious life in the curriculum. Kuntz (1986), himself a Jesuit and a student of Jesuit education, writes:

> In the Jesuit tradition, it is the teacher who must be responsible for the success or failure of education for justice. The teacher in the Jesuit school has a double purpose: to enable the students to appropriate Christian norms of morality even in the fact of external cultural pressures, and to encourage the students to conduct their lives in accordance with those norms. Jesuit educators place the primary responsibility for moral education on the teacher. (p. 113)

Convictions such as this are central to the Jesuits, but they are not nearly as critical for other Catholic orders. Thus, Catholicism as one variant of Christianity is itself varied, even pluralistic in its orientation to education. When it comes to other forms of Christian belief, evangelical Christianity, for example, the variability is just as wide within, not to speak of the differences between, evangelicals and Catholics.

Jews express their common faith in three major religious belief systems: orthodox, conservative, and reform. Members of each group embrace different ideas about what it means to be a Jew and therefore the kinds of personal attributes, beliefs, and behaviors children and adolescents ought to develop under the aegis of their schools. For orthodox Jews, only certain forms of adaptation to secular life are acceptable. For example, on the Sabbath it is not permitted for orthodox Jews to walk more than 2,000 "paces," a safeguard against using the Sabbath for purposes of work. The orthodox Jew must not only eat kosher food, he or she must keep a kosher home, meaning, among other things, that eating utensils for dairy and meat products must be kept separate. In addition, daily prayers are mandatory, and the Sabbath—the holiest day of the week—must also be kept.

For conservative and reform Jews, religious laws pertaining to daily life are, arguably, less demanding and the relationship between religious and secular life more forgiving. Thus even within the same religion, the meaning of what it means to be religious has considerable variance and those differing views find their practical expression not only in how their adherents behave in general, but also what is emphasized in schools. For example, in orthodox Jewish religious schools, it is estimated that about 60 percent of the time during the day is devoted to the study of religious texts. In reform Jewish schools, about 30 percent of the time is devoted to such materials. In orthodox schools, boys and girls are separated. In conservative and reform schools, the classes are mixed. Each group has a different view of what God requires, even though each of the three groups honors the "same" God.

At the upper reaches of secondary schooling, a special place of curriculum privilege is given to the interpretation of text. Religious texts are traditionally subject to various interpretations and the ability to discover God's meaning has been the ultimate aim of biblical and Talmudic scholarship. As a result, hermeneutic analysis has been one of the important intellectual practices in the development of religious scholarship. In this process, conflicting interpretations among authorities are sometimes employed to stimulate readers into participating in the intellectual puzzlements that emanate from competing, but at the same time plausible, interpretations of text. Such practices, when they occur, appear to have a paradoxical quality in the context of a dogmatically committed educational ideology, yet this apparent paradox can be said to reside at the very heart of a spiritual life.

As indicated earlier, the aim of an orthodoxy is to shape the views of others so that they are compatible with the views contained in the orthodoxy. Orthodoxies are not essentially about doubts, but about certainties. Indeed, to become orthodox is to become a true believer. The exploration of competing views regarding biblical interpretation is, at the very least, an admission that truths, even biblical truths, are uncertain. Hence, the cultivation in the young of attitudes that seek and even reward the exploration of ambiguity—for interpretation always requires some ambiguity in order to have the space to function—seems paradoxical. True beliefs revealed through dogma appear antithetical to ambiguity, yet biblical interpretation as *an intellectual process* requires it.

It is clear that at the elementary grades the propensity among the young to question, doubt, and criticize the basic tenets of religious orthodoxy is discouraged, particularly in evangelical schools where the mission of the institution is to pass on God's word, not to question it (Peshkin, 1986). In this environment the cultivation of a critical attitude is troublesome for it can undermine the very ideology directing the system and can erode the structure of authority it requires in order to maintain its intellectual hegemony.

In *Smith. v the Board of School Commissioners of Mobile County et al.* (N. D.), a suit filed by evangelical parents not only alleged that the Board omitted culturally appropriate Christian content from the curriculum, it also alleged that the attitudes fostered by instruction in the schools undermined parental authority by encouraging children to critically question traditions and their parents' conventional beliefs. Smith's attorneys argued in their brief to the Court:

> Plaintiffs Smith now seek relief from this Court from (1) the unconstitutional advancement of the religion of Humanism in the curriculum used in the Mobile County school system; (2) the unconstitutional inhibition of Christianity caused by the curriculum used in the Mobile County school system; (3) the unconstitutional violation of the free exercise of religion rights of teachers and students by the exclusive teaching of Humanism and the systematic exclusion from the curriculum of the existence, history, contributions, and role of Christianity in the United States and the world; (4) the unconstitutional violations of the rights of students to receive information, of the rights of teachers to free speech, and of the prohibitions against governmental disapproval of religion, inhibition of religion, and discrimination against religion caused by the systematic exclusion from the curriculum used in the Mobile County school system of the existence, history, contributions, and role of Christianity in the United States and the world; and (5) the violation of the statutory mandate to teach the "established facts of American history, tradition and patriotism." (p. 3)

What is clear is that at least some of the values embraced by the Mobile, Alabama, Board of Education were in direct conflict with the values held by evangelical parents. Parents embracing the evangelical ideology represented by their religion had no interest in developing in their children the kind of critical skepticism that is prized in rational or humanistic orientations to education. For them the development of such skills and attitudes could only serve to weaken the religious commitment that parents believed essential to salvation. In addition, parents argued that not only did the Mobile, Alabama, curriculum omit important factual content, such as attention to the influence of Christianity in the history of the United States, but also that the curriculum advertently or inadvertently promoted an alternative religious doctrine. Rational humanism, they argued, constituted this doctrine and the school board, therefore, not only violated students' rights by acts of omission, but also by direct acts of commission. The parents went to the Court to remedy what they believed to be a violation of their religious rights under the First Amendment to the Constitution.

In related cases, beliefs about the theory of evolution, which pertains directly to beliefs about the nature of human nature, has been subject to legal review motivated by people whose religious convictions find evolutionary theory antithetical to their own certainty concerning the human being's genesis on earth. When religious groups create and manage their own schools, the presence of strong religious views and the virtual absence of more widely held secular views pose no significant, overt problem. The public schools do what state education codes and their trustees think best and those directing religious schools follow their own path. To be sure, court cases and local pressures emerge from time to time and are resolved largely on an ad hoc basis. In general, though, secular and sectarian schools operate within their own sphere of influence and induct the young into the views their parents hold dear.

At first glance it seems that insulation and isolation from mainstream values is simply a form of benign neglect or a congenial way to cope with a potential problem of value conflict. One must, however, raise the question about how far a democratic nation can permit groups to inculcate into their children beliefs that, should their children achieve political saliency, would restrict the very freedoms that have been afforded them in their own schools. Peshkin (1986) raises this important question in his analysis of evangelical fundamentalist schooling in America. It is the issue that James Madison (1961) raised in *The Federalist Papers,* where he struggled with creating a set of principles that would provide for minority protection *and* minority rights, and that maintains a system of government "ruled" by the majority. The tensions that Madison identified in 1784 are still with us.

Although not itself a religious ideology, political belief structures can approximate some of the dogmatic features of religious views regarding the ways in which schools should function and the ends they should seek to attain. Teruhisa Horio (1988), a Japanese scholar, writes of the current tendencies of the Japanese Ministry of Education to promulgate educational policies for Japanese schools that are uncomfortably close to the militaristic policies promulgated by the Ministry of Education during the days of imperialist Japan prior to and during the Second World War. According to Horio, in Japan, local control of schools is being eroded and the scope of teacher authority is being diminished. In addition, Horio claims that textbooks have failed to provide Japanese children with the kind of balanced social view that he believes a viable democracy requires. As a result, the Japanese educational system, he says, is being guided by a subtle but influential array of authoritarian beliefs that may in the long run undermine the democratic potential of modern Japan. In Horio's view, business interests now dominate educational policies and traditional reliance on authority and status hierarchy in Japan is being recultivated by government. The same ideologies that led Japan astray in the early decades of the 20th century are, in Horio's opinion, reappearing today. He writes:

At about the same time, the then Vice-President of the United States, Richard M. Nixon, declared on an official visit to Japan that the Peace Constitution represented a major "mistake" in America's postwar policy for the reconstruction of Japan. Thus peace education was conceived of by both American and Japanese leaders as an obstacle to constitutional revision and remilitarization. Patriotic education was strongly advocated as the most desirable way to correct what were then being spoken of as the "excesses of democratization." Through their calls for a new emphasis on patriotism the anti-pacifist, anti-socialist, pro-American elements in Japanese society had found a new way to revive the prewar *kokutai* ideology and reassert what were ultimately anti-democratic values. (p. 148)

If one substitutes dogmatism for religious ideological views, the scope of the category increases considerably, for under such an umbrella can fall all types of dogmatic positions, especially those advocated at either end of the political spectrum. Both the ultra left and the ultra right are utterly convinced in the veracity of their own opinions and values.

Another example of ideological influence on curriculum can be found in the Waldorf Schools. These schools, and more important the programs they provide, were initiated in 1919 by German philosopher Rudolph Steiner. Asked by the owners of the Waldorf-Astoria Cigarette Company to create a school for the children of its employees, Steiner set about to design an educational program based on the principles of anthroposophy. Uhrmacher (1990) writes:

Anthroposophy might be thought of in two ways. First, it is a path of self-development for those who wish to follow Steiner's direction toward spiritual cognition. According to Steiner, human beings can develop latent organs of cognition so that they may directly perceive the spirit world. Second, Anthroposophy is also the fruit born from Steiner's ideas and methods. Biodynamic farming, Anthroposophic medicine, eurythmy and Waldorf schools are a few of the results from Steiner's spiritual knowledge. (Chapter 1)

Steiner tries to connect the life before birth to life after death, to conceive of human development in mystical yet optimistic terms. As an educational movement, Waldorf education has had an impressive growth throughout the world. At present there are about 330 Waldorf Schools functioning in 40 countries throughout the globe. In America alone, there are over 80 such schools. What we have in Waldorf education is a stunning example of a nonevangelical movement growing slowly but surely over a 60-year period. Waldorf Schools, largely neglected by mainstream educators and educational researchers, not only provide a curriculum based on philosophical and developmental principles, but also an organizational structure and teaching practices that reflect those principles. For example, it is the individual teacher who admits students to any particular Waldorf School. It is a teacher council that determines the educational policy for the school. Students remain with the same class teacher for an 8-year period rather than moving from teacher to teacher each year. Even the color of the classroom walls is determined by developmental principles that Rudolph Steiner articulated. These and other practices, such as a main lesson each day, an emphasis on myth and legend in the curriculum, and keeping of a log by each child, are a part of the educational regiment of Waldorf Schools. These schools, as much as any I know, attempt to relate classroom and school practice to philosophical beliefs. Given growth they have enjoyed, they are apparently succeeding.

All of the foregoing ideological views are in one way or another rooted in religious beliefs. They all share a belief in a supernatural being at the core of their philosophy and some permit no critical analysis of their basic value assumptions. For some ideologies, this prohibition of critical scrutiny of core beliefs leads to a form of dogmatism that could be regarded as the antithesis of an educational process. When the aim of an enterprise is directed toward the production of true believers, consideration of alternative sources of evidence in the weighing of belief is in jeopardy. Yet, those who hold dogmatic beliefs believe that their first obligation to children is to induct them into their belief structure. They claim that human rationality at its best is incapable of fully understanding God's plan; only arrogance and ignorance would suppose otherwise. It is precisely our inability to fully comprehend God's ways that leads to faith, a central tenet of any religiously oriented ideology. The result is a kind of stand-off between those who claim that orthodoxies of any kind lead to dogmatism and that dogmatisms are inherently alien to education, and those who say that faith in God's word transcends human rationality and that it is our overblown sense of self, our inflated conception of our own limited powers, that leads us to believe that we can "test" God's word.

When ideological beliefs make no difference in the content of educational practice or the conditions within which such practices occur, those beliefs can make no difference in the lives of the young. The fact of the matter is, however, that such ideologies are hardly ever without consequences for the practice of education.

Rational Humanism

Now we turn to a second ideology bearing on schooling—Rational Humanism.

Rational Humanism locates its modern roots in the Enlightenment and its ancient roots in Plato. Today, its most visible educational manifestation is found in Mortimer Adler's (1982) *Paideia Proposal* and, in the 1930s through the 1950s, in the Great Books Program promulgated by Robert

Maynard Hutchins and Mortimer Adler. There are some important distinctions to make regarding the aspirations of Enlightenment scholars such as Auguste Compte and modern day Rational Humanists.

Compte and others believed that the universe in which we live is, in principal, understandable and that through rational methods, best exemplified in science, the workings of the clocklike character of the world could be discovered. Mysticism and religious revelation were practices that for them were ill-suited to the human's rational nature and that that rational nature, as Aristotle had indicated, was to know. With the Enlightenment, a new optimism was cultivated and the promise of success was sufficiently attractive to lead scholars to believe that the order of the universe would someday be discovered by a rational mind. Scientific method was the procedure, par excellence, for achieving this enlightened status. With it came a new faith in the power of the human, particularly in the human's intelligence to guide and control his or her own future, to take control of his or her own life. The spirit that animated the Rational Humanism of Hutchins and Adler is broader than the methods of science. The laboratory was, according to Hutchins (1953), only *one* of the important resources for learning and knowing. There were others, and these were, at base, even more potentially powerful than science.

The pedagogical method that Hutchins and Adler espoused is based on their view that the distinctive feature of the human being is the capacity to exercise reason, and reason does not ultimately depend on empirical demonstration or on the conditions necessary for scientific knowledge, but on reflection and insight. Reflection and insight, in turn, could be fostered, they argued, by providing two educational conditions in the classroom. First, the content of the curriculum needed to offer students old enough to reason the very best that humans have written and created. *The Great Books of the Western World,* the program that Hutchins and Adler began in 1938, reflected this belief. Hutchins reasoned that because not all human works were "created equal," and because time in school is limited, students should study the very best rather than the mediocre. Hence, content inclusion and content exclusion decisions were of paramount importance (Walker & Schaffarzick, 1972).

Of equal importance was the method through which the great works were studied. In a great many schools, there is a heavy emphasis on the memorization of information, a process that is reinforced through the use of short answer and multiple choice tests (Cuban, 1988). When teaching methods emphasize the transmission of information and testing methods assess the extent of its recall, they are not likely to develop rational powers. To develop such powers it is necessary to employ what Adler (1982) calls *mieutic processes.* These are processes that engage students in in-depth reasoning about the material they study. Ideally, the teacher's behavior is dialectic rather than didactic. It is intended to enable students to provide reasons for their opinions and to find evidence and counterarguments to the views being expressed. For such matters the most useful pedagogical method is likely to be philosophical, literary, or artistic in character. It is likely to invite or stimulate analysis, even controversy. Rationality, according to Hutchins and Adler, is a potential achievement of human nature, but its cultivation is required in order for it to flourish.

The very principles that Rational Humanism advances—the centrality of human reason, man as the measure of all things, the contextualized nature of knowledge as a human construction although, at the same time, recognizing the existence of Truth—are principles that religious dogmatics reject. If God exists, and if God is truth, then to conceive of education in terms that make man the measure of all things is to lead children into spiritual damnation.

The practical educational implications of Rational Humanism center on curriculum content and teaching methods. As I already indicated, humanists believe that once students have learned how to read and cipher, they ought to be exposed to the best of the best. This, incidentally, does not mean reliance on secondary commentaries, but on the contrary, on the appropriate use of primary source material. It is much better to read Thomas Jefferson than to read about Thomas Jefferson. Indeed, from recent commentaries of contemporary critics of education regarding the vacuity and lifelessness of school textbooks, the admonition does not seem far off the mark. But, in addition, discussion, analysis, and debate are to be among the critical methods of instruction. As long as the issues students address are not cut and dried, debate is possible. As long as debate is possible, the higher mental processes can be stimulated and developed.

Rational Humanism, as an educational ideology, is often accused of being culturally parochial—only Western content is offered—and elitist. The former accusation is, in my view, unjustified, certainly at the level of principle. There is no reason why the content of the curriculum must necessarily be derived from works of the Western world, even if traditionally they have been so derived. If the premise that goodness adheres unequally in different works is accepted, there is no reason within Rational Humanism to restrict goodness to works created in the West.

As far as elitism is concerned, there are several ways to respond to this charge. One is that the proper aim of education is to expand the elite, that is, to enable all students to encounter and to be informed by the best works humans have created. A second is that if the best works that have been created are restricted to those now able to decode their meaning—the upper-middle and upper classes—then surely those in the lower socioeconomic classes will be consigned to a second-class intellectual status because of the second-rate curriculum that they will be offered. If it is argued that the quality of a work is simply determined by arbitrary judgment that has no possible justification or evidentiary base, then the selection of content becomes not only arbitrary, but relativistic, and if relativistic, there can be no basis for the appraisal of educational development. If *all* works are of equal value, *any* selection is as good as any other.

The cornerstone of Rational Humanism is a belief in the primacy of reason and in the human's ability to make rational and defensible judgments about the goodness of things. As long as this cornerstone remains intact, relativism must be rejected as a basis for the selection of curriculum content.

Although Rational Humanism has received much fanfare, mainly from its critics, its implementation in American schools is not widespread. Except for some private schools and those public schools that have attempted to develop Paideia Programs, the ideas of Rational Humanism are more like latent ideals than operating processes. The national penchant for evidence regarding educational attainment through measured performance does not sit comfortably with an orientation to education that celebrates reason, rationality, and extended explanation. Exegesis is difficult when the optical scanner must be used to score student responses. In short, our assessment technology imposes its own practical values and limitations on the content and methods of schooling. Those practical values are often incongruent with the values that Rational Humanists hold dear.

A few recent developments in American education reflect some of the values found in Rational Humanism, although the match is far from perfect. The developments I speak of are the efforts among some to define a curricular canon and to use original source material, especially in literature and history, to provide curriculum content. Hirsch's *Cultural Literacy* (1988), which in many ways is antiethical to Rational Humanism, nevertheless participates in the view that not all content is created equal. Knowing what counts matters and Hirsch and his colleagues have endeavored to identify what every American should know, best represented in their effort to create a cultural dictionary: Rational Humanism properly conceived places little emphasis on the idea of a dictionary of content, indeed such an emphasis, even tacitly, misconceives the meaning of content in Rational Humanism. Content is not to be construed as memorizing the facts, but as the development of a critical understanding of the values and premises that underlie important works. The implication of a fixed body of content to be found in Hirsch's "dictionary" runs counter to the spirit of the enterprise, even though it shares one of its important features.

Perhaps more closely identified with a rational humanistic ideology is the publication of the National Endowment for the Humanities, *American Memory* (Cheney, 1987). This public policy statement does echo much of the spirit of Rational Humanism: the emphasis on great works and humanistic forms of understanding, the desire for a common core curriculum for all, regardless of ability, and the promulgation of the higher mental processes through critical analyses of primary source material. These features of sound curricula are quite congruent with the humanists' educational values.

It should be said that although some might feel that the prescription of a common curriculum for a nation of 250 million is utopian, or naive, or ethnocentric, the case Rational Humanists wish to make is that without such commonality some children—most likely those of the poor—will receive an inferior program of studies, thus condemning them to a further life of poverty. Rather than to differentiate educational quality on the basis of ethnic, social, or economic criteria, all children should be afforded the very best culture has to offer. Where variability might be required is in method, not in content or educational aim. It is those who wish to accommodate group differences by differentiating content and aims that are the true elitists. Societies that differentiate the educational programs provided to the young on the basis of their economic or cultural roots deny opportunities to the less advantaged. As Hutchins (1953) has said, because in a democracy all who vote rule, all should have the education of rulers.

One other feature of rational humanistic ideology is important to mention. That feature pertains to matters of curriculum electives and vocational specialization prior to graduate school. To those who share the values of Hutchins and Adler, both options are anathema. Electives are undesirable, they believe, because the child is not in a good position to know what will best serve his or her educational interests. Because to know that requires that one have an education, something the child does not yet have, the child is not in a good position to make such decisions. As for vocational specialization, that option is appropriate only after the student's general education has been completed. Furthermore, it is inappropriate to attempt to provide such specialized content in public schools because the public schools are notoriously out-of-date regarding vocational matters. In addition, Hutchins asserts, the good schoolmaster is known by the important subjects he *refuses* to teach. Not everything that's important—and vocational skills are important—are the responsibility of elementary and secondary schools. But even if this were not so, it would be premature to focus a student's attention on vocational concerns before the course of general education has been completed. It is the virtual absence of a common intellectual culture that weakens the nation's ability to communicate: we lack a common cultural context. This is one of the major problems that Hirsch's *Cultural Literacy* (1988) was intended to solve.

Given America's current romance with the world of commerce—remember, regaining our "competitive edge" is the current catchword—it is unlikely that in the short term Rational Humanism will have much of a place in mainstream American schools. Where this idealized orientation is more likely to flourish is in those private schools that serve a social and economic elite, and perhaps in those schools that have for so long failed minority populations that virtually any new approach promising success will be tried. Currently, the appetite for approaches to education that appear noninstrumental to practical ends measured in standardized ways is not very large. A nation that has little toleration for ambiguity in its politics and a need for happy endings in its movies is likely to regard Rational Humanism as a bit too intellectual to be appropriate for today's world.

Progressivism

The third curricular ideology that I examine, progressivism, is most forcefully expressed in the writings of John Dewey and the large group of followers he and his ideas attracted. As Cremin (1970) and others have pointed out, Progressivism in education has had two related but distinguishable streams. One of those was rooted in a conception of the nature of human experience and intelligence, the other in social reform. Although Dewey addressed the romantic and reform side of his educational philosophy at different periods in his career, these two streams within American Progressivism are perhaps most clearly represented in the works of Harold Rugg and Ann Schumacher (1928) on the one hand, and George Counts (1932) on the other. Rugg and Schumacher's *The Child-Centered School* was influenced by the desire to create schools that addressed the covert, emotional life of the child, a life that Freud paid so much attention to. George Counts (1932), however, was concerned with the social and economic inequities of American society and thought schools had a positive obligation to "change the social order." Some of the manifestations of Rugg and Schumacher's orientation to education find expression in the work of A. S. Neill (1960) and are echoed in the present-day work of some curricular reconceptualists, particularly Grumet (1988) and Pinar (1988), while Counts's legacy appears in the writings of critical theorists such as Apple (1982) and Giroux (1989).

In one sense, the two streams within Progressivism can be regarded as on the one hand emphasizing the personal, on the other, the political. Dewey himself would never have made such a distinction because he believed the character of the political process inevitably influenced the kind of personal life the individual led, and the kind of individual life an individual was able to lead shaped the kind of politics he or she was able to embrace.

Because Dewey's work is so central to any analysis of Progressivism in American education, and because Progressivism, writ large, has been such an important ideological strain in American educational though, Dewey's works will be used to exemplify progressive ideology.

Dewey's work is rooted in a biological conception of the human being. By this I mean that he regards the human being as a growing organism whose major developmental task is to come to terms, through adaptation or transformation, with the environment in which he or she lives. Because the environment is not always hospitable to the comfort or even the survival of the organism, thinking is required. It is through the exercise and development of intelligence that the environment is reshaped. It is through the reshaping process that the individual learns and through which intelligence grows. In this sense, for Dewey, human life is a continuous process of constructive adaptation. Intelligence itself is not fixed, it grows. It is not a thing, it is a process. It is not restricted to a limited sphere of content—words or numbers—but manifests itself wherever and in whatever material problems can be posed and solved.

The development of intelligence—what Dewey called *growth*—does not emerge from biology or genetics alone, it requires the resources of culture. Young humans are notoriously dependent on adults for survival. The early manifestations of dependency are largely physical, but later, as biological development occurs, cultural resources are provided and the child begins to incorporate into his or her intellectual repertoire the variety of social skills and cultural tools—language, for example—that is made available. These cultural resources are, in a sense, intellectual amplifiers: they expand the individual's ability to cope with the objective conditions of the environment. Such coping includes the ability to conceptualize or pose problems through which constructive adaptation occurs. Indeed, one of the school's major tasks, according to Dewey (1902), is to create what he calls the *educational situations* through which a child becomes increasingly able to deal with ever more complex and demanding problems. What grows through this process of increasing competence is the child's intelligence.

The roots of Dewey's Progressivism are found in Darwin's (1897/1975) evolutionary theory in biology and in Hegel's (1900) ideas concerning thesis-antithesis. They were also shaped by the temper of the time. The turn of the century was an intellectually exciting period in America, indeed in the world. In the young behavioral sciences, a new optimism was emerging: the possibility of creating a scientific understanding of human nature. On the social side in America, waves of immigrants were populating American cities and workers were organizing to secure their rights in industry (Cremin, 1961). The schools were being both criticized for their lack of productivity (Callahan, 1962) while, at the same time, they were expected to do more and to serve a wider and more diversified population. In addition, a more dynamic view of human development was appearing among American intellectuals. The climate was right for educational change. Cremin writes:

> The same era that saw the rise of social Darwinism—both the conservative and the reform varieties—also witnessed the birth of a new psychology dedicated to the scientific study of human behavior in general and the phenomena of mind in particular. As with correlative developments in sociology, European influences were critical, but they were always tempered by the distinctive demands of the American scene. Thus, Edwin Boring has noted that the

paternity of American psychology was Germany, deriving from the work of Gustav Fechner, Hermann von Helmholtz, and Wilhelm Wundt; while the maternity was English, and is to be found in the work of Darwin, Francis Galton, and of course, Spencer. The child, however, was much influenced by the environment in which it grew up; for the Americans, as usual, borrowed selectively, and ended up fashioning a psychology clearly designed to serve the practical needs of their own civilization. (p. 100)

The conditions that Cremin described provided a fertile ground for the liberal ideas that Dewey advanced, particularly in that most optimistic of institutions, education. No longer was it appropriate to regard the child as a passive receptacle to be filled with curriculum content. No longer could mind and emotion be regarded as independent. No longer could the curriculum be thought of as a static, fixed body of content, created in administrative offices and handed down to teachers. The child acted on the environment, he or she did not simply digest it, and in the process, that environment was personally transformed. Emotion could not be disregarded in dealing with matters intellectual, because how children felt about what they studied influenced how they thought about what they studied. As for the curriculum, it could not be optimally developed by people who had never seen the child; hence, teachers needed to play a fundamental role in its creation.

As familiar and reasonable as these ideas may seem today, their introduction in the late 1880s was innovative, indeed radical. As they began to transform and develop in the first 4 decades of the 20th century, they took a direction that Dewey himself felt compelled to caution against.

Dewey's concerns about the excesses of American progressive education are most succinctly expressed in his 1938 publication *Experience and Education*. Simply stated, his small book is an effort to save his philosophy of education from his friends.

Despite Dewey's reservations concerning the ways in which his ideas were interpreted, his work provided then as it does today a powerful ideological view of what school, curricula, and teaching should be about. His conception of cognitive development—a term that he did not use—is consonant with the ideas of psychologists such as Piaget (1973) in Switzerland and Vygotsky (1962) in the once-Soviet Union. And his conception of intelligence as an active *process* rather than a static or fixed entity, as an event that is displayed differentially by individuals depending on the circumstances and the form of representation employed, is congruent with recent theoretical conceptions of intellectual ability (Gardner, 1983). In short, Dewey's work adumbrated many of today's most advanced notions pertaining to the intellectual and social development of children.

There are three points I wish to emphasize regarding Dewey's thought that are central to a progressive educational ideology. These pertain to his conception of the school as a whole, his view of appropriate curriculum content, and his view of the teacher's professional duties.

For Dewey, the "envelope" for the educational process was the school itself. Broader than the formal curriculum, it provided a shared way of life and social conditions that convey to the child the norms of social living. Although Dewey did not believe that there could be parity between adult and child in educational decision making—after all, the teacher did know more—he did believe that to the degree possible, the school and the classroom should reflect democratic principles. What this meant in practice was that schools and classrooms should offer children appropriate opportunities to formulate their own rules for social living, that internal and personal needs should be respected in the creation of learning activities, that group processes should be fostered so that children learned how to use collective intelligence to cope with problems in which their peers had an equal interest. It would be fatal, Dewey believed, to espouse the virtues of democratic life and to impose on schools an authoritarian form of management. The school, in a sense, was to be what the society under the best of circumstances was to become. This lesson, alas, is one that is yet to be learned in most schools.

As far as the curriculum itself, it was to display several features. First and foremost, it was to be problem-centered. By problem-centered, Dewey meant that the art of teaching was one that enabled the teacher to so construct the environment that children would be motivated to formulate problems or, in other terms, to make their situations problematic. The instantiation of a problem, itself an act of intelligence, provided the conditions for the use of experimental thought in pursuit of its resolution. For Dewey, the "complete act of thought" (1910)—the movement from purpose, to experimental treatment, to assessment of results—so exquisitely exemplified in science, was a model toward which curricula should aspire.

To create such problematic situations, the teacher not only needed to understand the intellectual potential of a body of ideas, he or she also needed to understand the child. "Start from where the child is" became a familiar admonition to Progressive teachers, an admonition that is not very distant from Vygotsky's (1962) notion of the zone of proximal development. The importance of starting from where the child is is directly related to the need to relate the problematic situation to the child's experience, as well as to his or her level of skill and understanding. The artistry in pedagogy is partly one of placement—finding the place within the child's experience that will enable her to stretch intellectually while avoiding tasks so difficult that failure is assured. To achieve this placement, the teacher needed to know the child.

As for teaching the "Progressive way," each child was to be a custom job. This implies an approach that required teachers to appreciate the child's background, to deal with the "whole child." "Whole" here meant the child was to be seen as a social and emotional creature, not only as an academic or intellectual one. The Progressives quite correctly recognized that children do not park their emotions on the threshold to the school as they enter. What a child had experienced and how he or she was feeling was directly relevant to the teacher's professional aims.

It should be noted that such attitudes toward teaching practice were far distant from the efforts being made during the same period to run schools like factories and to manage the teacher's performance in ways similar to those used in industrial settings. The efficiency movement in education did not speak of the child's needs, or of the child's wholeness (Callahan, 1962). Teaching was not viewed as a matter of artistry, but as a matter of efficiency. The outcomes of schooling were not thought of as the cultivation of unique talents, but the achievement of standardized goals. In short, the images of educational virtue reflected in progressive educational ideology and those reflected in what Callahan (1962) has called "the cult of efficiency" were almost opposite. It requires no great insight to recognize that these polarities concerning the aims and methods of education are still salient today.

In addition to the artistry that Progressives assigned to teaching at its best, the responsibilities of the teacher included in-context curriculum development. This meant that although a school district or even a state might provide a framework for curriculum development, the primary responsibility for designing educational programs, often on the wing, resided with the teacher. The reason this must be so is not only because it is the teacher who knows the child, but also because events within the classroom are often unpredictable and the need to exploit the teachable moment is always present. It is precisely the kind of intelligent pedagogical adaptability, this shifting of aims, that Dewey regarded as exemplifying what he called "flexible purposing."

It is more than of passing interest to note that much of the current debate concerning the improvement of schooling in both the United States and the United Kingdom is centered on the appropriateness of prescriptions by federal authorities of common national standards, or as is the case in the United Kingdom, a national curriculum. When the public becomes concerned about the quality of education provided in its schools, it tends to have two reactions. The first is to monitor more closely than it has in the past the performance of schools; this is called accountability. Second, it reiterates in the public forum its national (or state) goals for education. Through standardization of assessment and prescriptive curriculum, that is, by tightening up and reducing the professional discretionary space for teachers, efforts are made to create more educationally productive schools. Ironically, at the same time that such standardization is occurring, education policies are being promoted that urge that teachers, as the primary professional stakeholders, should have greater professional discretion in program planning and in monitoring and governing "their" schools (*Tomorrow's Teachers*, 1986).

These tensions are not unusual in nations that permit ideological pluralism. The efficiency movement in American education had its heyday during the very same period in which American progressive education was virtually at its peak. Perhaps one of the indices of democracy is its tolerance for ideological pluralism. Yet, pluralism in the name of democracy ensures neither the virtue nor the efficacy of the positions espoused. It seems to me unlikely that national standards, even national assessment, will be sufficient to improve American or British schools. The problems are more complex and the kind of investment needed much larger. If the public articulation of national goals was sufficient, *A Nation at Risk* (USA Research, 1984), perhaps the most widely disseminated statement on education published in America during the 20th century, should have done the trick. But who today can remember the five "new basics" given such vast publicity in 1983?

One final comment on progressive education as a curriculum ideology: given the visibility that progressive education has had—some laudatory, some hostile—one might conclude that during its peak period, say from the end of the 1920s to the end of the 1940s, Progressive education was a mainstream movement in American public schools. It was not. Where Progressive education did flourish was in small independent schools. Indeed, the first eight presidents of the Progressive Education Association were principals of such schools (Cremin, 1961). Like many other ideologically driven movements—the Plowden Report (1966), which oriented British primary schools of the 1960s, for example—there was more talk than practice. In England my search for Progressive British primary schools in 1972 proved to be more difficult than I anticipated before I left America (Eisner, 1974). I estimate that at the very most only 10 percent of the primary schools in Britain at the time could be said to reflect the spirit of the Plowden Report.

Perhaps the important lesson to be learned here is that it is unwise to confuse the public visibility of an idea in professional journals and in the public media with its practical application in the schools. Schools are remarkably robust institutions, slow to change; it is much easier to talk about innovation than to achieve it. Cuban (1979) describes the situation by making an analogy between the operations of the school and a storm at sea. Although the storm at sea might wreak havoc on the surface of the water— waves of 30 or more feet might be blown about—at the bottom of the sea the waters remain calm and quiet. Similarly, although the public press might have a heyday with new, even radical ideas about educational practice, teachers working alone in classrooms quietly go about business as usual; the most experienced have learned very well how to ride out the storm. Thus, if we want to know what schools are like, we need data closer to the phenomena than those described or promoted in print.

We turn now to the fourth ideology, one that has substantial visibility in scholarly circles: Critical Theory and its educational variants.

Critical Theory

With few exceptions, critical theorists, have not developed a coherent public statement pertaining to the aims, content, and methods of education. In this sense, Critical Theory is less of an educational ideology than religious ideologies, Rational Humanism, or Progressivism. Yet, Critical Theory provides one of the most visible and articulate analyses of education found in the pages of educational journals and in books devoted to the state of schools. It is for this reason—its salience in the intellectual community and its potential for reforming the current priorities of schools—that it is included here as an ideology affecting education in general and curriculum in particular.

What is Critical Theory and what is its "project"? Critical Theory is an approach to the study of schools and society that has as its main function the revelation of the tacit values that underlie the enterprise. The approach has been influenced by a hermeneutic orientation to texts; critical theorists often regard themselves as revealing the covert assumptions and values in the *social* text.

Critical theorists, almost always on the political left, are typically concerned with raising the consciousness of unsuspecting parents, students, and educators to the insidious and subtle ways through which an unequal and often unjust social order reproduces itself through the schools. In this sense critical theory is aimed at emancipating (their word) those affected by the schools from the school's debilitating practices.

The achievement of such ends typically requires careful attention to the structure of schooling, the ways in which roles are defined, the covert messages that are taught—in short, it requires an awareness of the school's "hidden curriculum" (Eisner, 1985a). The term *hidden* is used intentionally in distinction to the *covert* or *implicit* curriculum (Eisner, 1985a). The hidden curriculum consists of the messages given to children by teachers, school structures, textbooks, and other school resources. These messages are often conveyed by teachers who themselves are unaware of their presence. "Hidden" implies a hider—someone or some group that intentionally conceals. Concealment, in turn, suggests a form of subterfuge in order to achieve some gain. Hence, the hidden curriculum is often believed to serve the interests of the power elite that the school, often unwittingly, is thought to serve.

Within the context of critical theory, one of the important questions children are taught to ask of practices and policies in schooling and elsewhere is, "Whose interests are being served?" Although conspiracy theories are currently out of fashion, the political gist of the views of critical theorists is that the covert functions of schooling are rooted deeply in their beliefs that a capitalistic economy cannot, in principle, provide for either an equitable society or an equitable school system. As Bourdieu (1977) has written, the school is essentially an institution whose mission is cultural reproduction. When a society is believed to be inherently unfair, cultural reproduction through schooling is thought to be no virtue.

The roots of these ideas are found in Marx (1948/1987), particularly his views about the alienation of labor. For Marx the objective conditions of work define the realities that workers experience, and when work is organized to provide profit to those who own the sources of production, the working class is inevitably exploited. The essential problem that must be addressed, therefore, is to help the working class assume control of the sources of production, that is, to socialize the economy so that each individual receives according to his needs and contributes according to his ability. Social justice is essentially a function of economic conditions.

Although few Critical Theorists today would take such a doctrinaire view of the ills of the social order, the views they do embrace are descendants of Marx's view. As a result, they claim the school alienates labor—the student—and deskills him in the course of schooling by withholding opportunities for him to formulate his own aims and goals (Apple, 1982). In this way schools encourage in students a dependency on authority, foster one-way communication—from top to bottom—and in general provide a distorted view of American history that in turn undermines the kind of social consciousness needed to bring about change. One critical theorist writing of the deleterious influence of industry on school says:

> The industrial-capitalistic interests entertained a very different role of public schooling from that which had been though good under agrarianism and mercantile capitalism. As industry became more complex, the school also had to change to meet its needs. Compulsory schooling became essential and more accepted by the working class, and the compulsory schooling age rose. The high school (an urban school) became a necessity as did industrial education: manual training, vocational guidance, the enactment of child labor and additional compulsory education laws. These developments in public schooling were aimed at striving for greater efficiency in preparing children for occupational roles in the expanding economy. (Pratte, 1977, p. 99)

What is characteristic of this genre of writing is its "half-empty character." Almost always the emphasis is on the negative aspects of schooling, and although pulling weeds is helpful, their elimination in a garden does not ensure the presence of flowers; flowers have to be planted.

It should be acknowledged that depending on one's set of values, there is much to improve in the schools. Indeed, it is the mark of any respectable academic to be critical. Yet, the continually strident voices of so many Critical Theorists often becomes relentless and excessive. Consider, for example, the following comments on Bloom's *The Closing of the American Mind* (1987) and Hirsch's *Cultural Literacy* (1988).

> Read against the recent legacy of a critical educational tradition, the perspectives advanced by both Bloom and Hirsch reflect those of the critic who fears the indeterminacy of the future and who, in an attempt to escape the messy web of everyday life, purges the past of its contradictions, its paradoxes, and ultimately, of its injustices. Hirsch and Bloom sidestep the disquieting, disrupting, interrupting problems of sexism, racism, class exploitation, and other social issues that bear down so heavily on the present. This is the discourse of pedagogues afraid of the future, strangled by the past, and refusing to address the complexity, terror, and possibilities of the present. Most important, it is a public philosophy informed by a crippling ethnocentrism and a contempt for the language and social relations fundamental to the ideals of a democratic society. It is, in the end, a desperate move by thinkers who would rather cling to a tradition forged by myth than work toward a collective future built on democratic possibilities. This is the philosophy and pedagogy of hegemonic intellectuals cloaked in the mantle of academic enlightenment and literacy. (Aronowitz and Giroux, 1988, p. 194)

The tone of these remarks is not uncommon, nor are the code words that populate the text. It is almost as if an entire vocabulary had been developed to display to the world how capitalism has corrupted the schools.

As I have indicated, the major intellectual disposition of Critical Theorists is critical—in the negative sense. They are typically more interested in displaying the shortcomings of schooling than providing models toward which the schools should aspire. Nevertheless, some have described the sense of possibility they value, and in powerful ways. Giroux (1989), for example, emphasizes the importance of teachers and their potential role in defining the aims of schooling and in assessing its performance. Others speak of the potential coalition of teachers and parents as a way of creating a truly educational climate for their children, one free from the constrains of government bureaucracy. Others, such as Apple (1982), emphasize the importance of restoring to children a sense of personal meaning by allowing, indeed encouraging, them to define their own education ends and to relate these ends to the community in which they live. In some ways the directions in which Critical Theorists would take the schools resemble the social side of Progressive educational ideology.

Perhaps because a positive agenda for school programs has been underplayed in the writing of critical theorists, it is hard to say just where their implied agenda for educational reform has been implemented. Unlike the

Christian evangelicals who have created schools to reflect their ideology, or Progressive educators who have influenced school practice, even in public schools, or Rational Humanists who have a league of Paideia schools, there are no schools that I know of committed to critical theory. The primary locus of their writing is found in books and learned journals; their ideas have been lively and often extremely insightful and illuminating, but they speak essentially to intellectuals. As far as I know, they have had little impact on government education agencies or in local school boards. My sense is that if their material was less strident, more hopeful, more generous, and more concretely constructive, it would be much more likely to influence practice.

One example of a program that does share some of the values advanced by critical theorists, but is not itself associated with Critical Theory, is Lawrence Stenhouse's (1982) Humanities Curriculum. Developed in the United Kingdom in the 1970s, Stenhouse was interested in providing adolescents with opportunities to study and debate closed or controversial issues: matters pertaining to race relations, sex, politics, and church and state relations. With foundation support, he devised a humanities curriculum that invited students to debate sensitive issues; he did not take a position on these issues but prescribed a role for the teacher intended to deepen the students' level of discussion and through that his understanding of underlying value conflict. Stenhouse wanted to help students develop a more complex view of controversial issues so that their own value structure would be less secure and more open to examination. Although Stenhouse's curriculum was not *formally* an example of critical theory in action, it had features that critical theorists would, I believe, applaud.

Closer to Critical Theory in a formal sense is the work of Paulo Freire (1970). Working with illiterate peasants in Brazil, Freire devised an approach to the development of literacy that was based on the deep-seated and practical needs of his students. Reading materials were texts whose words and content were directly related to the world of work his students knew firsthand. But Freire died not stop with mere "literacy"; he also used his students' newly acquired literacy to help them understand the conditions of their labor and the interests being served by their work. In short, literacy was an instrument for political education. Freire's work provides a model for the educational development of critical consciousness.

What both Stenhouse and Freire have in common is their practical efforts to create materials designed to enable their students to understand better the values and conditions that affect their lives. Each, so to speak, rolled up his sleeves to demonstrate an approach to educational practice that reflects their educational ideologies. Critical Theorists, in the main, tell the world what schooling suffers from, but they have a tendency to emphasize criticism rather than construction. As a result, the debate has mainly been limited to scholars rather than to the reshaping of practice.

Given this emphasis, is it appropriate to regard Critical Theory as an instance of an educational or curricular ideology? I believe it is. There is no group I know more ardent about its beliefs or as outspoken about the right-eousness of its cause. It attracts adherents, it provides a common lexicon for its advocates, and it has a common canon. Its views on the ills of education are often exceedingly plausible; they are frequently both trenchant and accurate. What is missing is a positive agenda. Scholars who have directed their attention to practice, such as Adler (1982), Goodlad (1984), and Sizer (1984), have displayed the ways in which beliefs can be acted on—as did Dewey in his Laboratory School in 1896. This agenda is what critical theory needs to move from text to action. What would a school built on its beliefs and values look like? What would it teach? How would its effects be assessed? Such questions would form the core of an important project.

Reconceptualism

A fifth curriculum ideology is called by its advocates Reconceptualism. Emerging on the educational scene in the early 1970s, this view is far from complete, nor do its adherents wish it to be complete. It is more of an ori-entation than a dogma. That is, it is a way of thinking about education and the kind of programs that will serve its ends well.

The central ideas for Reconceptualists were implicit in the work of James Macdonald (1975) and especially Dwayne Heubner (1963), but in the United States the major spokesperson for this view is William Pinar (1975). Writing of *currere*, the conception Pinar embraces, he says:

> The questions of *currere* are not Tyler's; they are ones like these: Why do I identify with Mrs. Dalloway and not with Mrs. Brown? What psychic dark spots does the one light, and what is the nature of "dark spots," and "light spots"? Why do I read Lessing and not Murdoch? Why do I read such works at all? Why not biology or ecology? Why are some drawn to the study of literature, some to physics, and some to law? Are phrases like "structures of the mind" usable and useful? If so, what are these varying structures, and in what sense do they account for the form intellectual interests take or for their complete absence? What constitute "structures," and what are their sources?
>
> Such questions suggest the study of *currere*. The information our investiga-tions bring us is the knowledge of *currere*. It is its own knowledge, and while its roots are elsewhere, its plant and flower are its own; it is another species, a discipline of its own. (pp. 401–402)

Those familiar with Pinar's publications and those whose views partici-pate in its ideological orbit will recognize the importance that personal experience enjoys in their texts on education. What is missing from American schools, they argue, is a deep respect for personal purpose, lived experience, for the life of imagination, and for those forms of understand-ing that resist dissection and measurement. What is wrong with schools, among other things, is their industrialized format, their mechanistic attitudes toward students, their indifference to personal experience, and their emphasis on the instrumental and the out-of-reach. To provide children with a decent educational environment requires a reconceptualization of how we think about educational programs, who develops them, and what they are for. They are not primarily, in the view of Reconceptualists, for learning how to earn a living, but for learning how to live. To learn how to live the child must learn how to listen to her own personal drummer in an environment that makes such attention not only possible but desirable. Like the Critical Theorists, Reconceptualists tend to believe that American schools—perhaps most schools in Western industrialized societies—have been excessively influenced by a means-ends mentality that is modeled after a world that does not exist. Life is not like a scientific experiment or the operation of an assembly line. Schools that intend to prepare students for life mislead when they convey to them the idea that all problems have solutions and that all questions have answers. What is even worse, the message given to students is that not only are answers to all questions and solutions to all problems available, but also that there is a correct one for each. When this occurs the aim of schools for students becomes converted from the expansion of consciousness and the exploration of the possibilities of the imagination to successful adaptation to a technocratic routine.

For Reconceptualists the current dominant mode of curriculum theory, best represented perhaps in a narrow reading of Tyler's (1950) rationale, reinforces what is problematic and ill-conceived in schools. Such a rationale urges educators to regard curriculum planning as a type of experimental treatment: objectives are to be operationalized through measured procedures; treatment consists of the curriculum provided and is to be revised on the basis of its efficacy. After objectives are achieved, another set of objectives and curricular treatments are implemented. The entire enterprise is aimed at the achievement of specific, standardized goals. The efficient and effective convergence on what is a common aim is the ideal that guides the enterprise.

Reconceptualists regard such a view as seriously misconceived and oversimplified. What is needed, especially in a culture already characterized by high levels of alienation and personal indifference, is an approach to teaching that does not exacerbate one of our culture's major problems, indifference, but, on the contrary, compensates and helps students overcome it. What is needed is not more of the same, only better, but a basic reconceptualization of the aims and processes of schooling. Rather than attending solely to the child's behavior, Reconceptualists believe educators should try to understand the nature of the child's experience. In other words, the need is to turn from a behavioristic to a phenomenological attitude.

Although there are magnet schools and individual teachers that foster what might be called a phenomenological attitude, there is no unified, organized, or concerted program to create schools or teaching practices that develop or implement a Reconceptualist approach. In many ways, the virtual absence of organized efforts to create teaching practices congenial to Reconceptualism is understandable. Ideologies that lead to specific, more or less routinized procedures are indeed implementable; behavioristic teaching practices are examples. Reconceptualism is partly an attitude and unless teachers have acquired a disposition congruent with it, no routinized prescriptions are likely to be effective.

How then can such an approach to education be promulgated? Mainly through persuasion, it seems. Whenever an approach to practice requires artistry, even craft, standardized routines will be found wanting. Reconceptualization, like Critical Theory, is an orientation to schooling, indeed to living, that functions through the use of particular perspectives rather than through the application of rules.

Given the fact that in the United States there are over a 100,000 schools and more than 2½ million teachers, is it likely that a nonprescriptive, non-standardized approach to teaching will gain saliency? Probably not, unless there is an unforeseeable social change in the culture at large that supports its major tenets. The factors that drive schools—standardized testing and the maintenance of "our competitive edge"—are widely accepted. As long as this remains so, Reconceptualists will have an uphill battle to fight. After having said that, it also needs to be said that those associated with Reconceptualism have not simply stood by waiting for a miracle to happen. They have sponsored a journal, *The Journal of Curriculum Theorizing*, that publishes articles related to their interests and hold an annual conference, The Bergamo Conference, that explores educational problems from their perspectives. Intellectual interest is there and a community of scholars sympathetic to its ideological commitments has been formed. Whether these efforts will be sufficient to have a significant impact on schools is another question.

Cognitive Pluralism

The sixth curriculum ideology is called Cognitive Pluralism. Although the concept of Cognitive Pluralism is at least as old as Aristotle's distinctions among three different forms of knowledge—theoretical, practical, and productive—it has only been in the last two decades that a genuinely pluralistic conception of knowledge and intelligence have been advanced in the field of education. Cognitive Pluralism is a conception of mind and knowledge that has two different but related branches. As a conception of knowledge, Cognitive Pluralism argues that one of the human being's distinctive features is the capacity to create and manipulate symbols. These symbols are powerful cultural resources that are employed in mathematics, music, literature, science, dance, the visual arts, indeed, in any area of human life in which action or form is used to give expression or to represent experience or intention. Language, in the narrow sense of the term, is but one of the means through which the private, personal life of the individual is given a public presence; the symbol systems previously identified constitute a few of the others.

There are several functions that symbol systems or "forms of representation" perform that make them particularly important (Eisner, 1994). First, the ability to use a symbol system or form of representation makes it possible to stabilize evanescent thoughts and feelings: nothing is more elusive than an idea. Second, such stabilization makes it possible to reflect on what has been represented and to edit one's thinking. Third, the public transformation from what is private into a public form makes its communication possible. Fourth, the opportunity to represent through some material or device provides the occasions for the invention or discovery of ideas, images, or feelings that were not necessarily present at the inception of the activity. Put another way, the act of representation is also an opportunity for creative thinking. Finally, and most important, the features of the particular symbol system or form of representation used both constrains and makes possible particular types of meaning. Poetry, for example, allows one to represent or recover meanings that are inexpressible in mathematics or in prose.

Because the quest for meaning, it is argued, is part of human nature, the ability to represent or recover meaning in the various forms in which it can be experienced should be a primary aim of schooling. Some philosophers go even further. Symbol systems are regarded as so significant that Goodman (1978) goes so far as to say that they are foundational in the construction of our personal worlds. "There are as many worlds," he tells us, "as there are ways to describe them."

The roots of Cognitive Pluralism go back to Aristotle's tri-part distinction among the ways of knowing. Its modern variants can be found in the works of Ernst Cassirer (1961), Nelson Goodman (1976), and Susanne Langer (1976). In the curriculum field, similar ideas have been found in the work of Paul Hirst (1974) and Richard Peters (1960) in England and in Elliot Eisner's (1985a) and Phillip Phenix's (1964) work in the United States. The latter four curriculum theorists have all, in one way or another, emphasized the plurality of knowledge and the unique functions of different cognitive forms. These conceptions have, in turn, served as foundations for their views of what school programs should teach and what educational ends should be prized.

Related to the emphasis on the plurality of meaning is an emphasis on the plurality of intelligence (Gardner, 1983). The long psychometric tradition influencing American education has emphasized the identification and measurement of the general or "G" factor in intelligence. What most psychometricians have sought is the essential property or function that makes general intelligence possible. Further, they have eschewed the idea that intelligence was multiple, or that its presence depended on the context, material, or the circumstances in which individuals function. Related to the disposition to find essences has been a tendency to emphasize genetic rather than environmental influences. In some ways it is understandable that those who seek essences should have little appetite for measuring a process subject to the vicissitudes of the environment. What kind of mental science can be built on such a tentative personal feature?

During the past 15 years, the pluralism that has accompanied our conception of the nature of knowledge has also appeared in the way in which intelligence itself is conceived. Its meaning has shifted from a noun to a verb; intelligence for more than a few cognitive psychologists is not merely something you have, but something you do. Furthermore, these doings are precisely that: different ways of acting. Gardner (1983), one of the leading spokespersons for this idea, identifies seven intelligences that he believes individuals possess in varying degrees. For Gardner, these are not "simply" aptitudes or talents, but socially important ways of solving problems. Furthermore, he argues that environmental conditions have something to do with the particular kind of intelligence that will be valued and practiced. The relationship between knowledge types and forms of intelligence is an important one. If the kind of mind that children can come to own is, in part, influenced by the kinds of opportunities they have to think, and if these opportunities are themselves defined by the kind of curriculum schools provide, then it could be argued that the curriculum itself is, as Bernstein (1971) has suggested, a kind of mind-altering device. In this view it's easy to see how curriculum decisions about content inclusion and content exclusion are of fundamental importance.

I (Eisner, 1985a) have argued that what is omitted from the school curriculum—what is called the null curriculum—is every bit as important as what is left in. The kind of decisions that individuals make is not only influenced by what they know, but also by what they don't know. Hence, large areas of important but unexamined content can have a very significant influence on the kinds of decisions people make and the kinds of lives that they lead. Thus, symbol systems not only have the potential to provide unique forms of meaning, they also have the potential to practice and develop particular mental skills. Without these skills, the meanings made possible through the various symbol systems will be unrecoverable.

By opening the door to Cognitive Pluralism, a whole new array of *potential* consequences flow for curriculum. First, given this orientation, the concept of literacy would be expanded. Although the term *literacy* typically refers to the ability to read, it would be extended to include the encoding or decoding of information in any of the forms that humans use to convey meaning. (Eisner, 1982) At its broadest level, the concept merges with semiotics, the theory of signs. At a somewhat narrower level, it recognizes that each of the various cultural forms impose their own requirements on representation as well as on interpretation. In Phenix's (1964) words, each form of representation provides its own "realm of meaning." Because the pursuit of meaning is a basic part of human nature, and because meaning is in large measure achieved through the use of symbol systems, the ability to read symbol systems that mediate meaning is critical if meaning is to be secured. The kind of pluralism advocated in the curriculum writing of Phenix, Peters, Hirst, and Eisner leads to programs that intentionally provide for the development of multiple forms of literacy.

Another potential consequence of Cognitive Pluralism is the expansion of educational equity in the classroom. Given the fact that there are differences in aptitudes among children, the creation of programs that restrict the use of aptitudes for that dealing with curricular tasks provides an advantage to those children whose aptitudes are consonant with the tasks provided. Children whose aptitudes are not useful in dealing with the tasks schools emphasize are disadvantaged. By creating a wider array of curricular tasks, those that require the use of different forms of intelligence, for example, or depend on different aptitudes, opportunities for success in school are expanded. These opportunities are expanded *if* success on this wider array of tasks is regarded as having equal intellectual merit. If, for example, high level ability in the arts is regarded as laudable, but nonintellectual in nature, and if the school gives its most highly prized awards to what it regards as intellectual achievements, children who shine in the arts will never shine as brightly as those who are excellent in mathematics; the arts, like the children attracted to them, will remain second-class citizens in the hierarchy of curricular values.

Thus far, no consortium has been created to promote or implement programs reflecting a cognitively pluralistic orientation to curriculum, although individual schools can be found that do attempt to provide such an approach. The Key School in Indianapolis, Indiana, is currently attempting to develop a curriculum that is consistent with Gardner's theory of multiple intelligences and Malkus, Feldman, and Gardner (1988) have been attempting to identify what they call proclivities among preschool children. Although their efforts are still too new to assess, they do represent a move into the practical world of schooling.

Each of the foregoing curricular ideologies has a different degree of implementability. Rational Humanism and religious orthodoxy are two ideologies that have their counterparts in schools. Indeed, there are consortia and organizations whose primary mission is to expand and improve the practice of schools embracing these ideological positions. Progressivism is probably more prevalent in American schools than Reconceptualism, Cognitive Pluralism, or Critical Theory. The programs needed to implement a cognitively pluralistic approach to curriculum are scarce, and Critical Theory and Reconceptualism are, in some ways, more attitudinal in nature than methodologically prescriptive. In all, their ideological presence in curriculum is quite limited.

As I indicated earlier, in the public arena, ideas about priorities, goals, the allocation of resources must survive a tough array of competing proposals from those who feel equally convinced of the correctness of their views. Educational policies are modified not only behind the closed door of the classroom, but also in the arena in which they are debated. With 50 states responsible for educational policy and 16,000 school districts making and interpreting policies, homogeneity in micropolicy terms is hard to find. The local control of schools complicates the use of research in schools and classrooms: one never knows if the conditions that existed when the research was undertaken in one educational experiment also prevail in the school or district in which one wishes to implement the experimental practice. When national policy for schools is determined by a national ministry of education, the problem of implementing policy and the practices associated with it is not *quite* so complex, although it is very far from simple. Teachers still close the classroom door and do what they know how to do and believe is best for the students they teach. In this sense, changes in the teacher's ideology may be among the important changes that can be made in the field of education.

References

Adler, M. (1982). *The Paideia proposal.* New York: Macmillan.

Albertini, J., & Meath-Lang, B. (1986). An analysis of student-teacher exchanges in dialogue journal writing. *Journal of Curriculum Theorizing, 7*(1), 153–201.

Apple, M. (1982). *Education and power.* Boston: Routledge and Kegan Paul.

Aronowitz, S., & Giroux, H. (1988). Schooling, culture, and literacy in the age of broken dreams: A review of Bloom and Hirsch. *Harvard Educational Review, 58*(2), 57.

Atkin, J. M. (1989, November). Can educational research keep pace with education reform? *Phi Delta Kappan, 71*(3), 200–205.

Atkin, J. M., Kennedy, D., & Patrick, C. (1989) *Inside schools: A collaborative view.* London: Falmer Press.

Bernstein, B. (1971). On the classification and framing of educational knowledge. In M. Young (Ed.), *Knowledge and control* (pp. 47–69). London: Collier-Macmillan.

Bloom, A. (1987). *The closing of the American mind.* New York: Simon & Schuster.

Bourdieu, P. (1977). *Reproduction in education's society and culture.* London: Sage Publications.

Boyer, E. (1983). *High school.* New York: Harper & Row.

Bronfenbrenner, V. (1979). *The ecology of human development.* Cambridge, MA: Harvard University Press.

Bruner, J. (1964, January). The course of cognitive growth. *American Psychologist, 19*(1), 1–15.

Callahan, R. (1962). *Education and the cult of efficiency.* Chicago: University of Chicago Press.

84 ◆ THE EDUCATIONAL IMAGINATION

Case, R. (1984). *Intellectual development: Birth to adulthood.* Orlando, FL: Academic Press.

Cassirer, E. (1961/1964). *The philosophy of symbolic forms* (R. Manheim, Trans.). Preface and introduction by C. W. Hendel. 3 Vols. New Haven, CT: Yale University Press.

Cheney, L. (1987). *American memory.* Washington, DC: National Endowment for the Humanities.

Cole, M. (1974). *Culture and thought.* New York: John Wiley.

Counts, G. (1932). *Can the schools build a new social order?* New York: John Day.

Cremin, L. (1961). *The transformation of the school.* New York: Knopf.

Cremin, L. (1970). *American education.* New York: Harper & Row.

Cuban, L. (1979). Determinants of curriculum change and stability, 1870–1970. In John Schaffarzick & Gary Sykes (Eds.), *Value conflicts and curricular issues.* Berkeley, CA: McCutcheon.

Cuban, L. (1988). *The managerial imperative and the practice of leadership in schools.* Albany: State University of New York Press.

Cullen, J. (1982). *On deconstruction.* Ithaca, NY: Cornell University Press.

Darwin, C. (1975). *The origin of species.* New York: Norton. (Originally published in 1897)

Dewey, J. (1902). *The educational situation.* Chicago: University of Chicago Press.

Dewey, J. (1910). *How we think.* Boston: D. C. Heath.

Dewey, J. (1938). *Experience and education.* New York: Macmillan.

Dreeben, R. (1968). *On what is learned in school.* New York: Addison-Wesley.

Eagleton, T. (1983). *Literacy theory.* Minneapolis: University of Minnesota Press.

Eisner, E. W. (1974). *English primary schools.* Washington: National Association for the Education of Young Children.

Eisner, E. W. (1982). *Cognition and curriculum: A basis for deciding what to teach.* New York: Longman.

Eisner, E. W. (1985a). Aesthetic modes of knowing. In E. W. Eisner (Ed.), *Learning and teaching the ways of knowing: Eighty-fourth yearbook of the National Society for the Study of Education* (Part II, pp. 23–36). Chicago: University of Chicago Press.

Eisner, E. W. (1985b). *The educational imagination.* (2nd ed.). New York: Macmillan.

Eisner, E. W. (1985c). *What high schools are like: Views from the inside.* Stanford, CA: Stanford School of Education.

Eisner, E. W. (1994). *Conception and Representation.* New York: Teachers College Press.

Friere, P. (1970). *Pedagogy of the oppressed.* New York: Seabury Press.

Gallup, A., & Clark, D. (1987). The 19th Annual Gallup Poll of the public's attitudes toward the public schools. *Phi Delta Kappan, 69*(1), 17–30.

Gardner, H. (1983). *Frames of mind: The theory of multiple intelligences.* New York: Basic Books.

Geertz, C. (1973). *The interpretation of cultures.* New York: Basic Books.

Getzels, J. (1974, August). Images of the classroom and visions of the learner. *School Review, 82*(4), 527–540.

Giroux, H. (1989). *Critical pedagogy, the state, and cultural struggle.* Albany: State University of New York Press.

Goodlad, J. (1984). *A place called school: Prospects for the future.* New York: McGraw-Hill.

Goodlad, J., & Anderson, R. (1959). *The non-graded elementary school.* New York: Harcourt, Brace.

Goodman, N. (1976). *The languages of art: An approach to a theory of symbols* (2nd ed.). Indianapolis: Hackett.

Goodman, N. (1978). *Ways of worldmaking.* Indianapolis: Hackett.

Gruber, H. (1981). *Darwin on man.* Chicago: University of Chicago Press.

Grumet, M. (1988). *Bitter milk.* Amherst, MA: University of Massachusetts Press.

Hegel, G. W. (1900). *The philosophy of history.* New York: Wiley.

Heubner, D. (1963). New modes of man's relationship to man. In Alexander Frazier (Ed.), *New insights and the curriculum.* Washington, DC: Association for Supervision and Curriculum Development.

Hirsch, E. D. (1988). *Dictionary of cultural literacy.* Boston: Houghton Mifflin.

Hirst, P. (1974). *Knowledge and the curriculum.* London: Routledge and Kegan Paul.

Horio, T. (1988). *Educational thought and ideology in modern Japan.* Tokyo: University of Tokyo Press.

Hutchins, R. (1953). *The conflict in education in a democratic society.* New York: Harper.

Jackson, P. (1968). *Life in classrooms.* New York: Holt, Rinehart & Winston.

Jackson, P. (1986). *The practice of teaching.* New York: Teachers College Press.

Kuntz, J. F. (1986). *The transmission of values in two Jesuit high school classrooms.* Ph.D. dissertation, Stanford University, Stanford, CA.

Langer, S. (1942). *Philosophy in a new key.* Cambridge: Harvard University Press.

Langer, S. (1976). *Problems of art.* New York: Scribner.

Lepper, M., & Greene, D. (Eds.). (1978). *The hidden cost of reward: New perspectives on the psychology of human motivation.* Hillsdale, NJ: Lawrence Erlbaum.

Macdonald, J. (1975). Curriculum theory. In William Pinar (Ed.), *Curriculum theorizing.* Berkeley, CA: McCutcheon.

Madison, J. (1961). *Federalist Papers.* New York: New American Library.

Malkus, U., Feldman, D., & Gardner, H. (1988). Dimensions of mind in early childhood. In A. D. Pelligrini (Ed.), *The psychological bases of early education* (pp. 25–38). Chichester, U.K.: Wiley.

Marx, K. (1987). *Manifesto of the Communist Party.* Chicago: Charles H. Kerr. ((Originally published in 1948)

McKeon, R. (Ed.). (1941). *The basic works of Aristotle.* New York: Random House.

Meta, M. (1986). *Different by design.* London: Routledge and Kegan Paul.

Miller, J. (1983). A search for congruence: Influence of past and present in future teachers' concepts about teaching writing. *English education, 15*(1), 5–16.

Miller, J. (1987). Teachers' emerging texts: The empowering potential of writing in-service. In John Smythe (Ed.), *Educating teachers: Changing the nature of pedagogical knowledge.* London: Falmer.

Neill, A. S. (1960). *Summerhill: A radical approach to child rearing.* New York: Hart Publishing Co.

Neissre, U. (1976). *Cognition and reality: Principles and implications of cognitive psychology.* San Francisco: Freeman.

Olsen, D. (1980). *The social foundations of language and thought.* New York: Norton.

Olsen, D. (1988). *Developing theories of mind.* Cambridge, MA: Cambridge University Press.

Peshkin, A. (1986). *God's choice: The total world of a fundamentalist Christian school.* Chicago: University of Chicago Press.

Peters, R. (1960). *Authority, responsibility, and education*. London: George Allen and Unwin.

Phenix, P. (1964). *Realms of meaning: A philosophy of the curriculum for general education*. New York: McGraw-Hill.

Piaget, J. (1973). *The child and reality*. (Arnold Rosen, Trans.). New York: Grossman.

Pinar, W. (Ed.). (1975). *Curriculum theorizing: The Reconceptualists*. Berkeley, CA: McCutcheon.

Pinar, W. (1988). *Contemporary curriculum discourse*. Scottsdale, AZ: Gorsuch Scavisbrick.

Plowden Report. (1966). *Children and their primary schools*. London: H. M. Stationary Office.

Powell, A. G., Farrar, E., & Cohen, D. K. (1985). *The shopping mall high school*. Boston: Houghton-Mifflin.

Pratte, R. (1977). *Ideology and education*. New York: David McKay.

Rugg, H., & Shumacher, A. (1928). *The child centered school*. Yonkers-on-Hudson: World Book.

Sapir, E. (1962). *Culture, language and personality*. Berkeley: University of California Press.

Schoen, D. (1983). *The reflective practitioner: How professionals think in action*. New York: Basic Books.

Schwab, J. (1969, November). The practical: A language for curriculum. *School Review, 78*(5), 1–24.

Singer, M. (1990). *Senses of history: An inquiry into form, meaning, and understanding*. Ph.D. dissertation, Stanford University, Stanford, CA.

Sizer, T. R. (1984). *Horace's compromise: The dilemma of the American high school*. Boston: Houghton-Mifflin.

Smith, D. T., et al. (N. D.). *Douglas T. Smith et al. Plaintiffs vs. Board of School Commissioners of Mobile County et al.*

Smith, L., & Geoffrey, W. (1968). *The complexities of education in an urban classroom*. New York: Holt, Rinehart & Winston.

Stenhouse, L. (1982). *Teaching about race relations*. London: Routledge and Kegan Paul.

Sternberg, R. (1988). *The triarchic mind*. New York: Viking.

Tomorrow's teachers: A report of the Holmes Group. (1986). East Lansing: Michigan State University Press.

Tyler, R. (1950). *Basic principles of curriculum and instruction*. Chicago: University of Chicago Press.

Uhrmacher, B. (1990). *Waldorf schools marching quietly unheard*. Ph.D. dissertation, Stanford University, Stanford, CA.

USA Research. (1984). *A nation at risk: The full account*. Cambridge, MA: Author.

Vygotsky, L. (1962). *Thought and language*. Cambridge, MA: M.I.T. Press.

Walker, D. (1978). Approaches to curriculum development. In J. Schaffarzick and G. Sykes, (Eds.), *Value conflicts and curriculum issues*. Berkeley, CA: McCutcheon.

Walker, D., & Schaffarzick, J. (1972). Comparing curricula. *Review of Educational Research, 44*(Winter), 83–112.

Waller, W. (1932). *The sociology of teaching*. New York: Wiley.

Whorf, B. L. (1956). *Language, thought, and reality*. Cambridge, MA: M.I.T. Press.

Willis, P. (1977). *Learning to labor*. Lexington: D. C. Heath.

4

The Three Curricula That All Schools Teach

Perhaps the greatest of all pedagogical fallacies is the notion that a person learns only the particular thing he is studying at the time.
JOHN DEWEY

The Explicit and Implicit Curricula

In Chapter 3, six curriculum ideologies were described. These six ideologies provide a way of rationalizing what schools teach. But schools teach much more—and much less—than they intend to teach. Although much of what is taught is explicit and public, a great deal is not. Indeed, it is my claim that schools provide not one curriculum to students, but three, regardless of which of the six ideologies a school follows. The aim in this chapter is to examine those three curriculums in order to find out how they function.

One of the most important facts about schooling is that children spend a major portion of their childhood in school. By the time the student has graduated from secondary school, he or she has spent approximately 480 weeks, or 12,000 hours, in school. During this time, the student has been immersed in a culture that is so natural a part of our way of life that it is almost taken for granted. In that culture called schooling there are certain publicly explicit goals: teaching children to read and write, to figure, and to learn something about the history of the country, among them. There are, of course, other aims, many of which are associated with the explicit curriculum that the school offers to the students. There are goals and objectives for the sciences, the arts, physical education, social studies, and foreign language instruction. Not only do these goals appear in school district curriculum guides and the course-planning materials that teachers are asked to prepare; the public also knows that these courses are offered and that students in the district will have the opportunity to achieve these aims, at least to some degree, should they want to do so. In short, the school offers to the community an educational menu of sorts; it advertises what it is prepared to provide. From this advertised list, students have, at least in principle, an array of options from which to choose.

But is this all that schools offer? Does this advertised menu exhaust what schools teach? The answer to these questions is clear: no. Work by Apple (1979), Dreeben (1968), Jackson (1968), Sarason (1971), Vallance (1973–1974), and others have illuminated the ways in which the culture of both the classroom and the school socializes children to values that are a part of the structure of those places. Dreeben attends primarily to the sociological aspects of school learning, relating and contrasting school learning to the type of learning that takes place in the family. Jackson has discussed with great perceptivity how the structure of the classroom and the demands that it makes on teachers, in turn, affect the expectations of students and therefore shape the content of what they learn. For example, the fact that classrooms are crowded places and because teachers need the attention of students whom they teach, children, Jackson argues, must learn how to delay their gratification because teachers cannot satisfy all of the wants and needs of a child when he or she is in a group of 30 or more other children. The child who knows the right answer to a question raised by the teacher does not always—even usually—get an opportunity to provide it. Other children compete for a place in the sun. Hence, a child learns quickly that gratification and successes need to be shared with other members of the class.

Vallance's research has focused on the covert manner in which text material persuades. Materials as well as the structure of the classroom influence the values that are not recognized by students or teachers. These values are expressed in the kinds of illustrations that textbooks contain, in the language that is employed, and in the emphasis that is given to the characters that constitute the stories that are read. These messages are often numerous, subtle, and consistent. It requires a subtle critical analysis of text materials to discern the kinds of social values that are being promulgated within the materials that students and teachers employ. These investigators have helped us understand how schools socialize children to a set of expectations that some argue are profoundly more powerful and longer lasting than what is intentionally taught or what the explicit curriculum of the school publicly provides. Take, for example, that form of human behavior called initiative. It is possible to create a school environment in which the taking of initiative becomes an increasingly important expectation as children mature. In such an environment, as children get older, they would be expected to assume greater responsibility for their planning; they would be expected increasingly to define their goals and determine the kinds of resources that they would need to pursue the ends they have formulated. One general goal of such an institution would be to enable children to become the mappers of their educational journey, so that when they leave school they are in a position to pursue goals and interests that are important to them. If this were an important aspiration of schools, schools would make it possible in dozens of ways for initiative to be developed; it would be a part of the culture of schooling.

Critics of schooling point out however, that rather than cultivate initiative, schools foster compliant behavior. One of the first things a student learns—and the lesson is taught throughout his or her school career—is to provide the teacher with what the teacher wants or expects. The most important means for doing this is for the student to study the teacher, to learn just how much effort must be expended for an A, a B, or a C grade. How long should the term paper be is a question heard not only in secondary school; it is heard in graduate school, as well. Of course, such a request for information is not entirely unreasonable; one does want to know something about the general expectations. Yet, too often, the issue becomes the expectation and the need to meet it in the most expeditious way possible. This tendency to foster compliant forms of behavior is often exacerbated by programs that use behavior modification techniques. I was in one third-grade classroom in a wealthy San Francisco suburb where I noticed that on the wall of the room there was a chart on which each student's name was listed. Next to each name was a set of 20 boxes and in every fifth box was a picture of a smiling face. I asked one of the children what the chart was for, and he replied that after they completed reading a book they colored in one of the boxes. I then asked what the smiling faces were for. He replied that when they had read five books and therefore reached a smiling face, they got a goldenrod ticket, three of which were good for leave to go to lunch 5 minutes early.

There are a host of educational issues that could be identified and discussed concerning the use of such a reward system, but for now the point will remain with the fostering of compliant behavior. Such a reward system holds out to children something they apparently want and fosters a willingness to perform. In using such a system, the teacher or the school can, of course, increase or decrease the size or attractiveness of the reward to bring out the desired behavior at the lowest cost. Regardless of the type or size of the reward, the point remains the same: the school seeks to modify the child's behavior to comply with goals that the child had no hand in formulating and that might not have any intrinsic meaning.

Some interesting and useful research has been done in the hidden cost of reward. Lepper and his colleagues (1978) have found in a number of experiments that the use of extrinsic rewards can create a set of expectations on the children's part that dampens their future interest in activities if extrinsic rewards are not provided. In other words, if a group of children are consistently led to expect that they will receive a reward for engaging in an activity—even an activity that is inherently enjoyable—they are less likely to engage in that activity if they believe that an extrinsic reward will not be provided.

What this line of research implies for the use of rewards in schools is significant. Do we intentionally habituate children to satisfactions that are not a part of the process itself when we emphasize an extrinsic reward structure? Do we create "reward junkies" out of our children by using such a payoff system?

Now, in some respects, the use of rewards to reinforce or control behavior is a ubiquitous part of our culture, indeed of all cultures. Insofar as there are conventions, mores, customs, sanctions, and the like in culture, there will be forms of behavior that are positively rewarded and others that are sanctioned negatively. The question is not whether there should or could be a cultural institution without procedures for monitoring, rewarding, and punishing those who are a part of that institution. The major question deals with the pervasiveness of such conditions and their appropriateness, given the institution's explicit mission. If an institution uses expedient means for the management of students that, while doing so, interfere with the realization of some of its primary purposes, there is reason for questioning such "expedient" means.

I would not like to give the impression that the use of such rewards is the primary way in which compliant behavior is elicited and sustained. The factors that sustain such behavior are in a significant sense built into the ways in which roles are defined in schools. Take, for example, the expectation that students must not speak unless called on, or the expectation that virtually all of the activities within a course shall be determined by the teacher, or the fact that schools are organized hierarchically, with the student at the bottom rung of the ladder, or that communication proceeds largely from the top down. What does such a system teach the young, who must spend up to 480 weeks of their childhood there? What does it mean to children to engage in a wide array of tasks that often have little or no intrinsic meaning to them in order to cope with school successfully?

For those who have analyzed the implicit curriculum of the school and what it teaches, these lessons are among the most important ones that children learn. It is pointed out that most children will not have jobs in adult life that are intrinsically interesting. Most jobs do not afford an individual the opportunity to define his or her purpose. Most jobs depend on the use of extrinsic motivation to sustain interest. Most jobs do not provide for high degrees of intellectual flexibility. Most jobs depend on routine. From the standpoint of the type of work that most Americans will engage in during the course of their careers, one could argue that schools provide excellent preparation. Schools prepare most people for positions and contexts that in many respects are quite similar to what they experienced in school as students: hierarchical organization, one-way communication, routine—in short, compliance to purposes set by another.

Compliant behavior is only one of several kinds of behavior that schools foster. Some of these might be considered positive. I use compliance here simply for illustrative purposes. Take as another example competitiveness. Do schools teach children to compete, and do they encourage competitiveness? One way, and perhaps the most obvious way in which competitiveness is fostered, is through athletic competition. Athletic leagues engender a need to win by beating the other person or team. The metaphor is apt. One succeeds only at a price paid by another. But there are other forms of competition that are not as obvious that are also at work in schools. One of these is formal grading practices. When students are assigned grades based on the expectation that the distribution of scores or performance will be statistically normal, the relationship students are forced into is one of competition. If only students with the highest 10 percent of scores can receive an A grade, then clearly one student's A is another student's B. Again, one wins only at the cost of beating another. When the stakes are high, as they are when students are seeking admission to universities, medical schools, and law schools, it is not unheard of for some students to destroy the work of others or to check out or mutilate books needed by other students to compete successfully. Knowing well what will count, some students use whatever means necessary to gain an advantage.

Because it is extreme, such behavior is not characteristic in schools and universities and, depending on one's social vision, competitiveness could be viewed as the engine of human progress, something that schools would be well advised to encourage.

Competitiveness is not only fostered by the grading system: it is also fostered by the differentiation of classes into ability groups. For example, most comprehensive secondary schools and even a large percentage of elementary schools differentiate students into three or more ability groups, in, for example, Mathematics or English. Students who successfully compete for grades are rewarded not only by grades, but also by admission to honors classes. This assignment to classes in which one is honored by being in an honors class often becomes something highly valued by parents and students. Yet, why should students whose background or genetic makeup is advantageous be rewarded in this public way? Is it the case that the less able are less honorable or less worthy? This is not far from a cultural truth. The word *virtuoso* means someone who is good at something. The word *virtue* means good. The association historically and culturally between being good at something and being good is of long standing. Thus, combined with the Calvinist tradition of associating failure with sin and success with goodness, it is not surprising that quicker students are honored by being assigned to honors classes. Increasingly, school districts are providing a differential credit system for students who are enrolled in courses in different tracks within the school curriculum. Thus, the student in the highest track is given more credit for a grade than a student who receives the same grade in a lower track. What we do when we employ such a procedure in schools is to convert formally grades into commodities that have different exchange values for different students. We have, of course, been doing this for a long time. Different grades have different values. But this formalized procedure tells the A student in a second-level English class that his or her A grade is worth the price of a B or C for students in the first- or honors-track English course. Perhaps this is the message we want to give students. Perhaps the sooner they learn to cope with the competitiveness of the "real world" the better. Yet, I would hope that the values that animate education were rooted in a soil a bit richer and more humane than those of the marketplace.

Consider as still another example of the implicit curriculum the impact of time on the students' perception of what counts in school. In planning school programs one of the decisions that must be made is when various subjects will be taught and how much time will be devoted to them. Although such decisions are not intended to reflect to students value judgments about the significance of various subject areas, in fact, they do. Students learn in school to read the value code that pervades it. One of these coded qualities is the use and location of time. Take as a specific example the location and amount of time devoted to the arts in school programs. Virtually all elementary school programs devote some attention to the arts. But if one asks about how much and compares it to the amount of time devoted to, say, social studies, reading, mathematics, or the sciences, the proportion is quite small. But if one looks further to determine when the arts are taught, one will find that they are generally taught in the afternoon rather than in the morning and often on Friday afternoon.

What this conveys to the student is that the arts are essentially forms of play that one can engage in only after the real work of schooling has been finished. In the morning, students are fresh; they can cope at this time with the rigors of reading and mathematics. In the afternoon, the arts can be used as a reward, as a break from the demands of thinking. This reinforces the belief that the arts do not require rigorous and demanding thought and that they are really unimportant aspects of the school program. The idea that the arts deal with feeling and that reading and arithmetic deal with thinking is a part of the intellectual belief structure that separates cognition from affect, a structure whose consequences are as deleterious for educational theory as they are for psychology.

The major point I am trying to make here is one of illustrating the fact that schools teach far more than they advertise. Function follows form.

Furthermore, it is important to realize that what schools teach is not simply a function of covert intentions; it is largely unintentional. What schools teach they teach in the fashion that the culture itself teaches, because schools are the kinds of places they are.

The recognition of the impact of the hidden, implicit curriculum is relatively new. Aside from Willard Waller's *The Sociology of Teaching*, in 1932, there was little interest in the educational consequences of schooling, per se, until the 1960s. It was during that decade that work by Dreeben, Jackson, and Sarason was first published. What students of education began to recognize was what Lewis Mumford was talking about in 1938 in his *Technics and Civilization*. At that time Mumford wrote:

> One may define this aspect of the machine as "purposeless materialism." Its particular defect is that it casts a shadow of reproach upon all the non-material interests and occupations of mankind: in particular, it condemns liberal aesthetic and intellectual interests because "they serve no useful purpose." One of the blessings of invention, among the naive advocates of the machine, is that it does away with the need for the imagination: instead of holding a conversation with one's distant friend in reverie, one may pick up a telephone and substitute his voice for one's fantasy. If stirred by an emotion, instead of singing a song or writing a poem, one may turn on a phonograph record. It is no disparagement of either the phonograph or the telephone to suggest that their special functions do not take the place of a dynamic imaginative life, nor does an extra bathroom, however admirably instrumental, take the place of a picture or a flower-garden. The brute fact of the matter is that our civilization is now weighted in favor of the use of mechanical instruments, because the opportunities for commercial production and for the exercise of power lie there: while all the direct human reactions or the personal arts which require a minimum of mechanical paraphernalia are treated as negligible. The habit of producing goods whether they are needed or not, of utilizing inventions whether they are useful or not, of applying power whether it is effective or not pervades almost every department of our present civilization. The result is that whole areas of the personality have been slighted; the telic, rather than the merely adaptive, spheres of conduct, exist on very suffi range. This pervasive instrumentalism places a handicap upon vital reactions which cannot be closely tied to the machine, and it magnifies the importance of physical goods as symbols—symbols of intelligence and ability and farsightedness—even as it tends to characterize their absence as a sign of stupidity and failure. And to the extent that this materialism is purposeless, it becomes final: the means are presently converted into an end. If material goods need any other justification, they have it in the fact that the effort to consume them keeps the machines running. (pp. 20–21)

Mumford was concerned with the quality of life that technologically advanced societies were rapidly developing, and he believed that technology would get out of hand, becoming master rather than servant to man. Almost 40 years later we find Ivan Illich expressing a similar concern.

Speaking of the distinction between convivial and anticonvivial tools, Illich (1973) holds that most tools used in industrial societies restrict rather than expand human freedom. He believes their impact on society to be socially devastating and calls therefore for a reconstruction of society in a form that would make convivial life possible.

> A convivial society should be designed to allow all its members the most autonomous action by means of tools least controlled by others. People feel joy, as opposed to mere pleasure, to the extent that their activities are creative; while the growth of tools beyond a certain point increases regimentation, dependence, exploitation, and impotence. I use the term "tool" broadly enough to include not only simple hardware such as drills, pots, syringes, brooms, building elements, or motors, and not just large machines like cars or power stations; I also include among tools productive institutions such as factories that produce tangible commodities such as those which produce "education," "health," "knowledge," or "decisions." I use this term because it allows me to subsume into one category all rationally designed devices, be they artifacts or rules, codes or operators, and to distinguish all these planned and engineered instrumentalities from other things such as basic food or implements, which in a given culture are not deemed to be subject to rationalization. School curricula or marriage laws are no less purposely shaped social devices than road networks. (pp. 20–21)

Illich, a leading critic of formal schooling, is concerned with what he believes are the pervasive use of anticonvivial tools. He believes such tools— and the term *tool* refers to anything that can be used—impose themselves on the lives of individuals and groups in such a way as to close rather than open options, divide rather than unify the polity. The tool becomes a master that manages the lives of people. Furthermore, tools interlock and reinforce their power to control. If one is caught in a traffic jam, one misses one's plane at the airport. If this happens, the connection in Denver is also missed, which means that one cannot make an obligatory meeting in New York, which, in turn, will have other consequences.

Although Illich is writing about technological societies at large, the points he makes about them can be applied to schools. We divide time to create schedules that produce a degree of neatness and predictability for the use of school resources. When a school has 2,000 students, as many schools have, it is important to develop an organizational pattern that avoids chaos. The timetable and computerized class schedule regulate operations. At the same time, such procedures impose a kind of rigidity that requires that regardless of what one is doing, regardless of how well it is going, one must stop working and move on to the next class. Another class is waiting to move in. Every 50 minutes, an entire school population of 2,000 students and sundry teachers plays musical chairs.

Now clearly, one must weigh the benefits of using time this way against the costs. It might very well be that the benefits outweigh the costs. I am not arguing now that they do not. The point, however, is not whether such a schedule constitutes an educational vice or virtue; it is that the structure of the school day itself has educational consequences for both students and teachers. The timetable teaches. What the timetable teaches is interesting to speculate about. For one thing, it may teach students to be cognitively flexible, to be able to shift problems and adapt to new demands on schedule. It may teach students not to get too involved in what they do because to become too involved is to court frustration when time runs out. Such a schedule may teach students the importance of punctuality: they need to be where they are supposed to be, on time, eight times a day.

These aspects of the culture of schooling no school district advertises; indeed, there are few teachers or school administrators who conceptualize the latent lessons of school structure this way. The culture one is immersed in is often the most difficult to see. Yet, because these aspects of the life of schooling are so pervasive, their effects might be especially important. After all, the westward movement is studied for only a few weeks in the fall of the fifth grade, but the impact of school structure does not cease until one leaves graduate school.

It is usual to consider the implicit curriculum as having an entirely negative impact as far as education is concerned. But this is not necessarily true. The implicit curriculum of the school can teach a host of intellectual and social virtues: punctuality, a willingness to work hard on tasks that are not immediately enjoyable, and the ability to defer immediate gratification in order to work for distant goals can legitimately be viewed as positive attributes of schooling. They form no formal part of the curriculum, yet they are taught in school. Indeed, I believe that parents know they are taught, not perhaps at a critically conscious level, but more or less intuitively. This is perhaps best illustrated by two examples: the attractiveness of prestigious universities and the recent interest in more structured forms of elementary education.

What is it that makes Princeton, Yale, Harvard, Stanford, Swarthmore, University of California at Berkeley, Smith, and Radcliffe attractive places for so many aspiring middle-class students? A part of the reason might be the perceived excellence of the faculties at such institutions. The extensiveness of the libraries might also play a role. But one cannot easily discount the tacit appreciation of the general culture that pervades these schools. Colleges and universities with lesser reputations also teach most of the courses offered at these institutions. Indeed, the explicit curricula across universities in the United States are very much the same. But what does differ is the recognition that universities also present students with a way of life, a set of standards, a distribution of students coming from particular social classes, and levels of academic achievement that will have an important impact on entering students. If one visits university campuses across the country, one is struck by both their sameness and their differences.

Some universities monitor or attempt to monitor students' behavior in just the same way as some high schools. Others give the impression that within their hallowed walls reside the seeds of social revolution. Still others have a kind of cool intellectual pride, a sense of scholarly self-esteem that sets the institution aside from the more prosaic forms of cultural life. Such environments, developed through tradition, have selection procedures for staff as well as students that provide an implicit curriculum whose specific goals are not articulated and might not even be consciously recognized. It is something one senses. Many parents as well as students recognize such qualities and guide their children to places whose implicit curriculum is compatible with their values and with the levels of social, economic, and academic achievements to which they aspire.

Similar factors are at work in the motivation among parents to create within school districts more structured forms of elementary education. Although the return to the so-called basics movement is a part of this motivation, the back-to-basics movement cannot be easily separated from larger, more general values. For example, in a suburb near Stanford University, a small group of parents petitioned the school board to create a structured elementary school for their children. As a result of this petition and because some school board members were supportive of the proposal, the board offered to make a part of one elementary school a structured school, with a principal who was sympathetic to such a program. However, the board said that parents who did not want their children in such a program would have the option of having them attend parallel, nonstructured classes within the same school. This proposal by the board was not good enough. The parents seeking a more structured elementary school argued that what was necessary was for the entire school to be structured, not just a part of it, because "what happens to students on the playground is as important as what happens in classes." What the parents were correctly pointing out was that in order for the school to be optimally effective, in their terms, the entire environment needed to be taken into account. They did not want the values they thought would be fostered within the classroom vitiated by those that their children would encounter in the schoolyard.

The implicit curriculum of the school is not only carried by the organizational structure of the school and by the pedagogical rules that are established in school—in some high schools students must carry a pass to show hall guards that they have permission to use the washroom—but is also manifested in more subtle ways. Consider for a moment school architecture and the design of school furniture. Most school rooms are designed as cubicles along corridors and have a kind of antiseptic quality to them. They tend to be repetitive and monotonous in the same way that some hospitals and factories are. They speak of efficiency more than they do of comfort. Where, for example, aside from the teacher's lounge, can one find a soft surface in a secondary or junior high school? Schools tend not to be designed with soft surfaces. They tend to look like most of the furniture that goes into them. Most of the furniture is designed for easy maintenance, is uncomfortable, and is visually sterile. Plastics can be used in attractive ways, but instead wood-grained formica is used to make desks that restrict the ways in which one can sit and that yield to no form of body pressure. Rooms seldom have a soft relief; there are few places for enclosure or for privacy. The point here is not so much to chastise school architects but to point out that the buildings that we build do at least two things: they express the values we cherish, and, once built, they reinforce those values. Schools are educational churches, and our gods, judging from the altars we build, are economy and efficiency. Hardly a nod is given to the spirit.

Thus, the implicit curriculum of the school is what it teaches because of the kind of place it is. And the school is that kind of place through the ancillary consequences of various approaches to teaching, by the kind of reward system that it uses, by the organizational structure it employs to sustain its existence, by the physical characteristics of the school plant, and by the furniture it uses and the surroundings it creates. These characteristics constitute some of the dominant components of the school's implicit curriculum. Although these features are seldom publicly announced, they are intuitively recognized by parents, students, and teachers. And because they are salient and pervasive features of schooling, what they teach may be among the most important lessons a child learns.

The Null Curriculum

There is something of a paradox involved in writing about a curriculum that does not exist. Yet, if we are concerned with the consequences of school programs and the role of curriculum in shaping those consequences, then it seems to me that we are well advised to consider not only the explicit and implicit curricula of schools but also what schools do *not teach*. It is my thesis that what schools do not teach may be as important as what they do teach. I argue this position because ignorance is not simply a neutral void; it has important effects on the kinds of options one is able to consider, the alternatives that one can examine, and the perspectives from which one can view a situation or problems. The absence of a set of considerations or perspectives or the inability to use certain processes for appraising a context biases the evidence one is able to take into account. A parochial perspective or simplistic analysis is the inevitable progeny of ignorance.

In arguing this view I am not suggesting that any of us can be without bias or that we can eventually gain a comprehensive view of all problems or issues. I do not believe that is possible, nor do I believe that we would be able to know whether our view was comprehensive, for to know that would require that one know everything that was applicable to the problem. Such a perspective requires omniscience. Yet if one mission of the school is to foster wisdom, weaken prejudice, and develop the ability to use a wide range of modes of thought, then it seems to me we ought to examine school programs to locate those areas of thought and those perspectives that are now absent in order to reassure ourselves that these omissions were not a result of ignorance but a product of choice.

In identifying the null curriculum there are two major dimensions that can be considered. One is the intellectual processes that schools emphasize and neglect. The other is the content or subject areas that are present and absent in school curricula.

Consider first the intellectual processes that are now emphasized in school programs. Discourse in education, both in the public schools and in university schools and departments of education, has placed a great deal of emphasis on the development of cognitive processes. Cognition is supposed to be contrasted with affect, which in turn is contrasted with psychomotor activity. This trilogy is believed to exhaust the major parameters of mind. Cognition, the story goes, deals with thinking, affect with feeling, and psychomotor activity with acting or skill performance. Once these distinctions are made they tend to become reified, a process that is encouraged by the use of taxonomies for the formulation of behavioral objectives within each of the three "domains": cognitive, affective, and psychomotor. Aside from the problems inherent in the reification of distinctions among thinking, feeling, and acting, cognition itself has come to mean thinking with words or numbers by using logical procedures for their organization and manipulation and not thinking in its broadest sense. The term *cognitive* originally meant the process through which the organism becomes aware of the environment. *The Dictionary of Psychology* (Warren, Howard, & Crosby, 1934) offers this definition: "a generic term used to designate all processes involved in knowing. It begins with immediate awareness of objects in perception and extends to all forms of reasoning." Yet, in the literature of education the term has been impoverished, and in the process what we consider to be thinking has also been diminished. Thus there is the irony of cognition becoming increasingly important in educational discourse while it is being robbed of its scope and richness.

What school programs tend to emphasize is the development of a restricted conception of thinking. Not all thinking is mediated by words or numbers, nor is all thinking rule-abiding.

Many of the most productive modes of thought are nonverbal and illogical. These modes operate in visual, auditory, metaphoric, synesthetic ways and use forms of conception and expression that far exceed the limits of logically prescribed criteria or discursive or mathematical forms of thinking. When attention to such intellectual processes, or forms, of thinking is absent or marginal, they are not likely to be developed within school programs, although their development might take place outside of school. But the consequences within schools for students when such modes of thought and expression are absent or given low priority are significant. The criteria that are employed for assessing intellectual competence must of necessity focus on the forms of thinking and experience that are available and salient. Thus, not only does the neglect or absence from school programs of nondiscursive forms of knowing skew what can be known and expressed in schools, it also biases the criteria through which human competence and intelligence are appraised.

When we look at school curricula with an eye toward the full range of intellectual processes that human beings can exercise, it quickly becomes apparent that only a slender range of those processes is emphasized. When one also considers the fact that some of the most interesting work going on in the field of brain physiology is pointing out that the hemispheres of the brain are specialized, that the right and left hemispheres perform different intellectual functions, and that those functions can atrophy or strengthen with use or disuse, the neglect of what are erroneously referred to as affective processes is particularly significant. Researchers studying brain functions have demonstrated that the left hemisphere is the seat of speech—a fact known since the 19th century. But they have more recently demonstrated that what in previous years has been regarded as the minor hemisphere is not minor at all. The right hemisphere provides the location for much of the visualization processes; it is the seat of metaphoric and poetic thought, and it is where structure-seeking forms of intellectual activity have their home. Writing cogently about research on hemispheric specialization, Gabrielle Rico (1976) says:

These findings bespeak a partial redundancy in the two halves of the brain, operating to prevent the individual from being totally incapacitated should disaster strike one or the other hemisphere. But beyond redundancy of function, such evidence lends credence to Bogen's suggestion that a more fundamental distinction between the two hemispheres is not so much a distinction between material or content specificity (speech or faces) as between process specificity. How, then, can these differing capacities best be characterized? A question certainly far from resolved. But there are signs pointing the way:

1. If the left hemisphere is better able to process sequentially ordered information, the right is better at simultaneous patterning. Special tests by Levy-Agresti (1968) show a right hemisphere superiority for matching spatial forms, suggesting to her that it is a synthesis in dealing with information. Furthermore, one of the most obvious symptoms to follow right hemisphere damage is the patient's inability to copy block designs (Bogen, 1970) or to arrange blocks in a required pattern. There is also evidence that the left hemisphere tends to classify objects according to related linguistic categories, whereas the right tends to connect objects which are structurally isomorphic. Nebes (1975) writes "the left hemisphere tends to choose items which are similar in their use—i.e., if shown a cake on a plate

it might pick out a fork and spoon, while the right selects objects unrelated in use but structurally similar—a round straw hat with a brim" (p. 16).

2. If the left is better able to cope with familiar, learned, habitual configurations, the right is better able to handle unfamiliar configurations; in tests those which were unfamiliar and therefore not susceptible to verbal labels—random shapes, unusual textures—were processed by the right hemisphere, totally baffling the left. Furthermore, shapes easily categorized by language, such as ♡ or → were readily processed by the left (Nebes, 1975, p. 14).

   In addition, the right hemisphere is better able to reconstitute the whole of a figure after being exposed to only a small number of its elements (Bogen, 1972, p. 52).

3. If the left hemisphere is better able to handle time-ordered stimulus sequences, the right is superior for processing time-independent stimulus configurations (Gordon and Bogen, 1975). Carotid amytal injection is a method in which a drug is injected into one or the other hemisphere to immobilize it for 3–5 minutes. This method has confirmed that the left is specialized for time-ordered sentences, paragraphs, phrases which were retrieved according to grammatical rules and ordered into a specific temporal arrangement. In contrast, the right hemisphere was better able to retrieve songs and melodies which are remembered and produced as intact wholes (presentationally), not as units pieced together tone by tone, word by word. Gordon and Bogen suggest that the ability to store and recall intact such large units may be an important aspect of those tasks for which the right hemisphere of most individuals is dominant. (pp.41–44)

What Rico is pointing out are some of the major conclusions of a body of research on the functions of the brain that has been going on since the early 1970s. The research provides a useful perspective for examining what school programs provide, what they cultivate, and what they neglect. If we are concerned in schools with the development of productive thought, if we are interested in strengthening those processes through which invention, boundary pushing, and boundary breaking occur, then it seems reasonable that school curriculum should provide children with the opportunities to use those processes in the course of their work. It is not beyond the realm of possibility that every course that now occupies a position within schools could foster such processes. This would, of course, require that the curriculum activities planned, and particularly the kinds of tests that are used, elicit and reward such processes. The cultivation of imagination is not a utopian aspiration.

* * * * *

The neglect of such processes within schools, assuming they are not adequately fostered outside of schools, can lead to a kind of literalness in perception and thought that impedes the appreciation of those objects or ideas that best exemplify metaphorical modes of thinking. Take as an example the reading of poetry or literature. What will a strictly literal construction of the following poem by e. e. cummings (1926) render?

> *you shall above all things be glad and young.*
> *For if you're young,whatever life you wear*
>
> *it will become you;and if you are glad*
> *whatever's living will yourself become.*
> *Girlboys may nothing more than boygirls need:*
> *i can entirely her only love*
>
> *whose any mystery makes every man's*
> *flesh put space on;and his mind take off time*
>
> *that you should ever think,may god forbid*
> *and(in his mercy)your true lover spare:*
> *for that way knowledge lies,the foetal grave*
> *called progress,and negation's dead undoom.*
>
> *I'd rather learn from one bird how to sing*
> *than teach ten thousand stars how not to dance*

Now take the last couplet in that poem,

> *I'd rather learn from one bird how to sing*
> *than teach ten thousand stars how not to dance*

To penetrate the meaning of that couplet, to grasp the allusions it contains, requires one to free oneself from literal perceptions of meaning and to apprehend the import of the images in the poetry itself. Although these images are not literally translatable, there are a lot of things we can say about them.

Learning is a humble thing compared with teaching. To teach puts one in a superordinate position, to learn in the position of a subordinate. Learners are seldom philanthropists. But who would the poet rather learn from: not Einstein, or Marx, or Darwin, but from a bird. And what would he rather learn: to understand the universe, to be able to turn dross into gold, to be able to create atomic fission? No. He'd rather learn to sing. He'd rather learn to do something that gives joy to life from one of the most fragile of God's creatures than to teach the largest bodies of our universe itself how not to dance.

But who teaches stars not to dance? How does one teach stars not to do something? Astronomers do. Astronomers teach us that stars do not dance. What we see are simply the light waves that flicker as they traverse the atmosphere. The poet e. e. cummings chooses joy over knowledge. But to know *that,* no literal reading will do. An ability to allow one's imagination to grasp and play with the qualitative aspects of cummings's impression is a necessary condition for recovering the meaning the poet has created.

Schools have a role, it seems to me, to offer the young an opportunity to develop the kinds of intellectual processes that will be useful for dealing with the likes of e. e. cummings and other poets who have given the world its poetry.

Such processes are not restricted to poetry; they function in any sphere of human activity in which new patterns must be perceived, where literal perception will not do, when multiple meanings must be understood, where intimation, nuance, and analogy are at work. Consider the following passage from Aleksandr Solzhenitsyn's (1973) *Gulag Archipelago:*

> Spring promises everyone happiness—and tenfold to the prisoner. Oh, April sky! It didn't matter that I was in prison. Evidently, they were not going to shoot me. And in the end I would become wiser here. I would come to understand many things here, Heaven! I would correct my mistakes yet, O Heaven, not for them but for you, Heaven! I had come to understand those mistakes here, and I would correct them!
>
> As if from a pit, from the far-off lower reaches, from Szerzhinsky Square, the hoarse earthly singing of the automobile horns rose to us in a constant refrain. To those who were dashing along to the tune of those honkings, they seemed the trumpets of creation, but from here their insignificance was very clear.
>
> In the first place, it was very interesting to try to figure out the layout of the entire prison while they were taking you there and back, and to calculate where those tiny hanging courtyards were, so that at some later date, out in freedom, one could walk along the square and spot their location. We made many turns on the way there, and I invented the following system: Starting from the cell itself I would count every turn to the right as plus one, and every turn to the left as minus one. And, no matter how quickly they made us turn, the idea was not to try to picture it hastily to oneself, but to count up the total. If, in addition, through some staircase window, you could catch a glimpse of the backs of the Lubyanks water nymphs, half-reclining against the pillared turret which hovered over the square itself, and you could remember the exact point in your count when this happened, then back in the cell you could orient yourself and figure out what your window looked out on. (p. 212)

To understand this passage requires an ability and willingness to make the connection between spring and promises, to recognize its sense of growing life, and to appreciate how the experience of an April sky can be caught in "Oh, April sky!"—the tempo of the passage, the contrast of life and death, of heaven and prison, of the cacophony and the din of motor cars outside where life bustles and the cool systematic efforts to sustain that life in oneself by counting the turns en route to one's cell. An educational program that provides little or no opportunity for students to refine the processes that make such understanding possible is likely to yield a population ill prepared to read the world's great literature. But, perhaps even more importantly, it is likely to withhold from students the joys of intellectual discovery.

The major point I have been trying to make thus far is that schools have consequences not only by virtue of what they do teach, but also by virtue of what they neglect to teach. What students cannot consider, what they don't know, processes they are unable to use, have consequences for the kinds of lives they lead. I have directed my attention in the preceding section to the schools' general neglect of particular intellectual processes. Let me now turn to the content or subject matter side of the coin.

Why is it that the vast majority of schools in the United States at both the elementary and secondary levels teach virtually the same subject matters? Let us assume for the moment that basic reading skills, basic arithmetic skills, and basic skills of writing, including spelling, grammar, and punctuation, are necessary parts of virtually all elementary school programs. But even given this assumption, why are time, space, and energy given over to advanced forms of mathematics, history, the sciences, and physical education? Why do most secondary schools require 4 years of English, 2 years of mathematics, and 2 or 3 years of science? Why do they require 2 or 3 years of U.S. history or social studies? Why is it that law, economics, anthropology, psychology, dance, the visual arts, and music are frequently not offered or are not required parts of secondary school programs? Why do so few schools offer work in filmmaking, in the study of communication, in the study of war and revolution? In raising these questions I am not now suggesting that these particular subject matters replace those that now occupy a secure place in school programs. I am trying to point out that certain subject matters have been traditionally taught in schools not because of a careful analysis of the range of other alternatives that could be offered but rather because they have traditionally been taught. We teach what we teach largely out of habit, and in the process neglect areas of study that could prove to be exceedingly useful to students. Take, as an example, economics.

Economics is presently taught in less than 10 percent of all secondary schools in the United States. Now economic theory is not something one is likely to learn simply through the process of socialization. One does not encounter economic theory as one might encounter various forms of social behavior. Yet economics provides one of the frames of reference that enables one to understand how our social system operates. Indeed, to take advantage of the economic opportunities that this nation affords, it is useful to know something of the economic structure of the society, to understand how capital can be used to increase income, to know how to read a stock market report—in short, to have what is needed to make the most out of the resources one has. Yet such problems and the subject matters within which they appear seldom receive attention within schools, say, in comparison to sentential calculus or advanced forms of geometry. The null curriculum includes the study of economics.

Take as another example the study of law. What does a layperson need to know about the law to understand his or her rights, the basic ways in which our legal systems works, the rights and obligations incurred in the signing of a contract? What does it mean to be arrested? What is the difference between a criminal and civil suit? What is a tort and when has a crime been committed? Although I realize that such seemingly simple questions are extraordinarily complex, the same holds true for virtually all other fields in which a student works. Students could be introduced to the study of law first because the problems that it poses are interesting and rich—there is much that could be related to their lives in a fairly direct fashion—and second because it is important for citizens to know something about the legal system under which they live so that at the very least they will be in a position to understand the obligations of a contract and the remedies for its violation. At present, such knowledge is almost entirely within the province of the legal profession.

Take as still another example the study of what might be called the vernacular arts. In our society, a wide variety of visual forms are used to shape values, to influence aspirations, and in general to motivate people to do or not do certain things. The design of shopping centers, the forms of the displays that are created, the kinds of images that are shown in the mass media, on television, and on film, those images are, as Vance Packard aptly called them, the "hidden persuaders" in our culture. They are designed with skill and serve the interests of the manufacturer and merchant, politician, industrialist, builder, and salesman. How do these images work? In what ways do they impose themselves on our consciousness? Are we or can we become immune to their messages, or do we delude ourselves into thinking so? Are there ways students could be helped to become aware of such forms and how they function? Could they be enabled to learn to "read" the arts of the vernacular, to understand how they themselves use such arts to persuade and motivate? Is there a grammar to these images, a syntax that, although not following the forms of logic used in verbal and written discourse, nevertheless exists and can be revealed through analysis?

The study of popular images, the arts of the vernacular, could of course be offered as part of the school's program. The study of such arts would, at least in principle, help develop a level of critical consciousness that is now generally absent in our culture. Yet, as ubiquitous and as powerful as such popular images are, there are hardly any schools in the country that pay serious attention to them or help students learn to read the messages they carry at a level that subjects them to critical scrutiny. Writing about these images, Edmund Feldman (1976) says:

> One reason for this difference between the perception of visual and verbal imagery lies in the fundamentally sequential structure of speech and writing as opposed to the almost simultaneous perception of visual forms. Second, because of our phylogenetic heritage, the visual image established connection with different—one might say "older"—portions of the brain than verbal structures. The feelings experienced in the presence of visual images are more

difficult to control or resist than those dependent on language. Because language (especially the complex linguistic forms of modern man) evolved after the development of visual perception in the phylogeny of our species, we are equipped with older, possibly less sophisticated, biological equipment for the apprehension of images. We cannot so readily defend against what a picture seems to tell us to do or feel. Third, our knowledge systems and our educational institutions have been organized almost exclusively for the transmissions and reception of linear structures. It is obvious that these institutions find themselves in crisis when nonlinear, that is, visual, sources of imagery are perfected and made cheaply and instantly available. To complicate the problem further, it is possible that the most technically sophisticated mental operations on which an advanced civilization depends cannot be learned except through linear, sequentially organized meaning structures. But for the engineering of public assent, the encouragement of nonreflective behavior, visual imagery is ideal.

If visual images are relatively invulnerable to logical and semantic scrutiny, how can we account for the extraordinary influence of verbal slogans in religion, politics, and advertising? The explanation is simple, and it reinforces our argument concerning the compelling power of the visual image: the effectiveness of a slogan depends on repetition, and the function of repetition is to convert a logical sequence into an image. In fact, the repeated slogan becomes a motor image—one that we find difficult to forget, like the lyrics of a bad song or a frequently heard advertising jingle. So long as a slogan can be analyzed semantically it can be resisted. But once it has been drilled into the popular consciousness in the form of a patterned reenactment, there is no way to prevent many compelling transactions, that is, automatic acquiescence, from taking place. Thus the slogan becomes part of our involuntary behavior. (pp. 137–138)

It becomes clear that what we teach in schools is not always determined by a set of decisions that have entertained alternatives; rather, the subjects that are now taught are a part of a tradition, and traditions create expectations, they create predictability, and they sustain stability. The subjects that are now taught are also protected by the interests of teachers who view themselves as specialists in particular fields. There is no national lobby of teachers of law, or of communications, or of anthropology. Indeed, in the words of one individual (Hanvey, 1971) who tried to bring an anthropology curriculum into secondary schools, it was necessary to fly under false colors. In order for anthropology to be taught, it has to come disguised as history, a field already established and serving a well-defined professional interest group.

The strategy that we finally elected was chosen because it looked as though it might work, because it was consistent with our definition of the faults of the traditional social studies, and because it made sense in terms of what anthropology as a discipline had to offer. We decided to subvert a course very commonly taught in the ninth or tenth grade—the world history course. More specifically, we intended to offer materials that could be rationalized as world history and which would, in effect, substitute for a substantial segment of the traditional course. Many supporters of anthropology in the high schools urged us to design a high school–level anthropology course. We resisted this advice; we knew that such a program would never become a required course and we knew what happened to elective courses. The elective route was no way to bring large numbers of students into a meaningful encounter with anthropology. (pp. 145)

Take as still another example the general neglect of the arts in elementary and secondary schools. Although elementary schools are generally supposed to provide programs in the arts, few well-thought-out and competently taught art programs exist at this level. Elementary school teachers have little background in the arts and, in general, are not well prepared to teach them.

At the secondary level, where there are art specialists, the arts are taught in about half of all secondary schools and only 20 percent of the school population enrolls for as little as 1 year. This neglect of the arts, compared with, say, the sciences, leaves students unable, by and large, to deal meaningfully with sophisticated forms of the serious arts. One need not have special tuition to appreciate prime time T.V. When it comes to the music of Stravinsky, the films of Bergman, the paintings of Matisse, the architecture of Corbusier, the sculpture of Brancusi, the dance of Cunningham, tuition is needed. Yet, schools do not provide programs that develop such abilities, and, because such abilities do not develop on their own, millions of students leave schools each year without access to what such artists have contributed to the world. If in hundreds of years some archeologist wanted to understand something of the aesthetic level our culture had achieved, no more representative artifacts could be dug up than the Sears Roebuck catalogue and the *TV Guide*.

Law, anthropology, the arts, communication, economics: these are just a few of the fields that constitute the null curriculum. I am not here making a brief for these particular fields or subject matters, for in fact I believe that there can be no adequate conception of appropriate curriculum content without consideration of the context in which it is to be provided and the students for whom it is intended. I identify these fields and subject matters for purposes of exemplification and to highlight the point that what we offer the young in schools is largely bound by tradition. One could hope for more.

When we ask, therefore, about the means through which schools teach, we can recognize that one of the major means is through the explicit curriculum that is offered to students. But that is not all. Schools also teach, through the implicit curriculum, that pervasive and ubiquitous set of expectations and rules that defines schooling as a cultural system that itself teaches important lessons. And we can identify the null curriculum—the options students are not afforded, the perspectives they may never know about, much less be able to use, the concepts and skills that are not a part of their intellectual repertoire. Surely, in the deliberations that constitute the course of living, their absence will have important consequences on the kind of life that students can choose to lead.

Thus far, we have examined not only the major orientations that have guided thinking about what shall be taught in school, but we have also examined what schools teach that teachers do not realize they are teaching and what they neglect teaching, as well. The consequences of school programs emanate from values that are explicit and operational as well as those that are tacit and covert.

In the following chapter, we will deal with the problem of how curriculum objectives can be formulated, a problem that has been the center of great controversy since the late 1970s.

References

Apple, M. W. (1979). *Ideology and curriculum.* London: Routledge and Kegan Paul.

cummings, e. e. (1926). *Collected poems.* New York: Harcourt, Brace.

Dreeben, R. (1968). *On what is learned in school.* Reading, MA: Addison-Wesley.

Feldman, E. (1976). Art, education and the consumption of images. In Elliot W. Eisner (Ed.), *The arts, human development and education* (pp. 137–146). Berkeley, CA: McCutchan.

Hanvey, R. (1971). The social studies, the educational culture, the state. In Elliot W. Eisner (Ed.), *Confronting curriculum reform* (pp. 143–153). Boston: Little, Brown.

Illich, I. (1973). *Tools for conviviality.* New York: Harper & Row.

Jackson, P. (1968). *Life in classrooms.* New York: Holt, Rinehart & Winston.

Lepper, M., & Greene, D. (Eds.). (1978). *The hidden cost of reward.* New York: Halsted Press.

Mumford, L. (1938). *Technics and civilization.* New York: Harcourt, Brace.

Rico, G. (1976). *Metaphors and knowing: Analysis, synthesis, rationale.* Doctoral Dissertation, Stanford University, Stanford, CA.

Sarason, S. (1971). *The culture of the school and the problem of change.* Boston: Allyn & Bacon.

Solzhenitsyn, A. (1973). *Gulag archipelago.* (Thomas P. Whitney, Trans.). New York: Harper & Row.

Vallance, E. (1973–1974) Hiding the hidden curriculum. *Curriculum Theory Network (4)*1, 5–21.

Waller, W. (1932). *The sociology of teaching.* New York: Wiley & Sons.

Warren, H. (Ed.). (1934). *The dictionary of psychology.* Boston: Houghton Mifflin.

5

Educational Aims, Objectives, and Other Aspirations

*Finally, there should grow the most austere of all mental qualities;
I mean the sense for style. It is an aesthetic sense, based on admiration for the direct attainment of a foreseen end, simply and without
waste. Style in art, style in literature, style in science, style in logic,
style in practical execution have fundamentally the same aesthetic
qualities, namely, attainment and restraint. The love of a subject in
itself and for itself, where it is not the sleepy pleasure of pacing a
mental quarterdeck, is the love of style as manifested in that study.*
ALFRED N. WHITEHEAD

No concept is more central to curriculum planning than the concept of
objectives. The argument for its importance is straightforward. I will try to
provide it.

Behavioral Objectives

Objectives are the specific goals that one hopes to achieve through the educational program that is provided. In order for educational planning to be
meaningful, not only must goals be formulated, but they must also be formulated with precision and with clarity. To formulate them with precision
and clarity it is best not to use words that have referents that are difficult to
observe. Words such as *understanding, insight, appreciation,* and *interest* refer
to qualities that cannot be observed directly; they require one to make

inferences about their existence through the observation of manifest behavior. Thus, useful objectives should be stated in behavioral terms or, in more current jargon, performance terms. When objectives are stated behaviorally, it is possible to have specific empirical referents to observe; thus, one is in a position to know without ambiguity whether the behavioral objective has been reached. An objective that seeks to help students appreciate the insights of great poetry needs to be recast in terms far more specific and precise. What would a student *do* to demonstrate that such appreciation has occurred? What behavior would he or she display? What task is he or she to perform?

It should be noted, as it is by those who advocate the use of specific behavioral objectives in curriculum planning, that the objective is to be stated in terms of desired *student behavior*. It should not describe what the teacher is to do. If an objective stated that "the objective of the course is to introduce students to great ideas of the Western world," not only would the behavior be obscure—the term *introduce* for a behaviorist is vague—the objective would logically be achieved when the teacher introduced the material to the students. The objective in this case is stated in terms of teacher behavior, not in terms of the desired behavior of the students.

A further condition for formulation of meaningful behavioral objectives is that both the behavior and the content be identified. Appreciation, for example, is always of some thing or idea. Understanding always has a subject matter. One does something to something else and in some context. Thus, objectives that are adequately behavioral will not only refer to student rather than teacher behavior, will not only minimize the need for inference—the closer to manifest behavior the better—but meaningful objectives will also identify the particular subject matter in which the behavior is to take place. For example, the student will be able to identify the major causes of the Westward movement in the United States during the period 1840 to 1870.

Even with these criteria, for hard-line behaviorists, the foregoing objective is still too diffuse. What is missing is a statement of the specific criterion level the student will have to meet in order to demonstrate that the objective has been attained. There might be five major causes for the Westward movement. How many of these must a student identify—one, two, three, four, or all five? Thus, not only must an objective have the characteristics I have already described, but also, perhaps most importantly, it must specify the criterion level that must be achieved to demonstrate competency in reaching the objective. Perhaps the best spokesperson for this view is Robert Mager (1962):

> An objective is an *intent* communicated by a statement describing a proposed change in a learner—a statement of what the learner is to be like when he has successfully completed a learning experience. It is a description of a pattern of

behavior (performance) we want the learner to be able to demonstrate. As Dr. Paul Whitmore once put it, "The statement of objectives of a training program must denote *measurable* attributes *observable* in the graduate of the program, or otherwise it is impossible to determine whether or not the program is meeting the objectives."

When clearly defined goals are lacking, it is impossible to evaluate a course or program efficiently, and there is no sound basis for selecting appropriate materials, content, or instructional methods. After all, a machinist does not select a tool until he knows what operation he intends to perform. Neither does a composer orchestrate a score until he knows what effects he wishes to achieve. Similarly, a builder does not select his materials or specify a schedule for construction until he has his blueprints (objectives) before him. Too often, however, one hears teachers arguing the relative merits of textbooks or other aids of the classroom versus the laboratory, without ever specifying just what goal the aid or method is to assist in achieving. I cannot emphasize too strongly the point that an instructor will function in a fog of his own making until he knows just what he wants his students to be able to do at the end of the instruction. (p. 31)

What Mager and others holding this view are trying to do is to develop a highly precise technology for statements of objectives that they believe will improve the quality of teaching and learning. For many behaviorists, one of the major problems of goal statements is that they are vague, and because they are vague, they tend to be educationally meaningless. To have a meaningful objective, and by inference a useful one, one should be able to determine, usually through measurement, whether it has been achieved. To the extent that there is ambiguity in the statement, its meaningfulness and utility are diminished. Furthermore, if a curriculum planner knows exactly what kind of behavior he or she wants students to display, it is easier to select content and formulate activities that are instrumental to the desired end.

The Roots of the Objectives Movement

The tendency toward high levels of behavioral specificity is, of course, not new in American educational planning. Franklin Bobbitt, whose ideas we encountered earlier, listed ten areas for such objectives in his book *How to Make a Curriculum,* which was published in 1922. Although Bobbitt's objectives, too, are vague by today's standards, the spirit of behavioral specificity is the same. Indeed, the general thrust toward the study of behavior rather than experience has been characteristic of American educational psychology since the turn of the century. Thorndike, Watson, Hull, and Skinner participate in that tradition, and it provides the theoretical backdrop for this approach to the formulation of behavioral objectives.

There are two other traditions associated with the behavioral specification approach to objectives; one of these is found in industry, the other in military training. They have two features in common: the characteristics of the performance to be produced are known in advance, and, ideally, the specifications of the objectives and characteristics of the individual performance are isomorphic—that is, a perfect match between objective and behavior is desired. In industrial settings, such as in automobile production, the same conditions hold. A prototypical form is created for the cars to be assembled. This form is described both physically and mechanically for each model. Subsequently, a component analysis is made of the prototype, a task analysis follows that prescribes the steps to be taken in production and their sequence, and production begins. The manager of the assembly line has the task of ensuring that all operations are performed in the order specified. The goal to be achieved is the creation of an isomorphic relationship between the original prototype and each car coming off the line. If these cars do not match, there is a call-back, and the problem is identified and readjustments are made. An efficient and effective assembly line produces identical cars day after day that in every aspect match the model that was originally created.

Military training programs have similar features. New recruits are processed through a program that specifies in almost every detail what is to be done and how. The slogan "There is a right way, a wrong way, and an Army way" is not altogether inappropriate. When one has a training program, a program that intentionally attempts to help another acquire a known, specific performance system to be used to achieved a known goal, the acquisition of known behavioral routines might be appropriate. Personal ingenuity and idiosyncratic behavior are discouraged both on the assembly line and in the boot camp. The armed forces justify such an approach on the basis that it is of paramount importance for soldiers to learn to follow orders: prediction and control of troops are required in time of war. Industry employs such an approach because it is efficient; more cars can be produced in better fashion when systematic, routinized procedures are followed.

It is interesting to note that the earliest efforts at specifying goals and prescribing the methods through which those goals could be attained occurred during the so-called efficiency period in American education from about 1903 to 1925 (Callahan, 1962). During this period, school administrators were being criticized in the press for running slack schools, schools that had much waste, that did not give the public a fair return on its investment. These men, vulnerable as they were (and are), sought what they could to make schooling more rigorous and in the process discovered the work of Frederick Taylor, an industrial management consultant and the father of time and motion study. Taylor would go into industrial plants with a team of colleagues and study the movements of the work force, measure the current level of productivity, and then prescribe minute steps to be taken by workers to eliminate excess waste in movement. By using his methods, companies such as Bethlehem Steel were able to increase their level of productivity significantly. Raymond Callahan (1962), a historian noted for his work pertaining to this period, writes:

> The first element in the mechanism of scientific management listed by Taylor was time and motion study and the development of unit times for the various components of any job. This Taylor regarded as "by far the most important element in scientific management," and it was the basic element in achieving his first principle of the development of a true science for a particular job. Frank Gilbreth testified on this point by stating that "any plan of management that does not include Taylor's plan of time study cannot be considered as highly efficient. We have never seen a case in our work where time study and analysis did not result in more than doubling the output of the worker." Not only was time and motion study thus conceived by the engineers themselves, but also it was apparently identified in the mind of the average American as the key element of the system. Milton Nadworny notes, "Although scientific management employed many identifiable and characteristic mechanisms, its most prominent tool was a stopwatch, the popular symbol of the scientific management movement. The stopwatch symbolized the new approach to management: 'management based on measurement.'" (p. 28)

It is not surprising when one is in a vulnerable position, as superintendents of schools were and are, that one should embrace any new idea that promises to reduce that vulnerability. Scientific management, as Taylor called it, appeared to provide the mantle of scientific respectability that schoolmen needed and wanted. By wrapping themselves in a scientific cloak, they believed they could protect themselves from the criticism that they were inefficient stewards of the schools.

It is, I think, particularly important to take note of the language that was used during this period. The society was viewed as the consumer of the school's products. The children were the raw material to be processed according to specifications laid down by the consumer. And the teachers were the workers who were to be overseen by supervisors. All of this was to take place under a superintendent. Although the modern concepts of quality assurance and quality control were not used then, a similar spirit was at work in those "good" old days.

The analogy between industrial processes and educational processes is a deceptive one. When one is working with inert material for ends that are uniform and prespecified, the task of determining effectiveness and locating inefficiency or ineffectiveness is comparatively simple. After all, when 1,000 pounds of pressure is placed on 30-gauge steel within a 1-inch diameter, the reaction of the steel to the pressure is quite predictable. As long as there is no human error or mechanical failure, the results will be the same time and time again. Industrial managers bank on it. Such conditions, however, seldom are obtained in the classroom. Children are far from inert, and so are teachers. They respond differently to the "same" stimuli, because how the stimuli are perceived—indeed, *whether* they in fact stimulate—depends as much on the characteristics of the student as it does on the objective characteristics of the stimuli themselves. Furthermore, the realization of outcomes that are common to all students, the production of educational products all having identical features, at best suits only a small array of those aims that most educators seek in the course of teaching. One major problem I see in the admonition to teachers and curriculum planners to specify their aims in behavioral terms is that the limitations of such objectives are seldom acknowledged. They are offered as though one were not really professionally competent without a list of objectives that one could pull out for each set of curriculum activities formulated.

In identifying what I believe to be an oversimplified view of the character of educational aims, I am not taking the position that there is no place for clearly defined behavioral objectives in a school curriculum. When specific skills or competencies are appropriate, such objectives can be formulated, but one should not feel compelled to abandon educational aims that cannot be reduced to measurable forms of predictable performance. Conceptions of method should serve as tools and as heuristic devices for improving the quality of educational experience, not as constraints on teachers, teaching, or what students have an opportunity to learn.

Limitations of Behavioral Objectives

Let me provide a description of some other limitations behaviorally defined objectives have in the design of educational programs. I identify these limitations not as a wholesale condemnation of their use but as an attempt to increase the sophistication of the dialogue about them.

One limitation of discursively defined behavioral objectives deals with the limits of discourse itself. Much, perhaps most, of what we aspire to and cherish is not amenable to discursive formulation. Take, for example, our image of human sensitivity. Although we could describe discrete behaviors that were intended to characterize a sensitive human being—say, one who was responsive to the feelings of others and compassionate—discrete forms of human performance would ultimately fail to capture what we are able to recognize in others. Language is, after all, a surrogate for experience. We try to articulate in words what we know in nonlinguistic ways. For much of our experience, discursive language performs rather well. But for the subtleties of human experience, for our knowledge of human feeling, for modes of conception and understanding that are qualitative, discourse falls far short. How many words would it take to describe insight, perceptivity, integrity, self-esteem? How would one describe how water tastes? How would one describe the qualities of a late Beethoven quartet in precise, unambiguous, measurable terms?

The point here is not an effort to inject the mystical into educational planning but rather to avoid reductionistic thinking that impoverishes our view of what is possible. To expect all of our educational aspirations to be either verbally describable or measurable is to expect too little.

A second problem with the use of specific behavioral objectives is that those who evaluate them often fail to distinguish between *the application of a standard* and *the making of a judgment*. Dewey (1934) makes this distinction quite clear when he says the following:

> There are three characteristics of a standard. It is a particular physical thing existing under specified physical conditions; it is *not* a value. The yard is a yardstick, and the meter is a bar deposited in Paris. In the second place, standards are measures of definite things, of lengths, weights, capacities. The things measured are not values, although it is of great social value to be able to measure them, since the properties of things in the way of size, volume, weight, are important for commercial exchange. Finally, as standards of measure, standards define things with respect to *quantity*. To be able to measure quantities is a great aid to further judgments, but it is not itself a mode of judgment. The standard, being an external and public thing, is applied *physically*. The yard-stick is physically laid down upon the things measured to determine their length.
>
> Yet it does not follow, because of absence of a uniform and publicly determined external object, that objective criticism of art is impossible. What follows is that criticism is judgment; that like every judgment it involves a venture, a hypothetical element; that it is directed to qualities which are nevertheless qualities of an *object*; and that it is concerned with an individual object, not with making comparisons by means of an external preestablished rule between different things. The critic, because of the element of venture, reveals himself in his criticisms. He wanders into another field and confuses values when he departs from the object he is judging. Nowhere are comparisons so odious as in fine art. (pp. 307–308)

Standards are crisp, unambiguous, and precise. A person can swim five lengths of the pool or cannot. Someone can spell *aardvark* or cannot. Someone knows who the 27th president of the United States was or does not. Someone can multiply two sets of three-digit figures correctly or cannot. For such performances, standards are specifiable and applicable by anyone or by any machine that "knows" the rules through which the standards are to be applied. But what about the rhetorical force of a student's essay? What about the aesthetic quality of her painting? What about the cogency of his verbal argumentation? What about her intellectual style, the ways she interprets the evidence in a science experiment, the way in which historical material is analyzed? Are these subject to standards? I think not.

But to say that such qualities cannot be measured by standards is not to say that judgments cannot be made about them. It is not to say that one can have no criteria through which to appraise them. Judgments can say much about such qualities, not by the mechanical application of prespecified standards, but by comparison of the qualities in question to a whole range of criteria that teachers or others making the judgment already possess. How much weight does one give to insight and how much to logical argument? How does one compare this essay, or this statement, or this project, or this painting, to the one or ones the student did before? Judgments about such qualities are not will-o'-the-wisp, cavalier, irresponsible conclusions; they are complex appraisals that use an extraordinarily wide range of knowledge to arrive at what, on balance, is a warranted human judgment. The multiple-choice test is simply not adequate for everything.

A third problem with the demand that all objectives be behavioral and defined in advance deals with the assumption that the prespecification of goals is the rational way in which one must always proceed in curriculum planning. This assumption is rooted in the kind of rationality that has guided much of Western technology. The means-ends model of thinking has for so long dominated our thinking that we have come to believe that not to have clearly defined purposes for our activities is to court irrationality or, at the least, to be professionally irresponsible. Yet, life in classrooms, like that outside them, is seldom neat or linear. Although it may be a shock to some, goals are not always clear. Purposes are not always precise. As a matter of fact, there is much that we do, and need to do, without a clear sense of what the objective is. Many of our most productive activities take the form of exploration or play. In such activities, the task is not one of arriving at a preformed objective but rather to act, often with a sense of abandon, wonder, curiosity. Out of such activity, rules may be formed and objectives may be created.

The relationship between action and the formation of purpose is well known to artists. In a particularly telling passage describing the work of the abstract expressionists, Harold Rosenberg (1965), one of America's leading art critics, writes:

> At a certain moment the canvas began to appear to one American painter after another as an arena in which to act—rather than as a space in which to reproduce, re-design, analyze or "express" an object, actual or imagined. What was to go on the canvas was not a picture but an event.
>
> The painter no longer approached his easel with an image in his mind; he went up to it with material in front of him. The image would be the result of this encounter. (p. 25)

What Rosenberg describes of the abstract expressionists is to some extent an echo of Aristotle's remark more than 2,000 years ago. "Art," he said, "loves chance." "He who is willing to err is the artist." What both Aristotle and Rosenberg point out is that purpose need not precede action. Purposes may grow out of action. Unfortunately, our cultural tendency to eschew play and praise work makes it sometimes difficult to explain why play is justified in its own right and why in a broad sense it may be among the most productive forms of human activity.

Problem-Solving Objectives

What would a broader, more generous conception of educational aims look like? Are there ways of thinking about objectives and outcomes that are not constrained by the kinds of criteria that are prescribed for behavioral objectives? I believe there are. But before describing two other ways of conceptualizing educational aims, let me reiterate that I believe behavioral objectives to be appropriate for some types of educational aims, even though I recognize that they are in no way adequate for conceptualizing most of our most cherished educational aspirations. When it is appropriate to formulate specific types of educational exercises that aim at particular definable skills, the use of such objectives may be warranted: one must be able to swim four laps of the pool to be able to swim in the deep end. But one should not, in my view, attempt to reduce all of our goals in such forms. To do so robs them of the very qualities of mind one may be seeking to foster.

In Figure 2, two types of objectives and one kind of outcome are presented that can be planned in the design and evaluation of educational programs. The first of these, the behavioral objective, has already been described, and I will not restate its feature here. The problem-solving objective differs in a significant way from the behavioral objective. In the problem-solving objective, the students formulate or are given a problem to solve—say, to find out how deterrents to smoking might be made more effective, or how to design a paper structure that will hold two bricks 16 inches above a table, or how the variety and quality of food served in the school cafeteria could be increased within the existing budget.

In each of these examples the problem is posed and the criteria that need to be achieved to resolve the problem are fairly clear. But the forms of its solution are virtually infinite. Some students might increase food quantity and variety by finding new sources of supply or by establishing a student volunteer system to work with the kitchen staff. Others might decide that the most effective solution would be for interested students to set up their own kitchen facilities on school premises, and others might formulate an ordering system so students could place orders for some good Chinese and Italian food at a local inexpensive restaurant.

The point is that the shapes of the solutions, the forms they take, are highly variable. Alternative solutions to problem-solving objectives could be discussed in class so that the students could begin to appreciate their practical costs.

This form of objective is not unknown in the design field and in science laboratories. Designers, for example, are almost always given a set of crite-

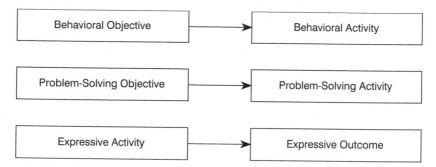

Figure 2   Relationship of Curriculum Objectives to Curriculum Activities

ria or specifications and asked to create a product that will satisfactorily meet those criteria. Often they are asked to create several solutions so that the client can compare alternatives and decide which suits his or her needs best.

In architecture, the client provides the architect with a set of specifications—budget, site, personal life-style, preferred architectural style—and the builder and municipal code present others. Finally, engineering requirements impose their demands: the building has to stand, the cantilevered deck must not fall, the foundations must not sink. Within these design constraints, the architect must create viable and constructive solutions.

In such situations the potential answers are not known beforehand. What is known is the problem; what constitute appropriate solutions remains to be seen after the work has been done.

In the sciences, this type of problem-solving activity is characteristic, at least for most scientists. The concept of *normal science,* a term coined by Thomas Kuhn, aptly describes the work of the typical scientist. Such a person works within a given theory, a theory that he or she does not question. The problem is to find solutions to problems posed within the terms of the theory. Kuhn (1962) writes:

> Mopping-up operations are what engage most scientists throughout their careers. They constitute what I am here calling normal science. Closely examined, whether historically or in the contemporary laboratory, that enterprise seems an attempt to force nature into the preformed and relatively inflexible box that the paradigm supplies. No part of the aim of normal science is to call forth new sorts of phenomena; indeed those that will not fit the box are often not seen at all. Nor do scientists normally aim to invent new theories, and they are often intolerant of those invented by others. Instead, normal-scientific research is directed to the articulation of those phenomena and the theories that the paradigm already supplies. (p. 24)

Like the architect, the scientist tends not to redefine the givens, in this case the basic theoretical premises by which he or she has been professionally socialized and that serve to define not only the problem, but also the scientist's expertise.

One very important difference between the problem-solving objective and the behavioral objective is that the solution to the problem in problem-solving objectives is not definite. The problem is, in a significant sense, a genuine one. Behavioral objectives have both the form and the content defined in advance. There is, after all, only one way to spell *aardvark*. Given the same set of behavioral objectives for a class of students, the successful teacher elicits homogeneous behavior at the end of an instructional period that is isomorphic with the objective. This is not the case with a problem-solving objective. The solutions individual students or groups of students reach may be just as much a surprise for the teacher as they are for the students who created them.

The issue concerning the form statements of objectives are to take is far wider than the character of the forms themselves. Although it is said that form follows function, the opposite is equally true: function follows form. The form, in large measure, reflects an underlying set of assumptions that might not themselves have been examined. The idea that goals should be specifiable in advance and that success in teaching consists primarily of bringing about predictable outcomes are themselves what is at issue. Such a set of beliefs, fostered not through an explicit educational rationale but rather embedded in the very techniques that one is encouraged to use, can have significant effects on the way the teacher's role is conceived and what educators believe they are after. Surreptitiously but inexorably, techniques that go unexamined with respect to the ideology that they reflect can be debilitating. Training comes to be substituted for education.

The use of problem-solving objectives places a premium on cognitive flexibility, on intellectual exploration, on the higher mental processes. It tends toward the formulation of curriculum activities that are likely to be taken seriously by scholars. The reason I make these claims is that not only have I seen this happen in classes where students had such objectives, but also it is reasonable to expect that when students have a set of clear criteria and are free to meet those criteria in ways that require ingenuity, they will take a deeper interest in coping with the problem. The opportunity to use ingenuity breeds interest.

Expressive Outcomes

A third type of educational aim is what I have called, in previous writing, expressive objectives (Eisner, 1969). Because I now see that the term *objective* implies a preformulated goal, something out of reach but to be attained, I think it desirable to change the term to *expressive outcomes*. Outcomes are essentially what one ends up with, intended or not, after some form of engagement. Expressive outcomes are the consequences of curriculum activities that are intentionally planned to provide a fertile field for personal purposing and experience. Take, for example, much of our ordinary activity—say, going to the movies. There is no one I know who formulates specific behavioral objectives before going to a movie. Nor do I know anyone who formulates a problem-solving objective. Most of us go to the movies because we think something interesting or exciting will happen to us there. We do not formulate specific goals that describe what our behavior will be after we leave. We do not establish criteria that the director and actors will have to meet in order to be successful. The fact of the matter is that we already have such criteria in ample abundance and retrospectively select from the ones we have those that appear appropriate for the particular movie we have just seen. If the movie is a comedy, we apply comedic criteria, if an adventure, dramatic criteria, and so forth.

But the problem of appraising the qualities of expressive outcomes is more complicated than I have just described, even in life outside of schools. If the movie we have just seen was billed as the year's funniest comedy or if it is being shown in the finest first-run theater charging the highest prices in town, we come to expect more than we would otherwise. If our favorite actor or actress is in the film or if it was directed by Fellini, Bergman, or Huston, we might make a more complex appraisal. If we have had the bad fortune of seeing a series of poor films during the last 2 months, our receptivity toward a somewhat better than mediocre film may be higher than it would otherwise be. The point here is that the appraisals we make as a result of activities we engage in are clearly complex and highly rational, employing a wide range of criteria that, although not explicit, operate in our judgments. The same holds true in classrooms.

I believe that it is perfectly appropriate for teachers and others involved in curriculum development to plan activities that have no explicit or precise objectives. In an age of accountability, this sounds like heresy. Yet surely there must be room in school for activities that promise to be fruitful, even though the teacher might not be able to say what specifically the students will learn or experience. Parents do this all the time. The trip to the zoo, weekends spent camping in the woods, the bicycle ride after dinner: no specific objectives or problems are posed prior to setting out on such activities, yet we feel that they will be enjoyable and that some "good" will come from them.

Curriculum planning and schooling in general need not always be single-minded in their pursuits, forever focusing on objectives that are by definition always out of reach. Purposes need not precede activities; they can be formulated in the process of action itself.

In Figure 2, not only is a distinction made among educational objectives, problem-solving objectives, and expressive outcomes, but they are also related to different types of curriculum activities. What we see in Figure 2 is that in both behavioral objectives and problem-solving objectives the formulation of the objectives precedes the curriculum activity. In this respect, they both participate in the standard means-ends approach to planning. However, expressive activities precede rather than follow expressive outcomes. The tack taken with respect to the generation of expressive outcomes is to create activities that are seminal; what one is seeking is to have students engage in activities that are sufficiently rich to allow for a wide, productive range of educationally valuable outcomes. If behavioral objectives and behavioral activities constitute the algorithms of curriculum, expressive activities and expressive outcomes constitute their heuristics.

These are not the only forms of language that are significant. The modifiers around the word *objective* have themselves changed significantly. In Tyler's (1950) curriculum monograph, *objective* was preceded by the word *educational*. Thus, what one was to formulate was an *educational* objective. Later the term was shifted by other writers to *instructional*. Still later the word became *behavioral,* and even later it was a *performance* objective that was to be formulated.

This shift in modifier is not an accident; it reflects an increased emphasis on the manifest behavior of the student and on discrete forms of student activity. It gradually moves from the general to the specific. But it is significant in other ways, as well. An educational objective supposedly has something to do with *educational* outcomes. An instructional objective, although not strongly normative, still participates in the context of education. But behavioral or performance objectives may or may not be educational; the normative aspect of education no longer is a part of the term. One can have a behavioral objective that aims at creating racists or paranoids. Such an aim could hardly be regarded as educational, unless of course, racism and paranoia were a part of one's conception of education.

These shifts in language are, in my opinion, no mere minor modifications. Words, of course, have connotations as well as denotations, and it is often the connotative meanings that influence significantly the way we come to think about things. For new students of education, students who do not have the benefit of perspective, the new term, normatively void as it is, might appear as a natural entity. History sustains our memory and provides for depth of field.

It would be erroneous to assume that some fields, such as the fine arts, have a monopoly on the use of expressive activities. This is not the case. Any activity—indeed, at their very best, activities that are engaged in to court surprise, to cultivate discovery, to find new forms of experience—is expressive in character. Nothing in the sciences, the home or mechanical arts, or in social relationships prohibits or diminishes the possibility of engaging in expressive activities and in the process of achieving expressive outcomes. The education problem is to be sufficiently imaginative in the design of educational programs so that such outcomes will occur and their educational value will be high.

What I hope comes through in the foregoing is the view that there is no single legitimate way to formulate educational aims. I have described three approaches or conceptions of objectives. Each has its virtues and utilities. The point of making the distinctions I have made among types of objectives is to expand the array of options that those who plan curricula can use in their work. Once a conception of problem-solving objectives is formulated, it is possible within each subject field—social studies, mathematics, art, English, physical education, and so forth—to plan activities related to such objectives. The same holds true for expressive outcomes. Such outcomes *are not* the exclusive domain of the arts. Even in a field that appears as rule-governed as arithmetic, expressive activities designed to yield expressive outcomes are possible.

A second utility of these three conceptions of educational objectives or outcomes is to ameliorate the unrelenting force and narrowness that a single view of what counts as a legitimate objective tends to have. If there is only one correct way to do something, those who hold other values or envision other means are going to be left out. If the scope of what is legitimate is broadened, the degrees of freedom for teachers and for others who plan curricula will be wider than would otherwise be the case. Indeed, it is reasonable to believe that the types of objectives, outcomes, or aims that can be formulated are not exhausted by the three types I have described. It is reasonable to expect that as our conceptual ability and creativity are applied further to this important aspect of curriculum planning, other options will emerge.

It is, as I have already indicated, possible to use the distinctions that have been made to plan curricula in the various fields that constitute the program of the school. It is also possible to use these conceptions as criteria for analyzing existing curricula, both teacher-made and commercial. To what extent are problem-solving objectives and expressive activities included? What is the ratio or rhythm among these types of objectives within a curriculum? Do the evaluation methods that are employed in the classroom or school district provide students with opportunities to deal with all three types of tasks, or do these evaluation methods provide only for behavioral objectives to be assessed?

At present in American education, criterion-referenced testing is becoming increasingly popular. Criterion-referenced testing is a procedure that directly relates the test content to the specific behavioral objectives that have been formulated for a course or a school district. The aim of criterion-referenced tests is to help educators determine whether or not students within a school or school district have achieved course objectives. This is unlike the norm-referenced test, which is designed to differentiate among students by sorting them out in relation to a normal distribution; the IQ test and most standardized achievement tests are norm-referenced. The criterion-referenced test is designed not to compare students with each other but rather to indicate which students have met the criteria—that is, the objectives. Because the objectives that are usually employed in school districts are behavioral in character, the use of criterion-referenced tests could inadvertently reinforce an emphasis on a limited conception of objectives. Testing for outcomes whose form and content are not easily predictable complicates the evaluator's task, yet it would surely be unfortunate to have educational aims determined by the technology of testing that is presently available. The educator who understands the alternatives and the issues involved in curriculum planning and educational evaluation is in a much better position to provide educational leadership to a school or school district than one who believes that there is only one way to plan curricula or to evaluate legitimately the outcomes of educational practice.

Some General Questions About the Use of Objectives in Designing Educational Programs

After all of the analyses of the various types of objectives and the criteria that each should meet, one is still left with some basic questions about their use in curriculum development and teaching. One of the questions deals with the matter of specificity and the educational "unit" for which they are appropriate or necessary. How specific should objectives be? Should they be formulated for the entire course, for parts of a course, for each curriculum activity that is formulated? It is clear that answers to these questions will differ depending on the view of educational planning that one holds. If one views curriculum planning and teaching, as, in their idealized form, an error-free type of program that moves a student as swiftly as possible from one condition at entry to another at exit—I use the technical jargon intentionally—it is likely that specificity in objectives and a large number of objectives would be desired. Yet I believe that in general one would do well to think through a set of objectives in some detail, particularly when one is not clear about the purposes or aims of teaching or when one needs for matter of public record a set of specific statements of educational goals. In other words, on the whole I see no compelling need for a teacher to formulate or to have formulated for him or her a highly specific set of behavioral objectives. For one thing, such a list, especially if prepared at the level of specificity that would satisfy a behaviorist, could easily run into hundreds of items for an elementary school teacher in a self-contained classroom. Assume for a moment that a teacher taught seven subject areas each week. Suppose further that the teacher divided the class into three ability groups and had one objective each week for 40 weeks in each subject area taught. Such a teacher would have $7 \times 3 \times 40 = 840$ objectives. Obviously no teacher is able to make explicit 840 objectives or be in a position to remember them if they were presented in the form of a guide or manual. How many objectives are feasible? Which ones should be omitted? For what scope of curriculum content are they appropriate? At present there are no quantitative research data that are adequate for answering such questions, nor do I believe there are likely to be.

What I want to claim is that teachers during the school year deal with far more than 840 objectives in the classroom. These objectives are not found in lists. They are not written (although some school districts have compiled such lists of objectives in notebooks the size of the New York City telephone directory). These objectives are a part of the personal and psychological repertoire that teachers draw on each day when working with students.

What I am referring to is the kind of intelligent activity that teachers typically employ in working with students, the kind of intelligence that gives motive and purpose to their teaching, that tells them when they should help a child feel better about himself, when she needs to work harder, when he needs a richer set of resources to work with, when a closer analysis of the text is appropriate. In thousands of ways, teachers draw on images of human virtue as criteria for the direction of their activity as teachers and for the directions they should take with their students. The storehouse of such images is large, and it needs to be. It is modulated according to circumstances and context and with regard to the particular student with whom the teacher interacts.

From this point of view, 840 objectives is a paltry sum. Consider for a moment the range of problems, content, contexts, and individuals with which a teacher must deal. Not only must there be some sense of purpose or direction to the activities in which teachers are engaged, but also the priorities among those projects must be considered, altered, or sustained. When does a teacher, for the time being, wisely forget about the goal of helping a student learn to spell a set of words correctly or learn how to punctuate an adverbial clause and instead attend to other aims, aims that are also a part of his or her aspirations for the student but not an explicit part of that particular segment of the curriculum? When does a teacher choose to make educational capital out of unexpected opportunities in the classroom—an offhand remark by a student or a keen insight by another—and in so doing depart from his or her previously specified objective? All of these happen in classrooms, at least those that are not rigidly tied to a set of single-minded aims. In particular, elementary school classrooms often acquire their own tempo; the students become immersed in what was to be a casual short-term project; and teachers often yield to such tempo, recognizing the need for an organic as contrasted to a mechanical treatment of time.

Thus, from one point of view, 840 objectives are far more than any teacher can reasonably be expected to focus on—420 would be equally difficult. Yet, at the same time, teachers operate with thousands of objectives in the form of their aspirations for the students with whom they work. The major difference is that their latter aims are implicit and contextual rather than explicit and prepared prior to the specific context in which they are to teach.

References

Bobbitt, F. (1922). *How to make a curriculum*. Boston: Houghton Mifflin.

Callahan, R. (1962). *Education and the cult of efficiency*. Chicago: University of Chicago Press.

Dewey, J. (1934). *Art as experience*. New York: Minton, Balch.

Eisner, E. W. (1969). Instructional and expressive objectives: Their formulation and use in curriculum. In W. James Popham (Ed.), *AERA monograph on curriculum evaluation: Instructional objectives*. Chicago: Rand McNally.

Kuhn, T. (1962). *The structure of scientific revolutions*. Chicago: University of Chicago Press.

Mager, R. (1962). *Preparing instructional objectives*. Palo Alto, CA: Fearon.

Rosenberg, H. (1965). *American painting today*. New York: Horizon Press.

Tyler, R. W. (1950). *Basic principles of curriculum and instruction*. Chicago: University of Chicago Press.

6

※

Dimensions of
Curriculum Planning

———————◆•◆———————

*We need, that is, both a way of passing from naked propositions
and their logical connections to the human activities that give them
their sense, and beyond those activities to the features of the world
and human life within which they are at home; and also a reverse
road, back from "forms of life" in the world to the specific activities
in question, and so eventually to the original propositions again.*

STEPHEN TOULMIN

———————◆•◆———————

Thus far, a variety of ideas, concepts, and theories have been discussed pertaining to the design and evaluation of educational programs. The ultimate
test of these ideas is determined by the extent to which they make educational planning more intelligent. As I have already indicated, education is
not a field that will yield to simple prescriptions or recipes. Each situation
in which educational decisions are made is significantly unique, not simply
unique in the sense of time and place—all situations are unique in that
sense—but unique in the sense that the goals, methods, people, and context
differ from each other in important ways and must be treated with respect
to those differences if decision making is to be effective. What we can
expect of ideas about curriculum planning is not that these ideas provide
formulas, but that they sophisticate our deliberations in planning programs
and, hence, contribute to educationally richer programs than might otherwise be provided. In short, we ought to view ideas as tools, not as blueprints; they are things to use, not things to follow.

What Is Curriculum Planning?

Curriculum development is the process of transforming images and aspirations about education into programs that will effectively realize the visions that initiated the process. I use the terms *images* and *aspirations* intentionally. The initiating conditions of curriculum development are seldom clearcut, specific objectives; they are, rather, conceptions that are general, visions that are vague, aspirations that are fleeting. Much of what we value, aspire to, and cherish is ineffable; even if we wanted to, we could not adequately describe it. Furthermore, what we value and seek is often riddled with contradictions—even within the context of schooling—and must be compromised or negotiated in context. We want children to master "the basic skills"; we would like them to be supportive and cooperative with their peers and with adults, yet we also would like to them to take initiative, to be able to compete and not feel bound by rules that might stifle their imagination, curiosity, or creativity. Our images of virtue are in flux; because images can never be translated wholly into discourse, to that degree they are always somewhat beyond the grasp of written or verbal expression.

Curriculum development in the context of education is, in this sense, a process that seeks the realization of certain ineffables. It is a process that is engaged in by anyone who attempts to make that translation. One group continually engaged in that process is teachers. Teachers inevitably have a range of options that they can exercise in the selection, emphasis, and timing of curricular events. Even when they are expected to follow certain guides or books in which activities and content have already been determined, there are still options to be considered and choices to be made by teachers with respect to how those materials will be used and the ways in which what is done in one particular area of study will or will not be related to what is done in other areas of the curriculum. These decisions are, of course, decisions bearing on the curriculum; they influence the kind of opportunities for learning and experience that children will have.

Who Plans Curriculum: The Teacher's Role

But more typically, the scope of teachers' freedom regarding what skills are to be taught, when, in what order, and how is far wider than what the most highly structured programs provide for. Typically, the teacher will have a general guide of topics in a subject field, a sequence among topics, a general set of aims, textbooks, and other instructional resources. With these materials and within the constraints set by time, school culture, and the characteristics of the students, the teacher builds an educational program. The decision making for that program may be a species of long-term, highly systematic planning; a teacher might try to develop a calendar of topics and activities that extend throughout the year, or the teacher might plan on a week-to-week basis, without making any attempt to follow a specified timetable. The extent to which one or the other plan is selected can depend on the teacher's need for order and predictability and on the teacher's view of the educational process. For example, if a teacher believes that students should play a role in the development of curriculum, that they should have opportunities to decide what they study and what ends they seek, then it is not so likely that it will be possible to predict where a class or an individual student is likely to be a month or two in the future. The point in such a view of educational planning is to encourage the student to develop increasing amounts of competence and initiative and thus to assume greater responsibility for planning his or her educational program. The control of student progress and the prediction of learning at specific intervals over time are, given this view of teaching, beside the point. But even so, the teacher plays an important role in curriculum decision making, because it is the teacher who decides to give or not to give students the opportunity to assume curricular responsibility, and it is the teacher who decides what kind of encouragement and guidance to provide in the selection of topics and areas of study.

In contrast to such a curriculum plan, consider the increasing tendency among school districts to specify particular performance objectives for students at intervals within each grade level. In such a system the scope for teacher or student flexibility in curriculum decision making is reduced significantly because the specified objectives define expected levels of student performance. The teacher and the students know what these expectations are, they know that they (both students and teacher) will be tested to determine their success in meeting these objectives, and hence their choices are circumscribed by the objectives. Options that might have otherwise been pursued are relinquished in favor of school- or district-wide goals.

Whether one works within a system that encourages truly individualized educational programs and that supports high levels of student planning or within one in which grade-level expectations and curriculum content are specified in great detail, the role of the teacher in curriculum decision making is always important. It is important because the teacher serves as the interpreter of educational policy and because the teacher is the major mediator of what shall be taught—if not learned—in the classroom.

Although curriculum development can and often does take form in the creation of materials, curriculum development more frequently yields no materials but, rather, plans that might be no more than sketchy notes. For example, a teacher might decide that a particular activity would be educationally beneficial in a classroom, say, a discussion of a book or film that students have read or seen. And the teacher might also decide that after the discussion he will ask the students to express their ideas about what they have read or seen in a painting or short story, a poem or a play. What the teacher wants to do is to help children recognize that ideas can be expressed in different ways and that they can have a choice in the way in which they choose to express what they know. Suppose further that the teacher thinks that it might be interesting and useful to follow up this activity by having a poet or a painter visit the class to talk with the children about her work. In this episode, the teacher is engaged in curriculum planning, but no materials are being created. It might be that the teacher prepares some notes to himself or develops a fairly elaborate lesson plan, but the latter is not a necessity. Teachers engage in such planning most of the time, and to do so is to make curriculum decisions, to engage in a form of personal curriculum deliberation. This, too, is one way in which curriculum development occurs. Indeed, it would not be possible to have a school without some form of curriculum development. The form might be as "loose" as is used in a neoprogressive school or as "tight" as a highly systematic training program that leaves virtually nothing to chance. The point here is not the form that curriculum planning takes, but the fact that it must occur.

District-wide Curriculum Planning

A second group involved in curriculum development is that working under the aegis of the school districts. Many school districts appoint committees made up of subject specialists and teachers to work jointly in the creation of curriculum materials that are considered singularly suitable for their particular school district or some portion of it. A school district under the leadership of the assistant superintendent for curriculum and instruction might decide as a result of the activities of a lay group that curriculum materials are needed in the area of human relations. The district serves a community that has a wide array of ethnic and racial minority groups and after having conducted a national search for available curriculum materials decides to create its own materials, materials that will draw on the talents and resources of people living in the community. A committee is appointed by the superintendent to work on such a project, and a budget is made available to compensate teachers and others for the additional work that they will be required to do.

Such a group might work two afternoons each week after school for 6 months to develop the structure and format for the curriculum, to create the activities, and to secure the necessary materials so that what is created can be used in the classrooms. At the end of its work, this committee will have prepared written, visual, and perhaps audio material relevant to the children living in the community the school district serves. Such work might be followed up with in-service education programs for principals and selected teachers, so that the aims of the project are gradually realized. If as a result of such a trial the materials are found to need revision, revision will occur. The expectation is that these materials, especially created for this particular school district, will become a regular part of the curriculum of each school. The materials represent the vehicles through which the initial aspirations of the lay group will be realized.

It is obvious that it is one thing to create plans for oneself and quite another thing to create plans and materials that others are to use. All teachers do the former; relatively few do the latter. What one can consider in developing materials for others to use will be described in detail later. For now it is important to recognize the difference.

State Curriculum Planning

A third major group to engage in curriculum development are the staffs of state departments of education or the committees that work under the aegis of the chief state school officer.

Curriculum development at the state level can take the form of specific curriculum materials to be used in the classroom, or, as is more typically the case, it can take the form of curriculum outlines that can be used as guides by local school districts. In California, for example, the state superintendent of schools appoints committees to develop new state guidelines, or, as they are called in California, State Curriculum Frameworks, for the teaching of particular subject areas prescribed in the state education code. These committees, made up of representatives from professional groups in education and laypeople, might be appointed for a 1- to 3-year period to meet, say, monthly, and to carry out the deliberations, consultations, and preparation of a new framework for teaching mathematics, social studies, art, music, the humanities, and so on.

The function of such statewide curriculum committees is to make use of knowledgeable people in the subject field in order to upgrade the quality of educational programs in the various fields of study. It provides an opportunity for the state to update what it offers school districts and in the process be instrumental in guiding the direction of educational change.

In developing a statewide framework for a field, a curriculum committee is faced with a variety of difficult decisions. How specific should the materials be? If they are highly specific, they might be inappropriate for particular populations within the state. If they are very general, the translation from the guidelines to practice might be very difficult. Who should be consulted in preparing such guidelines? In a statewide framework committee on which I served, a circuit of hearings was held throughout the state with relevant professional groups. We wanted reactions to the ideas we as a committee had created and we wanted the groups to feel that they, too, participated in the process of planning the framework they would eventually use. As it turned out, this process was a form of in-service education for those of us on the committee as well as for those who participated in 20-odd meetings that were held throughout the state. We learned a great deal about what teachers and university professors regard as appropriate goals and content, and they had the opportunity to reflect on some ideas about the content and goals of curriculum that they might not have otherwise considered.

This planning process lasted about 3 years, at the end of which a statewide framework for the visual arts was published by the state department of education and disseminated to all public schools and colleges in California. In addition, the work of the state curriculum framework committee was given a central place in regional and statewide conventions in art education. What occurred was a spin-off whose effects were much wider than the work that the committee did on the written document itself. The position the committee developed with respect to the curriculum for teaching art in the state had an intellectual set of consequences for the way in which art education was conceptualized.

One should not underestimate the importance of state-endorsed programs or curriculum materials. The ultimate legal responsibility for education belongs not to the local school district but rather to the state. The constitutions of the various states assign that responsibility to the state board of education, which in turn develops a state education code that provides the guidelines, standards, and mandates for local school districts. The state superintendent of schools, through his or her staff and with the assistance of the county school superintendent, is responsible for monitoring local school districts to assure that the requirements of the state education code are met. Although relatively few county superintendents execute primarily a monitorial function, the authority of the office and that of the state department of education carry weight. In many states, the withholding of funds to local school districts is possible if the mandates provided in the state education code are not heeded.

The point of all of this is to underscore the importance of state sanctions in the area of curriculum policy, particularly when a statewide educational policy is backed up by funding options that the state department of education holds.

It should be noted also that the state board of education is in some degree guided by the advice of the state superintendent of public instruction, particularly with respect to matters dealing with what should be taught and for what amount of time. In some states, the education code specifies which subjects will be taught at each grade level and how many minutes of instruction will be provided for these subjects each week. In addition, the state prepares a list of acceptable textbooks or provides state-adopted textbooks for the local school districts. Because many teachers build their programs around them, these resources have a great impact on the content with which students come into contact. If a textbook in science devotes three chapters to ichthyology, students using that textbook study ichthyology. If a textbook on the social studies presents a black perspective on the civil rights movement, students study that material. Because access to content is a condition to learning that content, questions of content inclusion–content exclusion are extremely important. In effect, they define much of the opportunity students will have within the school to deal with certain topics and ideas.

Research and Development Center

A fourth group that engages in curriculum development are those working in university research and development (R&D) centers and in regional educational laboratories. Research and development centers, all of which are affiliated with universities, conceive of their mission as conducting research and facilitating educational development by devising products and programs that are primarily experimental and, in principle, related to ongoing research. Educational laboratories do, however, engage in the creation and testing of curriculum materials, the marketing of which is handled by commercial publishers.

Educational laboratories engage in the development of curriculum materials in mathematics and in the area of aesthetic education. The main function of educational laboratories is to use federal funds to pioneer new methods and programs that require the skills of sophisticated curriculum specialists and others and the kind of risk capital that commercial publishers are unwilling to provide. Thus, with average annual budgets of millions of dollars, the laboratories conceptualize, develop, test, and document these materials for use in classrooms throughout the country. In addition, some laboratories have created teacher centers to train teachers in the use of the materials they have designed. Once produced, the materials are often published commercially, and school districts, with the aid of federal funds, may purchase from a commercial publisher what has been developed through the support of federal funds at the laboratory or the university-related R&D center.

Educational laboratories are generally larger and have larger budgets than R&D centers; they occupy often elaborate and at times sumptuous quarters and have a staff that consists not only of curriculum specialists, but also social scientists, designers, photographers, managers, secretaries, and the like.

In their ideal form, educational laboratories and university R&D centers should undertake programs of curriculum development that are high risk, forward looking, and based on the highest professional standards of the field. Agencies supported by the taxes of citizens have a special obligation in my view that exceeds that of commercial publishers. Unfortunately, the competition for federal funds has created in both laboratories and R&D centers a need to "look good," to project an image of success that too often hampers candor. Laboratories and R&D centers should be places where it is all right to fail. Indeed, a laboratory without failure is a contradiction in terms.

Commercial Publishers as Planners of Curriculum

A fifth group, and in many respects the most influential group aside from the classroom teacher in the area of curriculum development, are commercial publishers. And the most influential material published is the textbook. Textbooks are not typically looked on as curricula, but they are certainly important curriculum materials. In the first place, textbooks are, for many teachers, the hub around which programs are built. When a school or school district adopts a textbook in social studies, science, or mathematics, this book, de facto, defines a significant portion of the content of what students will study. Textbooks in these areas also contain suggestions to students and teachers for supplementary activities and in this way further define what students will do in the classroom. In addition, accompanying teacher guides provide guidance to the teacher regarding the kinds of questions or issues that can be used for discussion, and some contain tests that can be used to determine if the students have learned what the textbook taught.

Increasingly, however, publishers are developing not only textbooks, but also multimedia kits designed to teach what publishers believe will sell in schools. Most of these materials—and they come in video cassettes, film-strips, audiotapes, computer software, graphic displays, and educational games—are designed to provide short-term units rather than semester- or year-long programs. The creation of these materials originates from at least three factors: the possibilities that new technology provides, the marketability of the materials to schools and hence their profitability for publishers, and the realization that the channels through which students learn are multiple and the range of sensory modes that can be used for facilitating learning is wide. Yet, despite the plethora of such materials—a visit to a national convention of teachers and school administrators will provide a mind-boggling array of such materials displayed by publishers—the single most important resource influencing what children study in school, aside from the teacher, is still the textbook.

Federal Influences on Curriculum

There is another source that although seldom involved in planning curricula nevertheless has a significant effect on the curriculum that is offered. That source is the federal government. The government has access to two important resources for influencing the curriculum: money and publicity. When the government adopts a policy that will infuse $400 million into the teaching of science and mathematics in the schools and when the President of the United States speaks to the nation and says that science and mathematics education is a national priority, the conditions are created for bringing about a new emphasis in these fields in the nation's schools. With such funds, new curriculum development projects can be initiated, institutes for teachers to be retrained in the these fields can be created, scholarships to encourage students to select these fields of study can be provided, and increased salaries for science and mathematics teachers can be offered. These are not trivial considerations. But perhaps even more important is the rationale for more science and mathematics in the schools. The President provides the nation with an economic rationale: we must emphasize science and mathematics in school curricula in order to remain economically competitive with Japan, Germany, and other industrial nations. The reason is an instrumental one; students need to study in these areas for the economic well-being of the nation. There are, of course, other bases on which to justify the teaching of mathematics and science. One might wonder what a purely economic justification does to the public's understanding of education when such rationales are provided from the high office of the President of the United States.

Furthermore, what will happen to other aspects of the school curriculum when only two subjects receive such massive support? How is a balanced curriculum to be sustained—assuming one wants balance in the curriculum? Such questions and issues need to be asked and addressed by school boards and professional educators, even when they are neglected by policymakers in Washington. The federal government, despite our commitment to state control of education, plays an extremely important role in shaping the school curriculum.

What we find, then, when we look at who does curriculum development and where and when it is done are a variety of groups engaged in the task. Teachers develop curricula when they plan for their classes, school districts engage in curriculum development through the creation of materials to be used in classrooms, and professional and lay groups develop curricula when they create state frameworks for teaching in particular subject fields. Educational laboratories, R&D centers, and commercial publishers engage in curriculum development through the production of materials such as *Man: A Course of Study*, SRA Reading Kits, DISTAR, CEMREL's Aesthetic Education Program, and SWIRL's Basic Reading Series. Finally, the federal government is very influential in reshaping what schools teach. All of these groups and individuals engage in curriculum development as they attempt to transform aspirations and images of educational virtue into plans and methods they believe are useful for realizing such ends.

Dimensions of Curriculum Planning

What are the factors that one might consider in the design of an educational program? What can one take into account in curriculum planning? As I have already indicated, I do not believe it possible in the field of education to prescribe formulas that one is to follow, but it is possible to provide concepts and generalizations that can heighten one's sensitivity to issues, problems, and possibilities to which one might attend. What follows is the identification and discussion of some dimensions of curriculum planning that can be considered by those attempting to design educational programs. *The sequence of these dimensions is, to a large degree, arbitrary. One need not begin or end with the factors or aspects as they appear here.* Because for the purposes of writing some ordering is necessary, the sequence that follows seems to me to be reasonable, but one may proceed in curriculum development with a very different order.

It should be noted at the outset that the study of the processes of curriculum development as it actually occurs for individuals or groups is rare. It has only been quite recently that the process has been studied empirically. The reason for the general neglect is fairly clear. Individuals and groups interested in developing curriculum materials or formulating curriculum policy have had those goals as their major priorities. The study of the processes through which decisions are made is seldom a part of their mission. Hence, what groups actually do in different contexts and circumstances is at present largely known through recollection rather than through, say, naturalistic observation as an ethnographer might study the process. What is clear from the case studies of curriculum decision making that have been published is that the process is far more convoluted, circuitous, and adventitious than one might be led to believe by reading the formal literature on curriculum planning.

Goals and Their Priorities

Perhaps the area in curriculum planning that has received the most attention in the literature is that of how objectives should be formulated. If one looks into the literature in curriculum, one will find distinctions that are made among aims, goals, and objectives. Aims are the most general statements that proclaim to the world the values that some group holds for an educational program. "The aim of this school is to help students learn to participate effectively in the democratic way of life." From aims we sense a direction, a point of view, a set of values, to which the community or group subscribes. These statements form a kind of educational manifesto of cherished values, and, although such statements have been regarded by many as meaningless, if one were to contrast the statement of aims made in school districts in the United States with those found in the written material produced in China, Cuba, or Sweden, one would note significant differences in the spirit and outlook of what has been written. What such statements provide is an articulation of educational faith, in a sense in the way in which the Preamble of the Constitution or the Declaration of Independence expresses general but still meaningful beliefs about the individual and his or her relationship to the society.

A second kind of aim is referred to as a goal. Goals are statements of intent, midway in generality between aims and objectives. Goals describe the purposes held for a course or school program. "The goal of this course is to help students understand the causes of social revolution." "The goal of the course is to develop skills in copper enamel jewelry making." These statements are considerably more specific than aims, but insufficiently specific for, say, instructional objectives. Goals are intended to provide a greater focus on anticipated outcomes and to provide curriculum planners with the basis for the selection of curriculum content. In the standard curriculum literature, goals are supposed to be deduced from aims. Having deduced goals, one then deduces objectives. Having deduced objectives, one then proceeds to formulate curriculum activities. The planning process is supposed to be a step-by-step process from the general to the specific, from ends to means. The problem with this view, as I have indicated earlier, is that it assumes that curriculum activities that are educationally significant always have explicit goals or objectives, which they do not, and that the formulation of goals must precede activities, which is not always true.

Objectives are typically specific statements of what students are to be able to do after having experienced a curriculum or a portion of one. Objectives of the instructional variety are supposed to state with little ambiguity what particular forms of behavior the student will be able to display. Thus, "The student will be able to create a clay bowl on a potter's wheel that is at least 12 inches high, having walls no thicker than 1/2 inch," would be an example of an instructional objective.

Now the thrust of these comments is not essentially to restate the forms in which educational intentions are couched or even to describe their levels of generality but rather to point out that intentions are appropriate to consider in the development of an educational program and that priorities among goals must be determined.

The determination of priorities is influenced by the context in which programs are to function. For example, a school board, a community, or a school faculty might be convinced that a particular set of goals is of the utmost importance but at the same time recognize that the realization of these goals in this particular context is not possible at this time. Thus, goals, even those holding high status, are shifted in their operational importance. A faculty might believe that the critical study of local politics is crucial to the sound education of adolescents, but they might also recognize that the community would not allow such studies to be taught, or that there is in fact no one on the faculty who has the professional competence to teach such a course well. In this case, other areas and goals become practically more important.

Thus far, I have discussed goals as they relate to and across subject matters, but within fields, too, there is a host of competing goals. What kind of goals should be emphasized in mathematics: comprehension of the structure of mathematics as a system or skills in computation? What kind of social studies should be provided: those that emphasize history or those that emphasize the methods of inquiry of the social sciences? What sort of art program should be offered to students: one that enables them to appreciate the most significant works of art that have been created or one that aims at the development of skills needed to create art? Competent curriculum deliberation will consider the option within as well as among fields of study. In such consideration, educational values obviously come into play, and it is here that basic orientations to curriculum emerge among those who deliberate. But the ultimate resolution of those priorities always takes place within the constraints of the context. What one finally puts into practice is a function of the interaction of aspirations and existing constraints.

Although acquiescing to existing constraints in educational planning can lead to an inert form of educational conservatism, regard for the constraints of the context is necessary for an intelligent form of curriculum deliberation. Curriculum planning cannot adequately be treated in a simple piecemeal fashion; there are always trade-offs in time, expected outcome, human and fiscal resources, community support, and the like. To neglect the big picture is to court disaster, yet to regard the context only as a set of constraints rather than a set of opportunities is to embrace a maintenance model of educational management. Negotiating the balance between the desirable and the possible is one of the arts of school administration as well as curriculum planning.

The Content of the Curriculum

Because goals seldom prescribe the content that can be used to achieve them, attention to the selection of content is always an important curriculum consideration. If a curriculum development group working on the development of a curriculum in, say, biology agrees that the major aims of the program are to help students understand (1) that scientific inquiry always yields conclusions that are tentative and (2) that living organisms depend on the environment to survive, the specific content and the teaching methods that may be instrumental to such purposes are still not yet given. What the group must do is to identify the variety of potential content areas within biology or within the students' experience outside of biology that will help them grasp these ideas. A curriculum development group might, for example, choose a variety of content ranging from simple forms of plant life to complex forms of human behavior for exemplifying the relationship between organism and environment. Or the group might decide to create some analogies to nonbiological entities such as cities or nations in order to illustrate how similar principles operate in "nonliving phenomena."

The point here is that groups concerned with curriculum planning have options in content selection. The problem is one of deciding which of the possible content options should be selected. One possible criterion for content inclusion, in addition to whether there is some relationship between the content and the aim, is whether the content is likely to be meaningful to the children for whom the program is intended. Children bring to school wide varieties of experience that originate from the homes and communities in which they live. The kind of biological content that children living in a rural area might find meaningful can differ significantly from that which inner-city urban youngsters might find meaningful. One way of dealing with such diversity is to include in one's curriculum material options from which teachers and students can themselves choose. In other words, by providing different kinds of content to make the same point, the flexibility of the materials is increased.

In Sweden new curricula are being developed under the auspices of the Ministry of Education. Curriculum developers identify significant concepts and generalizations within particular subject areas. For example, in the social studies the concept might be *role*. Generalizations are then provided about role: "Societies tend to differentiate the roles people perform in order to deal with problems and social needs efficiently." Given the concept of role and the generalization in which it is embodied, the teacher, or the faculty of the school, works out the particular curriculum activities and specific curricular content that will make this concept and generalization meaningful to students. For students living in rural areas, exemplars of role may very well be different than exemplars for students living in urban areas. Thus, once the important concepts and generalizations are identified at a national level for a particular field of study, the way in which they are transformed into an operational curriculum for students is a task for the teacher or the faculty of the school. In this way both national and local needs can be met.

There are, of course, limitations on the number of options that can be provided. The physical size of the syllabus, for example, is not a trivial consideration—nor is the amount of materials teachers should be asked to read. More will be said about these considerations later; for now, the major point to be made is that goals do not prescribe content. Content selection, like goals, can be considered against a backdrop of options. Furthermore, curriculum developers, within the limits that seem reasonable, can provide teachers with the content of options that are related to the aims of the curriculum.

Types of Learning Opportunities

Goals and content are necessary but not sufficient for the development of a curriculum. The educational imagination must come into play in order to transform goals and content to the kinds of events that will have educational consequences for students. This transformation requires that an event be conceptualized and have sufficient educational promise for students to be used in an educational program. I say that the educational imagination comes into play because it is this task—educational transformation—that draws most heavily on the expertise of the teacher or curriculum designer.

If a group of citizens wanted to know what the most significant concepts and generalizations were in some branch of biology, the individuals most likely to provide such information would be biologists who know their field well and who were aware of the most recent developments within it. But to acquire such information from biologists is not sufficient for the creation of an educational program. Some educationally appropriate means must be created to enable students to interact with problems or situations that will yield an understanding of these concepts and generalizations. A biologist who has not worked with adolescents, who does not understand what teachers are able to do in a secondary school classroom, is not necessarily the best person to make such a transformation. It is here that curriculum expertise is crucial, for it is here that educational events must be planned and curriculum materials prepared to enable teachers and students to grasp those concepts and generalizations and to do it in a form that is consistent with one's view of education. For example, if one believes that the major mission of the school is to introduce students to the products of the best inquiry in the arts and the sciences, one might decide to use a moderately didactic approach to instruction in, for example, the biological sciences. Such an approach would emphasize the big ideas and theories that biological greats have created. In such a view, the work of Mendel, Darwin, Wall, Muller, and Dobzhansky would play a prominent role in content selection. The thrust of the curriculum would be to help students understand the theories and concepts these biologists created, say, within the context of their time. To do this one might provide lectures and films and perhaps have students read excerpts from primary source material. But if one were interested in having students understand the relationship between biological ideas and the methods through which those ideas were created, if one wanted to help students appreciate the tentativeness of scientific conclusions, then the type of learning opportunities one might use would give students experience in the conducting of biological experiments. The transformation of the "same" content would take different forms because the basic orientation to education would differ significantly.

The options available to the curriculum designers are numerous with virtually any body of content, and in the curriculum field, as in education at large, there has been a longstanding controversy on the relative importance of process as compared with product. Those who emphasize the importance of process tend to formulate learning opportunities that stimulate children to active inquiry. Such individuals want the student to inquire, to think, to act, and in the process to learn. The outcomes of the process are what children learn from the engagement. It is to be hoped that the product of such activity will be consistent with valid substantive knowledge in the field in which the inquiry occurred. But that is not necessarily the major aim. The main aim is to teach children to think, to act, and to learn from the consequences of their actions.

Those who emphasize the product are more interested in what children learn of the conclusions of mature inquiry in specialized fields. Does the student understand the relationship between random mutation and natural selection? Does the student grasp the concept of dominant and recessive genes?

These views of what counts educationally have an extraordinarily important bearing on the kinds of learning opportunities that are created in the curriculum. The advocate, for example, of learning by discovery will frequently be interested in helping children "learn to think like scientists." For such people the curriculum should be built around problems. The task of the curriculum designer is to create activities that help children either formulate problems or try to resolve the problems posed within the materials.

Although I have emphasized the relationship between one's orientation to curriculum and the kinds of learning opportunities that might be provided, in practice the relationship between activities and goals is neither linear nor unidirectional. Indeed, teachers are more inclined to focus on what they might *do* than on what goals they intend to accomplish (see McDonald, 1965). This is because practical decisions always relate to the utility of action. What teachers want and need are ideas that have practical payoffs; ideas that for the most part lead to action. Projects that appear interesting, activities that seem heuristic, events that will be attractive and engaging to students are valued by teachers. Once students are fully engaged in such activities, one can guide them so that various goals and aims are achieved.

But goals and aims, unless they can be transformed into educational events within the classroom in a form that is interesting to students, and within the capacity of teachers, are only empty hopes that have little educational reality. One means through which types of learning opportunities might be created is a matrix of intellectual processes. One such matrix has been formulated by J. P. Guilford, a psychologist long interested in creative thinking and in the structure of the human intellect. What Guilford has done is to conceptualize the variety of aptitudes or processes that the human mind is capable of. His scientific ambition has been not only to conceptualize these mental processes, but also to create instruments that can be used to assess them. We need not for our purposes try to evaluate the scientific validity of these instruments, but we can examine his model of intellect for its potential utility in the creation of learning opportunities within a curriculum. That is, we can use Guilford's model as a kind of mnemonic device to help us—if we so choose—to create learning opportunities that elicit different forms of thinking. These forms, once identified, could then be related to bodies of content considered important to so that sophisticated forms of thinking could be used to deal with educationally significant content.

Related to Guilford's structure of the intellect are the intellectual processes identified in the taxonomy of educational objectives in the so-called cognitive domain. The cognitive taxonomy lists not 120 mental processes, as does Guilford, but six. They are as follows:

1. Possession of Information.
2. Comprehension.
3. Application.
4. Analysis.
5. Synthesis.
6. Evaluation.

Although these terms refer to kinds of objectives that one can formulate and to the kind of test items or tasks on tests related to those objectives, the taxonomy can also be used to formulate types of learning opportunities that can be made available to students. For example, one could design learning opportunities that were intended to elicit each or all of these processes. Of course, there can be and often is a gap between intention and reality, but nevertheless, the taxonomy can help focus attention to enable one to convert a learning opportunity from one that is parochial and prosaic into one that has intellectual significance.

A word must be said about the potential hazards of classification systems, taxonomies, theoretical models, and the like. Such conceptual devices can be extremely useful for helping one differentiate and classify. In performing this function, they increase intellectual precision by helping us bracket the world in useful ways, but one must not forget that such bracketing is a construction of mind, that there are other ways to classify, and that one should take care not to reify concepts into realities and eventually constrain our understanding. Some of this has already occurred in the case of the taxonomy of educational objectives. These taxonomies differentiate the cognitive from the affective, the affective from the psychomotor, and the psychomotor from the cognitive. Individuals in education and psychology sometimes conclude the so-called cognitive activities are independent of affective ones, or that psychomotor activities are neither cognitive nor affective. In actual experience, there is no clear line between cognition and affect, except within the definitions of the taxonomy. For example, to have a feeling and not to know it, is not to have it. To think about a feeling is to know it. In short, the affective and cognitive pervade each other. Although in our culture we do find it useful to talk about our thoughts and our feelings, in education such talk can lead to theoretically devastating ideas and to practically questionable results. Some schools, for example, teach "cognitive" subjects in the morning and "affective" ones in the afternoons. My point here is not to argue that conceptual devices should not be used in the formulation of types of learning opportunities but rather to state that unless they are treated as tools, such devices can interfere with the ways in which aims and activities are conceptualized.

The Organization of Learning Opportunities

All educational programs occur over time. How events are planned within a period of time is one of the decisions curriculum planners can make. There are two images of curricular sequences that it may be useful to distinguish between. One of these is the "staircase" model already mentioned; the other is a "spiderweb" model.

The staircase model conjures up the image of a series of independent steps that lead to a platform from which one exits. This idea conceives of curriculum activities as building on what preceded them, preparing for what is to come. The movement, as is true in the climbing of a staircase, is always upward.

This conception is metaphorically consistent with terms such as *entry skills* and *exit competencies*. The route is well defined, mechanical in construction, and efficient. There is little room for wasted motion or exploratory activities. Perhaps the most pristine example of such a model in curriculum is to be found in linear programs used in computer-assisted instruction. The same image was used in teaching machine programs that were available several years ago. The task of the curriculum designer is to create a sequence of frames, that, like the staircase, leads the student to a predetermined destination whose features are known by the curriculum designer and the teacher. One of the major needs of educators who wish to use the computers is to secure or create programs that are sufficiently flexible to respond to the purposes and decisions of the student. Most programs put the student in a responsive position; the task is presented, the student responds, and then, if the response is correct, he or she proceeds along a fixed path that has already been predetermined. Much of the work is drill and practice. As programs become intellectually demanding and computers for classroom-use more sophisticated, intellectual processes that are truly important will be cultivated through computer-use. We are, as yet, still far from such a goal for most computer programs that are now being used in classrooms.

The spiderweb model is one in which the curriculum designer provides the teacher with a set of heuristic projects, materials, and activities whose use will lead to diverse outcomes among the group of students. The assumption used in this model of curriculum organization is that what is needed are projects and activities that invite engagement rather than control. With engaging projects or activities students will create ideas and develop skills that they want to pursue. The task of the teacher is then to facilitate the interests and goals that students develop as a result of such engagement. As children bring with them different experiential backgrounds, it is reasonable to expect that the kinds of meaning they make will also differ. This is seen as a virtue rather than a liability, for it is in the cultivation of those interests that truly personalized education resides.

To be sure, the kind of personalized education that is implied in a spiderweb model of curriculum organization places great demands on the inventiveness of the teacher. In this model the teacher cannot rely on stock responses to identical problems or tasks among students. Some students will work independently, others will work in small groups, but all will require a teacher who knows what kinds of problems and interests the students have and who is prepared to provide or point them to the resources that they need to develop those interests or to resolve those problems.

I do not believe it possible to conclude that one mode of curriculum organization is more educationally beneficial than the other. It depends on one's view of education and on the readiness of students—regardless of their age—to cope with different types of problems or tasks. It requires, as Whitehead (1929) implied, attention to the rhythm of education:

> Life is essentially periodic. It comprises daily periods, with their alternations of work and play, of activity and of sleep, and seasonal periods, which dictate our terms and our holidays; and also it is composed of well-marked yearly periods. These are the gross obvious periods which no one can overlook. There are also subtler periods of mental growth, with their cyclic recurrences, yet always different as we pass from cycle to cycle, though the subordinate stages are reproduced in each cycle. That is why I have chosen the term "rhythmic," as meaning essentially the conveyance of difference within a framework of repetition. Lack of attention to the rhythm and character of mental growth is a main source of wooden futility in education. I think that Hegel was right when he analyzed progress into three stages, which he called Thesis, Antithesis, and Synthesis; though for the purpose of application of his idea to educational theory I do not think that the names he gave are very happily suggestive. In relation to intellectual progress I would term them the stage of romance, the stage of precision, and the stage of generalization. (p. 29)

Yet, notwithstanding the argument that there is no intrinsic value in the abstract for either of these models of curriculum organization, I think that it is fair to say that the spiderweb model has more appeal to the progressives among educators, whereas the staircase model has appeal to those with the more conservative educational bent. Those holding a progressive, or child-centered, philosophy tend to emphasize the differences among children and the belief that children should be given ample opportunity to formulate their own educational aims. The teacher is not to "stuff the duck" but rather to facilitate the achievement of aims born out of the interaction children have with the stimulating resources the teacher provides.

Those with a more conservative view of education believe that there is a body of content that children should learn and that the sequential organization of this material is the best assurance that it will be learned. The staircase model fits the view nicely because it is systematic, well organized, and linear. When this view prevails, providing for individual differences usually means varying the pace through which children proceed to climb the same stairways rather than building different stairways leading to different goals for different children.

Historically these alternative models or conceptions of curriculum organization have been the subject of much dispute. In his classic book *The Child and the Curriculum*, John Dewey (1959) describes these camps this way. One groups says:

Subdivide each topic into studies; each study into lessons; each lesson into specific facts and formulae. Let the child proceed step by step to master each one of these separate parts, and at last he will have covered the entire ground. The road which looks so long when viewed in its entirety, is easily traveled, considered as a series of particular steps. Thus emphasis is put upon the logical subdivisions and consecutions of the subject-matter. Problems of instruction are problems procuring texts giving logical parts and sequences, and of presenting these portions in class in a similar definite and graded way. Subject-matter furnishes the end, and it determines method. The child is simply the immature being who is to be matured; he is the superficial being who is to be deepened; his is narrow experience which is to be widened. It is his to receive, to accept. His part is fulfilled when he is ductile and docile.

Not so, says the other sect. The child is the starting-point, the center, and the end. His development, his growth, is the ideal. It alone furnishes the standard. To the growth of the child all studies are subservient; they are instruments valued as they serve the needs of growth. Personality, character, is more than subject-matter. Not knowledge or information, but self-realization, is the goal. To possess all the world of knowledge and lose one's self is as awful a fate in education as in religion. Moreover, subject-matter never can be got into the child from without. Learning is active. It involves reaching out of the mind. It involves organic assimilation starting from within. Literally, we must take or stand with the child and our departure from him. It is he and not the subject-matter which determines both quality and quantity of learning. (p. 95)

For Dewey, the solution to the problem of how to sequence learning opportunities was to be found not in orthodoxies or in dogmas but rather in the concept of experience itself. The central question for Dewey was, "What kind of experience is a mode of curriculum organization likely to yield for students?" For Dewey, the experience was to be educative, rather than non- or miseducative (see Dewey, 1938). Yet differences of view as to what educational experience is and what conditions are likely to produce it still generate a considerable degree of acrimony in the field. Different parties may agree that students should have experiences in school that educate rather than its contrary, but they may differ radically in their conception of educational experience and in their judgment of what will bring it about. One task of the curriculum specialist is to facilitate the critical deliberations of such issues so that the choices that are ultimately made will rest on considered alternatives.

The Organization of Content Areas

Another task of the curriculum specialist is to help curriculum planners consider three ways in which content areas within the curriculum should be defined. One can, of course, maintain the traditional subject matter fields and make decisions about content within these boundaries. One might continue to teach arithmetic, history, art, music, science, reading, and the like. But one could also choose to teach communications, the humanities, the social studies, or ecological studies, problems of contemporary society, popular culture, and other areas that redefine or cut across the traditional subject matter fields within the curriculum.

The definition of these areas of study is a matter of what Bernstein calls "classification." Classification can be strong or weak, it can invite integration or discourage it. Bernstein (1971) writes:

> Classification, here, does not refer to *what* is classified, but to the *relationships* between contents. Classification refers to the nature of the differentiation between contents. Where classification is strong, contents are well insulated from each other by strong boundaries. Where classification is weak, there is reduced insulation between contents for the boundaries between contents are weak or blurred. *Classification thus refers to the degree of boundary maintenance between contents.* Classification focuses our attention upon boundary strength as the critical distinguishing feature of the division of labour of educational knowledge.
>
> If the model from which the curriculum is drawn is what is usually found among academic disciplines that occupy so central a place in the university, then it is likely that its classification will have strong boundary strength (Bernstein, 1971, p. 49).

Discrete subject matters will constitute the content and organization of the curriculum. But if the curriculum of the secondary school is considered not primarily as preparation for the university or as an effort to prepare students to become scholars in discrete fields of learning, then it is more likely that other forms of content organization will be considered. To develop programs that depart from traditional subject matter disciplines is easier to say than to do. In the first place, certification requirements may deter the educators of teachers from preparing prospective teachers who can deal with a range of fields or with problems that are not within single disciplines. Second, there may be no individuals on existing school faculties who are interested in cross-disciplinary teaching or teaching in areas that do not closely approximate the field in which they have been trained. Third, the political situation of professional educators often parallels disciplinary lines, and they may not wish to have competition for time and resources coming from programs outside of their particular fields. Finally, testing programs might penalize students who did very well in, say, the study of mass media in high school, but who knew little about English literature. In short, there are many social, political, and intellectual impediments to the development of new forms of content organization within the curriculum.

Yet, notwithstanding the practical difficulties of developing new forms of content organization, this is an area in which theoretical options exist. If the grounds for developing new modes of content organization are sufficiently compelling, one could try to make the changes or secure the resources to support it.

It is interesting to speculate on the possible grounds for such change. One of the arguments that has supported conventional approaches built around the disciplines is related to the so-called structure of the disciplines argument (Schwab, 1962). It is argued that each formal discipline has a distinctive structure. The syntactical aspect of the structure of a discipline defines the mode and criteria through which inquiry proceeds. The conceptual or substantive structure defines the concepts and subject matters inquired into. Because disciplines have a history and are well defined compared with general fields of study and because they offer the student organized concepts and theory, knowledge in these disciplines is easier to acquire, to store, and to retrieve than that available in fields that are less well organized. The order disciplines provide, the methods they employ, and the criteria they use make intellectual precision possible.

Yet it can be argued that the problems that citizens confront in their daily lives seldom come in the forms with which the disciplines can deal. Most practical problems of life are "messy." They require the use of diverse kinds of knowledge; they demand the application of practical judgment that is not rule-governed or accessible, using criteria that might be suitable for a single discipline. The argument proceeds that school programs, both elementary and secondary, should not be controlled by a propaedeutic theory of education. Schools should not decide what to teach or how to organize what they teach on the basis of what universities teach. What follows represents one secondary school's effort to offer courses that traverse disciplinary lines:

Junior and Senior Offerings
Courses in the upper two years are generally available to both juniors and seniors. Very few requirements are placed upon upper class students since they are expected to exercise mature judgment in choosing their areas of specialization. Students are expected to sign up for approximately 30 units of courses per year, except by special permission from the faculty scheduling committee.

Science
300   How to Fix it
Simple maintenance and repair of household items.   1 unit
301   Student Teaching in Science—3 W's or TBT (seniors only)
Students will teach science classes in consultation with science teachers. Credit for mini-teaching.   2 units per trimester
303   Intermediate Biology
An inquiry into life and a study of the basic structures and functions of microorganisms, plants, and animals with emphasis on evolutionary steps, patterns of heredity, animal behavior, and ecosystems.   4 units
304   Advanced Biology   4 units
305   TBT I—(theories behind technology)
Inter-disciplinary course of physics and chemistry. Emphasis on scientific processes rather than accumulation of facts.   4 units
306   TBT II
An advanced continuation of TBT I.   4 units

Social Sciences
310   Rebel
A study of the rebel in contemporary society—his reasons and his strategies.
                    4 units
311   Survival
Practical ways of understanding and surviving in the modern city.   2 units
312   Which Way America
An in-depth approach to key events and people that shaped America.   2 or 4 units
313   Backgrounds of Contemporary America
Course starting with contemporary events as a springboard into their root causes. Use of historical factual data along with American literature to capture the American consciousness of today. Will include some emphasis on means of communicating these ideas. Can be used in partial fulfillment of State History and English requirements.   4 units
314   Black Humanities   To be announced
A study of the writing of the Afro-American people with emphasis on the period from 1900 to the present, oral interpretation of recent Black writing in America and the African nations. (Course design could be a project of the interested students and faculty.) A Black teacher is being sought for this course.   2 units

What we see here is a set of course titles that reflect an interest in relating course content to the interests of adolescents. The topics chosen to serve as titles for the courses are not, as they are so often, U.S. History and Math 1. They are rather "Which Way America" and "Survival." Such course titles are in a sense symbolic of the faculty's desire to develop programs that address in a meaningful way the interests of students who are likely to enroll in them. In this sense, the faculty is making an effort both to capitalize on what students already are interested in and to tantalize them with descriptions that it hopes will satisfy.

These course titles are, for the most part, out of fashion in 1993. They were taken from a list of courses offered in a secondary school in Chicago in 1968. Our fashion today is more academic, demanding "less pizazz" and more convention. Whether one believes the shift from 1968 to 1993 is educationally beneficial or detrimental depends on the way in which one views the purposes of the secondary schools and the needs of the particular population in a school or school district.

Mode of Presentation and Mode of Response

One of the least-considered options in curriculum planning deals with the modalities through which students encounter and express what they learn. For the vast majority of subject fields in schools, the mode of presentation that students encounter is either verbal or written language. The teacher talks or students read textbooks containing the information and ideas they are to acquire. To demonstrate what they have learned, the students are expected to write or take examinations that are also presented in written form. Out of traditional expectations, we have inadvertently allowed one mode to so dominate how expression is to occur in school that we have come to believe that to have any understanding at all the student must be able to demonstrate it in verbal or written terms.

Yet the forms through which knowledge and understanding are constructed, stored, and expressed are considerably wider than verbal or written discourse. What can be known, say, about autumn can take form in scientific propositions that deal with chemical changes in trees, in astronomical propositions about the location of our planet in relation to the sun, in poetic expression disclosing the smell of burning autumn leaves, in visual images that present to our consciousness the color of a Vermont landscape, and in auditory forms that capture the crackle of leaves under our footsteps. Autumn, in short, is known in a variety of ways and the ways in which it can be known are expressible in a wide range of expressive forms.

Now the significance of this fact for the development of educational programs is considerable. What it implies is that educational programs that aim to help children gain an understanding of the world need to recognize that understanding is secured and experienced in different ways. What one is able to know through forms of musical expression cannot be known in discursive form, and vice versa. Humans employ different knowledge systems to acquire, store, and retrieve understanding, and they use different performance systems to express what they know about the world. For the curriculum designer this implies that if students are to understand phenomena in the variety of ways in which they can be understood, they need to have the opportunity to encounter forms that express ideas about those phenomena in different ways. Furthermore, it implies that if teachers are to understand what students know about something, then students should be given options in the ways in which they can express what they know. In short, students need not be restricted to one way of expressing what they have learned; curriculum designers need not use verbal forms of expression as the only means of presenting ideas to students.

When one also recognizes that there are aptitude differences among students with respect to the knowledge and performance systems they use best, the grounds for using diverse modes of presentation and response become even stronger. One could argue that by withholding such opportunities from students, a significant proportion of them are denied equal educational opportunity and that certain modes of presentation and forms of response deny them the opportunity to display what they have learned in the forms that most suit their aptitudes.

Although this might seem farfetched, I do not believe it is. We have created a culture in schooling that is so heavily pervaded by verbal and written performance systems that we take such performance systems for granted. In the process we forget that the culture at large depends on a much wider array of human competencies. We regard alternatives that are nondiscursive as "enrichment activities." We assign them to the margins of our concerns; they are events that are "nice to have" but not really of educational significance. Furthermore, we do not often recognize the unique epistemological functions that different expressive forms make possible.

The appreciation of this epistemological diversity allows the curriculum designers to create activities that may be experienced in one mode and expressed by the student in another. For example, a student might read a short story and express what she has learned or experienced from it in a painting, film, or poem. Or, conversely, a student might see a film and express his reaction in a short story. Although such activities do occur at present, they are seldom created intentionally and are seldom based on a realization of the interaction between knowledge and performance systems. What I am suggesting here is that curriculum designers can intentionally exploit the variety of modalities humans use to conceptualize and experience the world and to express what they have learned about it.

It is true, of course, that fields do have indigenous expressive modalities. Historians write prose, physicists express what they have learned in equations, musicians perform with voice or instrument, painters create visual images. To know whether someone knows history, we ask the person to speak or write. To determine whether someone knows physics, we ask the person to explain physical theory or to do a physics experiment. To the extent to which we would like students to express themselves within the mode that is indigenous to the discipline, *that* mode should dominate. But ideas secured from a discipline need not necessarily be limited to the mode indigenous to it. A study of history can lead to ideas that are best expressed by some students within the context of poetry rather than prose or within film or music. Ideas dealing with historical phenomena can be expressed in modes that are nonverbal. In addition, ideas that are not historical, per se, can be stimulated by the study of history, and, of course, these too can be expressed in modes that do not make use of what is indigenous to historical scholarship.

I use history only as an example. Other fields fit, a fortiori. Now this way of thinking about expression and response has some very interesting epistemological implications. We take history to be what has been written that meets, roughly, the criteria accepted within that field. By convention, historians expect history to be written and they expect historical scholarship to contain evidence, if not proof, of historical veracity. But such conventions need not necessarily foreclose other ways in which historical insight or generalization can be conveyed. Indeed, one might argue that written expression is a surrogate for what the historian knows in other ways, ways that often are not verbal. What I am suggesting is for curriculum designers to consider the potential of allowing students to use modes of response to historical ideas or experiences that might take shape in forms that are not indigenous to history as it is now conceived. I believe the exploitation of such possibilities has considerable potential for the education of the young. Indeed, to dramatize the limited scope of our expressive options, one has only to look at graduate programs. We seem to operate on the belief that the written word is the only means through which one can legitimately demonstrate that one knows something.

Types of Evaluation Procedures

Closely related to the type of presentation and response available to students is the type of evaluation procedures that are used to identify and assess what students have learned and experienced. Although subsequent chapters treat the problems of educational evaluation in detail, some preliminary remarks about the relationship between evaluation and curriculum development seem appropriate here.

In the first place, evaluation is a process that pervades curriculum decision making. Evaluation is not simply an activity that occurs after students have completed a unit of study. The very act of deciding on content, activities, aims, sequence, or mode of presentation or response requires one to consider the options and to evaluate the utility of the alternatives. Because more options exist than can be employed, selection is necessary. Selection requires choices, and choices require appraisals concerning strengths and liabilities of the alternatives with respect to some set of values; hence, evaluation occurs. The main issue with respect to evaluation centers around the care, the complexity, and the comprehensiveness with which the choices are made. In this sense, evaluation is a necessary part of any deliberate process. What we seek is that it be competent. Evaluation in the more traditional view often refers to the measurement of student performance. Here, too, there are important options that curriculum can consider. In terms of what I said earlier about the relationship between modes of presentation and response and student aptitudes, we may infer that how a student is able to express what he or she has learned will influence what the student can make public. What is made public in turn influences what conclusions teachers and others come to regarding how well the student has done. Although the provision of different student performance options for purposes of summative evaluation creates problems for classical test theory, I do not believe that the requirements of classical test theory should determine how we try to find out what students have learned and experienced at school. Let the test and measurement specialists follow our needs in education rather than we follow theirs.

With respect to the procedures for evaluation in the curriculum development process, groups often go through several steps or stages. As I have already indicated, evaluation occurs throughout the process of curriculum development. The determination that a new program is needed is, in part, the consequence of having judged that a lack exists or that some new program holds promise for significant educational gain. Needs assessment, the process through which educators and others determine existing needs, is itself pervaded by value judgments in the selection of items used on questionnaires and tests, of the format that is employed, and in the populations that are selected for assessment, not to mention the value-saturated process of interpreting the information once it is secured.

But even after the initial judgment has been made about the need for a new program, the selection of activities, goals, content, and the like require, as I have indicated, some form of evaluation. Any form of decision making requires judgment, and judgment requires evaluation of choices, options, and alternatives.

Stages in Evaluating Curriculum Materials

Taking this as a given, we can identify the stages or steps that many curriculum groups employ in the process of evaluating materials that are being developed. One such process is referred to as *hothouse trials*. In this stage, a group of curriculum developers will work with an evaluator to locate classrooms in which prototype materials may be tried. These prototype materials are usually in rough form, having enough finish for the teacher or, as is sometimes the case, a member of a curriculum development team to use them in a classroom. The purpose of the hothouse trial is to identify any major problems with the material, to determine if some important oversights have been made: are the problems suitable for children of this age? Can a teacher have easy access to the materials the way they have been designed? Do the tasks take longer than we expected?

To engage in hothouse trials, a curriculum development group, say, one working within an educational laboratory, will have established a network of schools around the laboratory that have agreed to cooperate with the laboratory in testing new material. For the school, such cooperation provides stimulation to teachers and creates a form of in-service education. In addition, some laboratories give cooperating schools free materials after they have been tested. For the laboratories, the schools provide the field site that they need to reality-test the materials. A network of schools with which the laboratory has a good relationship diminishes the need to locate and contact new schools each time materials have to be tested. Thus, the relationship can be viewed as a kind of symbiotic one: all concerned appear to benefit by meeting the needs of others.

The evaluator attached to the curriculum development group observes the materials being used in the hothouse trial. The evaluator's function is to locate difficulties that the teacher might not recognize and to feed back such information to the curriculum development team. Sometimes a member of the curriculum development team will actually teach with the materials in order to get a firsthand view of how the materials function, but even when this occurs, the evaluator may still be present to observe what the teacher might not see.

The function of the hothouse trials is to permit the curriculum team the closest possible scrutiny of how materials function in classrooms. The rapport between the member of the team and the teachers of the schools should be good; ideally they should see each other as colleagues. Although this rapport and relationship do not typify the field at large—teachers and curriculum developers are seldom seen as colleagues and they typically have no rapport—such a relationship is helpful for purposes of formative evaluation.

After hothouse trials have been completed and the necessary revisions made, the materials are then offered to a limited number of school districts for *field testing*. Field testing is done on a larger scale and is more impersonal in character than hothouse trials. In this stage of evaluations school districts agree to return to the laboratory their appraisal of the materials after they have had the opportunity to use them. Such appraisals might consist of evaluations that teachers complete or instruments that measure students' performance on achievement tests that the laboratory supplies. The function of the field testing is to approximate more closely the conditions under which the materials will be used but still to be in a position to modify the materials prior to their publication and dissemination. The materials at the field trial stage of development are often in a mimeographed or offset-printed form: they lack the kind of finished quality that they will receive when they are to be marketed.

As a result of field testing, final modifications of the material are done, and subsequently the materials are sent to a publisher who then mounts an advertising program to make their purchase possible by the 16,000 school districts in this country. This advertising program includes display of the materials at conventions attended by teachers and school administrators, mailing of brochures to school districts, placement of ads in journals read by teachers, and visits by salespeople to the school districts to demonstrate the materials at in-service meetings.

These procedures might give one the idea that testing curriculum materials is like testing new drugs before they are marketed, but the resemblance is slight. In drug testing, it is possible to isolate the relationships between the chemistry of a drug and the chemistry of individuals. For the testing of curriculum materials, the context and manner in which they are used by the teacher make a crucial difference in how they will be experienced by children. Poor teaching can render even the most attractive materials dull, and teaching that is imaginative can convert even the most banal materials into experiences that are stimulating. Curriculum materials are always mediated by the context, and the teacher plays a crucial role in that context. This is one reason why the notion of developing "teacherproof" curriculum materials is suspect. Not only does it demean the teacher and the profession of teaching, it also simply cannot be done in educational situations: training programs, perhaps, but educational programs, no.

I make a point of this because I do not believe that we can have standards for the evaluation of curriculum materials as we have standards to appraise food and drugs. We can use criteria, but criteria imply judgments that are flexible, that consider relationships between the materials and the context in which they are to function. What might be right for one situation will be wrong for others. The creation of a bureau of standards for curriculum materials could work only for the identification of their most egregious faults; such a bureau might function as a screening agency but not as a selection agency. What I believe we can provide through the evaluation of curriculum are judgments concerning the qualities the materials possess and information about some of their effects in a particular context, but not guaranteed results or even the implications of such results. In educational situations we do not have the luxury of substituting rule for judgment.

What I have tried to do thus far is to identify some of the factors that one can take into account in the process of curriculum development, in particular in the design of materials that may be of help to the teacher in his or her work. These factors, or considerations, are to be viewed as heuristic: they are tools to be used, not rules to be followed. There are no rules or recipes that will guarantee successful curriculum development. Judgment is always required, and if this task is a group effort, sensitivity to one's fellow workers is always necessary.

References

Bernstein, B. (1971). On the classification and framing of educational knowledge. In Michael Young (Ed.), *Knowledge and content.* London: Collier-Macmillan.

Dewey, J. (1938). *Experience and education.* New York: Macmillan.

Dewey, J. (1959). The child and the curriculum. In Martin S. Dworkin (Ed.), *Dewey on education.* New York: Bureau of Publications, Teachers College, Columbia University.

McDonald, J. (1965, May). Myths about instruction. *Educational Leadership, 22*(7), 613–614.

Schwab, J. J. (1962, July). The concept of the structure of the discipline. *Educational Record, 43,* 197–205.

Whitehead, A. N. (1929). The rhythm of education. In A. N. Whitehead (Ed.), *The aims of education and other essays.* New York: Macmillan.

7

On the Art of Teaching

First we see the hills in the painting, then we see the painting in the hills.

LI LI WENG

In the previous chapter I focused mainly on the dimensions of curriculum planning. In this chapter I wish to address another central aspect of the educational process: teaching. It is my thesis that teaching is an art guided by educational values, personal needs, and by a variety of beliefs or generalizations that the teacher holds to be true.

To argue as I will that teaching is an art is something of a paradox. We live at a time when virtually the entire effort of those who have attempted to study teaching has been devoted to the creation of a science of teaching (see Gage, 1963 and Travers, 1973). Yet, most of those who teach—indeed, even those who study teaching scientifically—often regard their own teaching as an artistic activity. For some, to say that teaching is an art is to say that it is poorly understood and that when it is understood a science of teaching will have been developed. I will have more to say about this issue a bit later, but for the present let us think about what it means to say that teaching is an art.

Four Senses of the Art of Teaching

There are at least four senses in which teaching can be considered an art. First, it is an art in that teaching can be performed with such skill and grace that, for the student as well as for the teacher, the experience can be justifiably characterized as aesthetic (see Dewey, 1934). There are classrooms in which what the teacher does—the way in which activities are orchestrated, questions asked, lectures given—constitutes a form of artistic expression. What occurs is a performance that provides intrinsic forms of satisfaction, so much so that we use the adjectives and accolades usually applied to the fine arts to describe what the teacher does while teaching.

Second, teaching is an art in that teachers, like painters, composers, actresses, and dancers, make judgments based largely on qualities that unfold during the course of action. Qualitative forms of intelligence are used to elect, control, and organize classroom qualities, such as tempo, tone, climate, pace of discussion, and forward movement. The teacher must "read" the emerging qualities and respond with qualities appropriate to the ends sought or the direction he or she wishes the students to take. In this process, qualitative judgment is exercised in the interests of achieving a qualitative end (see Ecker, 1963).

Third, teaching is an art in that the teacher's activity is not dominated by prescriptions or routines but is influenced by qualities and contingencies that are unpredicted. The teacher must function in an innovative way in order to cope with these contingencies. To say that prescription and routine do not dominate the teacher's activity is not to say that they are not present or play no part in teaching. Teaching requires for its artistic expression routines with which to work; the teacher must have available repertoires to draw on. It is through repertoires or routines that the teacher can devote his or her energies and attention to what is emerging in the class. Without such routines, an enormous amount of energy would need to be spent by the teacher to develop skills to use in the classroom. Thus, the presence of well-developed routines or teaching repertoires enables the teacher to deal inventively with what occurs in the class. It is precisely the tension between automaticity and inventiveness that makes teaching, like any other art, so complex an undertaking. Without automaticity and the ability to call on stock responses, energies are lost and inventiveness is hampered. Yet, if responses are too automatic or routine, if they become too reflexive, the teacher's ability to invent is hampered. Teaching becomes a series of routine responses rather than an opportunity for ingenuity.

Fourth, teaching is an art in that the ends it achieves are often created in process. Craft has been defined as the process through which skills are employed to arrive at preconceived ends. Art has been defined as the process in which skills are employed to discover ends through action. H. W. Janson, the noted art historian, has said, "Artists are people who play hide-and-seek but do not know what they seek until they find it" (Polanyi & Prosch, 1977). In a similar sense, teaching is a form of human action in which many of the ends achieved are emergent—that is to say, found in the course of interaction with students rather than preconceived and efficiently attained. This is not to say that there are no situations in which preconceived ends are formulated; most of the arguments advocating the clear specification of instructional objectives tacitly imply that the quintessence of teaching resides in the efficient achievement of such ends. It is to say that to emphasize the exclusive use of such a model of teaching reduces it to a set of algorithmic functions. Opportunities for the creation of ends in process or in the post facto analysis of outcomes require a model of teaching akin to other arts. Teachers do, at least in part, use such a model to guide their activities, not as a function of professional incompetence, but as a way of keeping their pedagogical intelligence from freezing into mechanical routine.

It is in these four senses—teaching as a source of aesthetic experience, as dependent on the perception and control of qualities, as a heuristic or adventitious activity, and as seeking emergent ends—that teaching can be regarded as an art.

Because teaching can be engaged in as an art is not to suggest that all teaching can be characterized as such. Teaching can be done as badly as anything else. It can be wooden, mechanical, mindless, and wholly unimaginative. But when it is sensitive, intelligent, and creative—those qualities that confer on it the status of an art—it should, in my view, not be regarded, as it so often is by some, as an expression of unfathomable talent or luck but as an example of humans exercising the highest levels of their intelligence. Dewey (1934) writes of the role of intelligence in art as follows:

> Any idea that ignores the necessary role of intelligence in production of works of art is based upon identification of thinking with use of one special kind of material, verbal signs and words. To think effectively in terms of relations of qualities is as severe a demand upon thought as to think in terms of symbols, verbal and mathematical. Indeed, since words are easily manipulated in mechanical ways, the production of a work of genuine art probably demands more intelligence than does most of the so-called thinking that goes on among those who pride themselves on being "intellectuals." (p. 46)

As Philip Jackson (1968) has said, rather than complain about the art of teaching, we should try to foster whatever artistry the teacher can provide.

The Role of Theory in Teaching

If we conceive of teaching as an art, does theory have a role to play in the guidance and conduct of teaching? Does artistic teaching vitiate the use of scientifically grounded theory? Theoretical frameworks, scientific or otherwise, are frames of reference that perform two extremely important functions. First, they serve as a means for identifying aspects of the reality to which they address themselves. Theories remind us of what to attend to by calling our attention to the theory's subject matter. For example, theories in sociology make vivid the social structure of the classroom, they illuminate class differences among pupils, and they describe friendship patterns and formal and informal sanctions. Psychological theory (depending on the specific theory being used) might address itself to questions of self-esteem or forms of reinforcement or the need to provide students with opportunities to practice the behavior they are expected to learn. What theories do in this regard is to help us focus attention on aspects of classroom life that we might otherwise neglect. They are tools that help us bring the world into focus (see Weitz, 1966).

But theories, in the social sciences at least, do more than this. They also provide rough approximations of what we might expect of certain pedagogical arrangements by the kinds of generalizations that they provide. Although no single theory in any of the social sciences is likely to be adequate to deal with the particular reality with which an individual teacher must cope, theories do provide generalizations that can be considered in one's reflective moments as a teacher. These moments, what Jackson (1968) calls "preactive teaching," occur prior to actual teaching: planning at home, reflecting on what has occurred during a particular class session, and discussing in groups ways to organize a program. Theory here sophisticates personal reflection and group deliberation. Insofar as a theory suggests consequences flowing from particular circumstances, it enables those who understand the theory to take those circumstances into account when planning.

In all of this, theory is not to be regarded as prescriptive but as suggestive. It is a framework, a tool, a means through which the world can be construed. Any theory is but a part of the total picture. Joseph Schwab (1969) describes the limits of theory this way:

> If, then, theory is to be used well in the determination of curricular practice, it requires a supplement. It requires arts which bring a theory to its application; first, arts which identify the disparities between real theory and theoretic representation; second, arts which modify the theory in the course of its application, in light of the discrepancies; and, third, arts which devise ways for taking account of the many aspects of the real thing which the theory does not take into account. (p. 12)

The point in Schwab's observation is not, as some seem to believe, to excise theory from curriculum planning or from teaching, but rather to hold appropriate expectations for its utility. What is dysfunctional is to regard it as a formula to be followed or as utterly useless. The former overestimates its function, the latter underestimates it.

In one sense, all teachers operate with theory, if we take theory to mean a general set of ideas through which we make sense of the world. All teachers, whether they are aware of it or not, use theories in their work. Tacit beliefs about the nature of human intelligence, about the factors that motivate children, and about the conditions that foster learning influence the teacher's actions in the classrooms. These ideas may not only influence their actions, they also influence what they attend to in the classroom: that is, the concepts that are salient in theories concerning pedagogical matters also tend to guide perception. Thus, theory inevitably operates in the conduct of teaching as it does in other aspects of educational deliberation. The major need is to be able to view situations from the varied perspectives that different theories provide and thus to be in a position to avoid the limited vision of a single view.

Thus far we have talked about teaching as an art and about some of the functions that theory performs in teaching. But what of the concept *teaching* itself? What does it mean "to teach"? What are the ways in which the term can be construed?

The Meaning of Teaching: Two Views

For John Dewey (1910) the term *teaching* was regarding as similar in form to the term *selling*. That is, one could not teach unless someone learned, just as one could not sell unless someone bought. Teaching and learning were regarded as reciprocal concepts. Although it was possible to learn without having been taught, one could not be said to have taught unless someone had learned.

The reason this view of teaching was embraced was because the term *teach* implied an end-in-view—namely, learning. Teaching was goal-directed and represented, in Gilbert Ryle's (1949) terms, an achievement, not merely the performance of a task. For example, to say that someone has run is to describe an activity—it is a task term. But to say that someone has won is to describe an achievement; it is an achievement term for Ryle. Thus, if a teacher attempts to teach but does not succeed in helping the student learn, then he or she may be said to have lectured, conducted a discussion, demonstrated, explained but *not* to have taught. To teach, in this sense, is known by its effects. Those effects are learning. Just as one could not be said to have sold something unless another bought, so too, one could not have been said to have taught unless another had learned.

When the study of teaching became a major interest among researchers in the early part of the 1950s, the view that teaching should be conceptualized in terms of its consequences presented something of a difficulty. To subscribe to this view of teaching means that one could study teaching only by first determining its effects on students, particularly with respect to the achievement of specified goals. This posed formidable problems in the study of teaching because it required that one must study two things: what teachers do and what students learn.

To simplify the research task, teaching was reconceptualized as a variety of acts performed by individuals called teachers as they work in classrooms with the intention of promoting learning. Whether they were successful was a matter to be studied separately. Thus, using this conception, it became possible to ask what teachers did in the classroom and to establish criteria, independent of their effects, that could be used to appraise the quality of what they did. Teachers, for example, lectured, demonstrated, explained, led discussions, introduced materials, and brought lessons to closure. All of these activities, regardless of their effects, could be evaluated by using criteria appropriate for each act. For example, the logic of lectures, the vividness of the examples provided, and the coherence of expression are considerations that could be used to evaluate aspects of teaching. The ability to ask questions in a discussion, to help the discussion move forward, to engage many participants, and to foster critical and analytical skills could be applied as criteria to appraise the teacher's skills as a discussion leader. It was believed to be too much to expect that both the quality of the acts of teaching and their consequences be studied simultaneously in a field just beginning to study teaching scientifically.

What we see here are two radically different conceptions of teaching. One regards teaching as a form of achievement directly related to learning. The other regards it as a set of acts performed by people we call teachers as they attempt to foster learning. To which of these conceptions shall we subscribe? Which one is "correct"?

It is both interesting and important to recognize that if we consider how we use the term *selling* it becomes clear that we do in fact use it not in one way but in two ways. Nel Noddings (in personal communication) has pointed out that when we talk about someone engaged in selling, we describe a series of acts and not necessarily a series of achievements. Someone is a salesman, is in the selling game, is selling cars. We use such phrases without necessarily implying that the individuals so engaged are successful. One is selling even though we might not have sold any cars today or even this week. Selling here designates a variety of actions that are guided by a set of intentions, not by a set of achievements. Similarly, we can talk about teaching as a set of acts guided by intentions, not as representing achievements.

At the same time, we also talk about teaching in the sense that someone has fulfilled an intention. Teaching also refers to the achievement of intended learning. We say, for example, "I taught you or I failed to teach you," implying that if one had not succeeded, teaching did not occur.

What can we do about this duality? I suggest that we can appropriately conceptualize teaching both ways. We do at present and have in the past used both conceptions of teaching, and I believe that they have served us well. We discern the meaning of the term *teach* not by referring to some operational or stipulated definition, but by recognizing how it functions in a context of other meanings. Much of our language functions in the same way. If under certain circumstances the context is insufficient to provide clarity of meaning, we can then stipulate what we mean by teaching so that others will know how we intend to use the term. In most cases, I believe, we can use the term *teach* in both ways—as an achievement term and as a task term—without a serious problem in communication.

Teaching and Instruction

There is, however, a tendency in our discussions to use *teaching* and *instruction* interchangeably. These terms are not interchangeable. Their connotative meanings are sufficiently distinctive to warrant attention because what they connote can lead to different conceptions of education and educational practice.

Perhaps the best way to illustrate the differences between *teaching* and *instruction* is to relate an episode that occurred to me when I was studying English primary schools (see Eisner, 1974). I was having tea in a common room of a London primary school with a group of primary school teachers. We were talking about how the school day was organized and in the course of the conversation I said that I was interested in the way in which they provided instruction. A group of incredulous expressions appeared on their faces. "Instruction?" they asked. I said yes, I was interested in how they provided instruction to the pupils. One of them said, "We don't provide instruction in this school, we teach. Instruction is provided in the church and in the army, but in this school we teach."

What they were conveying to me, and it was the first time I had reflected on the distinction, was that instruction was concerned with forms of training; it was harsher, less organic, more mechanical than teaching. To "teach" is softer than to "instruct." Perhaps this is why the term *instruction* is more likely to be used by those whose orientation to curriculum is technological and who want to maximize effective control over the content and form of what children learn in school. *Instruction* is a term more suited to a manual than is the term *teach*. Instruction is less apt to be associated with the adventitious, with what is flexible and emergent, in short, and what is artistic, than is teaching.

Now to draw this difference between terms might seem like quibbling, but it is not. It is precisely because we do not have clear-cut, stipulated definitions of these terms that their connotative meanings take on such importance. When terms are not formally differentiated, context and connotation significantly influence the kinds of meanings that individuals are likely to construe. To use the term *instruction* as an equivalent to the term *teach* is not to have an equivalent at all; each term carries its own conceptual baggage, and although there is some overlap, the significance of the terms resides in their differences because each implies a different image of what teaching should do.

It is significant, also, I believe, that the terms we use in educational discourse not only reflect different assumptions about the means and ends of education, but also that terms cluster—that is, individual terms tend to have conceptual links to other terms. In combination, they generate a view of what is educationally desirable. Consider, for example, the term *individual-*

ized instruction. Contrast this with *personalized teaching.* The term *individualized* is harsher and more bureaucratic in character than *personalized.* The latter is softer and more intimate. When combined with *instruction, individualized instruction* takes on a connotation that is more technological than *personalized teaching.*

Consider the following: "In this school system, individualized instruction is provided to learners after first having measured a learner's entry skills. Once these entry skills have been determined, appropriate exit skills are specified and measured at the end of the instructional period." Language of this sort communicates not only because of the specific denotations of the language used but also because of the images that the language conveys. *Entry* and *exit* conjure up something of an assembly line in which products are processed according to specifications. Education in this context is something that one does to another through a process called instruction. When such terms permeate our discourse they shape our view of the character and aims of education.

When it comes to discourse about teaching, perhaps no concept has had greater currency than the concept of individualized instruction. I have already pointed out that the concept itself participates in a tradition that is more mechanical than organic. If we were to study the ways in which individualization is provided in classrooms, we would find that in many classrooms the variable that is individualized for students is time. Individualized instruction in a great many classrooms means allowing children to take different amounts of time to arrive at the same destination. Yet, individualization (or personalized teaching, if you prefer) can be provided by altering the teaching method so that it suits particular children, by altering content, and by altering the goals themselves. Time is but one factor of many that can be modified to accommodate the characteristics or aptitude of different children.

What is not recognized—even by teachers who provide it regularly—is that the use of different kinds of explanations for different children, the variety of questions and types of examples teachers provide, the different ways in which motivation is engendered, the modulation of one's tone of voice and one's tempo to suit individual children are examples of individualized instruction. To be sure, these forms of pedagogical adaptation use no mechanical means—no workbooks, test forms, color-coded boxes of reading material—yet they reside, I believe, at the heart of individualization, for they represent one person's effort to try to communicate with another. Each child, so to speak, is a custom job.

Because of our national tendency to seek prepackaged and field-tested devices to make education efficient, we sometimes fail to recognize the extent to which some of the teaching practices employed daily reflect the most straightforward examples of individualization. Mechanical images too often intervene and hamper our recognition of the excellent things we already do.

Artistry in teaching is not a common occurrence. It is an ideal. The reasons for its importance are not self-evident, and although I have described the sense in which teaching is an art, I have not said much about why artistic teaching is so important to the educational development of the young.

The Importance of Artistry

Artistry is important because teachers who function artistically in the classroom not only provide children with important sources of artistic experience, they also provide a climate that welcomes exploration and risk-taking and cultivates the disposition to play. To be able to play with ideas is to feel free to throw them into new combinations, to experiment, and even to "fail." It is to be able to deliteralize perception so that fantasy, metaphor, and constructive foolishness may emerge. For it is through play that children eventually discover the limits of their ideas, test their own competencies, and formulate rules that eventually convert play into games. This vacillation between playing and gaming, between algorithms and heuristics, between structure-seeking and rule-abiding behavior, is critical for the construction of new patterns of knowing. Play opens up new possibilities, whereas games exploit these possibilities within a set of defined parameters, something that mature intellectual models do with their work. Playing with ideas that are transformed and guided by rules is as prevalent in the art studio as it is in the science laboratory. Although each area has its own syntax, each its own form and rules, they share the need for play as a source of invention and discovery. But for such a disposition to be cultivated, teachers themselves need to feel free to innovate, to explore, and to play. Teaching is not an act modeled after the sequences of a highly efficient assembly line. Teaching is more like what occurs on a basketball court or on a soccer field. Let me develop this analogy.

Basketball is a game defined by certain rules in which its players seek an unambiguous outcome: to end the game with more points than their opponents. In the former characteristic, basketball and teaching are similar: both have rules that define the activities of their respective games. However, in the latter characteristic, having unambiguous goals, the teacher is generally unlike the basketball player. Goals change in teaching, they can be ambiguous, and they are certainly not the same for all students. Still, basketball and teaching are alike in many ways. A basketball player must watch the court and understand emerging configurations; so must a teacher. A player must recognize productive possibilities and must know how to pass as well as to shoot; so must a teacher. The basketball player must also know how to slow down the pace, when to speed it up, and even when to stall for time; so must a teacher. He needs to know when to cut, how to slow down a pass, how to talk to his opponent, and how to provide support for his teammates; so must a teacher. The skills that he must have to play the game well require intellectual flexibility. Although good teams have a set of preplanned patterns, once they get on the floor they need to know both how to improvise within those patterns and when to give them up at a second's notice in order to exploit other options. Flexible purposing, Dewey (1938) calls it: knowing when to alter the goal, when to explore new interactions and when to shift strategies. In this sense, neither basketball nor teaching is optimized by chaotic abandon or rigid adherence to prespecified plans. Fluid intelligence, intelligence in process, is the hallmark of effectiveness in both arenas. Unlike the automobile assembly line where systemization, orderliness, predictability, and control serve the goals of efficiency, effective teaching, like effective basketball, profits from flexibility, ingenuity, and personal creativity, the last things desired on the assembly line.

To say that excellence in teaching requires artistry implies that the teacher is able to exploit opportunities as they occur. It implies that goals and intentions be fluid. But in many ways this is contrary to the belief that single-mindedness and clarity of one's ends-in-view are required for rationally guided activity. To be rational, one must be intentional. But what is not adequately appreciated is the limitation that such a conception of rationality places on the ways in which teaching can be undertaken. If teaching is regarded—at least in part—as a form of inquiry, as a process of exploring problems that one cannot always define or predict—problems of a pedagogical and substantive variety—the limitations of such a conception of rationality begin to become apparent.

Furthermore, the mandate to operationalize aims has the effect of frequently restricting the aims of teachers in curriculum development to those for which a technology of measurement is available. If such a technology is absent, the likelihood of relinquishing valued aims increases. The ability to measure provides a formidable restraint on what teachers come to believe they ought to do.

But perhaps the most insidious aspect of the belief that aims should always be clear and measurable is the coercive impact such a belief has on our conception of rationality and intentionality.

What counts as an intention? Must an intention be capable of linguistic formulation? Is it necessary that the aspiration one seeks be statable in discursive language? Given the admonition that teachers state their objectives behaviorally, it appears that objectives that cannot be articulated in discursive form are not objectives. Such a view is naive on several counts. First, much of what we aim for is held "in the mind's eye" as an image rather than as a proposition. The image is a visual form of knowing that is in many ways clearer than its discursive representation. Imagine an architect having to discursively describe the features of the structure she intends to create. Such a description is likely to fall far short of the architectural qualities she is after. The images of excellence in the arts and the sciences, in the social studies, and in the conduct of practice are often extremely difficult to articulate—and at times are ineffable. To expect all of what we prize to be capable of being translated into discourse is to make a second conceptual blunder: namely, failure to appreciate the modes of conceptual representation humans are capable of using.

One must ask further whether intentions must always precede action. Is it not the case that action breeds intention as often as intention leads to action? Regarding the relationship of action to ends, one of the foremost organizational theorists in the United States, James March (1972), has this to say:

> Goals are thrust upon the intelligent man. We ask that he act in the name of goals. We ask that he keep his goals consistent. We ask that his actions be oriented to his goals. We ask that a social system amalgamate individual goals into a collective goal. But we do not concern ourselves with the origin of goals. Theories of individual organizational and social choice assume actors with pre-existent values.
>
> Since it is obvious that goals change over time and that the character of those changes affects both the richness of personal and social development and the outcome of choice behavior, a theory of choice must somehow justify ignoring the phenomena. Although it is unreasonable to ask a theory of choice to solve all of the problems of man and his development, it is reasonable to ask how something as conspicuous as the fluidity and ambiguity of objectives can plausibly be ignored in a theory that is offered as a guide to human choice behavior.
>
> There are three classic justifications. The first is that goal development and choice are independent processes, conceptually and behaviorally. The second is that the model of choice is never satisfied in fact and that deviations from the model accommodate the problems of introducing change. The third is that the idea of changing goals is so intractable in a normative theory of choice that nothing can be said about it. Since I am unpersuaded of the first and second justifications, my optimism with respect to the third is somewhat greater than most of my fellows.
>
> The argument that goal development and choice are independent behaviorally seems clearly false. It seems to me perfectly obvious that a description that assumes goals come first and action comes later is frequently radically wrong. Human choice behavior is at least as much a process for discovering goals as for acting on them. (p. 420)

March's view of this matter seems clearly persuasive. Why then should a static, unidirectional conception of intentionality and rationality dominate our conception of responsible teaching and curriculum development? Largely, I believe, because we have taken our image of rationality from technologies that emphasize standardization, routine, and efficiency. As long as we conceive of the school as an institution with a static and common mission whose goals must be clearly specified, the belief that effective teaching must lead to the efficient attainment of such goals follows. The task of school administrators, or "program managers," as they are being called increasingly, is to see to it that teachers perform in ways consistent with those goals. Rational planning consists of articulating those goals, subdividing them into units, and casting them into operational forms. The next step is to attempt to discover or to create procedures known to be instrumental to the achievement of those goals. Once this has been accomplished, a monitoring system can be employed to control the performance patterns of teachers who, in turn, can control the performance patterns of students.

The failure to distinguish between education and training, between the school and the factory, between the algorithms and the heuristics of teaching accounts for the simplistic nostrums that are promulgated as ways of improving education. Intentions need not be statable to be held. Intentions need not precede action; they can grow out of action. Rationality includes the capacity to play, to explore, to search for surprise and effective novelty. Such activities are not necessarily contrary to the exercise of human rationality; they may be its most compelling exemplification. What diminishes human rationality is the thwarting of flexible human intelligence by prescriptions that shackle the educational imagination.

Happily, scholars are paying more attention to teaching as an art form. Faith in the power of technicism to eventually manage all classroom tasks has faded, at least among those who thought most deeply about the nature and complexities of teaching. This newfound realization for educational scholars is opening up new conceptions of what teachers need in order to improve their performance and how it is that they can make good judgments about how to teach. In the 1970s, much more confidence was placed in what was called "rational decision making." Some researchers believed that teachers consciously formulated decision trees with which to consider alternative courses of action or that they formulated hypotheses about action that were derived from theory. It has become increasingly clear that when teachers work "on the wing," the basis for action resides in the immediate judgment of constellations rather than through a detailed linear sequence of anticipated consequences from particular decisions being made. This broader view of teaching has implications for the kind of settings we create in schools for teachers to learn and grow and the kind of feedback and constructive criticism that can be provided to enhance their own understanding of their own work. From my perspective, this development has enormous potential *if* the organization of the school can be redesigned to make artistically grounded reflective teaching possible.

On the Relationship between Teaching and Curriculum Planning

Just what is the relationship between teaching and curriculum planning? For some, the distinction between teaching and curriculum is blurred. The argument is that if curriculum constitutes the content of what children learn, then it is not possible to separate the forms through which that content is conveyed from the content itself because form and content interact. How one teaches and what one teaches are inseparable.

This argument is not without merit. Indeed, one of the aims of this book is to encourage students of education to consider curriculum planning and schooling as an entity because each aspect of schooling has a bearing on other aspects. The timetable of the school, for example, influences the way in which teachers must plan the curriculum, pace lessons, and organize learning activities. Evaluation practices influence educational priorities as much as they reflect them. Yet, to say that teaching and curriculum interact or influence each other is to make a distinction between teaching and curriculum. I believe this distinction is a useful one for several reasons.

First, we already have a tradition of discussion regarding the term *teaching*. In the English language—despite the difficulties and differences in conceptions discussed earlier—we do talk about teaching and regard it as something other than curriculum. In the simplest terms—too simple to be sure—curriculum is the content that is taught and teaching is how that content is taught. This simple difference is important because all curriculum planning, insofar as it precedes its actual use in the classroom, requires a transformation of a set of plans or materials into a course of action. This transformation is what we regard as teaching.

Now it should be noted that in this view not all of teaching takes place when teachers talk to a group of students or lead a discussion. Teaching includes the setting up of conditions that do not require the teacher to be in an interactive relationship with students. Thus, a teacher who arranges a set of conditions, say a terrarium or a selection of books or art material with which students may work, and who provides a modicum of guidance to enable students to use these resources is engaged in teaching even though no lecture or discussion is provided. In short, teaching does not require either a didactic or a dialectic relationship between teacher and pupil. It can and does occur through the creation of an intellectually productive environment.

Earlier I pointed out that intentions and rational planning need not precede action, that intentions can develop out of actions as well as lead to them. How does such a conception bear on the relationship of teaching to curriculum?

The "standard" model of this relationship appears in Figure 3.

Figure 3

In this model, intentions are formed that set the direction and the constraints for curriculum planning. Once the curriculum is planned, it provides the aims, the content, and the resources that the teacher employs to transform intentions and curriculum materials into classroom conditions that promote learning. Although much pedagogical activity takes this route, not all of it does. Consider the diagram in Figure 4.

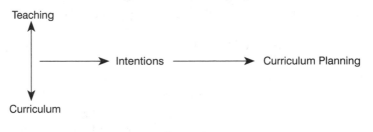

Figure 4

In this model, teaching, which always has a content because it is logically impossible to teach or to try to teach someone nothing, interacts with curriculum. One engages in teaching some content and out of action intentions develop that are then used as a basis for planning curriculum. In this model, action is the initiating agent that leads to the formation of intentions, which in turn leads to curriculum planning.

Both of the models presented here are unidirectional. One starts with intentions and terminates with teaching. The other starts with teaching and terminates with curriculum planning. Perhaps a more adequate representation of the process is found in Figure 5.

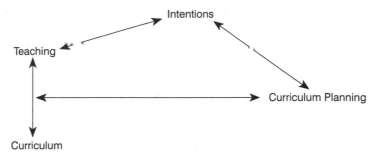

Figure 5

In this model, the process is circular—that is, one can enter the circle at any point in the model. Intentions lead to curriculum planning, which in turn provides the content and structure for teaching, which through the course of action leads to the formation of new intentions. One might start with curriculum planning and through it provide the content and structure for teaching, which in turn leads to intentions; or one might start with teaching and through action formulate intentions, which in turn lead to curriculum planning.

With such a model, one can begin to study the sources of intentionality in teaching and speculate on the kinds of value orientations that are more likely than others to encourage teachers to use teaching to formulate intentions and vice versa.

There is another comment worth making about the relationship of curriculum to teaching that has to do with primacy of curriculum in this relationship. By this I mean that it is no virtue to teach well what should not be taught at all. Put another way, what is not worth teaching is not worth teaching well. Thus, if the content to be taught is without redeeming features, it makes little sense to worry about how well it is being taught; teaching matters, so to speak, when what is taught is worth the student's time.

Looking at it from another angle, a curriculum composed of high-quality content and imaginative activities and materials can be scuttled by poor teaching. If the teacher is unable to use materials in the classroom effectively, regardless of how well planned they are, the virtues of the materials as far as the students are concerned go unrealized. But if the curriculum materials are without intellectual virtue, effectively teaching them constitutes a vice.

The virtues and vices of teaching are not only related to the quality of what is taught, but are also determined by criteria that are appropriate to the form of teaching that is provided. For example, the kinds of skills one needs to be able to give a lucid and coherent lecture are not the same as those needed to conduct a discussion. A teacher who is good at the former may be poor at the latter. To attempt to apply a single set of criteria to a wide variety of types and forms of teaching is to overlook what is distinctive about each type. Consider not only the giving of lectures and the leading of discussions, but the organization of small-group activity, individual counseling and guidance, and the ability to maintain a wide array of diverse but productive activities in the classroom; each of these forms of teaching requires the use of different skills. The criteria that are appropriate for appraising the quality of one kind of teaching are not necessarily appropriate for appraising the quality of another.

This admonition to apply to an art form the criteria appropriate to it is well known in the fine arts. We do not use criteria appropriate for tragedy to appraise the quality of melodrama and vice versa. What constitutes excellence in surrealist painting does not constitute excellence in impressionistic work. In teaching, too, excellence is related to the form of teaching being employed. It is probably too much to expect a high degree of excellence in all of the major forms of teaching that can be provided in a classroom. What we probably do want is a high degree of excellence in some.

I make this point—although it may seem obvious—because we often talk about excellence in teaching as though it were a single set of qualities. We sometimes tend to evaluate teaching with a single image of pedagogical merit. And research in teaching has tended to underplay the distinctive differences of different forms of teaching as well as the normative frames of reference or orientations to education that any set of criteria must in some way reflect. Yet these orientations are, in the last analysis, the crucial criteria for appraising the educational value of teaching. Excellence as a lecturer or as a discussion leader is not sufficient to constitute educational virtue if either the lectures or the discussions are regarded as educationally inappropriate. No judgment can be made about the quality of teaching as an educational event or performance without reference to some theory of education. It is ironic that the most neglected aspect in research on teaching is the very framework that would have made it possible for the researcher to say something about the educational significance of the findings.

In all of this discussion about the art of teaching, about differences between teaching and instruction, and about teaching as an independent or reciprocal concept, it is easy to neglect the fact that teachers have needs that must be met through teaching. Because teachers are *people* who teach, it is important that, in our efforts to develop self-instructional materials for students and prepackaged procedures for instruction, we do not eviscerate the classroom of those opportunities that teachers need to gain satisfaction from teaching. When such procedures begin to dominate classroom practice, opportunities to gain satisfactions from teaching can be seriously diminished. The teacher who wants the pride and satisfaction that come from having designed a reading program may be restricted from using such a program. Although schools do not exist primarily for the benefit of teachers, teacher who receive little or no satisfaction from what they do are not, I believe, likely to be educationally effective. The human need for pride in crafts and being able to put something of oneself into work is recognized even by companies that sell packaged cake mixes.

The need to get something out of what one does, aside from student achievement, is still very great for most of us. The school should provide the conditions where such needs can be met. Unless the school can provide the necessary life-space for the teacher's growth, the existence of optimal conditions for the educational growth of students is not assured.

References

Dewey, J. (1910). *How we think*. Lexington, MA: D. C. Heath.

Dewey, J. (1934). *Art as experience*. New York: Minton, Balch.

Dewey, J. (1938). *Experience and education*. New York: Macmillan.

Ecker, D. (1963, Spring). The artistic process as qualitative problem-solving. *Journal of Aesthetics and Art Criticism, 21*(3), 57–68.

Eisner, E. W. (1974). *English primary schools*. Washington, D. C.: National Association for Young Children.

Gage, N. L. (Ed.). (1963). *Handbook of research on teaching*. Chicago: Rand McNally.

Jackson, P. (1968). *Life in classrooms*. New York: Holt, Rinehart & Winston.

March, J. (1972, Fall). Model bias in social action. *Review of Educational Research, 42*(4), 413–430.

Polanyi, M., & Prosch, H. (1977). *Meaning*. Chicago: The University of Chicago Press.

Ryle, G. (1949). *The concept of mind*. New York: Barnes and Noble.

Schwab, J. (1969, November). The practical: A language for curriculum. *School Review, 78*, 12.

Travers, R. M. W. (Ed.). (1973). *Second handbook of research on teaching*. Chicago: Rand McNally.

Weitz, M. (1966). The nature of art. In Elliot W. Eisner & David Ecker (Eds.), *Readings in art education*. Waltham, MA: Blaisdell.

8

❦

The Functions and Forms
of Evaluation

———◆—●◗◖●—◆———

*Our discussion will be adequate if it has as much clearness as the
subject matter admits of, for precision is not to be sought for alike in
all discussions, any more than in all the products of the crafts. . . .
for it is the mark of an educated man to look for precision in each
class of things just so far as the nature of the subject admits; it is
evidently equally foolish to accept probable reasoning from a mathe-
matician and to demand from a rhetorician scientific proofs.*

ARISTOTLE

———◆—●◗◖●—◆———

Although many people regard evaluation as something analogous to the
giving of grades, in fact evaluation is used in education to perform a wide
variety of functions. This chapter identifies some of these functions and
describes the forms evaluation can take when directed toward various ends.
Of the functions of evaluation in education, five seem especially important:

1. To diagnose.
2. To revise curricula.
3. To compare.
4. To anticipate educational needs.
5. To determine if objectives have been achieved.

Let's examine each of these different functions. Evaluation can be used
to diagnose—but what? Three subject matters, each of which will be discussed in detail later, can be identified now as being the potential focus of
diagnosis. They are the *curriculum* itself, even before it is employed in a

171

classroom, *the teaching* that is occurring, and *the student* and his or her learning and experience.

Diagnosis

Diagnosis as an evaluative technique is most often used in the context of student learning, and the term itself has a medical connotation. Students are "diagnosed" in order to "prescribe" a "treatment" that is educationally effective. The medical analogy has its uses: it suggests that treatments will be employed that fit the nature of the student's difficulties. But there are limits to such metaphors. Students are not patients and they don't normally have illnesses to be treated. Furthermore, although there are standard forms of medical technique, controlled pharmaceutical formulas for medicines, and routine procedures for medical diagnosis, virtually none of the rigorous tools, treatments, or techniques available to the medical practitioner is available to the educational practitioner. To be sure, there are intelligence tests and diagnostic tests in reading and in some other subject areas such as mathematics, but the confidence one can place in these tools is limited and, in addition, performance on them is greatly influenced by the cultural conditions in which students live. Having said this, we can still talk about diagnosis as a function in evaluation. To diagnose can represent the effort to locate or try to locate the sources of difficulties students are having with particular learning problems. In the field of reading, in which many of the available diagnostic tools exist, it is possible to employ tests that assess word-attack skills, paragraph meaning, general comprehension, and vocabulary. The achievement profile secured from such instruments is designed to guide the teacher so that if a student is weak in a particular area, instruction in that area can be provided.

It should also be pointed out that the diagnosis of learning difficulties does not require the use of tests, and at its most general level is used by virtually all teachers to identify whether their students understand what is being taught. For example, an art teacher can look at a student's work or watch the student while working in class and "diagnose" the sorts of strengths and weaknesses that the student possesses. One student might, for example, be unable to control the material adequately to use it as a medium of expression, another student might be neglecting attention to his work's formal features, still another student might be inadequately wedging the clay with which she is working. In each of the foregoing cases, the type of problem the student has requires a different type of "solution" or educational "treatment."

But even more generally, any teaching attempting to explain something to students in class would attempt to determine whether the explanation was understood. To do so requires some form of diagnosis: a request by the teacher to a student to explain, to demonstrate, to draw relationships. The questions students ask also provide diagnostic information to the teacher. Indeed, if one looks at teaching dialectically, much of what teachers do will be seen as a result of their understanding of where students are and what they need. The use of an example to clarify a point that is not understood requires some conception of what is likely to make more sense to students than the explanation just provided. The good example provides the necessary bridge between the student's current level of comprehension, his or her experience, and the aims toward which the teaching is directed. The selection of the right example is, one might say, the result of a diagnostic evaluation.

Perhaps the classic example of such diagnosis occurs in the sixth book of Plato's (1956) *Republic*. Glaucon, after he asks about the nature of knowledge, is given an image by Socrates in an effort to help him grasp the hierarchy of truth that is used in Plato's epistemology. Glaucon fails to grasp the meaning of the image (in this case, a line divided into four segments intended to represent various degrees of truth), and so Socrates proceeds in the beginning of Book Seven to tell Glaucon the famous parable of the cave, which even more graphically depicts the relationships Socrates tried to explain earlier. What Plato gives us here is a telling image of both teaching and diagnostic evaluation.

Recognizing that Glaucon does not understand the abstract explanation he has provided, Socrates makes his explanation more concrete and uses the vivid imagery of the cave, the shadows, and the sun to help Glaucon grasp his point about the nature of knowledge. Like the good teacher, Socrates *individualizes* his example to help his pupil understand what he is trying to teach. To recognize the need for individualization, evaluation must occur. Evaluation here is used to diagnose and monitor. Thus, diagnosis in evaluation can be employed dynamically in the context of teaching or more formally in the context of specially designed tests that locate the students' strengths and weaknesses and, therefore, it provides a basis for curriculum change.

Curriculum Revision

A second function of evaluation is to revise the curriculum. If for the moment we conceive of the curriculum as a set of materials to be used by students or by the teacher in order to have educational consequences, then it becomes clear that such materials will need modification and improvements from the point of initial inception to the point where they are ready for general dissemination to the schools. This process—what Michael Scriven (1967) refers to as formative evaluation—has as its major aim the improvement of the program or curriculum that is being developed. In educational laboratories that develop curriculum materials, such evaluation goes through a variety of stages before the final product—in this case a package curriculum—is disseminated. One of these stages focuses on an evaluation of the content and aims of the curriculum. (Not all development processes start with aims and content. Curriculum activities themselves can provide a starting point for aims.) Before learning activities are created, there is some appraisal of the content that has been selected and the aims that have been formulated. This process, which itself is a part of the curriculum development process, lays the groundwork for transforming content and aims into promising learning activities: events that have as their intended consequences educational outcomes related to the subject matter or content employed in the first place.

Once the content has been appraised and learning activities have been formulated, the materials are hothouse tested, as described earlier. Among other things, this affords schools the opportunity to have contact with a developing educational enterprise that is stimulating to the school. It provides a type of Hawthorne effect for those teachers who elect to try the new material.

If the curriculum developer and an evaluator visit the classroom on appointment to watch the class use the materials and to observe the teacher and talk with him or her about the materials, the developer can gain some insight into the problems that exist and how they might be remedied. The materials might be too sophisticated for children of a particular age to use, the learning activities might turn out to be dull, the teacher might have difficulty handling the materials physically, the explanations might be misleading and therefore likely to be misunderstood, and so on. After the materials have been revised as a result of hothouse testing, the materials will be disseminated for field testing. Ideally, these stages of evaluation will yield curriculum materials that do not have major educational faults.

When the curriculum development movement got under way in the early 1960s, there was talk about the desirability of creating "teacherproof" curricula. That aspiration has, through the years, given way to the more realistic view that teachers are not mere tubes for curriculum developers. Teachers cannot and should not be bypassed. Materials guarantee nothing. What they do is to expand the range of resource with which teachers and students can work. They are not a substitute for teachers.

Using evaluation to revise the curriculum is in my view one of the central functions of evaluation. It is a type of feedback mechanism for educational improvement that diminishes the tendency to use evaluation practices simply as a means of classifying students, rewarding them, or selecting the able from the rest. Although classification, selection, and reward have been historically important functions of evaluation, when evaluation is used this way, the responsibility for performance shifts almost wholly to the student rather than the school. If students fail to perform, under conventional assumptions the fault lies with the students. (This assumption is widely prevalent in England and on the continent, where evaluation practices are designed to select the most able for the assignment to different forms of secondary schools and for university admission.) However, when student performance is viewed as an index of program effectiveness, the likelihood of curriculum improvement increases and a major contribution is made toward improving the quality of education.

Comparing Programs

A third function of evaluation is to compare programs, teaching, and other aspects of schooling such as forms of school organization. Educational policy is supposedly made with an eye toward improving the quality of educational experience the school provides. This means that when a school board decides that new school buildings will be designed on an open plan, there is implicit in that policy the belief that such a plan will have beneficial effects on the students for whom it is intended. Many, but not all, policy changes in school are based on certain values that the new policy is intended to realize. Often "new math" was adopted because people came to believe that it was important for students to understand the logic, or structure, of mathematics. The use of peer tutoring is embraced because it is believed that students teaching each other provide benefits that cannot be secured from a student-teacher relationship. Team teaching is used in schools because collaboration by teachers is thought to make it possible for them to exploit their strengths as teachers. Related arts programs are developed because such programs are considered to help students appreciate the common elements among the arts. Comparative approaches to evaluation ask whether these beliefs are true. Does the new math do more than the old math in helping students understand the structure of mathematics? Does peer tutoring have benefits that more typical teacher-pupil relationships fail to provide? And so forth. Insofar as educational policy rests on evidence concerning the effects of the alternatives being considered, the comparative evaluation of these programs, in principle, is one vehicle for making such evidence available.

There is, however, a set of paradoxes regarding the use of comparative methods for curriculum policy-making. In the first place, educational materials and modes of school organization are not susceptible to the kind of standardization that can be assigned to, say, light bulbs. If the electric company says that a light bulb will burn for about 740 hours, nine times out of ten its life will be close to that mark. Educational materials and new forms of educational practice cannot be standardized with the precision possible with materials that are inert; hence, a program evaluated as effective in one setting is not guaranteed to be effective in other settings. Moreover, the new setting will assuredly differ from the others in which the materials were originally used. Thus, a policy to adopt a new curriculum, to employ a new form of school organization, or to use a new procedure for scheduling must to a large degree be based on the attractiveness of such materials, modes of organization, and procedures rather than on "hard data."

Even if such data could be obtained, it might take several years to evaluate programs adequately to the point where hard data were available. By that time, the desire to implement the innovation might have run its course; its most ardent advocates might have left the district, the need for such innovation might have changed, or some new and even more promising innovations might have emerged on the horizon. Thus, comparisons of educational programs are difficult. They are difficult not only because of the reasons cited, but also because new programs most often tend to be aimed at the achievement of goals different from those that old programs were designed to achieve. It is seldom the case that the goals of existing programs are considered to be without merit. Hence, when one weighs the promise of a new program against that of an existing one, their effectiveness is found to be not strictly comparable. They aim at different ends. Because it is not a matter of one program doing better what another program does—that would be far easier—the problem of comparison is extremely complicated. Nevertheless, the effectiveness of different programs can be compared, if only in relation to their own goals and unanticipated consequences. Such a comparison will not provide simple and certain conclusions about what to adopt and implement, but it will expand the pool of considerations from which competent educational conclusions can be drawn.

Identifying Educational Needs

A fourth function of evaluation is to anticipate or identify educational needs. The concept of educational needs is directly related to the practice of needs assessment, in which various modes of data collection are employed with a community or school population in order to identify appropriate educational goals. For example, the U.S. Office of Education and later the National Institute of Education frequently required the writers of proposals for educational innovations first to do a needs assessment to demonstrate the existence of the need to be met through the proposed project. Writers of proposals would then employ tests of achievement and of attitude, conduct interviews, and determine public opinion by collecting statements from community leaders that there was a need for the program for which funding was sought. Needs assessment became the process for justifying the educational importance of educational innovation.

The practice of studying the community or the school population for which a program is intended is not unreasonable. At the same time, it is wise to be aware of the fact that educational needs are not like the clouds or the grass. They are not simply out there to be discovered by interviews or tests. Educational needs are the products of judgments about what counts in educational matters. What constitutes an educational need depends on the educational values one holds. In Chapter 3, some of the values that animate educational programs were identified. Clearly, someone who embraces academic rationalism will perceive educational needs differently from someone who is a social reconstructionist. The academic rationalist looks at the school population and concludes that the students are without an appreciation of the past, are ignorant of the major intellectual works of man, and cannot adequately reason. The social reconstructionist exclaims that students need to know that the environment is being poisoned, that bigotry and race hatred are rampant, and that the world needs a common government if it is to survive.

The influence of the values one brings to a situation is manifest in how one describes that situation. The selection of tests, the identification of relevant populations to study, the way in which data are secured and analyzed: these all reflect the values one considers important. If one values curiosity, imagination, and sensibility, it is possible to describe educational needs in these terms. If one values reading skill, arithmetical competency, and neatness, one looks for other types of data. In short, we look for data with which to determine educational needs by selecting subject matters to which we are already committed. In part, we find what we look for.

Determining if Objectives Have Been Achieved

A fifth function of evaluation, and the one most traditionally employed in curriculum theory, is as a means for determining whether educational objectives have been attained. The theory underlying this function of evaluation is straightforward. Educational programs should be purposeful; therefore, they should have goals. To be meaningful, these goals should be sufficiently specific to make it possible to determine whether they have been realized. The objectives once formulated at a meaningful level of specificity are the criteria through which student performance is assessed. Evaluation in this function is designed to provide the tasks and identify the situations that make possible the acquisition of data relevant to the objectives. Evaluation, therefore, can be used as a type of feedback mechanism to "recycle" the student if he or she fails to achieve the objectives, to pass him or her on to the next level if the objectives have been attained, to revise the curriculum if it is not effective for a particular student or group of students, or to alter the objectives.

This emphasis on use of evaluation conceives of clearly formulated objectives as a central and necessary condition for meaningful evaluation. It is argued, erroneously in my view, that there can be no evaluation without a "clear" statement of objectives. This assumption is embedded in much of the material on evaluation sent to school districts by state departments of education. Objectives are the criteria for determining whether the program has been effective. Evaluation is the means of collecting the data and analyzing them.

There is, of course, a reasonableness in the desire to have objectives in order to evaluate the effectiveness of an educational program. Yet, the evaluative net one casts can and ought to be much wider than the particular objective or set of objectives specified by a particular curriculum. The outcomes of educational programs are not completely predictable, and hence to evaluate only for those goals one has intended can lead one to neglect equally important, and at times even more important, outcomes that were unintended. Using objectives to serve as criteria for evaluating educational programs has an important function to perform, but a conception of evaluation that limits itself to what has been preplanned in terms of goals or objectives is likely to be educationally thin.

It should be noted that the use of objectives as a basis for evaluation has given rise to particular conceptions of educational practice. Mastery learning is one such practice (Bloom, 1976). Mastery learning theory posits that schools should not be primarily concerned with sorting out people through instruments that compare students to each other. Schools have historically performed the sorting role for society, and the result has been both frustration for those students who did not succeed and a loss of talented resources that society could have otherwise secured. Rather than attempt to sort out the able from the less able through evaluation procedures that are designed to compare students with each other, the school should formulate specific levels of mastery—particular objectives—and should evaluate students in relation to their mastery of these objectives, regardless of the amount of time it might take for particular students to attain mastery. Such a theory of educational practice would give virtually all students a sense of achievement and, in the long run, would contribute to their mental health as well as to their competence.

In describing mastery learning, I am simply pointing out the function that evaluation performs in such a view of educational practice. In this view, the form of evaluation called for requires a specific, operationally defined conception of mastery, hence, the need for a set of behavioral objectives.

The idea that evaluation should determine whether objectives have been achieved has given rise not only to the concept of mastery learning, but also to distinctions between two types of tests. These are *norm-referenced* and *criterion-referenced* tests (see Sax, 1976). In norm-referenced tests, of which IQ tests and most published achievement tests are examples, the performance of an individual or a group is compared with the performance of other individuals or groups. The test is constructed to discriminate between the performances of individuals and to enable the test maker or user to rank individuals within a group. Ranking can be individual or within groups, the most general being that of individuals whose performance places them in the upper half or in the lower half of a population of those who have taken the test. Rankings can be further refined into quartiles—the placement of individuals in the first, second, third, or fourth quarter of a population. Regardless of the particular scheme used, the distinguishing feature of norm-referenced tests is that the scores individuals achieve on such tests are reported and their meaning is interpreted in relation to the performance of others.

Criterion-referenced tests are designed to measure performance in relationship to some criterion (see Sax, 1976). The purpose is not to compare an individual with a group but to determine whether an individual has attained some criterion to which the test is referenced. An example might help illustrate this function.

When I was a boy of about 9 years of age I attended a summer camp located on a small lake in Illinois. On that lake there were three areas marked off by floats that were to be used for swimming by the boys in the camp. One area was for nonswimmers, a second for intermediate swimmers, and a third, which had a small wooden raft anchored to the bottom of the lake, for advanced swimmers. To get permission to swim to the raft that was in deep water, a boy had to be able to swim two laps of the intermediate section of the lake. If he could swim one and three-quarter laps, he had to use the intermediate section. It didn't matter whether a boy could swim three or 300 laps; all he needed to be able to swim to use the raft was two laps. That task, defined clearly in terms of a measurable competency, is an example of a criterion-referenced task or test. The issue was not one of comparing the swimming skills of the boys (although that inevitably happened)—it was to determine the presence of a competency.

Driver training programs, typing classes, and other skill-oriented courses use criterion-referenced tests. Indeed, contract learning—that form of educational practice in which teacher and student jointly form an agreement regarding the education task to be performed, the anticipated product, and the time of completion—is a not too distant relative of criterion-reference testing, which itself is related to the use of defined objectives as a basis of evaluation.

The Major Subject Matters of Evaluation

As I have indicated earlier, evaluation is a process than can be directed toward three important subject matters: the curriculum itself, the teaching that is provided, and the outcomes that are realized. Attention to the curriculum is justified on rather straightforward grounds. Unless one appraises the quality of the content and learning activities that constitute the curriculum, one has no basis for determining whether it is worth being taught. To paraphrase Plato, "The unexamined curriculum might not be worth learning."

Significance of the Content

But what are the aspects of the curriculum that can be evaluated, even prior to its implementation in the classroom? First, one can make some judgments about the educational significance of the content to which students will be exposed. Now the significance of the content can be determined only with criteria that flow from a set of values about what counts educationally. But whatever these criteria are, and they will differ for different groups and individuals, the application of such criteria is important for appraising the value of the curriculum in the first place. Some examples of how such criteria are applied might be helpful.

For years state boards of education and local school districts have engaged in the process of textbook selection. Textbooks, a fundamental element in most curricula, were adopted on the basis of attractiveness and feasibility as a teaching tool. It wasn't until the civil rights and women's liberation movements that states adopted specific criteria dealing with race and sexism to be used for evaluating textbooks and other curriculum material. Regardless of how attractive and significant the educational content of a textbook is, if it places minority groups in an unfavorable light or undermines the image of one of the sexes, it is to be rejected as suitable material for children in the schools. In California, the State Department of Education (1975) guidelines regarding the content of educational materials, including textbooks, state:

Male and Female Roles—Ed. Code 9240(a), 99243(a)

In order to encourage the individual development and self-esteem of each child, regardless of gender, instructional materials, when they portray people (or animals having identifiable human attributes), shall portray women and men, girls and boys, in a wide variety of occupational, emotional, and behavioral situations, presenting both sexes in the full range of their human potential.

Emotions—for example, fear, anger, aggression, excitement, or tenderness—should occur randomly among characters regardless of gender.

Traditional activities engaged in by characters of one sex should be balanced by the presentation of nontraditional activities for characters of that sex.

Ethnic and Cultural Groups—Ed. Code 9240(b) and 9243(a)

In order to project the cultural diversity of our society, instill in each child a sense of pride in his or her heritage, eradicate the seeds of prejudice, and encourage the individual development of each child, instructional materials, when portraying people (or animals having identifiable human attributes), shall include a fair representation of white and minority characters portrayed in a wide variety of occupational and behavioral roles, and present the contributions of ethnic and cultural groups, thereby reinforcing the self-esteem and potential of all people and helping the members of minority groups to find their rightful place in our society.

Obviously, these particular criteria, while important, represent only a limited range of those relevant to evaluate textbooks or curriculum. The intellectual significance of the content itself is, or ought to be, an important focus for appraisal. In the teaching of science, for example, what is the intellectual significance and validity of the concepts, generalizations, and subject matters with which students will deal? If the concepts are intellectually marginal and the generalizations trivial or so remote as to have little illuminative power for those other than specialists, it seems unlikely that schools should use their students' time to deal with that material. If ideas are being promulgated that are out of date, no longer valid, or simply insignificant, it makes little sense to spend a great deal of energy trying to help children learn such material. Some appraisal of the content of the curriculum in terms of its intellectual significance and the covert messages it might convey seems an appropriate focus for the evaluation for the curriculum.

But because curricula are intended for people and because people have different priorities, the appraisal of the curriculum needs also to be made with an eye toward its appropriateness for the population for whom it is intended. Determining the appropriateness of curriculum content takes at least two forms. First, it is important to determine whether the content and tasks the curriculum encompasses are within the development scope of the children who are to deal with it. Some kinds of content are inappropriate from a developmental point of view for the children of certain developmental levels. The concept of readiness, although at times abused in schools, can be employed to make judgments about the relationships between psychological tasks and content and the characteristics of the students. (The work of Jean Piaget is often used to support this view.) Thus, content within a curriculum might fare well from the standpoint of its significance within a discipline yet be rejected on the grounds that it is developmentally inappropriate for particular groups of children.

The second basis on which content may be evaluated deals with the experiential fitness of the content to the experiential background of the students. Curriculum content might be intellectually important and developmentally appropriate but still be ill-suited to the background or interests of the students. The importance of this criterion will, of course, vary with the curriculum orientation one embraces. To someone holding an academic rationalistic orientation, the need for students to be interested in a particular subject matter is likely to be less important than it is to someone concerned with personal relevance as a central condition of meaningful education. Yet this criterion can never be completely neglected. If the experiential background of students is so remote from the content encountered as to make it essentially meaningless, it is obvious that the curriculum, regardless of how defensible on other grounds, is inappropriate for that population. The point to remember here is that in evaluating the curriculum the educational significance of the content is a primary consideration. If the content is misleading or invalid, subsequent evaluation is not necessary. But even if the curriculum has been adjudged intellectually impeccable, one still has to appraise it both developmentally and experientially with respect to its suitability to the population for whom it is intended.

I have in the course of my work in education visited classrooms in Nigeria where 8-year-old Nigerian children were studying the Battle of Hastings. One can only wonder why out of all the possible subjects that those 8-year-old children might encounter they were studying the Battle of Hastings. There are good reasons why a former British colony should continue its traditions, but one might question the appropriateness and the meaningfulness of such content for those children. One does not have to travel to Nigeria to find similar situations in schools.

There are, of course, other criteria that can be used to evaluate the curriculum aside from the three already identified. As a matter of fact, any of the dimensions identified as relevant for curriculum development are also relevant for evaluating the curriculum after it is developed. Two examples should suffice.

You will recall that the forms used to display content and tasks to students and the forms through which their responses were elicited were identified as dimensions to be considered in curriculum development. If it is true that different forms of presentation provide different types of information, and that different forms of expression convey different types of understanding and insight, and if it is further assumed that the nurture of a wide range of human abilities is an educationally desirable goal, then it seems reasonable that educational materials, those materials that constitute a central portion of the curriculum, should employ the range of means available for both display and expression. This means in practical terms that curriculum materials can be evaluated with respect to the extent to which they employ visual, auditory, and kinesthetic modes of presentation as well as linguistic ones. It means also that the forms through which the students' competency is to be displayed can have a similar range. There is no intrinsic reason, except tradition, why curriculum materials must require a verbal mode of presentation and a linguistic form of response. Once we are willing to grant that the forms one uses to express oneself influence what one is capable of "saying" and that individuals differ with regard to their aptitude for using different sensory modalities for processing and expressing what they know, feel, or believe, the first steps are laid for justifying the use of diverse modes of presentation and response in the curriculum and classroom. To the extent to which we value this diversity and try to nurture it, it becomes important not only to construct, but also to evaluate materials with an eye to these values.

Quality of Teaching

The second major subject matter for evaluation is the quality of teaching that is provided. Although some educational theorists make no distinction between teaching and curriculum, I believe the distinction to be useful for several reasons. First, one can and usually does plan curriculum prior to using it in the classroom. Thus, curriculum development is a process, at least during some of its stages, that occurs outside of the classroom. Phillip Jackson (1968) refers to this as pre-active teaching. Second, and most important for the purposes of this chapter, the intellectual significance of curriculum can be appraised independently of how well it is taught. A teacher might do a brilliant job of teaching, but the ideas or skills being taught might be trivial, biased, or invalid. Conversely, a teacher might be using a faultless curriculum with respect to its intellectual merit and its appropriateness both developmentally and experientially for students, but that teacher might be teaching so poorly that only confusion and frustration result for the students. The educational problem in each of these cases is different, and without a distinction between curriculum and teaching I fear they will fail to emerge.

To evaluate the quality of teaching is, of course, easier to say than to do. Efforts at identifying the qualities that make for effective teaching have been many, but for the most part have not proved very illuminating. The approaches that have been taken to study and identify effective teaching have been scientific in character. The need for quantification, for explanation, for replicability, and for generalization has often led to a highly reductionistic approach to the study of teaching, one that attempts to locate specific causal relationships. The assumption is that by identifying specific causal units, eventually a holistic view of teaching will result. As yet this has not happened (Rosenshine & Furst, 1973). I will have more to say about the study of teaching later, but I would like to say now that there are aspects of teaching that can be evaluated by a sensitive student of classrooms: the type of relationships teachers establish with the classes, the clarity of their explanations, the level of enthusiasm they display, and the kinds of questions they raise. Although these specific qualities have not been demonstrated through quantitative empirical research to make for effectiveness, I believe that they are relevant considerations in evaluating what teachers do when they teach.

In stating that I believe they are relevant for evaluating teachers even though quantitative empirical research has not as yet demonstrated their efficacy, we approach the hub of an epistemological issue in education.

What is true? What counts as evidence? It is clear that scientific evidence about teaching or about most other aspects of educational practice is quite limited. There is very little in the way of hard data that can be used to justify educational practices, and even the little there is requires a nonscientific leap of faith because the sample from which the original conclusions were drawn is not likely to be identical to the population to whom the conclusion is to be applied. Indeed, if educational practitioners *had* to base their educational practices on hard data, we would have to close our schools. Yet, to assume that the only source of understanding is the laboratory is to render oneself helpless. There is much—to provide a gross understatement—that is useful from seasoned experience and critical reflection on that experience. The aspects of teaching that I have identified are only a few of the relevant dimensions that can be attended to and evaluated. Without evaluating teaching as well as the curriculum, one is not in a position to know, when there are difficulties, what their sources are.

Outcomes Achieved

The third major subject matter for evaluation and the most characteristically attended to is the evaluation of student outcomes. The selection of the term *outcomes* as opposed to *objectives* was not a casual one. Objectives are intended goals; they are the destinations one hopes to arrive at through the educational program. But roads taken do not always lead to the destination one intends, and even when they do, much can be learned en route. Thus *outcomes* is a broader term than *objectives*. The achievement of objectives can be included in the outcomes, but there is often much more to include as well.

Figure 6 presents a simple trichotomy of the kinds of outcomes that might be realized in a classroom. One segment of the circle deals with the outcomes that are subject-specific; a second segment deals with outcomes that are teacher-specific; and a third segment refers to outcomes that are pupil-specific.

Subject-specific outcomes are directly related to the content that is taught. Such outcomes can be, but are not necessarily, related to the objectives for the course. There are several reasons why subject-specific outcomes need not necessarily be related to course objectives. First, many courses in a field of study have no articulated objectives yet are educationally effective. Second, even when objectives are specified, outcomes may be realized that, although within the context of the subject studied, are not defined by the objectives. To evaluate with respect to subject-specific outcomes means to focus one's evaluation on the learning of the subject matter of a course or segment of the course. This is often done through the use of standardized or teacher-made achievement tests. Generally, such assessment focuses on outcomes within a subject that are common across students. A multiple-

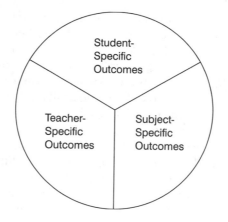

Figure 6

choice test, for example, presents to a population of students a common set of test items. Such items allow no scope for a personally constructed response; the alternatives are provided in the distractors from which the student must select. Thus, what such a test reveals is determined by the choice the test maker made during test construction. Hence, what one finds out about student understanding when such tests are used is what has been selected by the test constructor as being relevant. These are items sampled from the universe of content that the course has provided. And because in "objective" or multiple-choice tests little or no scope is provided for students to demonstrate their understanding of aspects of the course or content not sampled, those aspects simply fail to emerge for consideration.

Attention to what students learn about specific content within a course has been a primary and traditional concern of achievement testing. To find out what students have learned has almost always meant to find out what about the content taught they have learned. Such a focus is useful for evaluation, but it represents only one segment of a much more complex picture. Students learn not only what was intended, they also learn because of the unique intellectual relationships they make between the content and their other interests. They may be stimulated by the content of a course to learn things that are only tangentially related to the content. These outcomes, outcomes that are ripe for educational evaluation, are student-specific.

If one raises the question "What has a student learned in my class or course that is not about what I have been teaching?" one begins to move into student-specific domains. And if someone begins to develop procedures for obtaining some understanding of such outcomes, one is engaged in a student-specific mode of evaluation. Obviously, as long as the options presented to a student or group of students present no opportunity for the display of what might be called personalized learning, such outcomes will not be manifest. If we want to know what the personal spin-off is from the content or courses we teach, the tasks or methods used for evaluation have to be sufficiently open-ended to allow such personalized learning to emerge. Interviews, open-ended essays, and projects whose parameters provide opportunities for students to reveal what personal meanings they have constructed for themselves need to be made available. Such procedures will, of course, not be focused on providing comparative data. They are focused on the revelation of idiosyncratic outcomes.

Procedures that elicit idiosyncratic outcomes—in other words, personalized learning—are methodically distinct from procedures usually used in the construction of achievement tests. Typical procedures for the construction of achievement tests require not only that a common set of items be applied to a population of students, but also that items on which most students do well or items that systematically differentiate male from female performance be eliminated. The aim of typical achievement tests is to provide scores that make possible the differentiation of students. The type of differentiation sought arises from differences in performance on the same set of items for all students. In general, the closer the population's performance is to the normal curve, the greater the likelihood the test is statistically reliable.

Yet, applying a common set of items to assess a common content across a population of students can vitiate efforts to individualize teaching or to foster the development of students' aptitudes and interests. We often say that it is educationally desirable to encourage students to pursue particular interests within school and that teachers should be flexible and imaginative in developing programs particularly appropriate for the individuals with whom they work. However, the use of tests that seek only common outcomes from a content area common to all students can be and often is inconsistent with such aims. If we are really serious about curriculum differentiation for students, the need for student-specific forms of evaluation will become increasingly important.

The third segment of student outcomes is represented by those that flow from what the teacher teaches about him- or herself. The intellectual style the teacher displays, the standards that he or she upholds, the willingness to take risks, the tolerance for nonconformity, the type of precision and punctuality he or she values: these aspects of the teacher as a person are not necessarily trivial aspects of teaching. Indeed, because these features are likely to be more pervasive than the content studied, it might be that they have important consequences for what students learn. Studying with a really great teacher, whether in elementary school or at the highest levels of the university, can help a student more than exposure to some particular body of content.

What do the personal qualities of teachers mean for the elementary-school age children with whom they spend 5 or more hours each day for 40 school weeks? At present these questions are not answerable. Conventional conceptions of educational evaluation have seldom included them in the procedures used to assess the effects of schooling. Yet, these questions and others that could be raised, it seems to me, are nontrivial aspects of schooling. Unless one is aware of the possibility of educationally significant effects issuing from the characteristics, values, and interests of teachers, it is not likely that answers to such questions will be obtained. It would be interesting to ask students to characterize the contributions, other than those provided by course content, that their teachers made to them. What would students say about those contributions? Do those who work with particular teachers over extended periods of time display particular characteristics, interests, attitudes, or styles of inquiry that derive from characteristics of their teachers? A comprehensive theory of educational evaluation would include teacher-specific outcomes as at least one of three that warrant examination.

How Can Educational Evaluations Be Reported Artistically?

How can what occurs in a classroom or school be made vivid to a public that wants increasingly to know what it is getting for its investment in schools? The typical procedures for reporting the educational efficacy of schools have been twofold. First, parents have been led to believe that the grades their children receive adequately portray how well their children are doing in school and by implication how well the school is doing by the child. Good grades mean that the child is doing well; poor grades mean that the child is doing poorly, although as educational consumerism increases, poor grades might come to mean that the school rather than the child has done poorly.

The other major vehicle for reporting to the public how schools do is through the use of standardized testing. In many states, standardized achievement tests are mandated by the state legislature, and in some cities newspapers publish the mean performance by grade of students in schools within the school district. Parents and other citizens read such reports and draw conclusions about the educational quality of the school or school district by the rank that a school or school district occupies in some regional or national distribution. These scores are usually "unencumbered" by socioeconomic considerations or by any other factors of conditions that could influence test scores. Thus, the public has before it an array of test scores that provide a deceptive sense of educational precision. Although no competent educator would claim that performance on standardized reading and math tests adequately represents educational quality, these test scores, for all practical purposes, have become the major indices the public uses to judge the effectiveness of schools. And because the public uses such scores, school administrators feel the need to focus their teachers' attention onto activities that are likely to lead to high standardized test scores. A school that succeeds (and by extension an administrator who is effective) is one whose students receive high standardized test scores.

Thus, we have something of an educational irony. Most educators would say that neither letter grades nor standardized test scores capture the richness of educational experience, nor do they adequately disclose the quality of education provided and experienced in the school. Yet schools do reward students with honors classes and deans' lists based on such grades and therefore legitimize the importance of grades while recognizing their limitations. Although educators point out that standardized test scores do not necessarily represent what students are learning, the administration of such tests proliferates and the subsequent publication of their results has consequences that are as often as misleading as they are informative.

This state of affairs stems from several sources. First, the aspiration for precision in evaluation has manifested itself in the quantification of student performance, which in turn is translated into grades. Somehow a type of precise objectivity is implied when complex forms of learning are reduced to a single score or letter. Second, parents often want an unambiguous indicator of their child's or the school's performance. To suggest contingencies or qualifications concerning the performance of students or the school is for many parents to inject an uncomfortable degree of uncertainty and complexity. Simplicity, even if it is misleading, is often preferable to the kind of complexity that an educational connoisseur might perceive.

This preference for the simple and the neat is not unrelated to the correct assessment that parents make of the criteria that their children must meet if they are to have upward educational mobility. Admission to universities is heavily influenced by the rank students hold in high school. And class rank is a function of the grades received. In short, the criteria applied to students for purposes of selection and retention in the hierarchy of schooling reinforce the use of a grading system that can be easily translated into simple, numerical indices. Grade-point average, class standing, college board scores: these are far easier to compare in a competitive educational market than widely diverse, even if illuminating, forms of educational disclosure. We seek to reduce diversity in order to have a uniform scale on which comparisons can be made.

A third reason standardized test scores and grades have become the basis for judging educational quality is that we have not provided the public with alternatives. By neglect of such alternatives, a tradition of grading practices has been established. The public expects it. Yet, if we think about the reporting problem—helping parents and others to understand what has taken place in schools—a wide array of possibilities come to mind.

The problem of disclosing the character of educational events and the quality of what children are learning can, I am arguing, be conceived as an artistic problem. How can the results of educational evaluation be communicated so that the complexity *and* ambiguity *and* richness of what happens in schools and classrooms can be revealed?

Part of the answer to this question depends on the recognition that people communicate through different expressive modalities and that each modality has the power to convey different types of understanding. Quantitative indices are useful for some purposes but not for all. Written descriptions are helpful for understanding some events, but they cannot duplicate visual images for some purposes. Statistically derived norms are helpful for locating trends but neglect the unique occurrence. In short, if one considers the range of ways through which people come to express and understand and compares it with the range used for reporting the results of educational evaluations, it becomes apparent that only a slender slice of educational life is likely to be captured by the forms of reporting that are typically used. To capture this richness and therefore to help the public understand and appreciate the problems as well as the achievements of a classroom or school requires the construction of an evaluational landscape. Such a picture will probably employ a wide range of information secured from a variety of sources and revealed through different types of reporting procedures.

One of these procedures is likely to be what I referred to as educational criticism (see Alexander, 1977; Barone, 1978; Davidman, 1976; Fielders, 1979; Flinders, 1987; Greer, 1973; Hagberg, 1983; Hawthorne, 1988; Kuntz, 1986; McCutcheon, 1976; Sternberg, 1977; Taylor, 1993; Thornton, 1985; Uhrmacher, 1991; and Vallance, 1975). Such criticism would be aimed at helping parents, let us say, understand what has happened during the course of a school year in a particular school. What were the key events in the school? How did they come into being? In what ways did students and teachers participate? What consequences for the school did such events have? How could such events be strengthened? What do such events enable children to learn?

What is Mrs. Jones's classroom like? In what sorts of activities have the children engaged? What does Mrs. Jones provide that is uniquely hers? What is the character of the school day for children in her class? What are children deriving from her class that is not likely to be revealed by standardized testing? Questions such as these, if answered by a competent educational critic, would give parents an understanding of the school and the classroom that most at present do not have. Even parents who value education very highly have only the vaguest ideas about the kind of educational experience provided by the school their children attend. In the first place, report cards, if they are used, give no indication of the sorts of events I have described. The major focus of report cards is on how "well" the child is doing according to some criterion that itself is vague. And if the school is one where parent-teacher conferences are held in lieu of formal report cards, even then the discussion between parent and teacher is more likely to focus on the student's performance than on the program in which he or she is participating.

Another vehicle for disclosing the richness of educational programs to parents is through the use of film and videotape. One can capture on film or tape aspects of educational life that give a vivid picture to parents and others of what the school actually provides. The creation of such tapes and films will of course demand skills that most evaluators do not at present possess. Yet, the absence of such skills is no argument against developing them. The use of film and videotape, even the use of still slides and photographs, can be extremely informative if they have been taken with an artistic, educationally informed eye. The task of making such visual materials the sources of educational disclosure has scarcely been touched. There have been films made of schools, such as *High School* by Frederick Wiseman, that are powerful statements about the quality of life in an urban high school, and by extension in others. That film is extremely skillful in portraying certain aspects of high school life, but its strength is at the same time a source of its weakness. It exaggerates to make a point—it is a visual polemic. It does not attempt to disclose the strengths of the school it portrays, but instead accentuates its oppressive, mindless, military character. Informed educational criticism and the informed educational use of videotape and film would aim at a more circumspect view of educational life. Supplemented by critical narrative, such visual materials considerably expand the channels for communication.

The use of still photography is also potentially powerful in revealing aspects of educational life that measured achievement and even artful criticism cannot capture. Paradigm cases of such visual renderings already exist, perhaps the most notable being Alfred Stieglitz's *The Family of Man.* Since Stieglitz created that exhibition, numerous other portfolios of visual reporting have appeared. What these portfolios offer us, and what they could portray about the educational quality of life in schools, is a nondiscursive mode of disclosure capable, when artistically created, of helping us vicariously participate in the life that the school provides. At present, the use of such vehicles as an explicit form of educational reporting is virtually absent from the scene in American education. When it does occur, it is by accident, connected to a student yearbook or newspaper but not as part of formal resources the school uses to understand and report what it is doing.

During the past few years, increased attention has been focused on the use of nontext materials to portray schooling. This interest among educators parallels the relatively recent interest among anthropologists in what is called *visual anthropology.* Implicit in this newfound interest in both education and anthropology is the recognition that the form one uses to represent the world defines the parameters within which the content of expression and communication occurs. Not everything, even through the efforts of a highly talented writer, can be expressed in words. Some things, for example, need to be expressed through visual images. Pictures portray what words may never be able to reveal. Hence, to limit one's expressive options to words, particularly to propositional language, is to limit what can be conveyed about the world in which we are interested (see Smith, 1982).

Educational criticism and the use of videotape, cinematography, and still photography can be supplemented with still other types of information that would provide a more comprehensive and adequate picture of school life. One of these supplements is tape-recorded interviews of both students and teachers that deal with their work and its aims, their satisfactions, the situations and problems they encounter, their ideas about educational improvement, their aspirations in the school, the outcomes they value most and least, and so forth. Taped interviews on cassettes could be produced and edited in a way that would deal with ideas, beliefs, and feelings that seldom get expressed on written questionnaires and are never possible to express on achievement tests. The spontaneity of the interview, when it is conducted by a skillful interviewer, one who knows both interview techniques and education theory and practice, could yield data that are at present simply unavailable.

It should be noted that listening to tape-recorded interviews may itself require a type of connoisseurship that needs to be developed. What is said and what is not said, how something is said, the tone of expression, and so forth—all of the nonlinguistic cues that possess meaning—need to be penetrated if what one says is to be fully appreciated. Nevertheless, all of us have developed such skills to a considerable degree—they are survival skills—and even if they are not refined to an optimum level, we have learned how to listen sufficiently well to get much of what others say.

Additional information that could be used to construct an adequate evaluation of a school or classroom would include an analysis of the work that children produce. In typical evaluation procedures, examination scores, grades received on essays, and ratings of projects undertaken and completed are the data that are reported to parents about the progress their children are making in school. When this is done, it is seldom clear whether, for example, a grade of B on an essay refers to the quality of the essay in relation to other essays produced by students in the class, whether it is based on the efforts put forth by the student in writing the essay, whether it represents the amount of growth the student has achieved since the beginning of the semester, or whether it is based on a combination of all these criteria. These procedures for grading are not the ones I am referring to as an analysis of what children produce in school. The problem with such procedures is that they provide conclusions rather than disclosures about the character of the work done and the sorts of progress and problems children encounter. To do the latter would require, first, close attention to what a given child or class has created. If the work is an essay, one might describe how a child has organized his or her essay, the quality of the arguments or evidence he or she employs, the extent to which his or her imagination has been used to create the work. These aspects of the work could be treated comparatively with other work created by the child or the class and could be accompanied by a critique that would help adults or children understand what has been accomplished. If, for example, one wants to help a school board or a group of parents understand that human development is uneven, that children of the same age are at quite different places with respect to skills or understanding, it would be useful to display the range of work—not just the best work—that the children in class create. The display of only the best conceals the range of differences and distorts the real educational picture with which teachers must work. The visual display of such range when critically described and analyzed would do much to make apparent to a school board, for example, some of the realities of classroom performance.

The major point I am attempting to make here is that the problem of communicating to some public—parents, school board members, students, state agencies—about what has happened in schools, the problem of making known what is strong and what is weak, what needs support and what does not, can be usefully conceived as an artistic problem. It is a problem of putting together an expressive, sensitive, and revealing picture of educational practice and its consequences. The construction of such a picture can exploit both the various modalities that people have always used to communicate and also the new technology that can capture and hold even the most evanescent happenings in classroom life.

That this approach to educational evaluation is rare can be appreciated by examining evaluation studies. These studies virtually always are characterized by the attempt to be quantitatively "objective" and impersonal and to focus on measured achievement with no attention paid to the relationship between what was done (the process) and what ensued (the product). Conventional training in evaluation still bears the imprint of psychometrics. Although psychometric techniques are useful for describing some aspects of education performance, they by no means embrace the entirety of what counts educationally. When young evaluators are trained in psychometrics and neglect the normative and theoretical aspects of educational practice, the problem is compounded. Education is a normative enterprise. What counts educationally depends on one's educational values. The reduction of educational evaluation to a set of limited quantitative methods, ones that harbor their own values, which often go unacknowledged or unappraised, is to reduce educational evaluators to technicians and evaluation to a technical process. Educational evaluation is more than that, however. No narrow range of technical skills applied to educational settings is likely to reveal the richness of their context. To interpret the meaning of even that which is secured through parochial means requires some vision of educational virtue and some understanding of the history of educational practice.

It might seem strange to mention the importance of the history of education and educational theory in the context of discussing educational evaluation. These subjects are seldom found in such discourse, and when they occur as part of the educational program of prospective evaluators, more often than not they are there to meet institutional requirements rather than because they are considered important. Yet I hope I have made the point that education evaluation requires a sophisticated, interpretive map not only to separate what is trivial from what is significant in educational settings, but also to understand the meaning of what has been seen. Without a normative and historical perspective, the interpretation and appraisal of educational events are impoverished.

References

Alexander, R. (1977). *Educational criticism of three art history classrooms.* Unpublished doctoral dissertation, Stanford University, Stanford, CA.

Barone, T. (1978). *Inquiring into classroom experiences: A qualitative holistic approach.* Unpublished doctoral dissertation, Stanford University, Stanford, CA.

Bloom, B. (1976). *Human characteristics and school learning.* New York: McGraw-Hill.

California State Department of Education. (1975). *Guidelines for evaluation of instructional materials for compliance with content requirements of the educational code.* Sacramento: Author

Davidman, L. (1976). *A formative evaluation of the unified science and mathematics in the elementary school curriculum.* Unpublished doctoral dissertation, Stanford University, Stanford, CA.

Eisner, E. W. (1991). *The enlightened eye: Qualitative inquiry and the enhancement of educational practice.* New York: Macmillan.

Fielders, J. (1979). *Action and reaction: The role of an urban school superintendent.* Unpublished doctoral dissertation, Stanford University, Stanford, CA.

Flinders, D. (1987, June). *What teachers learn from teaching: Educational criticisms of instructional adaptation.* Unpublished Ph.D. dissertation, Stanford University, Stanford, CA.

Greer, W. D. (1973). *The criticism of teaching.* Unpublished doctoral dissertation, Stanford University, Stanford, CA.

Hagberg, H. (1983). *Don't be teachin Jovita wrong: An exploration of reading instruction in four urban third grade classrooms.* Unpublished doctoral dissertation, Stanford University, Stanford, CA.

Hawthorne, P. (1973, August). *Legislation by the states: Accountability and assessment in education* (No. 2). : Wisconsin Department of Public Instruction.

Hawthorne, R. (1988, March). *Classroom curriculum: Educational criticisms of teacher choice.* Unpublished doctoral dissertation, Stanford University, Stanford, CA.

Jackson, P. (1968). *Life in classrooms.* New York: Holt, Rinehart & Winston.

Kuntz, J. S. J. (1986, August). *The transmission of values in two Jesuit high school classrooms.* Unpublished doctoral dissertation, Stanford University, Stanford, CA.

McCutcheon, G. (1976). *The disclosure of classroom life.* Unpublished doctoral dissertation, Stanford University, Stanford, CA.

Plato. (1956). *The Republic.* (B. Jowett, Trans.). New York: The Modern Library.

Rosenshine, B., & Furst, N. (1973). The use of direct observation to study teaching. In Robert Travers (Ed.), *Second handbook of research in teaching.* Chicago: Rand McNally.

Sax, G. (1976). The use of standardized tests in evaluation In W. James Popham (Ed.), *Evaluation in education: Current applications* (pp. 243–308). Berkeley, CA: McCutchan.

Scriven, M. (1967). The methodology of evaluation. In M. Scriven, *AERA Monograph Series on Curriculum Evaluation* (Vol. 1). Chicago: Rand McNally.

Smith, N. L. (Ed.). (1982). *Communication strategies in education.* Beverly Hills, CA: Sage.

Sternberg, B. (1977). *What tokens and trophies teach.* Unpublished doctoral dissertation, Stanford University, Stanford, CA.

Taylor, L. (1993, June). *At home in schools: A qualitative inquiry into Christian home schools.* Unpublished doctoral dissertation, Stanford University, Stanford, CA.

Thornton, S. (1985, August). *Curriculum consonance in United States history classrooms.* Unpublished doctoral dissertation, Stanford University, Stanford, CA.

Uhrmacher, B. (1991, May). *Waldorf schools marching quietly unheard.* Unpublished doctoral dissertation, Stanford University, Stanford, CA.

Vallance, E. (1975). *Aesthetic criticism and curriculum description.* Unpublished doctoral dissertation, Stanford University, Stanford, CA.

9

❧

Reshaping Assessment
in Education

———————◆•◦•◆———————

All things that exist, exist in some amount.
EDWARD L. THORNDIKE

There are more things in heaven and earth, Horatio,
Than are dreamt of in your philosophy.
SHAKESPEARE

———————◆•◦•◆———————

If there ever was a time in which the calls were clearer or more strident for new, more authentic approaches to educational assessment, I cannot remember when. Yet, despite its saliency, the term *assessment* is more an aspiration than a concept that has a socially confirmed technical meaning. The older term, *evaluation*, although not particularly ancient in the literature of American education, is no longer as popular as it once was; the term assessment has given it a gentle but firm nudge.

Before discussing assessment, explaining why it has emerged, and proposing some of the new criteria it ought to meet, it is useful to examine the historical and ideological ground on which what we call educational evaluation emerged. Once having examined the terrain, we should have a better picture of the significance of current efforts to create new forms of educational assessment.

As most probably know, the early attempts to create a science of the social emerged during the Enlightenment. During the late 17th and 18th centuries, scholars such as Condorcet and Condillac (Berlin, 1966) attempted to grasp the order of nature by studying it through the scientific methods advanced by Galileo and his followers. The spirit that animated Galileo, Condorcet, Condillac, Newton, and later Auguste Comte was a conviction that the world could be studied through procedures that not only revealed its regularities, but also brought them under a theoretical net that would satisfy the human's need to know. No longer beyond our control, humans could come to understand how the world actually operated, beliefs about its features could be empirically tested and, in some cases, nature itself could be brought under control (Toulmin, 1990).

The psychological laboratories developed in Germany by Fechner and Wundt and in England by Galton in the latter part of the 19th century represented efforts to apply to the study of human beings the methods that had been applied to nature; humans were surely a part of nature and if nature could be understood, why not humans? American psychology in general, and American educational psychology in particular, were rooted in European soil and the ideas that guided their growth were essentially the same: to come to understand how nature works and through such knowledge to control its operations. Our aim in the West was not to create a partnership.

These ideals are themselves based on several core beliefs. First was the belief that nature was orderly; it possessed a pattern and this pattern could be identified. Second was the faith that rational procedures, epitomized by science, could be used to discover those natural regularities. Third was the belief that theoretical ideas about the regularities of nature could be constructed and that the truth of these ideas could be determined. Fourth was an admiration for the virtues of quantification. Mathematics had an order and possessed a precision that would diminish both subjectivity and the presence of untestable speculation. It lent itself to the dominant conception of rationality permeating the science of the social, and, in addition, the data it provided could be treated by the tools emerging from the newly developing field of statistics. Measurement, rationality, theoretical explanation, and eventually prediction and control were the hallmarks of the emerging science. The overall aim, rooted in the Enlightenment, was to create an objectively detached true description of the world as it really is.

American educators, and particularly American educational psychologists, saw promise in these methods, for with them educational practice itself could become a scientifically guided activity (Joncich, 1968). For the first time, educational practice could be grounded in true understandings of how humans learn and educational policy could be formulated by appealing to scientific knowledge. One of the most vivid manifestations of such beliefs is found in that practice invented by Fredrick Taylor called scientific management and, in education, its progeny, the efficiency movement, with its stopwatch efforts to measure human performance and its prescriptions to teachers on how teaching could be made more efficient (Callahan, 1962). It also manifested itself in the eugenics movement in its efforts to apply scientific principles to social policy. And it emerged in the powerful scientific legacy that Edward L. Thorndike left to American education (Joncich, 1968).

American educators found in Thorndike a useful ally, for unlike his contemporary, Sigmund Freud, Thorndike was interested in learning and his research and theories concerning learning had practical implications for both teachers and writers of textbooks. Thorndike's notions of *frequency*, *recency*, and *intensity* were guiding ideals for pedagogical practice and his theory of identical elements—namely, the belief that transfer of learning occurs only insofar as the elements in one situation were identical to those in the other (Thorndike, 1910)—became lawlike in their significance in the training of teachers.

It is not surprising that the new field of education, just out of its infancy, should look to science to provide what is intellectually respectable. The first normal schools in America were founded in the 1850s and they needed more than an apprenticeship model to secure intellectual legitimacy. The science of the social was there to provide it. The work that was done in Europe by Wundt and others provided the intellectual grounding for what American pedagogues needed.

The scientific conception of method and knowledge that was initiated in Europe and developed in America during the early part of this century has profoundly influenced how we think about education today. Much of this influence was carried by the test and measurement movement, which was given special impetus with Robert Yerkes' (1929) work on the Alpha and Beta tests. The Alpha and Beta tests were commissioned by the Army to identify levels of literacy among enlisted men during the First World War and to select those who were suitable for officers training school. These group tests helped demonstrate the practical utility and social relevance of the social sciences. In fact, they represented a conception of testing and evaluation that is only now beginning to change.

There is no doubt that educational measurement has become a highly refined and sophisticated field. It has not only its own distinctive history, it also has its own journals, its own training programs, and if Education Testing Service (ETS) is any example, its own industry. The creation of standardized achievement tests and the use of bubble sheets and optical scanners have made it possible for the American public to get a quick (if often illusory) fix on the state of schooling. Given the efficiency of new scoring methods, the public's desire to know how schools are doing, and the virtual absence of competing indicators, achievement testing has become one of the most visible and influential manifestations of scientific technology at work in education.

Yet as efficient as the optical scanner is, it became clear during the educational reform efforts of the 1960s that standardized achievement tests could not adequately assess the outcomes of the new curricula. The curriculum reform movement of the 1960s represented an effort not only to catch up with Soviet achievements in space, but also to rethink what was being taught in schools and to achieve aims that had not previously been conceptualized. These aims were formidable. For the first time, we wanted students to learn how to think like scientists, not just ingest the products of scientific inquiry (Bruner, 1961). We wanted students to understand the structure of mathematics, not just be competent at computation. Furthermore, the creation of new curricula was not a simple undertaking; even the best of our seemingly good ideas might not fly in third grade classrooms. We recognized that we needed to evaluate not only what students learn, but the program that was intended to enable them to do so. Michael Scriven's (1967) terms *formative and summative evaluation,* as much as any, became the new banners of the day. Evaluation, not merely testing, came into its own.

Educational evaluation had a mission broader than testing. It was concerned not simply with the measurement of student achievement, but with the quality of curriculum content, with the character of the activities in which students were engaged, with the ease with which teachers could gain access to curriculum materials, with the attractiveness of the curriculum's format, and with multiple outcomes, not only single ones. In short, the curriculum reform movement gave rise to a richer, more complex conception of evaluation than the one tacit in the practices of educational measurement. Evaluation was conceptualized as a part of a complex picture of the *practice* of education.

With this enlarged focus, there was a subtle but significant shift in epistemology. This shift is perhaps best represented in Schwab's (1969) seminal article on "the practical." The shift was from regarding evaluation as a predominantly knowledge-seeking activity to a decision-making one. Once evaluation was conceptualized as an important element within the complex of educational practice, it was expected to contribute to the enhancement of practice. Yet practical activities are not so much focused on trying to determine what is true as in making good decisions. To treat curriculum, teaching, and evaluation as practical activities is to shift not only focus, but also the *kind* of knowledge considered relevant: the meaning of knowledge slowly, but ineluctably, became related to what Aristotle (McKeon, 1941) called phronesis or, more simply, practical as distinct from theoretical knowledge. It was not concerned with identifying immutable patterns in nature, but providing context-dependent, tentative information useful for making defensible decisions.

At about the same time as the curriculum reform movement was in high gear (the late 1960s), another development emerged that also had a significant long-term effect on our views of assessment: the empirical, qualitative, interpretive study of what goes on in schools and classrooms.

Willard Waller (1932), a sociologist who worked in the 1930s, is often credited with making the first modern study of teaching in the public

RESHAPING ASSESSMENT IN EDUCATION   ◆   199

schools. But in more recent years, Philip Jackson's *Life in Classrooms* (1968) must be regarded as one of the most influential. Jackson's 1968 study is the result of over a year of observations of how teachers taught. It is rich in description, insightful, beautifully written, compelling. At about the same time, there appeared Lou Smith's and William Geoffrey's *The Complexities of an Urban Classroom* (1968). A beginning had been made. Returning to schools to find out what was going on, something Schwab had urged, became important—even stylish.

These early ventures revealed empirically what people like John Dewey had known and said years earlier. In *Experience and Education* (1938), Dewey remarked that "One of the greatest of educational fallacies is that the student only learns what he is being taught." What visitors to classrooms discovered for themselves is that classroom life, not to mention life in schools as a whole, is complex, unpredictable, and much less tidy than the systematizers and scientific managers had imagined. The early 20th century ideal of achieving scientific efficiency in the management of classrooms and teaching by following standardized procedures designed to eliminate wasted motion seemed quaint, indeed at odds with the unpredictable character of 8- or even 18-year-olds. The game was considerable more complicated.

To give order to such complexity some disciplined set of procedures had to be found. Enter ethnography.

It is not difficult to understand why ethnography is attractive as a way of studying educational practice. First, for those committed to the development of a scientific understanding of education, ethnography, as a branch of cultural anthropology, is within the family of the social sciences: the stretch is not wrenching. Second, ethnography, to paraphrase Clifford Geertz (1973), is about the inscription of cultural meaning. Inscription stabilizes thought and makes it available for inspection and correction. Such an aim seems appropriate to many of those who wish to understand schools. Third, ethnographic practices have almost as long a history as psychology. Although these practices seem much more tidy to outsiders than they actually are, the scientifically minded believed that ethnography could be employed to discover the basic patterns of classroom life and to systematically unearth its deep structure. Ethnographic-like accounts of schools and classrooms have, of course, emerged in not only Jackson's and Smith's work but in the work of Barone (1983), Erickson (1982), Lightfoot (1983), Peshkin (1986), Rist (1972), Wolcott (1984), and others. Indeed, many of the graduate courses offered in schools of education designed to teach students how to use qualitative methods in educational research employ ethnographers as teachers.

I will not now describe the strengths and limitations of ethnography as a way of studying and assessing educational practice. Both its strengths and limitations are many and they are significant. My main aim is to trace the ideological shifts in the study, evaluation, and improvement of education. We began with the aspiration to develop a science of the social, one that relied on mathematical accounts to describe natural regularities in the life of human beings. We moved to scientific management, represented in the efficiency movement, and next to the technology of testing intended to measure the educational productivity of schools and teachers. We then noted the shift from the reliable measurement of student achievement to a broader interest in evaluation as a way of understanding and enhancing educational practice, including the improvement of school curricula. From there we moved to the study of schools and classrooms as social-educational organizations through procedures resembling ethnography.

Although no description of the past ever has as much fidelity to actual events as the writer makes out, I believe the journey I have described so far adumbrates the general contours of the trip that has been taken and sets the stage for an examination of our current situation. It is to this situation— the emergence of new conceptions of educational assessment—to which I will now turn my attention.

The Recent Past and the Current Scene

To begin, one might reasonably ask why the broader conception of educational evaluation that was stimulated by the curriculum reform movement of the 1960s did not take hold and continue. Why are we now turning to an interest in what is called assessment, indeed not only assessment, but *authentic* assessment (Wiggins, 1989)? What happened between the end of the curriculum reform movement and the current interest in finding new and better ways to determine what students are learning?

What happened was the American public's growing concern about the quality of American schools. During the 1970s, it became increasingly clear that Scholastic Aptitude Test (SAT) scores were dropping (Harnischfeger & Wiley, 1975), and we were hearing from the armed forces that recruits could not read well enough to use the manuals prepared for the equipment with which they were to work. "Bonehead" English was oversubscribed, even in prestigious universities having selective admission policies, and the private sector complained that the recent high school graduates that they were hiring needed to be retrained—the schools had failed them.

As a result of such concerns, the remedy—at least to the American public and to government policymakers—seemed clear. Establish minimum standards for local school districts, design achievement tests to measure what students had learned, and monitor the system carefully. In a word, the operative term became *accountability*. Accountability was largely defined in terms of testing. Achievement testing became the means through which schools would become accountable to a concerned public. The decade between the mid-1970s and the mid-1980s was a decade that returned to the past. *Back* to the basics was the watchword. The broad view of educational evaluation that emerged with the curriculum reform movement of the 1960s could not withstand the criticisms stimulated by declining SAT scores, dissatisfied employers, and our inferior international position in mathematics achievement. Neither the public nor the policymakers were happy about the state of American education: it was time to get tough.

The demand for higher standards and demonstrated achievement began to soften in the mid-1980s. It became clear to some that educational standards are not raised by mandating assessment practices or urging tougher tests, but by increasing the quality of what is offered in schools and by refining the quality of teaching that mediates it. The problem is not one of correct policy formation. Policies are relatively easy to formulate and often easier to mandate. The problem is one of practice. Good teaching and substantive curricula cannot be mandated, they have to be "grown."

Furthermore, assessment (the new term) needed to be more generous, more complex, more closely aligned with life than with individual performance measured in an antiseptic context using sanitized instruments that were untouched by human hands. The model needed to be changed and the term assessment symbolized this ambition. In sum, the modern birth of educational evaluation as a field associated with the curriculum reform movement was not strong enough to withstand the public's need to get down to brass tacks, to go back to the basics, to measure, to monitor, to mandate. A decade later, however, we find ourselves exploring new routes to excellence, partly because we have recognized that mandates do not work, partly because we have come to realize that the measurement of outcomes on instruments that have little predictive or concurrent validity is not an effective way to improve schools, and partly because we have become aware that unless we can create assessment procedures that have more educational validity than those we have been using, change is unlikely.

Some Functions of Assessment

The exploration and development of the new approaches to assessment have made some things quite clear. Assessment, like educational evaluation, is not one but several things. It performs different functions and needs to be regarded in light of the educational functions it is intended to perform. For example, one function of assessment is a kind of *educational temperature-taking*. The National Assessment of Educational Progress performs a temperature-taking function. Its purpose is not to provide information about the performance of individual students or even individual school districts, but to describe "the educational health" of the nation. It does this by using a multiple matrix sampling technique that makes it possible to report to the

American public the performance of 9-, 13-, and 17-year-olds by gender and region of the country on tasks that are not limited to the specific content taught in schools.

A second function of assessment is a *gatekeeping* function. The Scholastic Aptitude Test is designed to measure individual students' aptitudes for work in college. Although colleges and universities claim that SAT scores do not *determine* who they admit, SAT scores do influence admission decisions. Other gatekeeping functions are served by bar examinations, medical board examinations, and many final course exams that are used to determine who passes and who does not.

A third function of assessment is to determine whether *course objectives have been attained*. In this, its classical use, assessment in schools is sometimes used for gatekeeping functions and sometimes to help teachers provided remedial help to students who need it.

A fourth function of assessment is to provide *feedback to teachers* on the quality of their professional work. Teaching is a complex and subtle art. What makes a lesson fly or flop may be due to the way in which information is provided, the way a teacher defines tasks for students, or by the way in which a teacher responds to students' questions. The teacher cannot or does not notice many of the subtle qualities of teaching that matter. The assessment of teaching can help a teacher become more informed and more reflective about his or her own performance so that it can be improved.

A fifth function of assessment focuses on the *quality of the program* that is being provided. Although the least prominent of assessment functions, this function is arguably one of the most important. What is the quality of the educational diet provided? What is the character of the activities in which students are engaged? What is the sequential nature of the events in the program as it unfolds over time? How attractive are the materials students and teachers use? All of the foregoing are questions designed to reveal the quality of the program as such. If the program's quality is poor to begin with, the quality of teaching does not matter much: if it's not worth teaching, it's not worth teaching well.

In a sense, all of the foregoing functions—and there are others I have not identified—can be reduced to the assessment of the program that is provided, the quality of teaching, and outcomes that result from the interaction of the first two. Program evaluation, teacher evaluation, and student evaluation are the major areas of focus for any form of educational assessment. One important realization that has emerged in the past few years is that different forms of evaluation—or assessment—are required for different functions. To help a teacher understand how he or she performs requires a form of assessment that is fundamentally different from an approach designed to describe the general contours of student outcomes. This realization is significant, for it contributes to the pluralism in method and knowledge that has been developing in American educational research since the late 1960s. This growing pluralism is likely to open up the field of assessment still further and will dramatically increase the array of data describing educational practice and its consequences. Ironically, the richness of this array is likely to complicate rather than to simplify our understanding of schooling. For simple conclusions, one wants simple data or data arrayed on a common metric. When neither the data are simple nor the metric common, complexity is virtually inevitable.

Features of the New Assessment in Education

Given the level of interest in "authentic assessment," what features might such an assessment possess? What criteria might be appropriate for guiding those designing new approaches to assessment in education? What follows are eight criteria that seem to me to be appropriate for creating and appraising new assessment practices in education.

1. The tasks used to assess what students know and can do need to reflect the tasks they will encounter in the world outside of schools, not merely those limited to the schools themselves.

One of the peculiar features of student evaluation as it occurs through the process of achievement testing is its remoteness from the kinds of tasks people engage in outside of school. Where except in school and in the most exceptional situations outside of school are people asked to fill in bubble sheets? In what occasions are they asked to provide bits and pieces of information regarding specific, content-oriented questions? In what encounters outside of school must they sift through a series of short answer questions and select among alternatives to find a single correct answer? I am sure that it is possible to identify such occasions—taking an examination for a driver's license, for example—but they are notable by their rarity. But even more than their rarity is the fact that what really counts as a measure of what students have learned in school is not what they can do in the context of school classrooms, but in the context of life outside of schools. The purpose of schooling is not to ensure excellence of schools, but to increase the student's ability to solve problems that are not limited to school tasks and, even more generally, to deepen and expand the meanings students can construe in daily living.

This aspiration, a long-held aim of progressive educators, is now referred to by some cognitive psychologists as *situated learning* (Greeno, 1989), by others as *grounded knowing* (Oliver, 1990). Situated learning refers to the realization that context matters and that test items that have little resemblance to life as normally lead may yield scores that have little predictive value with respect to that life. A student might know how to calculate equations on algebra tests and not know how to deal with quantitative problems in a nonalgebraic context. Furthermore, what a student *can* do is not necessarily an index of what a student *will* do, and it is what a student will do that matters in life. The new assessment practices need to provide tasks that resemble in significant ways the challenges that people encounter in the course of ordinary living. This requires an entirely different frame of reference for the construction of assessment tasks than the frame we now employ.

2. The tasks used to assess students should reveal how students go about solving a problem, not only the solutions they formulated.

Most tests in schools, particularly so-called objective tests, provide no information about the way in which students arrived at their answers. Alternative answers are provided by the test maker and the student's task is to select, not construct, a response. As a result, it is impossible to determine the quality of reasoning or the process of thinking, the answers considered and rejected, the hypotheses formulated, or the explanations entertained in scoring the student's answer. Although there are some achievement tests that do allow scorers to track the sequence of choices a student has made in the course of a solution, most preclude such information.

Understanding how a student arrived at an answer provides a basis through which teachers might be better able to modify their programs or alter their teaching strategies. Knowing what a student considered en route to a solution also implies knowing what a student neglected, and areas of neglect can be as important in furthering the development of problem-solving skills as determining if the answer is correct. Indeed, it is quite possible for a student to arrive at a correct answer for entirely irrelevant reasons.

The business of constructing tasks that make it possible to make valid observations or inferences about the course of reflection in problem solving is not easy, yet it is the process of reasoning that is essential to any conception of education concerned with increasing the transfer of learning and with the process of generalization. "Learning how to learn," as the slogan goes, is a fundamental educational aim and because learning is a verb, seeing it unfold, both haltingly and smoothly, is a prime aim of diagnostically useful assessment and therefore an important criterion for creating or appraising new assessment practices.

3. Assessment tasks should reflect the values of the intellectual community from which the tasks are derived.

In *The Process of Education*, Jerome Bruner (1961) comments that "[a]ny subject can be taught in an intellectually respectable way to any child at any age." Putting hyperbole aside, the ideas within subject fields or disciplines as they are called are a part of an intellectual community. They are a part of a specialized discourse. It is also true that ideas in the course of both teaching and assessment can be served from their intellectual moorings and trivialized in the process of assessment. Notwithstanding the aspiration to enable students to recognize the relationship between ideas learned in the context of a discipline and the social and personal uses to which those ideas may be put, ideas, concepts, and images are a part of a larger intellectual constellation. One of the significant achievements of intellectual life is appreciating their place in that constellation. This achievement is, in large measure, an aesthetic achievement. Like the appreciation of a pattern, ideas in their intellectual context are hooked to a network of related ideas. In a sense, they form an intellectual tapestry.

In the context of teaching, not all ideas are located in such a tapestry. When students are not taught or do not learn to see ideas as a part of a fabric—a changing fabric—ideas become, as Alfred Whitehead commented, inert. The challenge to assessment is to *somehow* create tasks that give students opportunities to display their understanding of the vital and connected features of the ideas, concepts, and images they have explored. In short, the aim is to help students demonstrate that they have grasped ideas as part of a larger field and as historically situated elements within a community of discourse.

The virtues of such learning are twofold. First, it increases both meaning and retention because it allows connections between intellectual networks and thus reduces the meaningless fragmentation of bits and pieces of information. Second, as more and more of the puzzle pieces come together to provide a coherent picture of the domain to which ideas are related, the probability is increased that learning will have aesthetic features.

One of the marks of expertise is the possession of highly differentiated schemata in some domain (Eisner, 1991). Both differentiation, which implies the ability to notice differences in qualities, and schema, which implies some form or gestalt, give the expert the ability to see what others with less expertise miss and allow the expert to retain through a coherent, schematic structure a set of tools with which to perceive, examine, and comprehend the features of some domain. Whether we can, in fact, construct the kinds of assessment practices that will reveal the existence of such intellectual competencies remains to be seen, but the aspiration to do so is more hopeful than an unwillingness to appreciate the intellectual and educational importance of such an ambition.

4. Assessment tasks need not be limited to solo performance. Many of the most important tasks we undertake require group efforts.

We have a tradition in America that puts a premium on individual accomplishments. Rugged individualism is a part of our national heritage. Yet many of the most important adult tasks that we encounter are tasks that require participation and cooperation with members of a group. If one of the important functions of schools is to assist the young in acquiring some of the skills needed for life in the adult community, it makes no sense to censor or proscribe tasks that best reflect the features of that life. This means that curricula will need to be designed so group tasks become part of the norms of acceptable classroom activity just as they are now a part of the norms of adult activity. It means also that the assessment of group performance *and* the contributions of individuals to that performance become a part of our assessment agenda. In many ways, this aspiration flies in the face of the dominant image we have of valid assessment: an individual student working on an individual test protecting his or her answers from the eyes of fellow students. We celebrate the individual, sometimes at the cost that might very well be both too high and inappropriate.

Determining the contribution of individual performance to group achievement has a long history in games such as baseball, football, and basketball. There is no comparable history in the realm of academic life in schools. Our tendency has been to measure individual achievement and to locate such achievement in relation to the achievement of others. Indeed, our grading practices, which are based on the normal curve, put the student in competition with his fellow student: one student's A is another's B. We define excellence as a scarce resource, hence confer it on only a few.

In recent years criterion-referenced tests have been designed to ameliorate the norm-referenced assumptions of the tests we have used for so long, but even criterion-referenced tests are designed to measure individual, not group, achievement of program goals. The new assessment will, I think, have to provide a place for assessing growth on group tasks and school programs will need to be designed to enable students to learn how to contribute to the realization of group goals.

5. New assessment tasks should make possible more than one acceptable solution to a problem and more than one acceptable answer to a question.

One of the pervasive beliefs in the methodology of educational research is the need for objectivity. Objectivity refers both to *ontological objectivity*, that state in which one's perception or understanding of the world is isomorphic with the world itself, and *procedural objectivity*, that method that allows little or no personal judgment or interpretation to enter the operations through which the world is described (Eisner, 1991). The former, within the beliefs of a constructivist account, is inherently untenable. The latter *is* attainable *if* instruments are available that can be applied without recourse to judgment. The use of the optical scanner for the scoring of test performance exemplifies a procedurally objective approach to the rating of performance.

Procedural objectivity became virtuous because of the fear that personal judgment, and therefore subjectivity, would enter into what ought to be an entirely objective account of a state of affairs. I will not in the context of this book discuss the implications and issues pertaining to this belief, except to point out that such a view of methodological virtue constrains in significant ways what can be asked of a student and the kinds of responses that can be considered legitimate. The multiple choice test, like the true and false test before it, stands as an encomium to procedural objectivity. Ironically, single correct answers and single correct solutions are not the norm of intellectual life, nor are they the norm of daily life. The problems that people confront in their intellectual endeavors, like the problems they confront in ordinary living, are replete with reasonable alternative solutions. To design tests that convey the message that most, or even all, correct answers and solutions are singular is to convey a message at odds with what people confront when they engage in serious inquiry.

The implication of the foregoing is the need to design tasks that permit and credit alternative ways of responding. This will, of course, create a labor intensive assessment task—the optical scanner is not a likely tool in considering a novel solution or appraising the cogency of an explanation. It is in the provision of tasks that make such options possible that we begin to approximate the twin ideals of practical relevance and intellectual authenticity. For large scale temperature-taking assessment tasks, the use of such procedures may be limited or even inappropriate, but when we want to know how or if a student is able to address problems, issues, or questions for which alternatives are not only possible but desirable, the use of such assessment practices is mandatory.

In addition to the foregoing benefits, tasks that present or even require alternative responses provide important pedagogical cues to students and guidance to teachers regarding what is educationally important. Students want to know what they will be held accountable for, as do teachers. Assessment procedures, more than teacher testimony, eloquently testify to what really matters. In this sense, the use of assessment procedures that put a positive value on alternative answers and solutions may not only provide information about students' thinking, but also may help alter the pedagogical priorities of classroom life.

6. Assessment tasks should have curricular relevance, but not be limited to the curriculum as taught.

Conventional approaches to evaluation emphasize the view that for a test to have content validity it needs to reflect the content to which students have been exposed. There surely is wisdom in such an approach. It would be unfair to hold teachers or students accountable for content that had not been taught. Yet, the relevance of tests to curriculum can be carried to an extreme. One of the major aims of education is to enable students to use what they have learned in settings other than the ones in which they were taught. This aim puts a premium on the transfer of learning, but even more, it emphasizes the importance of enabling students to modify or adapt a set of ideas or skills to materials and tasks that have a resemblance, but not an identity, to what was taught or studied. In other words, it is important for students to come away from their studies with a set of modifiable tools; the content they were taught will rarely be encountered in the form in which it was learned.

The implication, therefore, of this criterion is the need to design assessment practices that, although relevant to the curriculum, are not limited to it. That is, assessment tasks should make it possible for students to display intelligent adaptation of the ideas they presumably learned.

In constructing such tasks, there is a need for subtle types of judgment. How closely related should a set of problems be to the kind of problems students encountered in their classroom? Should a student who studied the structure and function of grasshoppers in a biology class be expected to employ those concepts on living creatures other than insects? What about human organisms? How far is fair?

Merely recapitulating content taught in schools is, at best, a test of memory, but even when it is more than this, it might not display the range of transfer that is desirable. Hence, the construction of tasks that reveal the student's ability to use at the level of principle of what has been learned is of critical importance in the new assessment. Put another way, assessment tasks that assess only what has been taught are too meager. Those that assess more than is reasonable are unfair. The key term—reasonable—is what is central to the construction of such assessment tasks. Reasonableness requires judgment.

7. Assessment tasks should require students to display a sensitivity to configurations or wholes, not simply to discrete elements.

The conduct of inquiry is seldom a series of single certain steps toward some unambiguous destination, except, of course, in its textbook version. In the real world, inquiry proceeds haltingly, uncertain about both means and ends, and displays the flexibility and the concern for pattern that enables the intelligent inquirer to create ideas or products that possess that elusive but precious quality we call coherence. It is the coherence or elegance of a solution that experts value. The sense of "rightness of fit," as Goodman (1978) calls it, is one of the most compelling indicators of our rationality. What does such an ability mean for assessment and how might it be displayed?

Although I do not have crisp answers to these questions, some seem to me to be promising. Creating tasks that require students to engage in larger problematic situations than are typically characterized by most standard achievement test questions might make it possible to observe their decision making in process and to interrupt that process at strategic moments in order to secure an explanation, as well as they can provide it, for the choices they have made and the strategies they have employed. The aim of such an exercise is to create the conditions through which the student's ability to decentrate perception and problem solving can be noted. It is to provide the kind of information to teachers that will enable them to assist students in widening the array of data they consider when working through a problem.

In artistic tasks, such skills are of the utmost importance. A student in a life drawing class must not only pay attention to the contour of an arm, but to its relationship to the body of which it is a part. But even more, the body or figure as a whole must be carefully related to the entire paper on which it is drawn. In other words, attention not only to the figure but also to the ground is critical if one is to create a coherent or satisfying drawing. Similar features hold in other forms of problem solving and understanding the extent to which they can be adequately addressed is an important aspect of the student's educational development.

8. Assessment tasks should permit the student to select a form of representation he or she chooses to use to display what has been learned.

One of the major assumptions used in group achievement tests is that all of the students taking the test should encounter the same items. The reason for this assumption is clear. When the items are identical, comparison among students is possible. Statistical procedures can be used to select appropriate test items and the bell-shaped curve can remain an ideal for distributing students' performance.

What this means in practice is that not only will the items be common across students, but also the form of their response. The multiple choice test provides a common set of questions and a common array of alternative possible answers. A group of students who have taken the test can have their scores arrayed within a distribution that approximates a normal curve.

When one of the major aims of testing is to sort students out, such a procedure has certain utility. In a sense, if one wants to identify winners in a race, it makes sense to have runners start at the same place, and if this is not possible (and it is not in academic contexts) they should at least run on the same track. But if one's view of the function of assessment is to determine the unique ways in which students interpret or apply what they have learned, then a common set of test items and a common set of response alternatives might not be appropriate. In new approaches to assessment, students will not only be given opportunities to construct their own responses to what they have learned, they will also be given opportunities to select the medium through which what they have learned can be made public. This means, for example, that after a unit of study in history or the social studies, some students might elect to create a ballad, or a poem, or write a short story. After a study in biology some students might elect to construct a three-dimensional model of evolution or write a speculative piece on the future of evolution.

Such options for students will surely create problems for assessors. Incommensurability among responses will certainly be pervasive. Each student's work will need to be appraised on its own terms. A common cookie cutter criterion will no longer be appropriate. Despite these difficulties, such a practice, at least as a part of the new assessment, will symbolize to students that personal proclivities matter, that productive idiosyncracies count, and that individual interpretation and creativity are values the school cares about.

It is well to remember that in "the real world" outside of professional specialization, individuals do create their own responses and their own preferred form in reacting to experience. After a trip to Paris, some people write poetry, others paint pictures, some show the photographs that they have taken and talk about their experience. It is precisely in the diversity of response to "common experience" that our cultural lives are enriched. The celebration of such diversity is congruent with the creation of a civilization in which what is unique about individuals flavors the common weal. The invention and use of new conceptions of assessment have important roles to play in the realization of that ideal.

As assessment leads to increasingly fine-grained, interpretive appraisals, it is less amenable to crisp, reductive measurement and comparison of student learning, experience, and performance. Can the public appetite for discrete certainty in assessment be satisfied by interpretive assessment practices? What vision of education must a public hold to accept less discrete indicators? Can a rationally oriented meritocracy embrace such a vision? Will a functionally differentiated conception of assessment increase the acceptability of approaches to assessment that are more personalistic in focus? If it does, will the reductionistic testing practices that now prevail marginalize the newer assessment as parents and others in the community continue to seek "the bottom line"?

I can only hope that with responsible and articulate interpretation, authentic assessment will be understood and valued by the public-at-large. If it is, assessment will not only contribute to better schooling for children, it will also contribute to a broader, more generous conception of education itself.

References

Barone, T. (1983). Things of use and things of beauty: The story of Swain County high schools arts program. *Daedalus, 112*(3), 1–28.

Berlin, I. (1966). The concept of scientific history. In W. H. Dray (Ed.), *Philosophical analysis and history* (pp. 5–53). New York: Harper & Row.

Bruner, J. (1961). *The process of education.* Cambridge, MA: Harvard University Press.

Callahan, R. (1962). *Education and the cult of efficiency.* Chicago: University of Chicago Press.

Dewey, J. (1938). *Experience and education*. New York: Macmillan.

Eisner, E. (1991). *The enlightened eye: Qualitative inquiry and the enhancement of educational practice*. New York: Macmillan.

Erickson, F. (1982). *The counselor as gatekeeper*. New York: Academic Press.

Geertz, C. (1973). *The interpretation of cultures*. New York: Basic Books.

Goodman, N. (1978). *Ways of worldmaking*. Indianapolis: Hackett.

Greeno, J. (1989). Perspectives on thinking. *American Psychologist, 44*(2), 134–141.

Harnischfeger, A., & Wiley, D. (1975). *Achievement test scores decline: Do we need to worry?* Chicago: CEMREL.

Jackson, P. (1968). *Life in classrooms*. New York: Holt, Rinehart & Winston.

Joncich, G. (1968). *The sane positivist*. Middletown, CT: Wesleyan University Press.

Lightfoot, S. (1983). *The good high school*. New York: Basic Books.

McKeon, R. (Ed.). (1941). *The basic works of Aristotle*. New York: Random House.

Oliver, D. (1990). Grounded knowing: A postmodern perspective on teaching and learning. *Educational Leadership, 48*(1), 64–67.

Peshkin, A. (1986). *God's choice: The total world of a fundamentalist Christian school*. Chicago: University of Chicago Press.

Rist, R. (1972). *The invisible children*. Cambridge, MA: Harvard University Press.

Schwab, J. (1969). The practical: A language for curriculum. *School Review, 78*(5) 1–24.

Scriven, M. (1967). The methodology of evaluation. *AERA monograph series no. 1 perspectives on curriculum evaluation* (pp. 39–83). Chicago: Rand McNally.

Smith, L., & Geoffrey, W. (1968). *The complexities of an urban classroom*. New York: Holt, Rinehart & Winston.

Thorndike, E. L. (1910). The contribution of psychology to education. *Journal of Education Psychology, 1*, 5–12.

Toulmin, S. (1990). *Cosmopolis: The hidden agenda of modernity*. New York: The Free Press.

Waller, W. (1932). *The sociology of teaching*. New York: Wiley.

Wiggins, G. (1989). A true test: Toward authentic and equitable assessment. *Phi Delta Kappan, 71*(9), 703–713.

Wolcott, H. (1984). *The man in the principal's office*. Prospect Heights, IL: Waveland Press.

Yerkes, R. (1929). *Army mental tests*. New York: Henry Holt.

10

❧

The Forms and Functions of Educational Connoisseurship and Educational Criticism

The transition from a paradigm in crisis to a new one from which a new tradition of normal science can emerge is far from a cumulative process, one achieved by an articulation or extension of the old paradigm. Rather it is a reconstruction of the field from new fundamentals, a reconstruction that changes some of the field's most elementary theoretical generalizations as well as many of its paradigm methods and applications.

THOMAS S. KUHN

The function of this chapter is to identify and discuss some of the assumptions, principles, and procedures used in educational connoisseurship and educational criticism. This form of educational inquiry, a species of educational evaluation, is qualitative in character (Dewey, 1931) and takes its lead from the work that critics have done in literature, theater, film, music, and the visual arts.

Interest in qualitative forms of research and evaluation has increased in recent years, but little of the work that has been done has been related to the fine arts. Most of those who have used qualitative approaches have related their work to ethnography. Yet, there is no area of human inquiry that epitomizes the qualitative more than what artists do when they work. Thus, it seems to me that if we seek to know what qualitative inquiry consists of, we can do little better than analyze the work of those who use it the most.

Artists inquire in a qualitative mode both in the formulation of ends and in the use of means to achieve such ends (Dewey, 1950). The result of their work is a qualitative whole—a symphony, poem, painting, ballet—that has the capacity to evoke in the intelligent percipient a kind of experience that leads us to call the work art. My claim is that the paradigmatic use of qualitative inquiry is found in the arts.

Another form of qualitative inquiry is found in the work of those who inquire into the work of artists, namely, the art critics. The art critic finds himself or herself with the difficult task of rendering the essentially ineffable qualities constituting works of art into a language that will help others perceive the work more deeply. In this sense, the critic's task is to function as a midwife to perception, to so talk about the qualities constituting the work of art that others, lacking the critic's connoisseurship, will be able to perceive the work more comprehensively. "The function of criticism," wrote Dewey (1934), "is the reeducation of perception of works of art" (p. 324). The critic's task in this view is not primarily the issuance of a judgment but rather the difficult task of "lifting the veils that keep the eyes from seeing" (p. 324).

There are two important points to be made about criticism. First, criticism is an empirical undertaking. The work *empirical* comes from the Latin *empiricus,* meaning "open to experience." Criticism is empirical in the significant sense that the qualities the critic describes or renders must be capable of being located in the subject matter of the criticism. In this sense, the test of criticism is in its instrumental effects on the perception of works of art. It is not abstraction that one understands through criticism but rather qualities and their relationships.

It is interesting to note that the studies we usually call empirical are studies whose findings are couched in terms that are not in the strict sense empirical at all. Take, for example, studies that report significant differences in variances or in means among groups of students. What we have in such studies are conclusions that may be four or five orders removed from the empirical qualities from which the conclusions were drawn. We tend to forget that individual students confront individual test items and answer them correctly or incorrectly. From the individual's response to individual items, a raw score is calculated for each student. This raw score is itself an abstraction that significantly limits the information on each student's performance. Two students, for example, can receive the same raw score for entirely different performances on the same test. These raw scores are then summed and averaged, a second-order abstraction. Following this procedure, variances are computed and compared and a probability is calculated to determine the relationship among variances across groups. These represent third- and fourth-order abstractions. In no way is it possible to reconstruct an individual student's test score from knowledge of a mean or from the differences between means. These latter quantities are in fact abstractions that, although derived from empirical performances, are not themselves empirical. One cannot locate a mean by looking for it in the world.

The second point I want to emphasize with respect to criticism is that *anything* can be its subject matter. Once again, by *criticism* I do not mean the negative appraisal of something but rather the illumination of something's qualities so that an appraisal of its value can be made. Although *criticism* is a term that is most frequently used in the arts, it also is used in sports, in the assessment of research, in the appraisal of human behavior, particularly in social settings, and in a host of other areas in which humans have intercourse with the world. There is nothing, in principle, that cannot be the object of criticism.

Although teaching is frequently referred to as an art, and although in our vernacular we recognize the artistic aspects of educational practice—the beautiful lesson, the exciting discussion, the well-made point, the elegant exposition—when it comes to our attempts to describe or understand educational practice, criticism is seldom appealed to as a possible method or approach. The reason for the neglect of criticism as a potentially useful vehicle for the description, interpretation, and evaluation of educational practice is, I think, a result of the ways in which educators have been professionally socialized, particularly those holding doctorates and working in universities.

Doctoral programs socialize students to believe that the most dependable procedure one can use to obtain knowledge is through science and that respectable inquiry in education, at least respectable empirical inquiry, is scientific in character. To use other methods, to employ metaphor, analogy, simile, or other poetic devices, is to lack rigor. Jeffreys (1961) tries to make the point this way:

> No matter what the subject matter, the fundamental principles of the method must be the same. There must be a uniform standard for validity for all hypotheses, irrespective of the subject. Different laws may hold in different subjects, but they must be tested by the same criteria; otherwise we have no guarantee that our decisions will be those warranted by the data and not merely the result of inadequate analysis or of believing what we want to believe. . . . If the rules [of induction applied in scientific inquiry] are not general, we shall have different standards of validity in different subjects, or different standards for one's own hypotheses and somebody else's. If the rules of themselves say anything about the world, they will make empirical statements independently of observational evidence, and thereby limit the scope of what we can find out by observation. If there are such limits, they must be inferred from observation; we must not assert them in advance.

Jeffreys's argument proceeds beyond the rejection of critical language; it also tends to include all forms of inquiry that do not translate the phenomena of interest into quantity. This is so pervasive a belief in educational research that educational research itself is identified not just with empirical inquiry but with quantitative empirical inquiry.

I mention this not as a condemnation of statistically oriented inquiry in education but rather as an example of its pervasiveness and of the relative neglect of other forms of inquiry that could be useful to the field. I believe that the creation of educational criticism, a form of criticism not unlike that found in the arts but directed to educational matters, could provide a kind of utility that scientific studies and quantitatively treated phenomena neglect. Indeed, I hope that one day we will have journals of educational criticism and critical theory that will seek to refine the quality of educational criticism and the methods and assumptions with which those doing such criticism work. During the past decade progress has been made toward that end, for example, *Curriculum Inquiry*, the *Journal of Curriculum Theorizing*, and the *International Journal, Qualitative Studies in Education*.

The Relationship of Educational Criticism to Educational Connoisseurship

Effective criticism, within the arts or in education, is not an act independent of the powers of perception. The ability to see, to perceive what is subtle, complex, and important, is its first necessary condition. The act of knowledgeable perception is, in the arts, referred to as connoisseurship. To be a connoisseur is to know how to look, to see, and to appreciate. Connoisseurship, generally defined, is the art of appreciation. It is essential to criticism because without the ability to perceive what is subtle and important, criticism is likely to be superficial or even empty. The major distinction between connoisseurship and criticism is this: connoisseurship is the art of appreciation, criticism is the art of disclosure. Connoisseurship is a private act; it consists of recognizing and appreciating the qualities of a particular, but it does not require either a public judgment or a public description of those qualities. The perception and appreciation of a particular requires a sensory memory. For example, if one is to develop connoisseurship of wine, one must drink a great deal of wine, learn how to attend to its qualities, and be able to recall from one's gustatory memory—and in the case of wine, the olfactory and visual memories also come into play—the qualities of other wines in order to have a backdrop against which the particular qualities of the wine being tasted can be compared and contrasted. In the case of music, the auditory mode provides the backdrop. A connoisseur could compare Arturo Toscanini's performance of Beethoven's Seventh Symphony with that of Herbert von Karajan. Only after a range of experiences are had in a mode of expression will sophisticated levels of connoisseurship be developed.

The same considerations apply with respect to educational connoisseurship. One must have a great deal of experience with classroom practice to be able to distinguish what is significant about one set of practices or another.

In saying that experience counts in the development of connoisseurship, whether in education or in the fine arts, it is important to recognize that the length of time spent in a classroom or the number of museums visited or the frequency with which one attends sports events is not necessarily an indication of the level of connoisseurship someone has achieved. Let us distinguish between recognition and perception, and let us agree with Dewey (1934) that recognition is perception aborted: looking is engaged in simply to be able to see enough to classify. That is an oak tree, the other is an elm, that dive was a half-gainer, that was a full twist with a somersault, and so forth. Perception based on recognition alone stops with assigning the particular to the class to which it belongs; it does not proceed to the sensory exploration of the ways in which *this* particular oak tree differs from other oaks, it does not locate the specific characteristics of *this* elm, *that* half-gainer, *this* full twist with a somersault. Recognition is not exploratory; it is focused on classification.

If one looks within a classroom primarily to recognize rather than to see, the number of years one spends in a classroom will contribute little to the development of connoisseurship. To develop connoisseurship one must have a desire to perceive subtleties, to become a student of human behavior, to focus one's perception. Looking is a necessary condition, but looking is essentially a task one undertakes; it is seeing that is an achievement.

It would be difficult to overemphasize the importance of connoisseurship in the creation of educational criticism. Connoisseurship provides the fundamental core of realization that gives criticism its material. Because it is so central to any understanding of practice, it is rather surprising that it has received so little attention. We tend to take it for granted, or we seem to believe that with the use of an observation schedule the problem of seeing what goes on in classrooms is cared for. This is simply naive. What is significant in a social setting might have little to do with the incidence of a particular activity or statement but a lot to do with a single act or statement or with the organizational structure of the classroom or with the character of an assigned task or with the way in which a reward is given. Observation schedules are tools that can guide one's attention, but their mechanical use can blind one to what is significant.

It may be that the neglect of connoisseurship is due to the fact that relatively few people doing educational research spend much time in classrooms. The general tendency in educational research is to use instruments that can be easily administered and scored and that are not susceptible to confounding through bias or long-term exposure to the vicissitudes of classroom life. The rigorous experiment in education is "clean." To achieve such cleanliness, experiments in educational research tend to be brief. The modal amount of time for educational experiments reported in 2 years of the studies published in the *American Educational Research Journal* is less than 1 hour. For 14 experimental studies reported during this period, six used a treatment period of less than 1 hour, three from 1 hour to 1 day, three from 1 day to 1 week, and one for over 1 year. No time was reported for one study. It is my view that such a conception of clean experimentation in education is likely to lead to work that has little significance for educational practice.

The development of educational connoisseurship requires an ability not only to perceive the subtle particulars of educational life but also to recognize the way those particulars form a part of a structure within the classroom. Erickson's (1967) discussion of the chess game is most apt. To understand a chess game, one must do much more than measure or even describe in qualitative terms the character of the physical movements made by each player. One must be able to perceive the structure of the game within which the physical movements take on social meaning. One must eventually be able to conceptualize the rules that give structure to the enterprise and define it as the game.

Similarly, the development of educational connoisseurship requires the ability to perceive the "rules" through which educational life is lived. Such a task is what Gilbert Ryle refers to as "thick description," about which more will be said later (Geertz, 1973).

The work that my students and I are doing at Stanford University is aimed at the development of educational connoisseurship and the ability to create useful educational criticism. Educational connoisseurship is to some degree possessed by virtually everyone who has spent some time in schools as a student or as a teacher, but it can be refined and developed. What is involved in the development of educational connoisseurship is, first, the opportunity to attend to happenings of educational life in a focused, sensitive, and conscious way. Second, it requires the opportunity to compare such happenings, to discuss what one sees so that perceptions can be refined, to identify events not previously perceived, and to integrate and appraise what has been seen. This is being done at Stanford through the direct observation of classrooms and through the careful viewing of videotapes of classroom life. When students jointly view such tapes, the basis for description and discussion is provided. Over time, descriptive language becomes less mechanical, more incisive, and increasingly literary or poetic as students try to get at the essence of what is occurring. To talk about essences and significance in the observation of educational events requires, of course, not only a sensitivity to the emerging qualities of classroom life, but also a set of ideas, theories, or models that enable one to distinguish the significant from the trivial and to place what one sees in an intelligible context. This process is not serial: we do not see and then assess significance;

the very ideas that define educational virtue for us operate within the perceptual processes to locate among thousands of possibilities what we choose to see. The essence of perception is that it is selective; there is no value-free mode of seeing.

Given the impact of our theories on our perception, the development of educational connoisseurship is much more complicated than simply a species of discrimination training. The problem of developing connoisseurship of the complex life of classrooms is not simply one of identifying the equivalent of Boeing 707s or DC-10s. Plane spotters have a comparatively simple task. The forms of such planes can be known in advance, and interaction effects are minimal. A 707 is a 707 is a 707. But in classrooms, interaction effects are the rule, not the exception. To discern what an event means requires an understanding of the context in which it occurs; that context requires not only some knowledge of the people involved and the circumstances within which the event occurs, but in many situations also something about the past, against which the particulars of the present can be placed. Again, memory is indispensable.

What we begin to recognize when we consider what connoisseurship entails is that the perceptual processes operate within an array of values and theoretical concepts that influence perception. Indeed, in both the social sciences and philosophy we use theories to organize our conception of the world. Individuals working with different theories—whether normative or descriptive—will attend to different phenomena within the "same" setting and interpret their significance differently. For the development of educational connoisseurship, an understanding of different social sciences, different theories of education, and a grasp of the history of education is not simply an intellectual ornament to be acquired within a graduate program but an essential working tool.

The cognitivist view that I am expressing with respect to the perception of educational practice has eloquently been expressed by a major American aesthetician concerning the role of theory in the perception and appraisal of art. Morris Weitz (1966) points out that although previous attempts to define the necessary and sufficient properties of art have been unsuccessful (because art is an open rather than a closed concept), the work of the great aestheticians is not useless. He writes:

> In spite of the fact that all of them [theoreticians] fail to accomplish what they set out to do—to give a true definition of works of art—these definitions are nevertheless helpful and well worth intensive study. For behind every one is a redefinition of "work of art"; i.e., an attempt to get us to concentrate on certain criteria or properties of works of art as against others. If we attend to these criteria or properties and forget the unsuccessful attempts as true, essentialist definitions, we can learn a great deal from the theories, especially as to what we should look for in works of art and how we should look at them. Indeed, the great contribution of theories of works of art is precisely in their

teachings, not in their definitions, of art: each of the theories represents a set of explorable criteria which serve to remind us of what we may have neglected or to make us see what we may not have seen. To do this, I should think, is the primary job of teaching. Here, then, is the relation between teaching and the nature of art or, to use the title of your conference, the nature of art and its implication for teaching: that the great theorists of the nature of art have served as the great teachers as well, in telling us, through their definitions of art, what we are to learn from them about the arts. (p. 10)

The same argument can be made—a fortiori—for theories of human behavior, culture, and education.

What Do Critics Do?

As I have already indicated, educational connoisseurship is a necessary condition for doing useful educational criticism. But what is it that critics do? What do they write about? And what kind of validity and generalizability does criticism have? Criticism is the art of disclosing the qualities of events or objects that connoisseurship perceives. Criticism is the public side of connoisseurship. One can be a connoisseur without the skills of criticism, but one cannot be a critic without the skills of connoisseurship. In using language to make public qualities and meanings that are not themselves discursive, something of a paradox exists. How can words express what words can never express? The successful resolution of this paradox lies at the heart of the critical act. To accomplish this feat, critics do not aspire toward a translation of an event from one modality to another, for in fact no such translation, at least in the literal sense, can be made. It is one thing to translate from one language into another. And even between languages there are difficulties. But to expect to translate what is known in a visual mode into a discursive mode is to use the term *translate* metaphorically. A more appropriate word, coined by Kozloff (1969) is *rendering:*

> For what criticism proposes to give, I think, is essentially an account of an experience, and never, as is sometimes supposed, a substitute for an experience. Though ideally it must be self-sufficient as prose, it can never be a stand-in for what has been perceived, lest it compromise a metaphorical with a literal fiction. Indeed, criticism's merit lies exactly in the fact that it is neither a work of art nor a response, but something much rarer—a rendering of the interaction between the two. Best, then, that it reconcile itself to virtual rather than actual meanings, the ambiguity of symbolic reference as opposed to the pidgin clarity of signs. (p. 10)

What critics do or should try to do is not to translate what cannot be translated but rather to create a rendering of a situation, event, or object that will provide pointers to those aspects of the situation, event, or object that are in some way significant. Now what counts as significant will depend on the theories, models, and values alluded to earlier. But it will also depend on the purposes of the critic. For example, an educational critic focusing on the learning patterns of a particular student will attend to qualities and circumstances different from those he or she would attend to if interested in the critical rendering of the character of classroom discourse, the qualities of the classroom's visual environment, or the meanings embedded in the treatment of time in the classroom. The point here is straightforward: what is rendered by someone working as an educational critic will depend on his or her purposes as well as the kinds of maps, models, and theories being used.

Discursive and Nondiscursive Knowledge

Of particular importance in understanding how critical language is illuminative is the distinction between discursive and nondiscursive forms of knowledge and that between representational and presentational symbols.

The conception of nondiscursive modes of knowing is not a new distinction among those schooled in philosophy, but it is new to those raised in the traditions pervading American educational research and its offspring, educational evaluation. American educational research has, since the early work of E. L. Thorndike, been largely behavioristic in its psychology and operationalist in its philosophy. To "know" has meant to make statements couched in the form of propositions and that therefore can be appraised by logical criteria. But because logic is essentially a tool for determining consistency between propositions, something more is needed if relationships between propositions are to be more than merely consistent. If propositions are to make true statements about the world, referents for those statements have to be located in the world. And because in empirical matters observation is subject to biases of one sort or another—biases in perception, in selection of population, and the like—observations need to be operationalized through standardized procedures that are reliable and quantitative and therefore supposedly least likely to suffer from unreliability and subjectivity. For generations, this conception of the meaning of knowledge has dominated inquiry into educational matters. Indeed, to do educational research has come to mean, by custom, to engage in inquiry having these characteristics. The idea that there are multiple ways in which things are known—that there is a variety of expressive modalities through which what is known can be disclosed—simply has been absent from the conversations that animate the educational research community.

A distinction between the respective contributions of the sciences and the arts to human understanding is made by Ernest Cassirer (1953) in *An Essay on Man*. Cassirer points out that a scientific perspective without an artistic one or an artistic perspective without a scientific one leads to monocular vision; both are necessary to have depth perception. Science, writes Cassirer, focuses on what is general and common across particulars, whereas art focuses on the unique characteristics of the particulars themselves.

> The two views of truth are in contrast with one another, but not in conflict or contradiction. Because art and science move in entirely different planes, they cannot contradict or thwart one another. The conceptual interpretation of science does not preclude the intuitive interpretation of art. Each has its own perspective and, so to speak, its own angle of refraction. The psychology of sense perception has taught us that without the use of both eyes, without a binocular vision, there would be no awareness of the third dimension of space. The depth of human experience in the same sense depends on the fact that we are able to vary our modes of seeing, that we can alternate our views of reality. Rerum videre formas is no less important and indispensable task than rerum cognoscere causas. In ordinary experiences we connect phenomena according to the category of causality or finality. According as we are interested in the theoretical reasons for the practical effects of things, we think of them as causes or means. Thus, we habitually lose sight of their immediate appearance until we can no longer see them face to face. Art, on the other hand, teaches us to visualize, not merely to conceptualize or utilize, things. Art gives a richer more vivid and colorful image of reality, and a more profound insight into its formal structure. It is characteristic of the nature of man that he is not limited to one specific and single approach to reality but can choose his point of view and so pass from one aspect of things to another. (p. 170)

Cassirer's plea for binocular vision through complementary forms of inquiry is one that I echo. One mode of conception and one form of disclosure are simply inadequate to exhaust the richness of educational life.

The notion that knowledge can be conceived and experienced in nondiscursive as well as discursive forms has been perhaps most eloquently expressed by an American aesthetician who was influenced by Cassirer's work—Susanne Langer. Langer (1957) argues that although propositions are among the most useful of cultural tools for expressing ideas about factual states of affairs, they are virtually useless when it comes to expressing what we know about the life of feeling:

> Yet even the discursive pattern has its limits of usefulness. An expressive form can express any complex of conceptions that, via some rule of projection, appears congruent with it, that is, appears to be of that form. Whatever there is in experience that will not take the impress—directly or indirectly—of discursive form, is not discursively communicable or, in the strictest sense, logically thinkable. It is unspeakable, ineffable; according to practically all serious philosophical theories today, it is unknowable. (p. 20)

Discursive language, the type used in science and in much of our ordinary speech, is our most powerful tool for classification, but when particular qualities of life must be revealed we have to appeal to a language more intimate, or, in Langer's terms, a language that presents to our consciousness what the feeling of those qualities is. Literature is, of course, a prime example of the nondiscursive use of language. So is poetry. What enables us to participate empathetically in the events, lives, and situations that the writer portrays is not mere factual description. If this were the case, everyone who could describe the facts would be a Dostoevsky, a Shakespeare, or a Bellow. What gives literature its power is the way in which language has been *formed* by the writer. It is the "shape" of language as well as the perceptive recognition of the metaphorical, connotative, and symbolic character or particular words and phrases that makes written language literature. What the writer is able to do, as is the painter, composer, dancer, or critic, is to transform knowledge held in one mode into another, namely, the mode within which the artist or critic works. Somehow the artist finds or creates the structural expressive equivalent of an idea, a feeling, or an image within the material with which he or she works. The material becomes the public embodiment—a medium, in the literal sense of the word—through which the life of feeling is shared. The arts are not a second-class substitute for expression; they are one of the major means people throughout history have used both to conceptualize and express what has been inexpressible in discursive terms.

Now the talk of the critic is in many respects similar to that of the artist. Both work within the limits of the material to create a form that expresses what has no name. The *particular* qualities of joy, grief, enchantment, irony, perseverance, or courage are never adequately revealed through the ordinary verbal classification of these terms alone. What was the character of this man's courage? What is the particular quality of her joy or grief? How does this classroom lead its life? What kind of personage does this teacher represent to his class? To reveal these particulars, to capture these "essences," one must not only perceive their existence but also be able to create a form that intimates, discloses, reveals, imports, suggests, implies their existence. In this process of transformation, metaphor is, of course, a centrally important device. Metaphor breaks the bonds of conventional usage to exploit the power of connotation and analogy. It capitalizes on surprise by putting meanings into new combinations and through such combinations awakens our senses. Metaphor is the arch enemy of the stock response.

The use of metaphor is not restricted to the creation of literature and the writing of poetry and criticism; it plays an extremely important role in our vernacular language. Take, for example, slang. "Cool," "dis," and "not," are only a few examples of metaphorical usage. We don't ask of such language what it literally means because literally its meaning is either absurd or nonexistent. Yet we all sense the rightness of the phrase when used in an appropriate context. Indeed, we use such language not simply because it is more economical than its discursive "equivalent" but because it has no discursive equivalent. Fresh conceptions find their expression in the inventive use of language. Even our discursive language is filled with words that once were metaphorical or had visual referents but through conventional usage have lost their initial power: Someone feels low, or high, or depressed; he has an inflated ego; she is being defensive; he is being slick; that painting is well balanced. The symphony is melancholy. Such words are so pervasive a part of our language that we seldom stop to reflect on the way in which they acquired meaning (Arnheim, 1969).

What is ironic is that in the professional socialization of educational researchers, the use of metaphor is regarded as a sign of imprecision; yet, for making public the ineffable, nothing is more precise than the artistic use of language. Metaphoric precision is the central vehicle for revealing the qualitative aspects of life.

The revelation of the qualitative aspects of life, particularly those aspects that deal with what individuals experience in various situations, has been a major focus of artists through the centuries. Let's assume for a moment that we wanted to know something about life in, say, a concentration camp. How would we find out? We could try to locate psychological and sociological studies of the inmates and of the organization of such camps, and if we could find such studies we might learn something about how new inmates were socialized, how they adapted to the conditions of the camp. We might learn something about social mobility, stratification, and class, about the various roles assumed, and about achieved and assigned status. We might learn about the use of sanctions and about the destruction of the ego. Such knowledge is, of course, useful. Based as it would be on concepts and theories within the social sciences, it would describe, through the concepts the theories employ, the various features of camp life and how they function.

But let us say we wanted to know what it was like to be taken to such a camp, to go through the initial screening, to work 14 hours a day in bitter cold, to have a wretched diet. To know these aspects of life in a concentration camp, one must go to the forms of expression that convey the qualities of such life to the reader. One could do little better than to read Solzhenitsyn's (1964) *A Day in the Life of Ivan Denisovich.* Through literature and through effective criticism we come to know what it feels like to be in prison, to be in ecstasy, to be in a particular classroom in a particular school. Through the arts we have the opportunity to participate vicariously in the lives of others, to acquire an empathetic understanding of situations, and therefore to know them in ways that only the arts can reveal.

If I dwell on these matters, it is because I believe they are crucial for understanding why educational criticism is such an important complement to the existing modes of inquiry in education.

The language of criticism, like the language of the arts, is essentially nondiscursive; that is, it informs not by pointing to the facts of the world but rather by intimation, by using forms to *present* rather than to *represent* conception or feeling. Representational symbols, the type used in conventional discourse, are like signposts: they point one toward qualities but are not themselves intended to possess expressive qualities. "Listen, listen to the bird" is a literal discursive expression, but "Hark! hark! the lark!" contains an energy absent in the former. The former is representational; it directs our attention so that a certain kind of experience can be had. The latter presents us with a form that itself generates the excitement of the experience. The former is a conventional utterance, the latter is poetic.

Thus far I have tried to identify the functions of qualitative inquiry in education and to distinguish between educational connoisseurship and educational criticism. Before describing in greater detail the major dimensions of educational criticism, it will be useful to examine a brief segment of art criticism written by the distinguished American critic Leo Steinberg (1972). From it, we can get a better sense of what one critic does in the course of one of his criticisms.

PAUL BRACH'S PICTURES

They are very near invisibility.

Invisibility is of various kinds, and to list its varieties while the pictures are up helps to focus attention.

Invisibility by disappearance. An object absent, remote or indistinct leaves a leftover emptiness and a straining to see. This seems relevant to Brach's pictures. Their vacant geometry suggests depleted voids, voided containers. Their huge suspended circles can look like extinguished suns. Solar cult emblems snuffed out. Empty icons.

Then, invisibility by extinction of light. This too seems relevant. Not actual darkness—which conveys a specific degree of reduced illumination—but a consistency or opacity that can be neither brightened nor deepened.

And invisibility due to dimmed vision; whether through blindness or the sightlessness of inattention. Brach makes his pictures easy to resist. They court unseeing indifference or disinterest; as if to remain invisible to the averted mind. (p. 286)

Although this constitutes only the first portion of Steinberg's criticism, we can use it to try to understand what he does. Consider first the title, "Paul Brach's Pictures." Steinberg does not write a long, complex title but a simple one, one that we shall find is in keeping with the works that he will criticize. Notice also that Steinberg does not refer to "Brach's Paintings" but rather to "Paul Brach's pictures." "Pictures" suggests more of illusion, of image, of icon. "Paintings" suggests a medium, the qualities of the material used, or technique, and as we find as we read on, paint and technique are not essential aspects of Brach's work; his are indeed images of a mysterious kind: *pictures* is more apt than *paintings*.

Steinberg's opening sentence, "They are very near invisibility," hangs there by itself. In some ways, it's an awkward sentence, yet is possesses some of the mysterious magical qualities of the paintings Steinberg is attempting to render. A lesser critic might have written, "Brach's paintings are nearly invisible." But such a sentence does not possess a spell.

Steinberg sets the mood of the work in his opening line and then shifts pace to suggest, in somewhat Aristotelian terms, that the classification of types of invisibility will be helpful to us in seeing Brach's work. And, abruptly, he repeats the fragmented tempo of the opening line, "Invisibility by disappearance." Because the issue is not grammar but mood and insight, the tempo works; it sets up a backdrop for the longer, more expository sentences to follow. Notice the nice contradictory quality of "leftover emptiness." Leftovers usually imply overabundance, not emptiness. Yet this, too, combined with "a straining to see," as Steinberg says, is relevant to Brach's pictures. What Steinberg is doing is depicting by implication and suggestion the pervasive quality of Brach's work. He is preparing the reader psychologically to see the point of the pictures, not only by specific verbal cues (which come later in the criticism), but also by the ambience in his language.

Steinberg then describes the "vacant geometry" of Brach's work, "depleted voids, voided containers," "huge suspended circles" that "look like extinguished suns." He then stops the paragraph as he began it, with a terse nonsentence: "Empty icons."

Again the illusion of Steinberg's language has its parallel in the works to which the language refers, not as an attempt to translate their visual qualities but rather, as Kozloff has suggested in his own writing, "to render" the works. Criticism works by implication, "the most appropriate devices at my disposal have been innuendo, nuance, and hypothesis, because what is peripheral to direct statement in language is often central to a pictorial encounter or its meaning" (Kozloff, 1969). Steinberg would surely agree.

Steinberg continues in his criticism of Paul Brach's pictures to combine nuance and innuendo with more literal references to the qualities of the work, but always the tempo of the writing epitomizes the suspense and mystery of the work itself. Steinberg ends the criticism as he began, tersely as though it were suspended in space. His last paragraph reads, "They are beautiful pictures, solitary and serious."

Four Aspects of Educational Criticism

Educational criticism is composed of four major aspects or dimensions. One of these is descriptive, another interpretative, a third evaluative, and a fourth thematic. Each of the distinctions that I make I am making for analytical purposes—to illuminate differences in language and intention—but the distinctions are sharper on paper than in fact. All description is in some degree evaluative inasmuch as only a fool would choose to describe the trivial. All evaluation is interpretive to the degree that one seeks to make some sense of what a situation or an experience means. Nevertheless, the distinctions are useful to the extent that they sharpen perception of the foci of criticism and therefore enable us to read or create criticism more intelligently.

The Descriptive Aspect of Educational Criticism

The descriptive aspect of educational criticism is essentially an attempt to identify and characterize, portray, or render in language the relevant qualities of educational life. Such qualities may be the general environment or cultural style of a particular classroom or school. How is life lived in Miss Held's fourth grade? What kind of tempo pervades Mr. Marco's algebra class? Or the descriptive aspects of educational criticism might focus on more limited or molecular characteristics. How does this particular child relate to his peers? What covert messages does the teacher give her students through the tone of her voice? What is the quality of the visual environment of the school, and what does it convey to the student about life in school? Although it is a piece of literature rather than a piece of criticism, the following passage from Dillard's (1974) *Pilgrim at Tinker Creek* illustrates how a perceptive and skillful writer can portray the sensory qualities of a complex environment:

> It was sunny one evening last summer at Tinker Creek; the sun was low in the sky, upstream. I was sitting on the sycamore log bridge with the sunset at my back, watching the shiners the size of minnows who were feeding over the muddy sand in skittery schools. Again and again, one fish, then another, turned for a split second across the current and flash! the sun shot out from its silver side. I couldn't watch for it. It was always just happening somewhere else, and it drew my vision just as it disappeared: flash, like a sudden dazzle of the thinnest blade, a sparking over a dun and olive ground at chance intervals from every direction. Then I noticed white specks, some sort of pale petals, small, floating from under my feet on the creek's surface, very slow and steady. So I blurred my eyes and gazed towards the brim of my hat and saw a new world. I saw the pale white circles roll up, roll up, like the world's turning, mute and perfect, and I saw the linear flashes, gleaming silver, like stars being born at random down a rolling scroll of time. Something broke and something opened. I filled up like a new wineskin. I breathed an air like light; I saw a light like water. I was the lip of a fountain the creek filled forever; I was ether, the leaf in the zephyr; I was fleshlike, feather, bone. (p. 31)

What the author has succeeded in doing is to enable the reader to participate vicariously in the auditory and visual qualities of the layered web of life at the creek. Such writing is in no sense a catalog of the number of trout, jays, or oak trees that populate the region; it is not a chronicle of happenings; it is the artistic reconstruction of events that may be more vividly experienced through that distillation called a work of art than in direct contact with the creek. This point is an important one, and one that is frequently overlooked. The artist, like the educational critic, does not write about everything that exists in a situation but rather about what he or she brackets, what he or she chooses to attend to. This bracketing of perception and its incisive rendering in an expressive medium allow the percipient of the artist's or critic's work to see, in part, through the bracket what the artist has created. Many have walked through places like Tinker Creek, but few have seen them with the clarity and sensibility of Annie Dillard.

The perception of both the pervasive qualities—those qualities characterizing a situation or object such as the upward thrust of gothic interiors, the scintillation of light in a Monet landscape, the vacuous mechanical regularity of an assembly line—and component qualities—those particular qualities within a whole, such as the tonal passages in the second movement of Sibelius's First Symphony, the supportive quality of a teacher's smile—are only two important subject matters for critical description. The nature of the "game" that is played is also a proper object of critical description. What are the rules by which educational life in this classroom operates? What are the regularities, the underlying architecture of social life in this school? What is the core value within this mode of school organization, or teaching, or evaluation? The description of these underlying qualities blends into the process of interpretation as well as description. Nevertheless, such structures can be conceptualized and described, and in a certain sense the effort to do so is reminiscent of the structuralist's attempt to locate the basic architecture underlying language. Again, Erickson (1967) makes this point well:

> There are many ways of describing what happens in a social event other than in functionally relevant terms. We could, for example, describe the playing of chess in terms of movement in millimeters forward, backward and sideways on a plane. The behavior of chess pieces on the board could be coded by observers this way with high inter-coder reliability, and the resulting data could be manipulated statistically. Yet such description and analysis would by itself tell us nothing about what was going on in terms of the game of chess. The descriptive categories would have no relevance to the game being played. For that we need descriptive categories with functional relevance for the game—checkmate, defense—terms that are meaningful in terms of an understanding (working theory) of the game as a whole. (p. 23)

All in all, the descriptive aspects of criticism can be regarded as making the most artistic demands on the critic. I say this because it is in the descriptive aspect of criticism that the critic's verbal magic must be most acute. Recall Steinberg's phrase, "An object absent, remote or indistinct leaves a leftover emptiness and a straining to see." To be able to express such an idea, one must not only be in touch with the qualities of a painting and one's response to it, but also be able to capture such qualities through the possibilities within words; a poet must speak. Such demands are not easy to meet, but they are not insurmountable. Indeed, one of the most striking things that has emerged in working with doctoral students at Stanford in educational criticism is the sensitive way in which they have been able to write such criticism. Even students who have had considerable difficulty writing in the traditional academic mode have produced educational criticism of impressive literary quality. To say this is not to imply that all will be the Leo Steinbergs, Max Kozloffs, or Susan Sontags of education. It is to say that the skills of critical writing can be developed and that there may be a good many students for whom this mode of writing is more compatible than the modes that many of them feel compelled to use in order to complete their dissertation.

It is of interest to speculate why some students take to this mode of writing and conceptualization more than others and why some students who do not do well in one mode do well in the other. It *might* be that the kinds of intellectual processes that nondiscursive forms of conceptions and expression require are possessed to different degrees by different students. Present work in the study of the hemispheric specialization of the brain might be relevant to such an explanation. As mentioned earlier, it has long been known that the left hemisphere is the seat of speech, and in the last 30 years neurophysiologists have determined that the right hemisphere plays a distinctively important role in dealing with nonlinear, nondigital, nonconventional forms of conception and expression. Gabrielle Rico (1976) distinguishes between the functions of the hemispheres this way:

> I suggest this fundamental difference lies in the left hemisphere's susceptibility for *order-abiding* capacities and the right hemisphere's susceptibility for *structure-seeking capacities.* The distinction I have in mind which may underlie all the others is clarified by a look at the etymology of "order" and "structure," two words often incorrectly used interchangeably.
>
> *Order,* from the Latin, *orde, ordini,* literally means "in a straight row, in a regular series." The definition of order encompasses anything from "arrangement," "a regular or customary procedure," "established usage," "settled method," to "a precept or command," or "a regulation." Order, therefore, like discourse defined in Chapter I, suggests receptivity to linear, established, regularly patterned, rule-governed activity. Order is imposed from without. Wrote Wittgenstein: "Following a rule is analogous to obeying an order. We are trained to do so: we react to an order in a particular way. . . . When I obey a rule I do not choose."
>
> *Structure,* on the other hand, from the Latin *struere,* means "to heap together" to give the quality of wholeness, totality. Structure does not imply seriality or linearity; it does imply coherence, holism. Structure can be discerned even when only a limited number of relevant elements become apparent, as in a motif of a Beethoven sonata or as in a configuration of a Street Figure Completion test item. Moreover, structure can be independent of a lin-

ear sequence between what comes before and what comes after because it is simultaneously grasped.

Perhaps those students who are best able to work in a critical mode are those whose strongest aptitudes are located in the right hemisphere. At present, the case cannot be demonstrated, yet it is striking that some students take to educational criticism with a sense of ease and competence that seem to fit almost naturally the way in which they encounter the world. Indeed, one student told me that until he encountered the notion of educational criticism and the possibility of doing it within the School of Education at Stanford, he was living two lives. One was the life he led outside Stanford, which was responsive to the arts, to the poetic and romantic aspects of experience, and the other he encountered at Stanford, which presented a different view of reality and required that he substitute Stanford's reality for his own. He now finds he can draw on his sensibilities and on the modes of thinking with which he is most comfortable for doing his work at Stanford. A cognitively schizophrenic existence is no longer necessary.

The Interpretive Aspect of Educational Criticism

Although there is no sharp and clear line to be drawn between the descriptive and the interpretive, there is a difference in emphasis and focus. The interpretive aspect of criticism asks: What does the situation mean to those involved? How does this classroom operate? What ideas, concepts, or theories can be used to explain its major features?

In the interpretive aspect of criticism, ideas from the social sciences most frequently come into play. These ideas form the conceptual maps that enable the educational critic to account for the events that have occurred and to predict some of their consequences. For example, let's assume that someone functioning as an educational critic observes a classroom in which the use of contracts is pervasive. What we have are children of 8 or 9 years of age signing written agreements with teachers to plan and monitor their assignments in school. The use of such contracts creates a particular level of involvement in the classroom that the critic characterizes with sensitivity and vividness. But what do these contracts mean to the students and to the teacher? And what are their long-term effects? What kinds of concomitant learning are the children experiencing? What type of social relations do contracts create, and how do contracts, when they are ubiquitous in a classroom, affect a child's concept of purpose in school?

To answer these questions, one can refer to a host of theoretical ideas within the social sciences to explain the ancillary consequences of contractual relations in face-to-face groups. One can refer to reinforcement theory to explain why contracts might increase dependency rather than autonomy. One can use cognitive field theory to deal with the importance of ambiguity in learning and the effects of contracts on the student's ability to tolerate

ambiguity. The point here is not that there is one theory to be used to interpret the meaning of events within classrooms, but that there is a variety of
theories. No one is interested in the facts by themselves but rather in the
facts interpreted. What theory provides is not single-minded, certain conclusions regarding the meanings secured in school but rather frameworks
that one can use to gain alternative explanation for those events. If theories
in the social sciences can be regarded as games consisting of rules or structures one lays on a field of phenomena for purposes of making some sense
of the phenomena, the interpretive mode of criticism can be regarded as
the application of those games in whatever numbers appear to be useful for
getting on with the business of education.

To be able to apply a variety of theories from the social sciences to the
events occurring within schools and classrooms is no simple task. First, one
must know the theories that are to be applied. Second, one must be in a
position to determine that this particular instance or situation is one for
which a particular theory is appropriate. In legal theory, the process of recognizing that a particular case falls within the province of a law is called
casuistry. And casuistry is a complex art that melds both theoretical knowledge and practical wisdom. No less is called for in seeing the connection
between, say, Maslow's stages of human development and the kinds of
social situations created in classrooms. In the education of teachers and
educational researchers, practice in making such applications has been
rare. We seldom use films or videotapes of classrooms, for example, in the
education of doctoral students, despite all of our talk about the importance
of "multimedia." We do not typically use case material as is used in schools
of law, social work, and schools of business to which theory in the social sciences could be applied. We operate as if the ability to apply the theoretical
ideas one learns in university classrooms is automatic, that no practice is
necessary, that such skills take care of themselves. I wonder on what theories such beliefs are based.

The role of interpretation in criticism is related to the concept of "thick
description" as used by Clifford Geertz (1973) in anthropology:

> Ryle's discussion of "thick description" appears in two recent essays of his
> (now reprinted in the second volume of his Collected Papers) addressed to the
> general question of what, as he puts it, "Le Penseur" is doing: "Thinking and
> Reflecting" and "The Thinking of Thoughts." Consider, he says, two boys
> rapidly contracting the eyelids of their right eyes. In one, this is an involun-
> tary twitch; in the other, a conspiratorial signal to a friend. The two move-
> ments are, as movements, identical; from an I-am-a-camera, "phenomenalis-
> tic" observation of them alone, one could not tell which was twitch and which
> was wink, or indeed whether both or either was twitch or wink. Yet the differ-
> ence, however unphotographable, between a twitch and a wink is vast; as any-
> one unfortunate enough to have had the first taken for the second knows. The
> winker is communicating, and indeed communicating in a quite precise and

special way: (1) deliberately, (2) to someone in particular, (3) to impart a particular message, (4) according to a socially established code, and (5) without cognizance of the rest of the company. As Ryle points out, the winker has done two things, contracted his eyelids and winked, while the twitcher has done only one, contracted his eyelids. Contracting your eyelids on purpose when there exists a public code in which so doing counts as a conspiratorial signal is winking. That's all there is to it: a speck of behavior, a fleck of culture—and voila!—a gesture. (p. 6)

The distinction between thick description and thin description is a useful one. Geertz regards it as the anthropologist's work to explicate social phenomena. "It is explication I am after, construing social expressions on the surface enigmatical" (p. 5). Seeking the deep structure of social events, the rules or modes that give them order, is what ethnographers should do, according to Geertz. It is an enterprise that has its place in the interpretive aspects of educational criticism as well.

The Evaluative Aspect of Educational Criticism

It is, perhaps, the evaluative aspects of educational criticism that most clearly distinguish the work of the educational critic from that of the social scientist. Education is, after all, a normative enterprise. Unlike schooling or learning or socialization (all of which are descriptive terms), education is a process that fosters personal development and contributes to social well-being. This is not necessarily the case with respect to learning, schooling, or socialization, to use only three examples. One can learn to become neurotic, be schooled to become a scoundrel, or be socialized to become a bigot. Education implies some personal and social good. But to say this is to raise the knotty question of what kinds of values to apply to phenomena that aspire to be educational. On this matter there is a wide range of different views. The five curriculum ideologies described in Chapter 3 represent some of the values that different groups bring to the development of educational programs and the assessment of educational practice. Yet, even though different individuals and groups hold different conceptions of educational virtue, and even though their judgments of the value of the processes and outcomes of schooling might differ, the need to make these judgments is inevitable. One must inevitably appraise the value of a set of circumstances if only because, in the process of description, selective perception has already been at work. Evaluation, as I have already indicated, pervades the perceptual processes themselves.

But even if this were not the case, the point of educational criticism is to improve the educational process. This cannot be done unless one has a conception of what counts in that process. Are the children being helped or hindered by the form of teaching they are experiencing? Are they acquiring habits of mind conducive to further development or are these habits likely to hamper further development? What is the relative value of direct learning to ancillary learning within this classroom? Questions such as these require the use of *educational* criteria. The educational critic, unlike the social scientist who has no professional obligation to appraise the educational value of a culture or group, has this obligation as part of his or her work.

To make such judgments requires, as I have already indicated, the application of educational criteria. Where can such criteria be found? They can, of course, come from arbitrary, uncriticized preferences. But the truly competent educational critic is aware not only of the educational values to which he or she subscribes, but also of the values that are rejected. The educational critic will be able to provide grounds for the value choices made while recognizing that others might disagree with these choices.

The grounding of such values not only requires knowledge of the history and philosophy of education, it also benefits from practical experience in the schools. Many things the pedagogically uninitiated might be quick to criticize negatively would give an experienced teacher pause. Teaching tactics that might appear inappropriate to someone fresh out of a graduate school of education and untouched by the trials and tribulations of classroom life might be viewed with greater sympathy by one who has taught. One of the first things that the teachers whose classrooms have been the subject of educational criticism want to know is whether the critic has ever taught. Some things can be known only by having acted. Teaching, like swimming, is one of them.

One of the questions that often arises when the evaluative aspects of educational criticism are discussed is whether the critic should make his or her values known in advance. Should one's educational values be laid out—up front, so to speak? To this question I have a mixed response. On the one hand, it might be useful in preparing an educational criticism to describe the kinds of values that the critic holds so that readers can understand where the critic is coming from. A manifesto of one's educational position insofar as it is describable could, in principle, be provided as a critical prologue to educational criticism. On the other hand, the values one holds permeate the writing one does, just as they permeate the conversations people have about value-saturated issues. After a while those values, even when not explicit, become clear, and after several contacts with a critic's work a prologue might seem redundant. Those who read William F. Buckley, James Kilpatrick, or John Kenneth Galbraith know where these men stand on political and economic matters. I suspect that the same will hold true in reading educational criticism. Indeed, the issue is not whether such values are present but rather whether they should precede the writing of the actual criticism. At this stage in the development of educational criticism as a species of educational evaluation, it appears to me reasonable to have it both ways.

The fact that two critics might disagree on the value they assign to a common set of educational events is not necessarily a liability in educational evaluation; it could be a strength. For much too long, educational events have been assessed as though there were only one set of values to be assigned to such events. The drop in test scores is perceived as a problem, the increase in grade-point average is believed to be a problem, but little or no analysis or few countervailing views are offered. Thus, through a lack of professional leadership, the public takes our lack of analysis and debate on the meaning and significance of such events as tacit assurance that they are indeed indicators of poor-quality schooling. One of the virtues of differences among educational critics with respect to the meaning and significance of educational events is that they could open up the kind of discussion that educational practice should but does not now receive. Virtually every set of educational events, virtually every educational policy, virtually every mode of school organization or form of teaching has certain virtues and certain liabilities. The more that educational criticism can raise the level of discussion on these matters, the better. What I believe intelligent and professionally responsible deliberation calls for is the application of multiple perspectives on an issue or policy, perspectives that view the phenomena from different angles, weigh the costs and benefits, and lead to the core considerations as well as to the ramifications of alternative policy decisions. The denial of complexity, in educational matters, as in politics, is the beginning of tyranny. Educational criticism could contribute to the appreciation of such complexity and therefore provide a more adequate basis for the making of educational judgments.

The fourth aspect of educational criticism is called *thematics*. Thematics is the distillation of the major ideas or conclusions that are to be derived from the material that preceded it. What is the larger lesson or lessons that this particular educational criticism has to offer? What specifically can be learned from it? What does it all add up to? The thematic aspect of educational criticism provides the reader with a kind of summary that enables the reader to grasp the essential point. In a sense, the themes within an educational criticism not only provide a distillation of the essential features of that criticism, but they also provide naturalistic generalizations that can guide one's perception of other classroom, schools, or teaching practices. Although no classroom is identical to any other, the distilled features of a particular classroom have some relationship to features that might be found in others. The identification of themes not only summarizes the essential points of the criticism, but it also enables one to use the criticism as a way of understanding other educational situations.

What then can we say thus far about the characteristics of educational criticism and how it differs as a mode of qualitative inquiry from the kind of quantitative inquiry that is conventionally used in educational research? First, educational criticism is focused essentially on the events and materials that purport to be educational. Its function is to expand one's awareness of such events and objects so that they are more fully appreciated. Appreciation in this context does not refer to the liking of something, although one might like what one sees, but rather to the achievement of a heightened awareness of the subject matter.

To achieve such ends, an educational critic must possess a high level of connoisseurship within the area that he or she criticizes. Criticism can be only as rich as the critic's perceptions. To create such criticism, educational critics prepare material having three major aspects: description, interpretation, and evaluation.

Although there is no sharp line between these aspects of educational criticism, there is a difference in focus and emphasis. The descriptive aspect aims at the vivid rendering of the qualities perceived in the situation. The interpretive attempts to provide an understanding of what has been rendered by using, among other things, ideas, concepts, models, and theories from the social sciences and from history. The evaluative aspect of educational criticism attempts to assess the educational import or significance of the events or objects described or interpreted. The major function of the critic here is to apply educational criteria so that judgments about such events are grounded in some view of what counts within an educational perspective. In the performance of this task, knowledge of the history and philosophy of education is crucial. The former provides the context necessary for purposes of comparison and the latter the theories from which grounded value judgments can be made. An understanding of the variety of orientations to education makes it possible for the educational critic to appreciate what he or she rejects as well as what he or she accepts within educational practice.

Differences between Quantitative and Qualitative Modes of Inquiry

Given these characteristics of educational criticism as both a species of educational evaluation and a qualitative inquiry, we can now ask what the distinctive differences are between qualitative and quantitative modes of inquiry in education.

It is patently clear that quantitative- as well as qualitative-oriented inquirers attend to qualities emerging within educational settings. For example, the investigator who is interested in the incidence of teacher approval in the classroom must attend to qualities in order to detect approval and secure data. Furthermore, both quantitative and qualitative inquirers interpret the information they secure from the classroom, and both will, in general, make some value judgments about its educational meaning—although the qualitative inquirer may be more likely to do this than the quantitative inquirer, whose scientific orientation is less likely to emphasize *explicitly* the appraisal or valuative aspect of the inquiry.

I believe the major differences between quantitative and qualitative inquiry to be two. *The more important difference resides in the language of disclosure that each uses.* The quantitative inquirer is obliged to transform the qualities perceived into quantitative terms so that they can be treated statistically. In this translation the information is altered; differences between qualities are placed on a common scale to make them comparable. This process requires the use of a coding system—number—that is not structurally analogous to the forms that were initially perceived. The number symbol is a representational rather than a presentational symbol.

The qualitative inquirer uses a mode of disclosure that allows the percipient to participate vicariously in the qualities described because the symbols used to describe such qualities are structurally analogous to the event or object. The qualitative description allows the reader to envision and experience what he or she has not experienced directly. Poetry and literature are linguistic paradigms of such description, whereas the other arts—painting, music, dance—provide knowledge in other modes. What most radically distinguishes qualitative from quantitative inquiry is not that the former attends to qualities and the latter does not; they both do. What most sharply differentiates them is how they choose to inform the world about what they have seen.

The second feature that distinguishes quantitative from qualitative inquiry is the tendency of the former to prescribe procedures and to define in advance what shall be attended to. For example, the experiment in education has sought as its ideal procedure one in which all of the variables that might influence an outcome are brought under control. The lack of such controls is considered a confounding factor that makes interpretation difficult. Surprise and uncontrolled variation in educational experimentation are regarded as an epistemological liability.

Take as another example, not the experimental model, but that of systematic observation. Observation schedules are used to predefine what one is to look for; they prescribe to a very high degree what counts and what is to be counted. A qualitative approach to classroom observation is more open-ended and flexible; the investigator or critic, rather than the prestructured schedule, is the major instrument through which observations are made.

In distinguishing between qualitative and quantitative approaches to education, I am in no way attempting to argue that one approach is always superior to the other. One approach *is* superior to the other, but only with respect to the nature of the problem one chooses to investigate. Quantitative methods have clear-cut virtues for some types of questions for which qualitative approaches would prove to be weak and inappropriate. And vice versa. It is this judgment—when and for what purposes each mode of inquiry is appropriate—that poses the toughest intellectual task in laying out a strategy for the investigation of educational problems. It is precisely around such judgments that disagreement is the greatest, because the tools investigators are skilled in using also serve to determine the parameters of their perception and thus how they define the problem itself.

Reliability, Validity, Generalization, and Other Matters of Inference

One of the central reasons given for scientific inquiry is that such inquiry makes it possible not only to secure warrant for belief, but also to establish empirical generalizations. Such generalizations, a product of drawing inferences from a sample, help one anticipate the future. Description, explanation, and prediction are the trinity that scientific inquiry makes possible.

But what of qualitative forms of inquiry that do not employ a scientific model? Can such forms of inquiry yield generalizations? To what extent are the claims they make valid? How is reliability determined? How can we know if educational criticism can be trusted?

The conceptual tools, the statistical procedures, and the research designs available for testing the inferences, reliability, and validity of conclusions in the social sciences are of long standing and highly elaborate. Donald Campbell and Julian Stanley's (1966) classic monograph on experimental and quasiexperimental design is an example of existing canons for the conduct of scientific inquiry in education. Distinctions between Type I and Type II errors, between internal and external validity, between random selection and random assignment, between experimental and quasiexperimental designs, among construct, content, predictive, and concurrent validity, between stability and reliability—these are some of the technical terms that have been created to make scientific inquiry into human affairs more rigorous. Does inquiry in the qualitative arena have similar tools? If so, what are they?

Let's examine first the question that is most frequently raised concerning qualitative inquiry in general and educational criticism in particular: is it objective? Perhaps the first response that should be raised is another question: what is meant by "objective"? Does objective mean that one has discovered reality in its raw, unadulterated form? If so, this conception of objectivity is naive. All of us construct our conception of reality by interacting with the environment. What we take to be true is a product not only of the so-called objective conditions of the environment, but also of how we construe that environment. And that construction is influenced by our previous experience, including our expectations, our existing beliefs, and the conceptual tools through which the objective conditions are defined. To hold that our conceptions of reality are true or objective to the extent that they are isomorphic with reality is to embrace a hopeless correspondence theory of truth—hopeless because to know that our conceptions correspond or deviate from reality would require that we have two conceptions operating. One is an unmediated view of reality, the other our conception of that reality. Only in this way would we know anything about correspondence. If we knew the former, however, we would not need the latter.

What so-called objectivity means is that we believe in what we believe and that others share our beliefs as well. This process is called consensual validation. It operated as powerfully in once-held beliefs in the existence of phlogiston, ether, and a geocentric universe as it does in the religious convictions held by the religiously orthodox. Although a scientifically oriented individual might object and say that scientific beliefs are testable and religious beliefs are not and that the differences therefore are crucial, the religiously orthodox would counter by pointing out that scientific criteria do not exhaust the means through which beliefs can be held to be true. Indeed, they would argue—correctly, I believe—that scientists themselves hold beliefs, even within science, that cannot be warranted by scientific methods. In the social sciences, this most clearly is the case. The differences in basic assumptions among Freudians, Rogerians, Skinnereans, Heiderians, Eriksonians, Piegetians, and the like are not resolvable through science. The fundamental theoretical structures through which each defines psychological reality differ, and there is no critical test that will resolve the truth or falsity of their respective belief systems. Each has a community of believers who reaffirm the beliefs of those working within the system.

My point here is simply this: objectivity is a function of intersubjective agreement among a community of believers. What we can productively ask of a set of ideas is not whether it is *really* true but whether it is useful, whether it allows one to do one's work more effectively, whether it enables one to perceive the phenomenon in more complex and subtle ways, whether it expands one's intelligence in dealing with important problems.

Given this view, what can we say about the means through which educational criticism receives consensual validation? Two processes are important here. One is called structural corroboration and the other referential adequacy.

Structural Corroboration

Structural corroboration is a process of gathering data or information and using it to establish links that eventually create a whole that is supported by the bits of evidence that constitute it. Evidence is structurally corroborative when pieces of evidence validate each other, the story holds up, the pieces fit, it makes sense, the facts are consistent. Take as an example of structural corroboration the work of Inspector Poirot in Agatha Christie's (1974)

Murder on the Orient Express. The inspector finds himself with a dead man, murdered on a train, and the problem of solving the puzzle of who murdered him. Little by little, Poirot succeeds in putting the pieces together so that there are no contradictions, the pieces support one another, and the problem of who killed the man is solved. In the case of the Orient Express, the murdered man once had contact with everyone on the train. The final scene in the book finds Poirot presenting his case to the murderers in the lounge car of the train as it speeds toward Calais. Poirot's brilliant use of evidence works; his conclusions hold up.

The use of structural corroboration is found in jurisprudence as trial lawyers attempt to present to a jury the evidence that will exonerate or convict a defendant. The prosecution tries to create a structurally corroborative set of facts that will persuade a jury to convict, while the defense tries to construct a set that will convince it not to convict. In such circumstances, one has a combination of both structural corroboration—the evidence that the respective attorneys try to muster—and *multiplicative corroboration*—the use of a jury of peers to pass judgment on what has or has not been structurally corroborated. The jury in this case provides the consensual validation for the cases that the attorneys have presented.

When we write or read educational criticism we can ask about the extent to which the facts presented or the interpretation of those facts is corroborated by the way in which they support one another. Does the teacher really play favorites in class or was his behavior in that particular circumstance atypical? Is the teacher genuinely supportive of the students or is she merely using a superficial stock response that gives the illusion of caring? These questions and questions like them can be adequately answered only by securing other evidence that would structurally corroborate the conclusions one has drawn from observation.

The process of structural corroboration is not some exotic process that is used in special circumstances in courtrooms and in doing educational criticism, but it is a ubiquitous part of our daily lives. We all use such processes to make judgments about people, to determine whether they are fake or authentic in their relation with us, to understand their limits so that we can effectively relate to them and to cope with the situations in which we find ourselves. We use this process to negotiate the environment. It is a far more characteristic way of dealing with the world than conducting a controlled experiment. In the flux of events and in encountering new situations—a new classroom, for example—we try to read its code, to find evidence for our impressions, to structurally corroborate our initial observations so that our expectations for that situation are appropriate.

Referential Adequacy

Nevertheless, structurally corroborated conclusions can be false. As Geertz (1973) points out, nothing is so persuasive as a swindler's story. Something more must be added to validate the observations of the educational critic. That something more is the determination of referential adequacy. The end of criticism, as I have already indicated, is a reeducation of the perception of a work of art. For *educational* criticism, the end-in-view is the education of the perception of the educational event or object. We can determine the referential adequacy of criticism by checking the relationship between what the critic has to say and the subject matter of his or her criticism. What the critic does, whether in painting, drama, or schooling, is to write or talk about the object or event he or she has seen. If the talk or writing is useful, we should be able to experience the object or situation in a new, more adequate way. We use the critic's work as a set of cues that enable us to perceive what has been neglected. When the critic's work is referentially adequate we will be able to find in the object, event, or situation what the cues point to. It is in this sense that criticism is a highly empirical undertaking. We look to the phenomena to test the adequacy of critical discourse.

Now it might be objected that the critic might lead us to see certain things in a situation because the criticism biases our perception, that criticism is in a sense something like a self-fulfilling prophecy. I would point out that we all bring to events, situations, and objects certain preconceived ideas; none of us approaches the world with a blank slate. The issue is not whether we come to the world empty-minded, because we have no alternative, but whether what we bring to the world is useful for the purposes we consider important. Criticism is a kind of advance organizer, just as theory in general is an advance organizer.

Others might object and say that educational criticism may lead us to neglect aspects of the situation that the critic might not see or write about. This can occur. We never know when we have a comprehensive view of things, because, as in the correspondence theory of truth, we would need to know the thing itself in its comprehensive form to know whether our view of it was comprehensive. Again, if we knew the former, we would not need the latter. Yet, criticism might lead us to neglect certain aspects of the situation, but that is true of any theory, set of cues, or road map. Take as an example the services of a good travel agent.[1] He or she provides the client with information about what can be seen, but that does not foreclose the possibility of seeing other things as well. In the process of providing such guides, the travel agent readies us for sites and sights that we might otherwise overlook if left to our own devices. When the terrain is new or complex, guideposts help. Effective criticism provides such guideposts.

It is frequently pointed out that critics disagree on the characteristics and merits of the events and objects to which they attend. This claim is in some respects exaggerated. Critics in general achieve a high degree of consensus

---

1. I am indebted to Gail McCutcheon for this example.

on objects or situations that have a reasonable amount of variation in quality. When critics do disagree, it is usually because the objects or events constituting the group to be judged present to critics a narrow range of unusually high-quality work.

But even when this occurs, the issue of differences among critics with respect to, say, the characteristics of classroom life is not crucial. In standard statistical procedures, interjudge agreement is critical. Low levels of interjudge agreement make a study invalid. What one usually does to ensure such agreement is to simplify the phenomena to be counted and to train the judges extensively. If judges are asked to count the incidence of, say, negative verbal statements given by the teacher, the probability of achieving high interjudge agreement is good. The tendency to focus on what can easily be counted is used as a way of achieving high interjudge agreement, even when what is easily counted might be of marginal educational importance.

The need for unanimity among critics is not characteristic of criticism, because it is recognized that complex phenomena—works of literature, painting, film, and the like—have several layers of meaning and that the greatest works seem inexhaustible in the meanings one can secure from them. What is sought is not the creation of one final definitive criticism of a work; rather, the goal is to have our perception and understanding expanded by the criticism we read. Classrooms and schools are at least as multilayered as works of art, and we should seek, therefore, not a single definitive criticism but rather criticism that is useful. Indeed, we should anticipate that critics with different educational orientations and interests will find in situations as phenomenologically dense as classrooms different things to describe, interpret, and evaluate. The cultivation of such productive diversity is a virtue, not a vice. As in education itself, we do not seek to create an army marching in step to the same tune but individuals who follow their own drummer as long as the beat is interesting.

The specter of having to consider for purposes of educational evaluation a variety of educational criticisms is likely to frighten some people. There is often the temptation to seek simple, clear-cut, unambiguous answers to complex problems. Having to consider alternatives, to deal with dilemmas, to resolve contradictions, to think in a complex way about complex issues may seem to be more of a challenge than some are willing to take. The seductiveness of simplicity is worth resisting. Not everything—whether we like it or not—can be scored using an optical scanner.

These two processes, the determination of structural corroboration and referential adequacy, are the two major procedures with which to determine the validity of educational criticism. Structural corroboration seeks to determine the extent to which criticism forms a coherent, persuasive whole. It seeks to determine if the pieces of the critical story hold together, make sense, provide a telling interpretation of the events. Referential adequacy is the process of testing the criticism against the phenomena it seeks to describe, interpret, and evaluate. Referential adequacy is the empirical check of critical disclosure.

The task of determining the referential adequacy of a critical description of a piece of sculpture, painting, or work of architecture is to some extent different from determining the referential adequacy of a criticism of a classroom or other social situation. Works of art such as paintings, sculptures, and buildings do not change over time; classrooms do. How can one be sure that what the critic has created actually fits the phenomena a month or two later? How can a piece of criticism be tested against something that has a dynamic, changing quality? This problem is not unique to educational criticism. Ethnographers face similar problems, and even in the arts, such as in music and theater, two performances are never identical. What one assumes in doing educational criticism, as in doing ethnography, is that the salient and significant characteristics of a situation do not radically alter over brief periods of time. Classrooms and schools do have idiosyncratic characteristics that distinguish them from other classrooms and other schools. One of the reasons it is important for someone functioning as an educational critic to have an extended contract with an educational situation is to be able to recognize events or characteristics that are atypical. One needs sufficient time in a situation to know which qualities characterize it and which do not.

This need for familiarity with the educational situation before a dependable critical account can be rendered is something that virtually all teachers recognize. Teachers do not believe it fair for someone to make a judgment about their teaching on the basis of one 15-minute visit or even one full day's visit. Teachers, like everybody else, have good and bad days. One cannot know which is which on the basis of one observation.

To say that competent educational criticism requires familiarity with the classroom or school to which the criticism is directed is to say that criticism as a form of educational evaluation is not a quick and easy procedure. Unlike the administration of standardized tests that are machine-scored and computer-analyzed, educational criticism requires time. But from my point of view, we have underestimated the amount of time useful educational evaluation requires. Easy test administration and test scoring have been seductively simple tools for evaluating what children learn and experience and what teachers and schools teach. We might very well have to face up to the fact that the kind of evaluation that will be useful to the teacher will need to pay attention not only to the outcomes of teaching and learning but also to the processes. Without careful attention to those processes, we will not be in a position to account for the consequences of our activities. Indeed, the sooner educators help the public to understand the need for forms of evaluation that attend to the processes of teaching and learning, the better. The more we legitimize forms of evaluation that we really believe to be inadequate, the more difficult it will be to provide children with the kind of educational programs to which they should have access.

Can Generalizations Be Drawn from Educational Criticism?

Scientific inquiry yields generalizations that help us to anticipate the future. What can be learned from a form of inquiry that is not scientific in its aims and procedures? What lessons can be learned from doing educational criticism? I believe educational criticism yields two types of generalizations. One of these is the generalization of more refined processes of perception. The other is the creation of new forms of anticipation.

The consequence of using educational criticism to perceive educational objects and events is the development of educational connoisseurship. As one learns how to look at educational phenomena, as one ceases using stock responses to educational situations and develops habits of perceptual exploration, the ability to experience qualities and their relationships increases. This phenomenon occurs in virtually every arena in which connoisseurship has developed. The orchid grower learns to look at orchids in a way that expands his or her perception of their qualities. The makers of cabinets pay special attention to finish, to types of wood and grains, to forms of joining, to the treatment of edges. The football fan learns how to look at plays, defense patterns, and game strategies. Once one develops a perceptual foothold in an arena of activity—orchid growing, cabinet making, or football watching—the skills used in that arena build on themselves for other objects and events within that arena. One does not need the continual expertise of the critic to negotiate new works, or games, or situations. One generalizes the skills developed earlier and expands them through further application. Once having learned that there is something to see or to do, one attempts to see and to do. A child does not need to be taught everything. Once a child learns that there is something to be learned in an area, the child not only learns those things but also learns that he or she can learn even more. This process is not unlike what John M. Stephens (1967) refers to as "spontaneous schooling." If you teach children half of the names of the state capitals of the United States, it won't be long before they know most of the other half.

The point here is that skills generalize. Their use becomes more flexible and sophisticated. As educational criticism contributes to the development of connoisseurship, the generalization of skills occurs. Indeed, that is what is meant by connoisseurship. It is not the ability to appreciate a single object or event but the ability to appreciate a range of objects or events within a particular class or set of classes. No one is regarded as a connoisseur if only one particular object can be appreciated. What generalizes, therefore, in the case I have just described is a process rather than a proposition. This process we refer to as connoisseurship.

The other type of generalization that is fostered by educational criticism is in the acquisition of new forms of anticipation. Educational criticism illuminates particulars, but it is through particulars that concepts and generalizations are formed that are then applied to new situations. What educational criticism does is to help us appreciate the uniqueness of a set of circumstances; but this uniqueness can be appreciated only if we consider it against a backdrop of other instances and circumstances. For example, to recognize the distinctive or unique quality of mind displayed by a particular student we must be able to recognize the ways in which that distinctiveness manifests itself. To do this, some conception of typicality is required. Once having recognized distinctiveness, we are in a position to look for it in subsequent situations. Thus criticism creates forms of anticipation by functioning as a kind of road map for the future. Once having found that such and such exists in a classroom, we learn to anticipate it in other classrooms that we visit. Through our experience we build up a repertoire of anticipatory images that makes our search patterns more efficient.

The potential liability of such a repertoire is that classification and recognition abort perception. We may overlook what is unique by the precocious application of preconceptions. To avoid this, what we seek is a balance between the inclination toward perceptual exploration and the use of a repertoire of expectations that makes exploration fruitful. Kant put it well when he said, "Concepts without percepts are empty, and percepts without concepts are blind."

The kinds of generalizations that criticism yields are much more like those created during the course of ordinary life than those produced through controlled scientific inquiry. In the first place, no one ordinarily sets up the conditions for producing generalizations by randomly selecting objects or events and then randomly assigning them to some treatment. This is not to say that such procedures are not useful. It is to say that we do not negotiate the world in that way, and yet all of us form generalizations. The central question deals with the dependability of the generalizations we form. As a basis for dealing with complex problems of practical decision making, ordinary experience is far more effective than the attempt to design scientific procedures for creating generalizations from situations whose characteristics might no longer be the same after the scientific work has been completed. The point I wish to argue here, however, is not primarily about the virtues and vices of the practical and the theoretical; rather, I wish to argue that useful generalizations are made from particulars all the time. Criticism is one of the means through which the particular situ-

ation can be more effectively experienced and from which useful generalizations can be drawn.

Who Is the Educational Critic?

Although school districts, universities, and other institutions concerned with
the practice of education might eventually employ on their staffs an individual designated as an "educational critic," educational criticism is, as I conceive of it, not so much a role as it is a function. Anyone—student, teacher,
supervisor, school administrator, university professor, school board member—might provide educational criticism to enable a colleague or institution to pursue aims more effectively. In fact, to some degree, each of such
individuals now provides an incipient type of educational criticism. The
teacher provides it when feedback is given to fellow teachers or principals
on the character and quality of their work. Supervisors are professionally
responsible for such criticism when they consciously attempt to provide
pedagogical guidance to teachers. Principals provide it as they appraise the
teaching competency of the school staff, and school boards provide it when
they attempt to assess the work of the school administrator.

Although the perception and appraisal of such work are not considered
forms of educational criticism, the roots of criticism are present. The supervisor, for example, tries to see what goes on in the classroom and attempts
to provide useful feedback to teachers. When principals meet their responsibilities as educational leaders, they, too, attempt to perceive, describe, and
assess so that the quality of educational practice is increased. What has been
lacking is a model with which such practice could be conceptualized, legit-
imized, and refined.

In making the point that existing forms of professional colleagueship
provide incipient forms of educational criticism, I am not suggesting that
what is now done is always adequate or useful. It is to say that both professional and laypeople responsible for the improvement of educational
processes have relied on their own perceptions, sensitivities, and ability to
articulate what they see as a way of improving those processes. The refine-
ment of such dispositions is something that should be encouraged. I prefer
this to the formal designation of an "educational critic" within a school or
school district. I prefer the broad utilization of the concept as a tool for
educational improvement that all involved in the process could learn to use
with skill and sensitivity.

I make this observation because schools are already sufficiently bureaucratized and teachers already too isolated from one another to create the
kind of environment that breeds trust and respect. The nonspecialized use
of educational criticism within classrooms, schools, and school districts
might contribute to the kind of community among staff, students, and par-

ents that would help make schools the kind of supportive and humane places that they can and should become.

Although most of what I have had to say about the subject matter of educational criticism has focused on the activities of teachers and students, educational criticism can be applied to any set of objects and events that one considers relevant to the aims of educational practice. For example, Elizabeth Vallance (1975) focused her efforts on the educational criticism of textbooks used in the social studies. The aim of her work was to identify the ways in which textbook writers and publishers conveyed messages to students, messages that were not simply explicit but instead a function of the ways in which books were designed, color was used, words were employed, emphasis was given in the text, and the like. She writes of one textbook:

> Lacking any central focus other than the general subject-matter, the text develops meanings primarily through the images it creates. These general impressions are perhaps the strongest messages conveyed by the materials. There are several of these, some created by the visual qualities of the text and some by the written content itself. The first and strongest is the image of the city as a clean, well-scrubbed, nicely lighted world. It is an image created entirely through the illustrations. The cheerful colors, the comic-book flavor of fantasy in the drawings, the rich photographic tones, and the wholesome scenes which these portray—all contribute to a feeling of good cheer. Most (though not all) of the few pictures of urban grime manage to look clean and tonally rich, and the factory in the drawing of air and water pollution is quite likeable—the gray, thick and bulbous smoke puffing from the smokestack looks as friendly as the smoke of *The Little Engine That Could.* (pp. 174–176)

What is curious is that all of us living in the United States in the latter half of the 20th century know firsthand how design, packaging techniques, forms of advertising, and types of emphasis given to certain products influence our own behavior and attitudes. The advertising industry is built on the fact that the forms used to market a product have an enormous influence on its success. Exposure, although important for a product, is not enough; the way in which that exposure occurs is important and the characteristics of the qualities that constitute the advertisement are critical. Yet these considerations have, until quite recently, never been applied by educators to textbooks, or, as far as I know, to other instructional tools. The recent exceptions, of course, are in the areas of race and sex stereotyping. But there is considerably more that can be attended to in order to discover the covert messages of the materials that children use in school. These, too, are proper subjects for educational criticism.

Take, as an example, the kinds of images used in illustrations for texts. What sort of men and women are portrayed? What kinds of settings do they work in? What type of emphasis do they receive? How much white space, how much color, what kinds of layouts are used to give emphasis to various aspects of the book? The use of such qualities might seem trivial, but they play on and with the images we hold of people, places, and ideas. The portrait of George Washington on a dollar bill and his heroic image at the bow of a small boat crossing the Delaware amid ice and threatening sky, surrounded by his weary but loyal soldiers, have created an indelible image in the minds of many Americans. Such images influence the ideas we hold, and as such they should warrant our professional attention; yet, educators have given these matters little conscious attention.

Consider as still another example of the objects that ought to receive critical attention the school buildings that we design for students and the furniture we use to fill them.

Buildings represent our ideals about the ways we want to live. State capitols throughout the nation hark back to Greek architecture to express the ideals of government—justice, stability, and historical presence—that citizens believe are conveyed by domes, columns, and white marble. Factories are most often designed with a no-nonsense quality about them. They present an image of work; surfaces are hard, right angles predominate, little is done to refine, embellish, or soften the forms within which people spend a major portion of their waking hours. The factory building expresses what it is, a place of work. Consider bank buildings as another example; although there are exceptions, of course, bank buildings tend to look like the Rock of Gibraltar, having massive shapes and often Greek columns so that they, too, can reap the benefit of association with the past. People who bank their money want a place that looks solid; a fly-by-night image will not do.

And what of schools? What image do schools present to children and parents and the teachers who work there?

School architecture has come a long way since the days when many urban elementary and secondary schools were built, during the 1910s and 1920s. The best of contemporary school architecture is as congenial to the senses as almost anything else that has been built. However, most school buildings, particularly those in cities, are characterized by long vacant halls with nests of well-insulated rooms opening onto them. The rooms are usually identical: strong, rectangular boxes, drab in color and not given to amenities. The rooms speak of functionality but do not address themselves to the aesthetic needs of either students or teachers. They are not places in which one would choose to spend a lot of time.

What do such places say to students? What values do they convey? How do they affect the student's image of the school itself and the experience of schooling? These questions, too, are appropriate ones for educational criticism.

And what of the furniture used in schools? Why the ubiquitous use of formica? Where in the school can one find a soft surface? Where can one encounter a cozy place, somewhere where it is quiet? Where can a student create a place of his or her own? Is a desk large enough for such a purpose?

When in the 1920s the German Bauhaus gave us machine-made furniture that exploited the aesthetic as well as functional possibilities of steel, glass, chrome, and plywood, the concern for proportion, detail, finish, and comfort was critical. The modern furniture of *that* era was so classic in its proportions and style that is still being sold. What is used in most schoolrooms today is furniture that is neither comfortable nor aesthetically satisfying. What passes for modern furniture is too often so unattractive that we learn how to avoid looking at it. Instead of using the environment of the classroom as a source of psychological nourishment, we try to shut it out of our consciousness. The same environmental qualities exist in most college classrooms. The critic of education who can help us to see what we have learned to shut out may be helping us acquire the kind of critical consciousness that is necessary for bringing about change.

Finally, it is appropriate to direct our attention to the works and performances of the student as proper objects of educational criticism. One of the characteristics of standardized testing is that it describes student performance on a common scale. On norm-referenced tests students are differentiated from one another on a common scale of test items and on criterion-referenced tests in relation to their ability to perform at criterion level. In either case, a set of criteria common to all students taking the test is applied and differentiations are made in relation to those criteria.

But what is the distinctive style of a student's ideas, his or her verbal expression, the quality of his paintings, her analytic abilities, the way in which students respond to new opportunities? Is the student perceptive? Is he sensitive to the implications of new ideas or to the feelings of others? Is her written expression lean, logical, and classical or is it romantic, analogical, and baroque? What qualities of mind differentiate this student from the rest? What is it that uniquely characterizes the student's mode of thinking?

Surely attention to the qualities that uniquely distinguish a student from his or her peers is an appropriate consideration for educators to attend to. Surely what we want to know about students and what we wish to cultivate are not only those qualities that they share with every other student, but also the qualities that give them individuality. Because educational criticism focuses on the particular, because it does not require that the particular be characterized on a common scale, its potential for rendering these qualities in a language that makes them vivid is especially great.

In these pages I have tried to describe what I believe qualitative inquiry is in the context of education. The work needed to demonstrate the promise of such inquiry is under way not only at Stanford but also elsewhere in various parts of the world. Indeed, since the 1980s, qualitative inquiry as a form of research has flourished. Dozens of books have been published that address various aspects of qualitative research and the uses of narrative as a way of revealing what only stories can tell has become increasingly important. Connelly and Clandinen, Maxine Greene, Tom Barone, Philip Jackson, David Flinders, Egon Guba and Yvonne Lincoln, and Sarah Lawrence Lightfoot are only a very few of the growing numbers of educational researchers that use artistically grounded and other qualitative approaches as a way of understanding the forms and consequences of teaching.

What has changed in the past decade is not simply the introduction of methods that serve as alternatives to conventional, quantitatively oriented approaches to research, but the realization that humans represent experience through fundamentally different forms and that each of these forms can make a unique contribution to human understanding. Poetic forms of understanding are not the same as those found in propositional discourse. To understand aspects of the world through descriptions of quantity is different than seeing those aspects made vivid through a film or a literary narrative. In short, a new appreciation for cognitive pluralism has developed in the research community and it is beginning to find a place in the schools.

In many ways, experienced teachers have long known what educational researchers steeped in the traditions of the social sciences are only recently discovering: there are many ways of understanding the world and each makes its own special contribution. This new development in education and in research methodology is, in my view, one of the most promising developments for educational inquiry that has emerged in the 20th century.

References

Arnheim, R. (1969). *Visual thinking.* Berkeley: University of California Press.

Campbell, D., & Stanley, J. (1966). *Experimental and quasi-experimental designs for research.* Chicago: Rand McNally.

Cassirer, E. (1953). *An essay on man: An introduction to a philosophy of human culture.* Garden City, NY: Doubleday.

Christie, A. (1974). *Murder on the Orient Express.* London: William Collins Sons.

Dewey, J. (1931). Qualitative thought. In J. Dewey, *Philosophy and civilization* (pp. 93–116). New York: Minton, Balch.

Dewey, J. (1934). *Art as experience.* New York: Minton, Balch.

Dewey, J. (1960). *Experience and education.* New York: Macmillan.

Dillard, A. (1974). *Pilgrim at Tinker Creek.* New York: Harper's Magazine Press.

Erickson, F. (1967, July). *Some approaches to inquiry in school/community ethnography.* In a workshop exploring qualitative/quantitative research methodologies in education, Far West Laboratory for Educational Research and Development, in cooperation with the National Institute of Education and Council on Anthropology and Education, Monterey, CA.

Geertz, C. (1973). *The interpretation of cultures.* New York: Basic Books.

Jeffreys, H. (1961). *Theory of probability* (3rd ed.). London: Oxford University Press.

Kozloff, M. (1969). *Renderings: Critical essays on a century of modern art.* New York: Simon & Schuster.

Langer, S. (1957). *Problems of art.* New York: Charles Scribner's Sons.

Rico, G. (1976). *Metaphors and knowing: Analysis, synthesis, rationale.* Doctoral Dissertation, School of Education, Stanford.

Solzhenitsyn, A. (1964). *A day in the life of Ivan Denisovich.* (Max Hayward and Ronald Hingl, Trans.). New York: Praeger.

Steinberg, L. (1972). *Other criteria: Confrontations with twentieth century art.* London: Oxford University Press.

Stephens, J. M. (1967). *The process of schooling: A psychological examination.* New York: Holt, Rinehart & Winston.

Vallance, E. (1975, July). *Aesthetic criticism and curriculum description.* Doctoral Dissertation, School of Education, Stanford University, Stanford, CA.

Weitz, M. (1966). The nature of art. In Elliot W. Eisner and David Ecker (Eds.), *Readiness in art education.* Waltham, MA: Blaisdell.

11

❧

Some Examples of
Educational Criticism

Technique is the means to the creation of expressive form, the symbol of sentience; the art process is the application of some human skill to this essential purpose.

The making of this expressive form is the creative process that enlists a man's utmost technical skill in the service of his utmost conceptual power, imagination.

SUSANNE K. LANGER

In Chapters 8, 9, and 10, I dealt with some of the important general considerations in the design of educational evaluations. Chapter 10 presented a conceptual overview of educational connoisseurship and educational criticism. In that chapter I tried to provide the rationale underlying this approach to educational evaluation, to make clear its purposes, and to identify the "parts" that constitute the approach. From Chapter 10 you should understand that educational connoisseurship and educational criticism are related, but not identical, to the approaches to criticism used in the fine arts, that educational criticisms are directed to different audiences, that the way in which an educational criticism is written will depend on the audience for whom it is intended, and that criticism includes writing that is descriptive, interpretative, and evaluative in character.

But as you well know—if you have grasped the underlying theme of this book and the two preceding chapters especially—words do not tell all. Between words, sentences, and stories, there often exists an unbridgeable chasm. Hence, one important way to grasp the meaning of educational connoisseurship and educational criticism is to encounter examples of them, to read them, and then to reflect on how they are constructed. This chapter provides five examples of educational criticism, one written by an educational psychologist who "enrolled" in a medical school as a second-year student in order to learn about the ways in which future physicians were trained. A second criticism was written by a professor of education whose specialty is curriculum and evaluation. He was asked to write an educational criticism about a school that had an art program judged by experts to be particularly outstanding. A third criticism was written by a graduate student at Stanford School of Education who attended high school for a full 2 weeks, every day and all day, in order to "shadow" a low-achieving senior male student. The other two criticisms, also written by graduate students in the School of Education at Stanford, are observations of visits to classrooms at the middle and senior high levels. The criticism written by Burchenal was written as a class project. In the case of Porro and Catford, the criticisms were written as a part of an evaluation project with which they were affiliated. In each case the audience for whom the educational criticisms were intended consisted of their peers and their professors in the School of Education at Stanford.

Barone's educational criticism was prepared at the request of *DAEDALUS, Journal of the American Academy of Arts and Sciences*, for publication. Cohen's criticism of a second-year medical school program was initially prepared for a presentation at a symposium at the American Educational Research Association.

As you read these works it will become clear that they differ not only in focus but also in style. Unlike most research articles appearing in psychological journals, educational criticism does not display a single legitimate style of writing: there is no dogma of form to which writing must pledge allegiance. On the contrary, the particular visions and views of the writer, the specific manner in which the piece shall be done, the desirability of leaving one's own thumbprint on the work created are encouraged rather than discouraged. Critics in the fine arts are not voiceless creatures who have gone mute in the service of objectivity. In educational criticism one wants space for one's own subjectivity to operate, for it is from the subjectivities of the world that we learn. The vision of an officially sanctified form or style (the ubiquitous *we* in impersonal "objective" social science writing is largely sham) is an anathema. Let there be but one criterion: the criticism as written and read should provide insight and understanding. Through its form and content (the two cannot in the last analysis be separated) it should broaden and deepen our view of what is going on: it should help us get on with the processes of education.

It has been suggested to me several times during lectures in America and Europe that it would be wise to provide a framework—a set of dimensions or variables—that writers of educational criticism could use to observe and describe classrooms. It would not be a difficult task to provide such a framework, or indeed even a matrix. One can readily make a list of criteria to include: the quality of teaching, the intellectual character of the curriculum, the nature of classroom discourse, the forms of evaluation, and so forth.

One can as easily imagine a scale on the horizontal axis that might easily be converted into a matrix, a scale from 1 to 7. Such a grid or matrix would again be a vehicle for the kind of reductionism that educational criticism is intended to replace. Counting the incidence of behaviors or assigning numerical ratings on a scale of 1 to 7 is not what educational criticism is about, and although there might be a place for such schemes in conventional approaches to classroom research and *even as a part of educational criticism,* there is no exhaustive set of categories, dimensions, or variables that needs to be employed by those who go to classrooms, schools, or communities hoping to learn what their own perceptivity reveals. Well-prepared observers of educational practice already have a head full of grids! The observers take into account far more than can ever be portrayed within a simple classification scheme or taxonomy. More important is the ability to judge wisely which aspects are relevant to which situations, and what in any particular situation is important to see, know, and comment on. Conjure up the image of an art critic or a literary critic approaching a painting or a novel with a mimeographed form affixed to a clipboard. Imagine the critic assigning appropriate numbers to parts of the work. If such an image appears strange, it is because it is. In the end, what I have sought is an approach that exploits rather than buries one's unique perceptivity, that makes educational capital out of the subtle but significant, that recognizes that what is significant can very well be unique to particular situations, that places a premium on the inventiveness of the writer (or photographer) to reveal through the skilled use of word and image what he or she has seen. There are no recipes, no rules to follow, no formulas for writing a report. In educational connoisseurship and educational criticism we start with our own freedom. The work stands or falls, like all criticism, on its capacity to open our eyes and to help us understand. I believe the five criticisms that follow make important contributions to this end.

Meta-criticism is the criticism of criticism. What has a critic done? What has he or she intended? How does the critic convey meaning? What has been emphasized? In Chapter 12, I shall examine one of the educational criticisms in order to reveal how the critic's language, tone, and structure perform work within the criticism itself.

Playing the School System: The Low-Achiever's Game

BARBARA PORRO

"So much of adolescence is an ill-defined dying,
an intolerable waiting
a longing for another place and time,
another condition."

ROETHKE (1956)

1.   As part of my recent training at Stanford, I was sent to Claremont High to follow Bob and to discover what high school is like for a low-achieving sophomore. I came to this experience having spent 9 years as an elementary teacher in nonpublic schools. So although I have an insider's view of education, both the high school level and the public school setting were new territories for me.

2.   I was first introduced to Bob on the side lawn, that place on the Claremont High School campus designated as the smoking section. Students who meet on the side lawn are drawn together for a number of reasons. Besides the fact that they smoke, many of the students are close friends who enjoy being together. I was immediately struck by how friendly and playful these students are toward one another. They share food, bum cigarettes, play cards, swap personal stories, keep each other warm on cold days, flirt, joke, and generally have a good time. As one student from the side lawn put it: "We have a reputation of being tough, but really we probably have better friends that any one else on this campus. The thing about the side-lawners is—we hang together. If somebody messes with one of us, they'll have to take on the whole side lawn."

3.   In addition to being stereotyped as "tough," members of this group are also characterized as the low achievers, those students who will never amount to much academically because they lack the skills, the interest, or both. The low-achiever label, like the "tough" label, fits this group of students from an outsider's perspective. If you ask the side-lawners what they are about, however, you will find with a high degree of consensus that they are seriously engaged in getting through high school by doing the least amount of academic work necessary to pass their courses. I came to realize in my 2 weeks as a pseudo–side-lawner that not only does this require a substantial amount of concentrated effort, but also that they are highly successful at achieving their goal. It is quite possible to get through high school without doing much, at least at Claremont. I was lucky to have been paired with Bob because of his uncanny knack at playing the low achiever's game and because of his willingness to share "inside" information. You can't tell by looking at Bob how bright and perceptive he really is. He's bigger and older than the other sophomores and has a sloppy but "cool" look about him. Typically he wears a baseball cap, "shades," jeans, and a t-shirt that says "The Moose is Loose." His peers and teachers are naturally attracted to his warm, playful spirit and charming sense of humor. His savvy is perceivable only if you discover how masterful Bob is at playing every situation to his advantage. By following Bob, I gained access into the kind of high school experience most teachers and administrators would rather sweep under the carpet. Bob, in his single-minded effort to avoid school work, pointed out all the loopholes in a system loosely designed to educate.

> The district office calls low-achieving students *terminal,* meaning that their education will terminate with a high school diploma.

> Me: What's going on in school?
> Side-lawner: Nothing . . . it's boring . . . same thing every day . . . excitement level zero.
> Me: So, you're trying to get through high school the easiest way possible?
> Side-lawner: Actually it'd be easier if we just did the work. . . . The work's not so hard. I'd just rather not do it.

> Bob is a Title I student, which means he is 2 years behind in reading and math according to test scores. Bob's counselor told me that Bob is a capable student, but he's never really tried very hard. "He took over my office one day and did a fine job. He's really quite perceptive and smart."

The Outside Game

4.   High school is played in two main areas—outside on the patios and lawns, and inside the classrooms. Like many of the side-lawners, Bob prefers the outside area because it is here he can avoid school work most effectively. School officials permit student to legitimately visit the outside area for 15 minutes during "brunch," 30 minutes during lunch, and 5 minutes between classes. There are, however, many

additional ways to stay outside if one is clever enough to know when to skip class. "Stealing" additional outside time is one of Bob's strong suits.

5. At first I carefully noted the details surrounding Bob's "cutting" behavior in an effort to discover a pattern. Then one day, while snacking with the side-lawners, I asked them outright: "How do you decide which classes to go to and which classes to cut?" They collectively offered these general cutting tips: (1) Seventh period is a good one to cut because Edwards (the dean who prowls the campus looking for delinquent students) is never around; (2) don't skip second period because that's when the roll is sent to the office and if you're absent, they call your home to find out if you're really sick; (3) forge a note from your parents saying you have a doctor's appointment, show it to the teacher, and then cut the class; (4) get an appointment card from the counseling office, write yourself an appointment for the period you wish to cut, present it to the teacher, and walk out; (5) determine which teachers do not penalize you for an "unexcused" absence and cut their classes at your own discretion. (Penalties include lowering your grade or sending you to detention.) Bob used this last strategy most frequently because he had several teachers who accepted his cutting behavior without penalty. In the 8 days I followed Bob, he cut six classes and was late to five.

Several teachers remarked that the rainy weather had helped promote good attendance. On sunny days students are more inclined to go to the beach than to class, especially in the afternoon.

Mr. Edwards, dean: "Skipping class is the most difficult problem of all to control. When I have time, I pop up unexpectedly in different places around the campus and send students to class. This creates the illusion that I'm always watching."

---

6. The only other way to get out of class is by being suspended. None of the students recommended this method because you can only be suspended for committing a serious offense and this is often upsetting to parents. The students quickly pointed out how counter-intuitive suspension is as a punishment: "It's stupid to kick you out of school when you do something wrong. We don't want to be here anyway, and you can't learn anything when you're not at school." I saw the logic in this a few days later when Bob was suspended for getting into a fight. Although he was suspended on Tuesday at 10:30 in the morning, he had no way of getting home so he spent the rest of the school day lounging on the side lawn, talking and smoking with his friends. The lecture he missed in Health class that afternoon described the damaging effects of smoking on the body. When Bob and I met back at school Thursday morning, he informed me that he had made $30 mowing lawns on his "day off." Because Bob's absence was "excused," none of his teachers penalized him for missing nearly 2 days of class.

The Inside Game

7.   Teachers and students met in an assigned room to conduct class seven periods each day for 45 minutes each. The first thing I noticed about most of the classrooms is that no one seems to live in them. The rooms are furnished with the bare essentials: 30 to 35 desks lined up facing a teacher's desk, chalkboard, clock, filing cabinet, an occasional stack of dusty books, bulletin boards. None of the bulletin boards contain information that is currently relevant to the material being presented to students; some of the information is not even relevant to the class. For example, in the room where Psychology meets, the walls are decorated with a map of Vietnam, a poster of San Francisco, and a picture of a girl dancing. Perhaps it is because the rooms are shared by a number of teachers that no one has bothered to set up a learning environment.

8.   Students, too, move in and out of the space without regard for the mark they leave. Although there seems to be a generally accepted set of ground rules for appropriate classroom behavior, whether the rules are enforced or not depends on individual teachers. In one classroom the rules are posted on a wall. Even in this room, however, desks are scribbled on and food wrappers often litter the floor.

PLEASE!

*Do not eat in class.

*Do not drink soft drinks or hot chocolate in class.

*Do not write on the desks.

*Do not bring skateboards or tape decks to class.

---

9.   The most colorful aspect of classroom life is the students themselves, who are generally accepted on a "come as you are" basis. Students wear their culture proudly—miniskirts, sweat shirts, punk rock mohawk hair-dos, baseball caps, sneakers. Everyone carries a comb and uses it. The girls have additional beauty aids they apply regularly—lipstick, eye makeup, perfume, nail polish. Students saunter into class, take a seat with friends (which sometimes involves moving furniture), and do their own thing: the fun-loving types toss paper balls and peanuts across the room; the hungry ones eat apples, bananas, and potato chips; the sexy students massage each other's hands in the back of the room; the new-age adolescents arrange dope deals. Whatever students bring to class gets passed around—lollipops, candy bars, cans of coke, magazines. Then the bell rings, the teacher calls for quiet, and (for students like Bob) the waiting begins.

Bathroom Graffiti

"This school system is going down the tubes."

"Does anyone know how it feels to be pregnant?"

"Yeah, I've already had 4 kids and I'm only a sophomore."

"At least you don't get your period"

"When you're p.g. you feel kind of sick in the morning, sometimes all day. You get some cramps, and you feel tired."

Thanks!

10. Although there is a fair amount of variation in what takes place during the 45 minutes between bells, watching the clock is a popular activity in all classrooms. This was perhaps most obvious in Bob's math class where the clock was broken. Whenever students wanted to know the time they asked Bob, the only person in the room with a watch. During the last 20 minutes of one class, students asked Bob on five occasions for the time. Bob's answers were direct and to the point: "only 20 more minutes," "10 minutes to go," and finally "9:28 school time," at which point students stood up and walked toward the door. It was not uncommon for students to stand up 1 or 2 minutes before the bell, even while the teacher was talking. Teachers respect this as a signal to stop talking, and wait with students for the bell to ring. The clock, it seems, controls teachers as well as students.

"School time" is 5 minutes slower than time outside of school. The clocks have been set back 5 minutes to help students be more punctual. Students still come late to class, however, because they know the clocks are slow and they also know how to tell time.

Cartoon on the chalkboard in math class:

11. The classes Bob attends are different in a number of ways, depending on how individual teachers interpret their role. The teachers have different perceptions of what school is about, different modes of conducting class, and different expecta-tions of students—all with different effects on Bob's behavior in the classroom. When I asked myself the question, "What's going on in this room?" I discovered that the classes fell roughly into three broad categories that sketch a continuum.

12. *Pretend School.* The first category, marking an extreme end of the contin-uum, is "Pretend School," which describes those classes in which teachers and stu-dents go through the motions of conducting school without considering educational consequences. These teachers seem to gear their courses in response to the attitudes of the low-achieving students rather than to their academic ability. The predomi-nant teaching style used in these classrooms is lecturing, though I use the term loosely to refer to teacher talking, students listening. (Films are often substituted for the teacher at the front.) The "Pretend School" classes are a good match for Bob because it is in these rooms that teachers are most cooperative in helping Bob "get by without doing much."

13. Three of Bob's classes fit the "Pretend School" category. The first class, Mythology, is taught by Mr. Arnold. Although this course counts as an English credit, students read/wrote on only 1 of the 8 days I observed. The rest of the time students listened. During three class periods Mr. Arnold told the story of the Greek myth *Odysseus,* and on three different days students watched the full-length film of the same story. These listening activities accomplished the goal Mr. Arnold had set for himself—to expose students to Greek mythology in an exciting way. As he put it, "You've got to be realistic when teaching a group of students who are terrible at writing and who don't put out much. Even though these students can't read, they can appreciate a good story, and if you're a good story performer, they'll be good listeners." Mr. Arnold was an outstanding storyteller and the students responded by sitting quietly. Not only was he well-informed about Greek mythology, but also his delivery was entertaining. He brought the stories to life by inserting dialogue, often in the students' vernacular, and by acting out the exciting battle scenes.

Me: What do you like least about teaching?

Mr. A: My salary. . . . Any other professional who gives four shows daily gets paid much more than I do.

---

14. Another priority of Mr. Arnold's is to relate to students in an open, easygo-ing way. "If you don't maintain good relations with students," he cautioned, "they'll turn off." Mr. Arnold remained cheerful and friendly even when students came late to class, socialized at inappropriate times, or chose not to work on class assignments. During one in-class assignment, Mr. Arnold circulated among half the students who were working, while the rest of the class openly talked, looked at magazines, combed their hair, or sat quietly doing nothing. Mr. Arnold made no attempt to bring the nonproductive students to task.

15. Mr. Arnold also was lenient when it came to homework. The "major paper" he assigned asked students to write three diary entries that might have been written by one of the people involved in the Trojan War. When he introduced the assignment, he let students know that "if you weren't here when I told the story, you'll have to read the book because the movie version isn't accurate."

This was my fourth day of observation and the first time I heard a book mentioned in this class. Mr. Arnold later explained that he was basing the course on Hamilton's *Mythology,* but unfortunately there weren't enough books for every student to have one.

---

16. The day the assignment was due, 1 week later, Mr. Arnold reminded students that he would be filing progress reports on the following day, and because this was the only paper he had assigned that term, it was important that they turn in something. He gave students the period to work on their papers and circulated among them doing whatever was necessary to get students working.

17. Bob had no paper, no pen, and no idea what the assignment was. When Mr. Arnold realized his predicament, he gave Bob a piece of paper, offered him a pen, and suggested he write his diary from Hector's perspective. "Was Hector on the Trojan or Greek side?" Bob asked, hoping for additional clues. "Hector was the greatest of the Trojan fighters," said Mr. Arnold in a friendly tone, and with that he began to dictate a few lines from Hector's diary. "Can you do it now?" Mr. Arnold asked in the end.

During my 2-week stay, this was the only class in which Bob was assigned a piece of homework.

---

18. Twelve minutes before the assignment was due, Bob made his first mark in the page. Although he did not hand in a paper at the end of the class, Bob later informed me that Mr. Arnold had not sent him a negative evaluation. "How did you get away with that?" I asked Bob. He smiled wide: "I just told him that I had to work and didn't have time to do the paper. [Bob works 29 hours per week at a sandwich shop.] Besides, Mr. Arnold likes me." Bob had taken a risk and won. He figured Mr. Arnold would not grade him down on the midterm evaluation even though he did not write the "major paper," and he was right.

Me: What do you think about Mythology?
Bob: It's boring but okay because it's not hard. You don't have to read the book . . . just listen to the lecture and watch the movies. . . . Mr. Arnold is a nice guy.

---

19. Bob's General Science class, taught by Mr. Cleary, is easier than Mythology in that less is expected of him, but harder to sit through because it is "dead boring."

Although the period often begins with students reading from the science textbook, Mr. Cleary usually dominates class time by telling personal stories that are unrelated to the lesson in the text. As one student put it, "I like science, but Mr. Cleary gets off the track real easy." Dr. Pinot, a visiting scholar at Stanford in the area of science education, accompanied me to class one day and shared these observations: "The lesson consisted of two parts: A student read aloud a page and a half devoted to genetic counseling and then the teacher began to talk, telling all kinds of stories on marginal issues such as his acquaintance with a genetic counselor and with epileptic people. There was no discussion of the real issues and no attempt to explain the biological principles presented in the text. In fact it was clear that the teacher himself knew very little about these biological principles. I had the impression that initially the students were interested in what they read, but when the teacher began to talk they 'switched off.'"

20. In an interview with Mr. Cleary, I learned that he does not expect students to take notes during class and that he does not assign homework. When I asked how he determined grades, he said he does not give tests because "they don't tell me anything I don't already know. I grade on what I think they've learned and if they're involved."

Mr. C had recently received notice that he would not be asked to return the following year. Mr. C has been teaching science for 25 years.

---

21. Mr. Cleary's perception of low-achieving students reveals his priorities and helps explain why he teaches in this way. In his mind the students' low self-esteem is the primary cause of their academic failings. Mr. Cleary said that, more important than teaching science, he wants to change the way students feel about themselves. "I'd like to break the chain that goes back a long time with these students . . . that they're no good. I want them to learn that the authority is not cruel and unreasonable, that they are not helpless, that they can affect the outcome."

22. Mr. Cleary's manner of conducting class demonstrated a sincere concern for students. He repeatedly told students how much he respected their opinions, listened carefully to what students had to say, and responded to their comments in a caring manner. Unfortunately, Mr. Cleary's affective agenda did not have much to do with science and often lost students' interest and attention along the way. It was not uncommon to see students whispering to their neighbors, reading other books, passing notes to friends, or sitting with their heads down.

During one class meeting Mr. C reached down from where he was sitting and gently roused a sleeping boy.

---

23. Bob often skipped science class because "we never do anything. He just sits up there and tells stories like an old lady." Bob could easily get out of class by telling

Mr. Cleary that he was working on a project he was making in Woodworking II, the class Bob attends the period before. One of the days Bob skipped class, Mr. Cleary explained to me that although he supported Bob in his shop work, Bob had been "overdoing it lately."

24. The third class that fits the "Pretend School" category is Health, 7th period. This is a particularly difficult class to teach, according to Ms. Morton, because it's the last period in the day and "no one wants to be here." Ms. Morton usually begins class by reminding students how to behave: "Stop talking please . . . take your feet off the table . . . the next time I see food in here I'm going to ask you to leave . . . put the ball away please." Ms. Morton often relies on audiovisual materials to keep students focused during this difficult period. Films, videotapes, or slides were shown in over half the classes I attended, including two full-length movies about schizophrenics, lasting 3 days each. The films, *Sybil* and *Five of Me,* were presented to students at a time when the class was studying Red Cross First Aid techniques. When I asked Ms. Morton why she was showing *Sybil* she said that if she showed it earlier when they were studying mental health, the students would have nothing to look forward to.

> Bob: I'm cutting 7th.
> Me: Why?
> Bob: Why not.

> At the end of class one day, Ms. M put in one final request: "Will you please remember to go to the bathroom *before* you come to class tomorrow?"

25. When students were not viewing audiovisual materials, they either listened to Ms. Morton lecture or worked on assignments and tests. Both activities served to run students through the course; rarely did the exercises allow students to discuss the material. For example, on two occasions students were asked to fill out a questionnaire prior to a lecture. Five minutes later the teacher read the true-or-false answers without reading the question or presenting any kind of explanation. In a similar way, lectures were formally delivered without any attempt to involve students, even when the material seemed relevant to their personal lives. In one lecture on alcoholism, for example, she named groups of people who experience problems with drinking, statistically speaking. Included in her report was the fact that alcoholism is the "biggest teenage health problem today." The teacher listed the nine signs of being an alcoholic on the board and asked students to copy the list because "it will be on your quiz tomorrow." When she read the list out loud to students, she mentioned that one of the items—"drinking alone"—may not apply to them because "you're underage and can't legally drink in public . . . so if you drink alone, it does not necessarily mean you have a problem." Although Ms. Morton seemed to be aware that students in the class probably drank alcohol, she was not interested in opening up the topic for discussion. Her tacit acknowledgment that the students drank alcohol and her unwillingness to deal with the issue almost seemed to condone the activity.

> One day when we arrived late to class, we found a note on the door: "In library, 7th period." Bob ripped the note from the door and stuffed it in his pocket explaining, "Here's another way to cut class. When she says 'Didn't you read the note that we were meeting in the library?' I'll say, what note?"

26. There appeared to be two types of students in Ms. Morton's class: those who did what the teacher said and those who didn't. Academic work was completed on time by the diligent students, while the others (including Bob) generally ignored the assignments. Ms. Morton responded to the nonworking students by extending all deadlines in the hope that they would eventually turn something in. Even tests were negotiable. On one day, for example, students who were not ready to take a quiz were invited to go to a neighboring room to study. The ten students who remained in the room were apparently the only ones in the class who were running the course on time. (Twenty-one students are enrolled.) Ms. Morton later warned students who were "getting behind" that if they hadn't turned in 60% of the assigned work by the following week, they would receive a negative progress report. Although Bob did receive a failing midterm evaluation, he invented an excuse that convinced Ms. Morton to change her report. Once again, Bob had managed to remain in good standing as a student without doing any academic work.

> A poster on the wall reads:
> SILENCE is the only successful substitute for brains.

> "Are you going to study?" I asked Bob as he raced out the door. "Are you kidding?" Bob replied, lighting a cigarette and walking to the side lawn.

27. *High Standards Classroom.* A second broad category of classroom types, positioned at the opposite end of the continuum, is the "High Standards Classroom" or "Simulated College." Unlike "Pretend School" teachers who take their cues from the reluctant learner's attitude, the "High Standards Classroom" teacher bases the curriculum on some external consideration—what students *should* be able to handle, for example, or what students will need when they go to college. This type of classroom is not a good match for Bob because the curriculum is delivered above Bob's head. Fortunately Bob is taking only one "High Standards" class, Psychology. Bob was forced to take this Psychology course because it is the only class he could get into that would fulfill the "History" requirement. (Bob's first choice, Film Literature, was already filled.)

28.   Mr. Kelly's goal in teaching the course is "to expose students to all the difference areas of psychology that they might be interested in pursuing in college." The instructional style Mr. Kelly uses is similar in some ways to Bob's other teachers. Lectures were used to deliver the bulk of course material. During Mr. Kelly's classes, however, students were expected to take notes and participate in discussion (though Bob didn't do either). Mr. Kelly dictated his lectures slowly enough for students to copy the material verbatim, even spelling out the more difficult psychological terms for students. Mr. Kelly was quite willing to interrupt his lecture to answer students' questions. He always switched from psychological jargon to students' lingo in addressing their remarks, and often succeeded in getting a discussion going with students. This was the only class I observed where dialogue between teacher and students lasted more than a few moments.

> Mr. Kelly: We're trying to get this course to be a senior elective again. There's a real mix in here now, and it's impossible to meet all their needs. . . . The problem with public education is they're trying to educate *everybody*. As a result, all the programs have to be watered down.

29.   Mr. Kelly also relied heavily on films to fill class time. In fact, he showed two of the same films we saw in Health—*Sybil* and *Five of Me*. Unlike the Health showing, however, Mr. Kelly related the films to the Abnormal Psychology unit they were currently studying. Mr. Kelly liked these films about schizophrenics because they vividly showed a wide variety of bizarre behavior. Although the students were obviously fascinated with these psychotic characters, I couldn't help but feel that the teacher was exploiting a sensational aspect of psychology for the sake of keeping his audience's attention. Why should teenagers be asked to learn the difference between hebephrenic and catatonic forms of schizophrenia when they are experiencing their own pubescent problems? (The syllabus indicated that the unit dealing with abnormal psychology took up nearly half of the 9-week course.)

> This was not the only class in which the curriculum overlapped. Near the end of my visits, sex education was introduced in both Science and Health.

30.   Mr. Kelly expected students to attend class, participate in discussion, and perform well on tests in order to pass the course. According to Mr. Kelly, Bob is in danger of failing the course because "he doesn't do anything; he just shows up." Bob does show up because he knows his grade will be lowered if he doesn't. According to Bob, Mr. Kelly is hard to outfox because he's young and "knows how kids are these days." Although Bob received a negative evaluation from Mr. Kelly in the midterm report, Bob later got a "B" on the abnormal psychology unit test. "How did you manage to do that?" I asked Bob. "It was an easy test," he explained, "Multiple guess and true/false, the kind made up by the textbook. I just skimmed the chapter before taking the test." Part of playing the low-achiever game skillfully is knowing when to become involved in the academics to secure the long-range goal: passing the course. The failing midterm report had alerted Bob to the fact that it was time to start acting like a student.

Bob worked out an arrangement with his sister to intercept the "progress report" from the mailbox before his parents got home from work.

---

31. *Real School.* The last category of classes is where "Real School" takes place. By this I mean that the majority of students spent a fair amount of time actively engaged in academic learning. The two classes that fit this description are different from Bob's other classes in several ways: the teachers gear instruction to the students' actual academic ability (rather than the students' lackadaisical attitude or some external standard); the teachers' instructional mode is private, 1:1 tutoring (rather than lecturing); and in both "Real" classes, students spent the majority of time doing an activity (rather than passively listening). In General Math and Woodworking II, the two classes in which these conditions were found, Bob stopped playing the low-achiever's game and became a real student.

32. Why does Bob choose to work in math rather than goof off? The most obvious answer is that in math, unlike most of his other classes, there is something for Bob to *do*. The teacher, Ms. Golden, organizes class time around a daily assignment she has specially designed for low-ability students. Each period follows the same pattern: Ms. Golden announces the assignment for the day, places it on a shelf, and circulates among individuals, offering help and encouragement; students pick up the assignment, work independently or with friends, and call on Ms. Golden for assistance.

33. Another way in which math differs from Bob's other classes is that the teacher does not adjust her expectations of students in response to their attitude. Her approach to students communicates a clear sense of her role and theirs: "It's your responsibility to do the work, not mine to make you do it. If you want to pass this course, that's up to you. I'm here to help those who are here to learn." Ms. Golden's expectations of students are stated in the syllabus and are non-negotiable: students must complete 75% of the assignments or they will receive an incomplete; students who do not finish the assignments in class are expected to finish them as homework; students with unexcused absences or tardiness must make up the missed time or they will lose points; students may not leave the room to go to their locker or to the bathroom until after the bell rings.

Ms. Golden: Math I and II are really the same course, but students can take it twice for credit. This is Bob's second year with me.

> Bob: I tried to take Algebra I but it was all lecture, and the homework you had to do at home. I don't do homework, so I flunked Algebra and switched back into Ms. Golden's class.

34. Establishing clear expectations with students does not wholly account for Ms. Golden's success, however. When I asked Bob why he worked in Ms. Golden's class, he said, "because she deserves it." Bob is one of many students who describes Ms. Golden as his favorite teacher. What is it about Ms. Golden that students like? Students responded to the question in this way: "because she cares about you," "because she knows what she's doing," "because she helps you learn," "because she's not too hard and not too easy." Ms. Golden seemed to have the right combination of qualities as a person and as a teacher to win her students over.

35. As I listened to Ms. Golden's conversations with students, I realized that she treated them individually and related to them on two different levels—as their teacher and as their friend. The way she talked to students depended on what the situation called for. To one student she issued an ultimatum: "We went over this stuff yesterday. If you feel you know it well enough to cut, you can figure it out yourself." In the next moment she complimented a boy on his new mohawk haircut. To the student who does a good job, she gives a pat on the back, "oh yes, you're so smart." And always, very patiently, Ms. Golden answers whatever question students ask. During one class period, I heard her explain how to do the assignment to five different students. When I asked why she repeated the directions to individuals rather than insist that students listen the first time, she explained that "only a few students get it from the lecture; the rest need to hear it individually." In this sense, Ms. Golden had adjusted her style to meet the needs of students who habitually "tune out" teacher talk, except in answer to a direct question.

36. Ms. Golden lectured one time, on the day she introduced new vocabulary words for the geometry unit they were beginning. She spoke slowly, used simple language, demonstrated her main points on the board, maintained eye contact with students, and asked them repeatedly if they understood the material. Her remarks were addressed to this particular group of students. Students listened attentively and were obviously "with it."

> Ms. Golden: Okay. If I asked you on a test to circle the "endpoints," show me what you'd do.

37. Bob never skipped math and worked hard on the daily assignments. When Bob got behind in completing one of his assignments, he finished the work at home. This was the only class in which I observed Bob taking a test. Before my very eyes, Bob had transformed himself into a real student.

38. The other class where Bob consistently worked is Woodworking II, taught by Mr. Teicher. Like Math class, students spent the period actively applying the skills they have learned to a specific task. In shop class, however, the projects are chosen and designed by the students themselves. Some of their projects included building dressers, bookcases, skateboards, and wine racks. Bob was making a kitchen cupboard for his neighbor who often takes him fishing. It is easy to sense the students' high level of involvement. They are busy with their hands and bodies the entire class period—sawing, hammering, sanding, staining. While students work, Mr. Teicher circulates among them, answering questions, checking the quality of their work, offering suggestions for improvement. He takes time to lead the students through the thinking process rather than simply telling students how to solve their construction problems.

39. The students respect Mr. Teicher's skill as a craftsman and as a teacher. When I asked students what they thought about Mr. Teicher they said: "He's a real good teacher. He knows what he's doing. He'll let you make a mistake and then he'll teach you how to fix it. He can fix anything. And he jokes around a lot." Bob never skipped Mr. Teicher's class and on a few occasions worked overtime on his project. Although it is true Bob used his shop work as an excuse to get out of science, it was also obvious that Bob was wholly invested in constructing his cupboard.

What Does It Mean?

40. The close-up view Bob has provided says a number of things about the high school experience. Perhaps most obvious is the fact that Bob is winning his game. During the 2 weeks I observed, he carried no books, he seldom had paper, he rarely read or wrote (except numbers in math class), he almost never knew what the teacher was talking about, he skipped many classes, and he's passing his courses. You may find this difficult to believe, as I did at first. You may wish to call Bob the exception. But, in fact, Bob is one of many students I observed who is opting out of learning and is "getting away with it." If you talk to people at Claremont High, you will find that this is not unusual. It is simply the way things are; everyone has adapted accordingly. The way they adapt varies from person to person, but generally speaking, all "ways" are acceptable. Some play pretend school, other maintain high standards, and a few provide real educational experiences. Students and teachers alike have the option of playing school whichever way makes sense to them without upsetting the status quo and without jeopardizing their personal goals. Thus we see Bob faking it at the same time we see pretend teachers keeping their jobs at the same time we see gifted teachers stimulating Bob. The two teachers conducting "Real School" are not responding to any pressure they feel within the system to do a good job, but rather to their own personal commitment to make something educational happen. These exceptional teachers are exceptional individuals.

> Me: How did you get so good at avoiding school work?
> Bob: It comes with experience.
> Me: Oh yeah? How long have you been doing it?
> Bob: Ever since I figured out I could get away with it . . . about second grade.

> Me: Are you trying to graduate?
> Senior: I'm not trying, but I'm going to graduate.

> Me: How can you stand to sit here all day?
> Bob: You get used to it.

41.   The Claremont High School system is not so exceptional, however. Although it appears to be running smoothly, like a good machine, the way in which it operates is not necessarily related to educating. The system merely sets up an opportunity for education to take place. Whether or not real education happens is up to individual teachers and students.

42.   I brought Bob to Stanford one day to show him my school. At the end of the tour he told me he was thinking of going to Foothill College after he graduates. "What!" I said in disbelief. "I can get a better job if I go to Foothill. The only problem is I hate to read."

> Me, during the Stanford tour: There's no way to fake it at this place.
> Bob: Yeah? That's what they said when I was in junior high . . . "wait till you get to high school, then you'll *really* have to work." What a joke! High school turned out to be *easier* than junior high.

43.   My guess is that Bob doesn't like reading because he can't read very well. Bob is not learning to read better in high school because he is not participating in the academic life there and because he has not been lucky enough to get an English teacher who knows how to motivate Bob to learn. The cost Bob will pay as a result of these unfortunate circumstances is high: many doors will be permanently closed by Bob's "terminal" high school diploma. Bob has not yet figured this out—that there may be something in school for him. He is too busy "beating the system."

> Me: What do you want to be when you grow up?
> Bob: I don't know. . . . Maybe a machine operator like my Dad, or a truck driver like a friend of mine.

44.   Why is Bob playing this self-defeating game? One possible reason is that school is so boring for Bob. He plays his game in order to liven things up. It is much more interesting to try to "get away with stuff" than to do what "they" want you to do. Bob's game adds a little challenge to an otherwise dull day, and because he is successful, it gives him a sense of personal power, a feeling of being in control.

Me: What do you like to do at school?
Student from the side lawn: Get away with stuff.
Me: What can you get away with?
Student: You name it.

Me: Why do you suppose you're so good at getting away with stuff?
Bob: Because I am AWESOME, and the teachers are lame.

45. Another guess is that Bob doesn't want to do school work because it is not something he has personally chosen. School is compulsory. Bob doesn't like being told what to do, so he rebels in any way he can. Whatever "they" want becomes what Bob rejects.

46. My last hunch is that Bob plays his game because that is what he sees adults doing. It is quite possible that Bob is mimicking the approach to life we unconsciously teach through our actions. How do we play the game? By *avoiding* the unpleasant ... by going through the motions for someone else's sake ... by passively waiting for a better time, always in the future? (Life is compulsory, something we must all go through, but you'll get used to it.)

"Not once had he been present for his life. So his life had passed like a dream.
    Is it possible for people to miss their lives in the same way one misses a plane?"

(Percy, 1980)

47. Another way of life we endorse through our behavior is the success route. High-achieving students seemed to have picked up on this message. They fill their days worrying about being good enough, making the grade, getting into the right school. But like Bob they are putting off real life for now in the hope of finding a brighter tomorrow. How can we expect our youth to invest in their present lives when we are unwilling to do the same? How can we convince them to live in this moment when we act if there's nothing in it for us?

"As long as success is our goal we cannot be rid of fear for the desire to succeed inevitably breeds the fear of failure."

(Krishnamurti, 1953)

(from Liften)

> When Dr. Lewis looked closely at his personal experience with four dying friends, he became aware of the ways in which a total life-style can be seen as a mechanism for avoiding the death issue: "I refer here to what can be thought of as a compulsive life-style that so focuses on tasks, accomplishments, and productivity as to exclude a broader consideration of life's meaning."
>
> (Becker, 1973)

Ernest Becker, author of *The Denial of Death,* considers this preoccupation with trivial tasks a central defense against the fear of death.

48.   What else can be said about Bob's high school experience? There is one more thing that stands out for me. Bob voluntarily stopped playing his game a few moments every day. Even Bob, under the right set of circumstances, is capable of rising to the occasion and bringing himself to task. This tells us it is possible to reach a student like Bob. He is not a hopeless case. When we examine the classrooms where Bob became a real student we find that teachers taught him on a personal level. The condition that seems to have made a difference is the feeling Bob received from his teachers that they cared enough to teach *him,* 1:1. Bob responded by working for them.

> Me: Why do you work in math?
> Bob: Because she deserves it.

49. I could see that other teachers also cared about their students. In fact, one of the most surprising aspects of life at Claremont was the feeling I got that teachers and students were "on the same side." Regardless of which schooling game they played, student-teacher relationships were warm and genuine. It was almost as if there were two levels of experiences running tandem—a formal schooling dimension and an interpersonal dimension. Although the schooling experience was often ineffective, the human dimension was fully functional.

50. Maintaining positive relations was a priority for both students and teachers. For example, there was rarely any need for teachers to discipline or reprimand students. The tone of the class was informal, friendly. Students and teachers laughed at the same jokes. There was a feeling of mutual respect. Even when students rejected the curriculum, they were polite about it. Teachers accepted students as they are, rather than demanding that they become something else. There was no need for students to lie about what they were doing. There were no negative consequences for getting the wrong answer. Teachers respected the rights of students to work in school or not. They did not set themselves up as the adversary. They did not use fear to control. They were simply there to help students get through school. Students and teachers were working together to accomplish the same goal. Their relationships were honest. The integrity was intact. The contrast between the way school looks—barren, cold, unkempt—and the "feel" of the place clearly indicates that the human experience is most valued here.

> "One of the dangers of discipline is that the system becomes more important than the human beings who are enclosed in it. Discipline then becomes a substitute for love . . . discipline guarantees a result . . . but the means determine the end."
>
> (Krishnamurti, 1953)

> "Conformity and obedience have no place in the right kind of education. Cooperation between teacher and student is impossible if there is no mutual affection, mutual respect."
>
> (Krishnamurti, 1953)

> Whenever teachers walked out of the room, I noticed that the students' behavior did not change.

> "I call it the paradoxical theory of change . . . that change occurs when one becomes what he is, not when he tries to become what he is not. Change does not take place through a coercive attempt by the individual or by another per-

> son to change him, but it does take place if one takes the time and effort to be what he is—to be fully invested in his current positions."
>
> (Beisser, 1970)

51. As we have seen, warm, human relations between teachers and students do not necessarily mean that education is taking place. Only two of Bob's teachers were able to teach him in addition to caring about him. The appearance of positive teacher-student relations in the classroom, however, is nonetheless important. I do not believe it is possible to educate without genuinely caring about those we seek to educate. The fact that relations between students and teachers are based on mutual respect rather than fear may be the most promising aspect of Bob's schooling experience. That people are not going through the motions of being human is a significant step in the right direction.

"Systems, whether educational or political, are not changed mysteriously; they are transformed when there is fundamental change in individuals . . .

teachers who are really interested
in education, the main problem is
how to develop an integrated individual.
To do this, the educator himself must obviously be integrated . . .

love is essential to the process of integration

without love no human problem
can be solved . . ."
(Krishnamurti, 1953)

SEEING IS BELIEVING—
I wouldn't
have seen it
if I hadn't
believed it.
(Brilliant, 1979)

References

Becker, E. (1973). *The denial of death.* New York: Free Press.

Beisser, A. (1970). The paradoxical theory of change. In J. Fagan and I. L. Shepherd (Eds.), *Gestalt therapy now.* New York: Harper & Row.

Brilliant, A. (1979). *I may not be totally perfect but parts of me are excellent.* Santa Barbara, CA: Woodridge Press.

Krishnamurti, J. (1953). *Education and the significance of life.* New York: Harper & Row.

Percy, W. (1980). *The second coming.* New York: Farrar, Straus & Giroux.

Roethke, T. (1956). Random lines from "I'm Here."

Things of Use and Things of Beauty

The Story of the Swain County High School Arts Program*

THOMAS BARONE

———————◆•◎•◆———————

> *"It is clear that children should be instructed in some useful things
> . . . (but) to be always seeking after the useful does not become free
> and exalted souls."*
>
> ARISTOTLE (cited in McKeon, 1941, p. 1308)

> *"Weaving, hit's the prettiest work I ever done. It's asettin' and
> trampin' the treadles and watchin' the pretty blossoms come out and
> smile at ye in the kiverlet."*
>
> "AUNT SAL" CREECH of Pine Mountain, Kentucky
> (Eaton, 1937, p. 4)

The Appalachian Mountains of western North Carolina are aging gracefully. Thousands of years ago (geologists tell us) they possessed the kind of brittle, angular, energetic majesty of the Rockies. But with an infinite patience, Nature has rounded their formerly pointed peaks into gentle curves, and cushioned them with

* The preparation of this essay was supported by a grant from the Rockefeller Brothers Fund. Reprinted by permission of *DAEDALUS, Journal of the American Academy of Arts and Sciences, 112*(3), 1–28, Summer 1983, Cambridge, MA.

a lush green canopy. Underneath this blanket of vegetation, one can observe the aging process up close, as the mountain streams etch wrinkles into the face of the earth. The centuries of erosion have worn down this land, but strength and dignity clearly remain: even at their age they are still able to lift themselves into the grandeur of the clouds.

Somewhere within these ancient hills lives a young man named Donald Forrister. Every weekday morning around 7:30, he leaves his wooden frame house, climbs into his pickup truck and heads north. Down a narrow dirt road to the highway, he rambles, through the town of Bryson City and a few miles later, into the parking lot of Swain County High School.

Don is an art teacher—the only art teacher—at the school, and the old Smoky Mountains provide, in many ways, an apt metaphor for what he has accomplished here. Slowly, carefully, patiently, Forrister has succeeded in sculpting formless adolescent talents into aesthetic sensibilities of impressive maturity. Almost singlehandedly he has created a high school arts program that is not only outstanding, but (perhaps even more remarkable) cherished by both the school and county communities. Any such embrace is, we know, quite rare in an era in which the arts are often treated like (in Jerome Hausman's [1970] phrase) "unwelcome boarders in a burgeoning household" (p. 14). And so even though the Swain County story is, in many respects, a singular one, I believe that we might learn from its telling much that is pertinent to the general survival and flourishing of the arts in our schools.

An Introduction to the Program

It was on one spring morning in 1982 that I first met the central cast of characters in the Swain story: the students. That morning as usual they flowed down from the mountains like individual drops of dew that had coalesced into a stream. Along the way they were joined by teachers like Don Forrister, members of the Swain administration and staff, and me. Together we poured through the school doors.

The mountains looming above Swain County High School provide a sense of locale, but move inside and where are you? Many places you have been before. In the more-or-less standard Modern American School Plant circa 1978. The building's right-angled innards seem familiar to me: the variously sized cubicles of space that stare blankly at the newcomer, the prolonged rectangular corridors that invite without a hint of destination. I am surprised to find a school building from near where I reside, in the Cincinnati suburbs, here in rural North Carolina, partly (I confess) because of my preconceptions about the level of financial support for education in a county so rural and with such a small economic base. But there it is: the same charmless modernity, the refreshing lightness of the glass and brick, the airiness of the pleasingly massive open chamber that dominates the heart of the building and serves primarily as a reading area and media center. But a startling difference, so crucial to our story, becomes vividly apparent as one's eyes move inevitably to a boldly executed (and placed) 5' by 5' abstract expressionist painting on the brick wall near the lobby to the administrative offices. And in several other spots—from the cloth wall-hangings (stuffed tubes intertwined playfully into serpentine knots) that dangle above the stairwells, to a remarkable set of drawings displayed near a side entrance (including a carefully composed and brilliantly colored still life of red and green apples)—there is art. To be sure, space exists for many more pieces, but the presence of any student artwork of such quality adorning the inside of a high school is unusual and exciting. They serve to whet one's appetite for learning more about these students and their Arts program.

There are approximately 500 students in Swain County High School; an average of 80 (or 20%) elect to take Art. During their freshman or sophomore year (in Art I class) students are introduced to what Forrister considers the foundations of aesthetic awareness: line, form design, color. These concepts are broached not only through examination of the works of major artists, but also through a number of individual projects completed under the critical eye of the teacher. The forms of arts and crafts offered in Forrister's program include these: macrame, pottery, fibers, weaving, drawing, photography, silkscreening, papermaking, batique, stichery, quilting, lettering, and airbrush. According to Forrister and his students, it is from this broad exposure to a smorgasbord of possibilities that a student will sense a proclivity toward one or more areas. The student will then usually select a set of major projects in those areas for Art II and III. It seems probable that the range of activities enhances the overall success of the program by increasing the chances of students finding an agreeable specialty.

But training in every area of the arts is certainly not provided in this program. Notice, first, that the emphasis is on the visual: musical talent is under the aegis of the school band, literary and theatrical performance are to be developed, if at all, by the English Department. The gaps in the list of visual art forms, including all forms of painting, are due to the primary source of funding for the program: it is largely federal vocational funds that pay for the supplies, equipment, and the services of Don Forrister. Hence the emphasis on the commercial arts and crafts (although not a totally exclusive one, as we shall see) provides the program with a strong local Appalachian flavor. To paraphrase Oscar Hammerstein, "the hills are alive" in the Swain County High School Arts Program. This fact certainly accounts for some measure of the program's success as well as its local support. This vital link with the community deserves documentation, and to do that we move back outside into the hills.

Community Context: Natural Richness/Economic Poverty

Swain County, North Carolina, is by and large a national park. Or more precisely, over half of the county is situated in the Great Smoky Mountains National Park, and over half of the Park is in Swain County. As such, the county in the western wedge of the state, borders on Tennessee. About one half of the Cherokee Indian Reservation, including the town of Cherokee, is also within the county lines, but, like the Park to the north, outside of the county's governmental jurisdiction. Because the Federal government controls 82% of Swain County, only 18% is left for local taxation.

In the lower third of the county sits Bryson City, the county seat by default, and hardly a city—it is a town of 1,500 people, the only (except for Cherokee) municipality in the county. The texture of life in Bryson City is, of course, to some degree influenced by its locale, but in other ways seems quite typical of Small Town America. In evidence here are, no doubt, some of the qualities that Carol Kennicut, the protagonist of Sinclair Lewis's *Main Street,* found so dismaying in turn-of-the-century Gopher Prairie, Minnesota: perhaps a self-satisfied provincialism in values and mores, certainly a cultural bleakness that even rules out most forms of public entertainment (save a games arcade and one "last picture show").

There is, to be fair, this rebuttal by a local newspaper (*Smoky Mountain Tourist News*, 1982, p. 8): "No, Bryson City ain't very fancy, but it's real." And if that sounds like a cliché, it also has the ring of truth. I observed among the populace a genuinely courteous and friendly demeanor with no hint of pretense. And although much of the town's commercial property is incessantly drab, many of the residences exude a homemade charm lacking in the dour architecture of Gopher Prairie.

And further unlike the folks of *Main Street*, a curious ambivalence is detectable among some of Bryson City's natives concerning its small town status. The local press may insist: "If you're looking for a place with a lot neon [sic], fast food restaurants and crowds of people, don't come to Bryson City" (p. 8). And rightly so, for Bryson City has indeed managed to elude some of the cultural blight common to the 20th century. But one detects a note of false bravado, perhaps even thinly disguised desperation, in that quote. For one thing, there is an unmistakable feeling of pride among the locals in their newly opened "Hardee's"—the first national fast-food chain to locate a franchise in Bryson City. But more importantly, consider the source of the quote: it is excerpted from an article in *The Smoky Mountain Tourist News*. So its mock disdain of crowds is in reality an open plea for carloads of tourists, and a suggestion that in coming to Bryson City they will somehow manage to escape from each other. My clear impression is that there are those in Bryson City who would love nothing more than to see it swell to the size of Gatlinburg, Tennessee, the overwhelmingly commercialized tourist mecca across from the Park—no matter that currently Bryson City's major selling points are those virtues (the peaceful isolation, the wilderness sanctuary, and the small-town charm) that Gatlinburg has chosen to prostitute. But because the Bryson City area is on the edge of the tourist belt, miles from the nearest interstate, it must be carefully sought out by vacationers for the attractions it offers: hiking, picnicking, white-water rafting, and above all, the natural splendors of the mountains.

I was not really surprised to hear Don Forrister speak one night of the spirituality he perceives in these mountains, for in them, I too had experienced a rare communion with nature. Sitting on the porch of Forrister's mountain home after a twilight thunderstorm, I watched the fireflies painting in watercolor on a gigantic canvas, their speckled phosphorescent moments of light diffused and softened by the mist. I recalled a poem by William Cullen Bryant, "Thanatopsis," which I had been forced to memorize in high school long ago, but which was only now helping me to see and hear "the voice of gladness, the smile, the eloquence of beauty, the mild and healing sympathy" that is the lavish gift of Nature.

This natural richness must surely suffuse the lives of the inhabitants of these mountains and hopefully it compensates somewhat for economic poverty of so many of them. That poverty pervades Swain County. The average capita personal income in 1979 was $5,705, as compared with the national average of $8,773 (Country Development Information for Swain County, 1981). In April 1982, when the national unemployment rate was a whopping 9.2%, Swain County's jobless rate was 26.2% ("Swain Jobless Rate Climbs"). But poverty in Swain County has a long history—which may be why (as some Bryson City townsfolk insisted to me) "folks here is poor, but they don't feel poor." One suggested that, because of a tradition of self-sufficiency—including vegetable gardening, canning, building one's own furniture and often one's own home—hard times in these hills are less painful than in city or suburb. Perhaps. It is a sociological truism that the poor have less to lose to a depression. But many from the middle class are also out of work in Swain County, and the testimony of several (in a local newspaper article) concerning their emotional shock and alienation sounds like an echo from far off Detroit or Akron.

Of the 4,000 in the labor force who *are* employed, nearly half are either tradesman or workers in furniture and clothing factories. (A blue-jean factory closed in early 1982.) Most of the others work in a level of government, or service-related businesses. The latter include the motels, gas stations, cafes, and gift shops that cater to the tourist dollar. The tourist business is seasonal, of course, but still important to the Swain County economy.

The Craft Heritage: Aesthetics and Functionality

The tourists are lured by the wilderness of the mountains and once there attempt to preserve their memories by purchasing souvenirs of the mountain culture. The countryside is speckled with craft gift shops—the River Wood Craft Shop, the One Feather Craft Shop, and (within a stone's throw of the pink and white Teddy Bear Motel) Miller's Groceries and Crafts. The shops contain tons of mass-produced bric-a-brac, but items handcrafted by the Cherokees and the white mountaineers also abound—baskets, pottery, quilts, rugs. The genuine handiworks are a fundamental part of the Southern Appalachian heritage. Recently popularized in the series of Foxfire books, the crafts of the white Southern Appalachia Highlanders have evolved for generations since the arrival of the first pioneers in the 1790s and the early 1800s. It is possible, I believe, to discern several qualities of life among these people by considering their cultural artifacts. I will suggest only three.

The first, perhaps the most obvious, has already been mentioned. It is an almost totally *self-sufficient* life-style, demanded of a people kept apart from the rest of civilization by distance and even isolated from neighbors by a rudely intervening mountaintop. Once, in these hills, everything was handmade: cabin, furniture, clothing, utensils. . . . Second, one senses the enormous *care* invested in these artifacts. It is surely patient people who were (and are) willing, for example, to wash and straighten animal and vegetable fibers, to stretch, twist, and spin them, then to dye and weave the yarn into cloth. It could only be someone inspired to create a thing of beauty and excellence who would produce from that hard-earned cloth the intricately patterned Appalachian "Sunday Quilts." And that inspiration must surely have arisen, as did Bryant's, from the "various language" spoken by their natural surroundings. One senses a link between the aesthetic pleasure that must have pervaded the creation of these artifacts and the satisfaction derived from the beauty in these hills.

But ultimately, there is *pragmatism*—indeed, the traditional pragmatism of the American frontier. These early mountaineers were not artists in any full-blown technical sense—they were craftspeople. The aesthetic character of their work was clearly subordinate to its functional nature. Their generally harsh circumstances strongly suggested a utilitarian channel for release of any artistic tendencies: "direct your need for the creation of beauty toward the things of survival." And so their pride in a cabinet built or a basket woven must surely have sprung not only from aesthetics—an appealing form, a pleasing design, an interesting texture—but also, perhaps primarily, from the presence of more practical attributes, such as strength, and durability, and general usefulness.

The Official, Vocational Orientation

One escape route from the malingering poverty in Swain County nowadays is through the production and sale of arts and crafts. The people of Swain County are aware of this fact and a rationale for an arts program that rested on it should be viewed quite sympathetically, for it would be the latest manifestation of the pragmatism that has lived in this region (and indeed, this country) for decades. And the Swain County Arts Program does in fact have a strong vocational nature. The program, as mentioned, is funded with Federal monies, and administered by the North Carolina Vocational Education Department. Its official raison d'etre, therefore, is to equip students with the knowledge and skills needed to become commercial artists, artisans, and craftspeople.

Within the school the thrust of the program is also seen as primarily vocational. Mr. Frizell, the school principal, for example, spoke of it strongly in those terms. Written documents also ascribe to the program's vocationally oriented aspirations. Consider the Swain County High School Arts Program booklet (Forrister & McKinney, n.d.) prepared for a school accreditation process. At one point, there is the unequivocal assertion that "Crafts as a Vocation is an individualized program concerned with occupations in the crafts industry. (Craft as a Vocation is taken as Art II and Art III by graduates of Art I who so choose). The greatest portion of time is spent in laboratory activities while increased emphasis is placed on developing skills for local crafts industries" (p. 2).

And again in the booklet's description of the Commercial Art courses one reads: "At least 50% of the allocated time for this class will be used in the lab or shop for hands-on experience, *illustrating their relevance to the work world* [emphasis added]" (p. 7). And why are the "basics" such as color and line, design, layout, balance and proportion taught in that course? "In order for the student to develop competencies relative to the occupation" (p. 7). Likewise, two of the major objectives of the Photography course (taken as Art III) are: "To prepare individuals for gainful employment in occupations relating to photography," and "To become aware of sales potential and prepare and practice selling photographs" (p. 11). And so it goes: one cannot escape an awareness of the program's official orientation.

The Roots of Vocationalism   This curricular pledge of allegiance to commerce is, of course, hardly novel—whether in the area of the arts or in terms of the overall agenda of the American school. Indeed, one of the first influential Americans to suggest that schools should pay serious heed to the needs of the marketplace was Benjamin Franklin. Franklin's utilitarian approach was embodied in his plans for an academy in which classical scholarship was to become a curricular bedfellow to subjects of a more commercial interest to the newly emerging middle class: natural science and its applications, agriculture, bookkeeping, the history of technology, and so on.

Franklin suggested that the study of art (especially drawing) be assigned a purpose in addition to developing creative expression, namely, as a useful tool for improving the design of the work of ship builders, engravers, cabinet makers, and mechanics. Franklin's academy never became a reality but his utilitarian notions of the general curriculum—and the place of art within—were the beginning of a lasting trend. Schooling, especially on the secondary level, would gradually divest itself of a large portion of the classical curriculum, often in favor of subjects and approaches more vocationally oriented. Several years later there appeared perhaps the original segments for actual course offerings of handcraft art such as embroidery, quilting, drawing, painting, and needlework, in terms of an expanded economic opportunity. These were in the form of newspaper advertisements for the private "English" schools that were favored in the mid-18th century by many of the middle class over the stuffier Latin grammar schools, and indeed, some of the logic in the Swain Arts Program booklet is reminiscent of them.

But only in the last half of the 19th century was the marriage of art and industry in the school curriculum finally consummated. These were the years of robust industrial development and expansion, decades that witnessed the rise of American iron and steel, the expansion of the textile industry, and the growth of the railroads and shipping that opened up both foreign and domestic markets for American goods. It was also, if we are to believe a bulletin of the U.S. Bureau of Education (quoted in Eisner & Ecker, 1970), a time of increased opportunity for artists willing to serve as handmaidens to the newly crowned lord of manufacturing:

> In addition to the increased competition arising from the steam-carriage, new and cheaper methods of manufacture and increased productiveness, another element of value has rapidly pervaded all manufacturers, an element in which the United States has been and is woefully deficient—the art element. The element of beauty is found to have pecuniary as well as aesthetic value. The training of the hand and of the eye which is given by drawing is found to be of the greatest advantage to the worker in many occupations and is rapidly becoming indispensable. This training is of value to all the children and offers to girls as well as boys opportunity for useful and remunerative occupations, for drawing in the public school is not to be taught as mere "accomplishment." The end sought is not to enable the scholar to draw a pretty picture, but to so train the hand and eye that he may be better fitted to become a bread-winner. (p. 14)

Another indication of the importance of art training for industry during this time was the intense lobbying used by leading industrialists to ensure passing of an 1870 Massachusetts law that required all cities with a population exceeding 10,000 to provide art instruction to teenaged boys.

The last half of the 19th century was thus the heyday of the vocational rationale for the teaching of drawing and the crafts in the public school. John Dewey and the Progressive Education Movement finally provided a rationale for the fine arts as an activity central to the educational process, and both the justifications for and the methods in courses of the fine arts and the practical (or industrial) arts grew more disparate, as they are today.

And so in Swain County (according to Mr. Frizell), "it was not easy to get the crafts and commercial art into the Vocational program" back in 1973. The school administration decided to make the attempt when the state-funded arts teacher/counselor retired. The intercession of the State Superintendent of Public Instruction was required, but the Swain County Commercial Arts and Crafts program was finally accepted by the state Vocational Education Department. Today only one other such program in North Carolina—a strongly craft-oriented one at Robinsville—also receives funding through the state from the federal government.

The Swain program must be resubmitted every year, with projections of courses to be taught and numbers of students, along with follow-up studies of program graduates. This last process is apparently crucial, for the survival of the program depends in large measure on the percentages of Art III graduates who choose to pursue arts and/or crafts as a vocation, or as a major in a technical school or 4-year college. The required percentage fluctuates, but according to Ms. Alice Lance, the school's Vocational Guidance Counselor, it usually hovers around 50%. "It is totally up to the Vocational Education Department," said Ms. Lance. "They go by the numbers. . . . What's saving the program is that the students have been using [their arts and crafts training] . . . but it's scary."

This number seems astonishingly high to me, especially considering the traditional disinclination of the region's people toward higher education, and it stands as testimony to Forrister's profound influence on the career choices of his students. So despite its slightly tenuous future status, the program has indeed proved successful in terms of its official mandate. And although that accomplishment itself is interesting, there are, I believe, achievements in the Swain High School Arts Program even more fascinating and compelling. To consider those we need to look more closely at the program in action.

The Arts Program's Non-vocational Outcomes

There are really three "arts and crafts" rooms presided over by Don Forrister. The main classroom is located fittingly in the school's Vocational wing, and the other two—the photography darkroom, and the weaving room—require considerable transit through those right-angled corridor tubes. Forrister's classroom is L-shaped (the lap of the "L" is an adjoining arts material storeroom), but its angularity is somewhat softened by the layers of student crafts and artworks that cover the horizontal surfaces and cushion the walls. Entering this room is like exiting from the building: one leaves the nowhere-land of the school plant and slips back into Appalachian hill country. The sense of place returns, thanks largely to the local flavor of objects like the baskets woven of birch twigs, the large intricately designed Sunday quilt and the drawings of hill country still life. Many of these exhibit the same curious blend of the aesthetic and the functional seen in the artifacts of the southern Highlands pioneers.

And the longer one remains, the stronger wafts the aroma of the hills. Not only in the distinctive accents of the students, but soon also in the open and friendly demeanor that is a reflection of their elders on the sidewalks of Bryson City. And certainly the perseverance and the care one observes as the students tussle with their materials are the qualities one can observe fossilized in the artifacts of the mountain pioneers. It causes one to ponder whether the same fuel that fired the engines of the mountain craftsmen is moving these students in Don Forrister's classroom. Is it indeed a struggle for economic survival that motivates them? Are the scarlet threads woven into that rug merely to supply a tangential beauty, placed there primarily to catch the eye and only secondarily to please it? Not as an end in itself, but as a means of ringing the cash register?

Just what does motivate these teenagers? It is an important question because its answer can provide a clue to the *educational* meaning and significance of the Swain County Arts Program's outcomes—the character of its impact on the lives of these students. Having spent only 4 days in the school, I will avoid pronouncements, and instead share my reasons for some strong suspicions. They are based on observations of student comportment, on their informal comments, on mass "whole-class" discussions over which I presided, and on interviews with individual students.

An Eclecticism of Purpose   First, it is apparent that a motivational eclecticism exists here—as in most human endeavors there are a variety of prevailing causes and reasons for actions. There is indeed a degree of the career/economic/commercial incentive, although the amount seems startlingly small considering the program's stated intentions and sources of funding. Consider, for example, the case of Robert, the senior voted "most talented in art" by the graduating class, an adolescent whose sensitive and technically accomplished drawings are an emphatic testimony to that talent, and whose family (according to Forrister) is of extremely modest means. I was quite moved by one of Robert's drawings and was interested in acquiring it, but when I asked him if it was for sale, his refusal was absolute: "I like to keep all of my drawings." Don Forrister assured me that this disinclination to part with their work, even for money, is quite common among his students—and their parents. Only a few of them (including the craftspeople) will merchandise their handiworks. More often the creations will either adorn their homes or become gifts, providing lasting pleasure to themselves, their kin, and friends.

And their plans for future employment? The current crop of upperclasspeople appear to fit the pattern of the past: of the 14 I surveyed 8 (57%) expressed an intention to work at an arts-or-craft-related job. For some, following in the paths of former students like John Herrin, a truck driver who "moonlights" in macrame, crafts may provide a supplementary income. But for the preponderance of Forrister's students, different motives seem to dominate. Their interest in their arts and crafts is not based primarily on the acquisition of a saleable skill. Here is the question I posed to an assembly of 16 Arts II and III students: "Suppose it were impossible to use what you have learned in this class in terms of a job, would you still have taken this class, and would you still enjoy it as much?" A show of hands indicated a nearly unanimous affirmative response.

So although the image among much of the Swain County public, members of the school administration and faculty, and the distant bureaucrats in Raleigh and Washington who administer and fund the program may be of students learning to draw, reality begs to differ: the economic imperative, the prevailing practicality of their ancestors, is, for the most of these students, clearly subordinate to motives more compelling. What are they?

A Personal Pride   One discerns a personal pride emanating from their accomplishments. There are several facets to this pride, including a degree of vanity from the attention their talents attract. Occasionally a sense of self-importance could be detected among some of Forrister's senior students, an awareness of a kind of privileged status usually associated with talented athletes, or found among high school thespians backstage before the senior play. This status, as far as I could tell, was certainly not flaunted—and part of it might be explained by the fact that so many of Forrister's senior students were already part of (in Philip Cusick's [1973] term) the school's "power clique" (p. 153). But this status was also derived from the recognition of and admiration for their many awards and honors that the students (they readily admit this) welcome. That thrill of victory is heady stuff. The scent from a drop or two can apparently provide the momentum for many a painstaking and time-consuming project. This attention and excitement may be particularly impressive to the large percentage of Forrister's students who are (according to Ms. Lance) in other subjects less than academically able. Can we imagine the impact registered on the psyche of an 11th grader who after years of frustration, boredom, and perhaps even derision in Math and English classes, is suddenly flown to New York to receive a national award for his drawings?

Nevertheless, many junior and senior students insisted to me that visions of plane trips to exotic locations, or even the regional trophies and blue ribbons, did not lure them into Art I. As freshmen or sophomores they could not imagine that they might possess such talent. Just a few years later, however, the pride in creating (in their words) a "thing of excellence"—or, more accurately, the accolades received from those creations—does seem to partially explain the students' reluctance to sell them.

An "Expression of their Art"   But again, many students are unwilling to part with their "lesser" works as well. Could this perhaps indicate a more intrinsic satisfaction in their creation? In that regard, a closer inspection of the SCHS Arts Booklet (Forrister & McKinney, n.d.) contains a beguiling passage:

> A great many people work at crafts as a hobby or avocation and a growing number are becoming craftsmen and producing crafts as a vocation. For some, craft work is an "alternative" vocation which the craftsmen prefer above the nine-to-five job. For others it is their sub-occupation and expression of their art for which the benefits can seldom be [sic] calculated in dollars and cents. (p. 1)

A priceless "expression of their art"? Is there really a nonvocational incentive producing outcomes infinitely more valuable when measured with the economic kind of yardstick implied in the program rationale? The phrase suggests a purpose more concerned with the needs and development of the individual, as opposed to an exploitation of the needs of the marketplace. There are, of course, many rationales for aesthetic education that pertain to the personal well-being of the individual, such as the development of artistic talent, aesthetic appreciation, the therapeutic value of the artistic process, and so on. "Expression of their art," in the context used here, however, inspires two thoughts in me: first, it is reminiscent of the aesthetic pleasure which was an important by-product of the time-honored process of crafts-making in these hills. And second, it is a phrase that evokes a particular branch of art theory—the expressivist. These theorists see art as an expression, an embodiment of the artist's inward feelings and images into an objective, outward "expressive" form. They often speak of a subjective "inner life"—"the life of feeling" is Susanne Langer's (1957) term for it—and the aim of art, in their view, is to promote insight into and understanding of this inner realm. As Wordsworth saw art, it is "emotion recollected in tranquility." But according to the expressivists, this recollection is also a publication: a work of art is a transmutation of personal feelings and imagery into a unique sensible form—an objectification of the subjective. Objects of art, said Langer (1957), articulate and present "ideas of feelings" for our contemplation.

But aren't we placing an overwhelming burden on the shoulders of a single phrase in a single paragraph in a single program booklet? Is the development of the students' creative self-expression really a significant feature of the daily activities in

Forrister's classes? The evidence leans strongly toward the affirmative, especially for the more advanced students.

According to Forrister, the Art I students (perhaps reflecting their heritage) are more interested in functional items, or in decorating things to be used—like the silk screen designs for their t-shirts. With maturity, however, expressing oneself through the creative process also becomes important: In the private conversations I had with senior students, several told me of how they inform their materials with "a part of myself." Perhaps most telling was a discussion with a verbally (as well as visually) articulate son of a Baptist minister. Jim was an Art III student then pursuing the art of paper making, a process of sifting pulp through a wire screen and painting it with colors, often including other materials such as straw, newspaper photos, and so on, for a kind of collage effect. In one sensitive piece a photo of a pensive old woman in a rocking chair sits among brooding clouds of purple, green, and yellow-gray.

Tom: Why do you like papermaking?

Jim: I like to be able to . . . it's not so defined. I like the freedom of it more than anything.

Tom: What do you mean by "it's not so defined," that you can make abstract sorts of things?

Jim: Yeah, like lots of times you'll make something that you're not sure why you're doing it, but when it gets finished, you really like it.

Tom: When you do your papermaking, do you ever think "well, that has a certain feeling to it"? . . . like it's expressing an emotion? . . .

Jim: Oh, yeah, I think it depends on when I come into class what kind of mood I'm in. I think that comes out in some of my work.

Tom: Like, for example, the one that you're doing now of the old woman. What kind of feelings does that express?

Jim: Kind of a lost feeling. You see, I graduate in about a week . . . and I feel kinda worried about it. I guess that's coming out in it [the piece]. At least I think so.

Tom: You probably wouldn't have done that one . . .

Jim: Earlier on? No, I wouldn't have done that one. . . .

Tom: When was the first time you realized [you were expressing yourself through your art]?

Jim: Probably sometime last year when I was a junior.

Tom: But in Art I it . . . was just techniques?

Jim: Yeah

Tom: Do you think other art students . . . also express themselves like that?

Jim: Oh yeah, a lot of them . . . 'cause basically you [are allowed in Forrister's class] to do what you want to.

By the freedom "to do what you want" I don't believe that Jim meant a license to angrily scratch and scrawl on a drawing pad, or to giddily splash paint on a canvas at random. Although such behavior might be "expressive" in a primitive sense, it is not artistic expression. I believe that in Forrister's class the individual student is pre-eminent, but the individualism that develops there has a distinctly Deweyan cast to it. In lieu of a mindless outpouring of unbridled emotion, there is a considered channeling of impulses into purposeful actions. Their artistic activity is in fact composed of careful negotiations with their materials, ardent attempts to create forms that communicate ideas and images. Degrees of success vary, of course, but in this process qualitative forms of intelligence can clearly develop.

"Working Hard" at Self Expression   Several students described this process as "fulfilling" and "enjoyable," but they also insisted that it was "hard work." No question that I asked of Forrister's class was greeted with more chuckles of affirmation than this one: "Is art as hard a subject as the others you take?" Some admitted to electing Art I with hopes of coasting through with minimal effort. They apparently harbored a notion quite common in our society—the one that associates crafts like basket weaving with extremely low rates of mental taxation. But to their astonishment, these students soon found Art, in their own words, "harder than other subjects." Reason: they had not anticipated a "striving for perfection." Who, after all, would have expected this newfound desire to "make your next project better than your last"?

But in Forrister's class the nature of the "work" is different from the Calvinistic notion of work implied in Max Weber's famous critique of the Protestant ethic, the conception that has prevailed throughout American schools for centuries and that remains today the image of educational virtue held by parents, schoolpeople (including many at Swain), and much of the general public. Such "work" demands a deferment of present interests and needs for a vision of future rewards, an imposition of self-discipline to doggedly outlast the tedium of (in today's educational lingo) the "time on task." The result is said to be the development of certain personal attributes, as noted in this description of the weaving process of the mountaineers by Frances Goodrich, an early 20th-century preservationist of the hill country artifacts (Dykeman & Stokely, 1978):

> In the younger women who were learning to weave and keeping at it, I would see the growth of character. A slack, twisted person cannot make a success as a weaver of coverlets. Patience and perseverance are of the first necessity, and the exercise of these strengthen the fibers of the soul. (p. 107)

Patience and perseverance are indeed personal qualities helpful in overcoming the monotony of the production phase of the weaving process or the boredom of the assembly line. For further implied in this notion of work is the mindless replication of a prototype—and thus a personal distancing, an alienation from the process. Indeed, any intellectual engagement with one's materials could be harmful to the reproduction of a standardized end result. What is needed instead is the skill for precision in copying—and in the arts and crafts, the "training of the mind and eye" (mentioned in that Bureau of Education Bulletin) might provide such skill.

It is not surprising that during the late 1800s—the period of maximum coziness between art education and industry—this image of work was most clearly reflected in the methodology of art instruction. The methods originated, as did the Industrial Revolution, in Britain. The British National Course of Art Instruction (a.k.a., the Cole System, after Henry Cole, head of the South Kensington Training School for Art Masters) was transported to the United States and its aim was, indeed, to manually train students in copying.

Stuart MacDonald (1970) has described this Course:

> Exact uniformity was insured by the National Course of Instruction, each of which had several stages, the sum of which comprised the twenty-three Stages of Instruction. The Stages . . . were mechanical steps to the acquisition of "hand-power." Twenty-one were successive exer-

cises in copying . . . intended . . . to be strictly initiated until States 22
and 23 were reached—a most unlikely eventuality. (p. 188)

This manual training approach to drawing was brought to America by another
Englishman, Walter Smith, and soon the art instruction in American schools was
pervaded by these alienating exercises of meticulous reproduction of master
designs.

The activities in Forrister's class, however, provide a stark contrast with the Cole
System. Technique is indeed mastered there, but as a means to a greater goal,
rather than as an end in itself. And the students do seem to be "working," but in a
sense different from that implied in the Protestant ethic. Patience is certainly present, but it often seems less imposed than arising from a more immediate gratification. The effort appears to be generated from within the activities themselves, and
directed toward an original transformation of the ideas and experiences of the individual student.

One can observe in this process a dialogue between the students and the materials being shaped, a qualitative problem-solving process in which the
student/worker/artist struggles with possibilities, tentatively moves on the material,
encounters resistance, manipulates the component parts. For example, at one point
in working on his paper collage, Jim incorporated some torn pieces of white paper
above the head of the woman in the rocking chair, hoping to achieve a daydreaming
effect. The "product," however, spoke back to him: "Perhaps too bright, distracting
the eye from the central figure." Jim listened, reconsidered, added a more yellowish
cast that reflected the woman's sallow facial tones, and that skirmish ended successfully.

Thus was the aesthetic tension between creator and creation resolved, as Jim
used his freedom to work hard at publicizing through his artistic medium his own
distinctive ideas, feelings, values, and ends-in-view. Aestheticians are prone to words
like *authenticity, self-actualizing, liberating,* and *emancipating* in describing the effects of
this creative process. It is a process that celebrates individual growth, as the student
wrestles with his materials in order to create meaning, to make sense of his life.

Expressiveness in Crafts   The result of this process—a result Maxine Greene (1970,
p. 41) has called the "recovery of the self"—is obviously a far cry from what one
might expect in a vocationally oriented arts program—especially considering those
of an earlier day. Nevertheless, this kind of "personal unfolding" occurs not only in
the more obviously artistic endeavors of Forrister's students, but also sometimes in
their craftmaking as well. There are many similarities in the processes: the same
attitude of caring, the personal attachment to their products, the pleasure in their
creation. Of course in craft production the intended function or use of the object is
a design source that imposes limitations on shape and form. Some aestheticians
would disqualify most crafts from membership in the realm of fine art on this basis:
they are not (in Langer's [1957] term) "virtual objects," objects whose only function
is to "create a sheer vision, a datum that is nothing but pure perceptual form"
(p. 32).

Nevertheless, it is clear the craftmaking can involve aesthetic judgments, as
argued by Edward Mattil (1971), who could have been speaking of the early
Southern Highlanders in this passage:

> We must assume that the earliest tools and utensils of man were restricted to the considerations of utility. As their efficiency improved, there was a steady evolution of form. In any situation where people were first required to produce the necessities of life by hand, the useful concern was of prime importance and as long as impoverished or stringent conditions continued, the art quality of the object rarely exceeded the functional design of the object. However, as soon as time and skill permitted, the craftsman was fairly sure to elaborate or decorate his objects and it was at this point in man's development where the matter of choice entered into the picture. For example, when man became able to create a variety of clay bowls, each good for holding grain or water, he found himself engaged in the process of making judgments—practical *and* aesthetic—in determining form and decoration. (p. 3)

Today's Swain County High School students also often create meaning in their crafts—arranging elements of color, form, texture into imaginative relationships that communicate feelings. Indeed, they told me so: When I asked the assemblage of advanced students to divide into two groups—art students to the right, crafts people to the left—no one moved. There was a nearly unanimous insistence that any arts/crafts dichotomy would be an unimportant one. The students whom I had observed "working" at crafts like weaving, quilting, and batik-making, clearly perceived themselves as "doing art." Indeed, distressed by their inability to effectively respond to the question in a group setting, two such students sought me out later for private discussions, and one of them said this: that although some minor distinctions may exist, nevertheless, there is "art in crafts" and that she was able to "express my emotions" especially in the design phase of her weaving. (I was able to extract an admission that in the production phase, there was some "work" required, as Frances Goodrich has assured us, but even that process was often filled with the excitement of seeing one's design "come to life" with the personal qualities placed in it.)

Interestingly, the Arts Program booklet (Forrister & McKinney, n.d.) suggests that it is those once tangential, individually produced aesthetic qualities that today provide the craft products with their functional value:

> In our age of mass production where a certain "sameness" marks most products, there is a growth market for goods that are unique and distinctive. The craftsman who can design and produce articles that have aesthetic value and brings [sic] distinction to their owners, have access to a market with which mass production cannot compete. (p. 1)

Thus the "functional" value of today's craft objects may be defined less by their practical usability than by their ability to visually persuade a prospective purchaser. (The mountain-folk of yore could have survived a winter under an ugly quilt, but today's Appalachian craftsmen must be aware of the frigidity of the disinterested consumer.)

Recall, however, that Forrister's students are generally disinterested in selling their wares, and are therefore freer to consult with their own personal aesthetic values in the construction of their objects. Individual self-expression thus seems central not only to the activities of Forrister's future artists but to the craftmaking as well and is surely one of the sources of a profound satisfaction which attracts them to Don Forrister's class.

Here then is what we have learned thus far about the Swain program: that there exists within the program major nonvocationally related motivational factors, attributes, methods, and outcomes; that these include a thirst for self-esteem and a need for individual self-expression; that these are generally recognized (at best) as ancillary, and (at least) as officially unsanctioned facets of the program; but that these same outcomes are viewed by a preponderance of the students as the most compelling features of the program.

These findings are especially intriguing when viewed in the light of a particular ongoing dialogue among some educationists. Radical critics of schooling have long portrayed schools as extensions of the modern technocratic state, as agencies ideologically committed to the corporate social order. Through both the overt and covert (or "hidden") curriculum, it is said, the institution of the school transmits the dominant cultural system. Schooling thus promotes a subversion of individuality in favor of attitudes and a worldview that further the mechanistic purposes of business and industry. In the rather pessimistic critique of some of the radical determinists, any piecemeal reform of this monolithic apparatus of control is extremely problematical. Teachers in particular are seen as ineffective change agents, enmeshed as they are in the technocratic superstructure of the school.

The official vocational rationale of the Swain program seems to pay homage to this point of view, but the program in action suggests the possibility of a more complex and attractive model—one in which the deviant values and beliefs of individual participants (in our case, a teacher) can, through an infestation of activities and events, yield personally liberating rather than oppressive outcomes. A further articulation of our counterexample to the radical critique will require a description of this history of the program and the role of its chief architect.

An Appalachian Artist Designs an Arts Program

Donald Forrister knows these hills and their people, for he is one of them. Now a tall, slim, 33-year-old, he was born and raised in Appalachia and attended college at Western Carolina University. And reflections of those qualities found earlier in the mountain artifacts are clearly visible in Forrister's personality. There is, for example, his strong *self-reliance* and independence of thought and action. These manifest themselves in a variety of ways, including personal appearance. The beard and long hair of a couple of years ago were perhaps for some of the teachers an unwanted reminder of the stereotypical mountaineer and helped to solidify Forrister's image among them (at least according to some students) as something of a "weirdo." The beard (though trimmed) remains today, but Forrister's consistent casualness of dress, as well as his general life-style and values, are reminiscent of the "back to nature" movement among middle class youth in the late 1960s and 1970s. (The difference may simply be that Forrister never left.)

But his independence is evidenced in other ways as well. He particularly disdains gossip and is intentionally uninformed about the politics within the school faculty and administration. Though Forrister does not seem disliked by other faculty members, some of them may mistake his aloofness for disdain. Forrister, for example, often lunches with students in the cafeteria rather than with his peers—perhaps only a slight breach of the etiquette of collegiality, but surely a habit (again according to students) deemed irregular by some teachers. These qualities of independence and a loose definition of his role status are greatly admired by some of Forrister's students, and seem instrumental in gaining their trust and respect.

"Hard-working" is the trait cited most often by Swain teachers and administrators. And a large measure of his success is due to his enormous investment of time and energy in the program. In class he is a blur of movement from student to student for seven class periods a day, and even, during some periods, from classroom to weaving room to darkroom. On closer inspection, the blur becomes a mosaic composed of individual exchanges between Forrister and students—such as mini-critique of a choice of subjects, a quick nod of affirmation concerning a color mixture, or a one-on-one demonstration of a new technique. An arts course consists of an untold number of such interactions, each a piece of an emerging pattern. And Forrister's dedication extends well beyond the school grounds and class time. He can be found on weekends escorting a group of students to an art exhibit in Asheville, consulting with an individual student on a photographic project and so on.

The students prefer the word *caring* to describe this "hard work." But the latter, it seems to me, is simply a manifestation of the former, just as the perseverance of the early spinners and weavers followed their desire for beautiful coverlets and quilts. That Forrister does indeed care very deeply about his program was exceedingly obvious. One anecdote in particular highlights this quality: In attendance at an award ceremony honoring the Arts program was the mother of a former Swain student who had won a $10,000 scholarship to a prestigious art institute, thanks, she said, to "that man."

"And when we telephoned him to tell him the news, do you know what he did?" she asked.

"He cried."

Forrister himself admits to "getting emotional" whenever a student creates a particularly beautiful work. That emotionality is touching, of course, but it is important mainly insofar as it illuminates that which lies at the heart of the Swain County success story: the simple but intense mission of a single teacher to enhance the lives of his students through art. And it is a cause that achieved fruition not only through the unswerving dedication of that one man, but also by his shrewd intelligence as well.

Which brings us to our final commonality between the character of the Appalachian people generally and Don Forrister in particular: namely, a deep-seated *pragmatism*. We saw that pragmatism in the hill folks' ingenious combinations of the useful and the beautiful, the melding of aesthetic qualities into the utensils of everyday living. Forrister's work of art was his program, and his method for assuring not only its survival but also its flourishing in terms of its own values and definition of "success" were also pragmatic.

Part of what Forrister did was to make the program famous. This high visibility was achieved through active participation in a wide variety of arts and crafts contests. Of course the students' talents won the awards, and the incentive produced by the recognition was developed in the classroom through the teaching process described above. But Forrister also played a leading role in the selection of student work for entrance in competitions, a tactic that often resulted in a legitimation of his expertise. One senior described to me the growth of his respect for Forrister's judgment:

> I would want to enter one of my drawings in a contest, and he would say
> "Why don't we try this other one"—because he thought it was better—and
> he would tell me why he liked it more—and I would say "Well, okay"—

and . . . when he chose the ones to put in [the contest] I would win [an award], and when I chose which ones, I wouldn't . . . a lot of the time that happened. . . . So I figured he must really know what he's doing.

Forrister's primary aim in emphasizing competitions, I am convinced, was to heighten student interest in art, not to increase the visibility of the program. Furthermore, I believe Forrister's assertion that his students' career decisions are of secondary importance to him. Nevertheless a significant side-effect was also spawned by these two measures of success. Both the obvious vocational influence and especially the contest results greatly impressed many parents and the school's administrators. The regional and even national recognition stirred local pride (and, according to Ms. Lance, has been noticed in Raleigh). As a result, Forrister had acquired a little of the aura of a winning football coach. His job certainly seems secure: Mr. Frizell has stated that, even if the vocational funds were slashed, "we would find the money to keep Forrister here."

Such a change in funding sources would probably increase Forrister's autonomy, and a few changes might ensue (such as the inclusion of "nonvocational" art forms like painting). But these should be minimal because Forrister already possesses freedom to pursue his own aspirations under the existing arrangements. The acquisition of much of this freedom seems less a result of forethought than of fortune. This is how it came about: During the 1970s, said Forrister, a regional representative from the State Vocational Education Department would visit his classes to monitor the orientation of his pedagogical methods and choice of curricular content. "For 1 or 2 years I wouldn't hear anything and then a new person would take over (in the regional office), and complain about my emphasis, and I would have to concentrate on commercial art, and lead them more into the crafts."

In the last 3 or 4 years, however, Forrister says that he has acquired greater latitude in his choice of content and methods, with more emphasis on generating intrinsic interest and less on vocational. What has brought this about? A "reduction in force," a decrease in the staffing of the regional office, that has forced the Vocational Department to rely on a less direct, more quantitative, and less informative program evaluation procedure. I have only Forrister's word for this shift in emphasis but the irony in such an occurrence would be rich indeed. Is there any other example of a budget cut possibly resulting in the enhancement of artistic self-expression in students? I know of none.

Thus have the seeds sown by Forrister sprouted in the cracks of a concrete technocracy. The success of his efforts belie any notion that schools are necessarily the kinds of "total institutions" posited by the radical critics. Indeed, as institutions become more complex and cumbersome, their management and the monitoring of official mandates tend to become more problematical. Corporate hegemony tends to diminish and individual prerogative is enhanced.

So although Forrister's actions may in some respects resemble the kind of "resistance" in educational institutions described by Jean Anyon (1982) and others (King, 1982; Miller, 1982), that is, an individual agent's direct contestation of the systematic imposition of the technocratic will—a metaphor less antagonistic in tone seems more appropriate—one that suggests an accommodation of aims from a variety of sources. Direct contestation is not necessary in an organizational arrangement whose unwieldiness allows for a peaceful coexistence between formally sanctioned aspirations and those held by individuals charged with conduct of the program.

Note that in the Swain County program official criteria are indeed being met. The development of individual self-expression has not been accomplished at the expense of the mandated vocational outcomes. On the other hand, neither has Forrister allowed the vocational imperatives to overwhelm the curricular decision making and pedagogical processes—even though compromises (already documented) were sometimes necessary. Even early in the program's history, Forrister certainly never resorted to any methods even vaguely resembling the essentially anaesthetic Cole System of training students. He has shown us that preparing students for an occupation in the arts and crafts does not, today, require an alienating, spiritually exhausting regimen of mindless exercises. Indeed, evidence suggests that the personal rewards flowing from the creative activities often encourage a lasting devotion to the artistic process and therefore an inclination toward an arts or crafts-related career. (And it seems fitting to learn of the potential compatibility of aesthetic and vocational program outcomes from a native of the Southern Highlands where functionality and aesthetic pleasure have traditionally cohabited within the "arts-and-crafts.")

On Effectively Arguing for the Arts: A Hint from Swain County

This demonstration of a successful eclecticism of purpose has, I believe, important implications for the manner in which those of us close to the arts argue for their inclusion in the curriculum. Too often we display (as has, for example, Jacques Barzun [1979]) a tendency to dismiss the necessity of justifications less "rudimentary" than those involving self-expression and aesthetic appreciation. The sources of this tendency are surely noble: an acute awareness of the intense satisfaction to be derived from the aesthetic experience, and a desire to enhance the capacity of members of the younger generation for engaging in such experiences. Such an acquisition might even lead (as Harry Broudy [1951] has hoped) to "the good life . . . the kind of life that finds its expressions in the so-called good works of art (p. 192)." I would suggest, however, that it is an overreliance on the "art-for-art's sake" arguments that has, regardless of their intrinsic validity, partially contributed to the sadly consistent relegation of the arts to the curricular caboose. Despite the lip service sometimes paid to the arts, the American public (including legislators and many educators) obviously does not share our devotion to a belief in their intrinsic worth. Perhaps a generally low level of aesthetic literacy prevents a sizable number from appreciating the profundity of the life-enhancing capacities of the arts. Or perhaps not. At any rate, the survival of school arts programs may, especially in the era of economic stringency, require emphasis of rationales more sensitive to the fundamentally pragmatic character of the American people.

How much, for example, would the people of Swain County value a program—even an award-winning program—that served, in their eyes, no "useful" purpose? Even in this region steeped in a tradition of folk art would there be widespread and sustained enthusiasm for a program that educated solely for "worthy leisure time activities" or "aesthetic appreciation"? My hunch is that the American-style pragmatism of these economically distressed people would ultimately deem such a program frivolous and of low priority.

The Swain County example, therefore, suggests the judicious employment of *additional* arguments, pragmatic ones that present the arts as instrumental in, and indeed as fundamentally essential to, the development of competent individuals capable of functioning in our society. It is beyond the scope of this essay to identify and articulate all such rationales, but we should note that they include others beside the obvious career-education justifications.

One particularly intriguing and, I believe, potentially fruitful argument sees the growth of aesthetic awareness as fundamental to the development of the "basic skills" of reading and writing. As set forth by Elliot Eisner (1982), it goes thusly: There exists a variety of forms of public representation of privately held concepts and images. We need to increase the literacy of students in a variety of these forms by developing their aesthetic awareness and artistic expression, and therefore a more sophisticated perceptual system, one with greater power for the imaginative perception of qualitative relationships among empirical phenomena. This is important, says Eisner, because:

> Information developed out of a highly differentiated perceptual system can then be used as content for a form of representation, often in a form other than that in which the information was initially acquired. For example, consider the writer of literature. To be able to write, the writer must have something to write about. To have something to write about, the writer must be able to "read" the environment in which he lives. He must become aware of qualities of gesture and nuances of voices, he must have subtlety of vision. . . . For those who are unable to see, or to hear, or to taste, or to smell, the content of literature will be little more than something that other people enjoy. School programs that neglect developing the child's literacy in forms of representation that sharpen the senses ultimately deprive the student of the very content he needs to use well the skills of reading and writing. (pp. 76–77)

I wish to stress that I am not advocating a total abandonment of those rationales that point to the intrinsic delightfulness of the aesthetic experience, or that emphasize personal growth and self-expression—especially for audiences that seem, to any degree, potentially receptive to such arguments. But the approaches that emphasize the instrumental value of the study of art would seem to hold greater potential for persuading a skeptical and frugal American public (and American educators who should already know better) that the arts are indeed worthy members of the curriculum household.

And, finally, this: regardless of justifications engaged in, and the program's stated objectives, once a program is in place then the successful attainment of the truly fundamental aim of art education, that is, the intellectual and emotional growth of the individual, will obviously occur only through the hard "work," the dedication, the caring, the talent and the intelligence of those in charge. Don Forrister has exhibited these qualities in fashioning a program that, although undergirded by a utilitarian rationale, results in the flourishing of that fundamental aesthetic purpose. His program reveals that, although caution is certainly in order, we need not fear the presence of such rationales to the degree that we might have in an earlier era.

The discovery of that truth has been, for me, both instructive and inspirational. Indeed, I will remember that discovery—as I will the artifacts of the pioneers of the Southern Highlands and those of their descendants, the students of Swain County High School—as, itself, a thing of general usefulness and of a simultaneously singular beauty.

References

Anyon, J. (1982). *Aspects of resistance by working class and affluent fifth grade girls to traditional sex-role demands.* Presented at "Resistance in Education," American Educational Research Association Annual Meeting, New York.

Aristotle. (1941). Politics, Book VIII. In Richard McKeon (Ed.), *The basic works of Aristotle.* New York: Random House.

Barzun, J. (1979). Art and educational inflation. In *Art in basic education* (Occasional Paper 25). Washington, DC: Council for Basic Education.

Broudy, H. S. (1951, November). Some duties of an educational aesthetics. *Educational Theory, 1,* 192.

County development information for Swain County. (1981, August). Center for Improving Mountain Living, Western Carolina University, Cullowhee, NC.

Cusick, P. (1973). *Inside high school: The students' world.* Holt, Rinehart & Winston.

Dykeman, W., & Stokely, J. (1978). *Highland homeland: The people of the Great Smokies.* Washington, DC: Division of Publications, National Park Service, U.S. Department of the Interior.

Eaton, A. H. (1937). *Handicrafts of the Southern Highlands.* New York: Russell Sage.

Eisner, E. W. (1982). *Cognition and curriculum: A basis for deciding what to teach.* New York: Longman.

Eisner, E. W., & Ecker, D. W. (1970). Some historical developments in art education. In George Pappas (Ed.), *Concepts in art and education: An anthology of current issues.* London: Macmillan.

Forrister, D., & McKinney, G. (n.d.). Art. *Arts program booklet.* Swain County High School.

Greene, M. (1970). Teaching for aesthetic experience. In *Toward an aesthetic education,* A Report of an Institute sponsored by CEMREL, Inc., Music Educators National Conference, Washington, DC.

Hausman, J. J. (1970). The plastic arts, history of art and design—Three currents toward identifying content for art education. In George Pappas (Ed.), *Concepts in art and education: An anthology of current issues.* London: Macmillan.

King, N. (1982). *Children's play as a form of resistance in the classroom.* Presented at "Resistance in Education," American Educational Research Association Annual Meeting, New York.

Langer, S. (1957). *Problems of art.* New York: Charles Scribners' Sons.

Macdonald, S. (1970). *The history and philosophy of art education.* New York: Elsevier.

Mattil, E. (1971). *Meaning in crafts.* Englewood Cliffs, NJ: Prentice-Hall.

Miller, J. (1982). *Resistance of women academics to curricular and administrative discrimination in higher education.* Presented at "Resistance in Education," American Educational Research Association Annual Meeting, New York.

Smoky Mountain Tourist News. (1982, May 21). Bryson City, NC, p. 8.

Swain jobless rate climbs. (1982, April). *Asheville Citizen,* Asheville, NC.

The Natural Laws of Teaching: A Study of One Classroom

MARY H. BURCHENAL

———————◆●●◆———————

My apologies to Bill Cresta,
who's been in the ring far longer than I.

The Natural Laws of Teaching

I. Increasing Entropy

The entropy of the universe tends toward a maximum.
SECOND LAW OF THERMODYNAMICS

The "order," the trivia of the institution is, in human terms, a disorder, and as such, must be resisted. It's truly a sign of psychic health that the young are already aware of this.
THEODORE ROETHKE (1965)

I find the last seat in the last row, next to the wall and put my coat over the back of the chair-desk (a furniture hybrid produced by grafting the two species together). Except for the teacher, a girl asking some assignment questions, and me, the classroom is empty. Feeling somewhat awkward in the lull before class, I take out the official notebook and the official pen and pretend to be jotting with serious intent; I try to look the engaged university scholar. For lack of livelier activity, I note the posters I see on the walls: Einstein, American Realism in painting, Half Dome at Yosemite, Sam Shepard's play "True West," the New American Library ("Broaden Your Horizons," we are advised), and the English Royal Lineage are all represented on posters around the room. I also notice a formal-looking College Info board along the opposite wall with notices and brochures tacked up for viewing. The chair-desks are in five rows of six, and like Robert Frost's beachgoers, "all turn and look one way": toward the teacher's desk and the front wall of blackboards. I am struck by the light fixtures that, instead of resembling huge metal ice trays as did the lights in my high school, they resemble large white ladders hung parallel to the floor and they glow with light. I don't know if the metaphor was a planned one, but the resemblance is unmistakable. I briefly turn to look at the wall against my right shoulder and am almost physically startled by computer sheets that display numerical student grades on all assignments. I notice that the A.P. sections are not part of the posting system. I am somewhat relieved to see that students are listed only by I.D. number, but it makes me slightly uneasy nonetheless. I shift and turn in my seat the way I do when I'm feeling unsociable and a stranger sits next to me on a train.

The bell rings and students begin to drift in, talking and laughing in jagged rhythms. I am surprised at how eager I am to see them, how relieved I am to have them fill the room with that remarkable intensity of adolescent life that is conspicuously absent from graduate school. The contrast it makes with my current educational atmosphere strikes me almost painfully, even as I realize how I am romanticizing it. I turn back to my official notebook.

I feel like an intruder in the classroom, yet simultaneously I feel back in my school element. Students toss some casual curiosity my way, but on the whole go on with business as usual. Two girls with carefully coiffed hair and dangling earrings have settled themselves and are looking through a photo album. A red-faced blonde boy in a black Giants jacket attempts to lift a chair-desk along with its female inhabitant and she squeals her protest-delight. Suddenly I am startled by a tinny rendition of Scott Joplin's "The Entertainer." It is being piped in over the loudspeaker at the beginning of school announcements. The students don't skip a beat, and seemingly ignore the disembodied voices throughout announcements of upcoming events, Chicken Cup o' Soup for lunch, awards, etc. I ask one boy if he knows who is speaking. "Someone who likes to hear himself talk," he answered with a smile.

I wait for class to begin.

II. The Shortest Distance Between Two Points Is a Straight Line
The warm smell of eucalyptus will forever remind me of my year at Stanford. On this wet Thursday morning, it was particularly strong, and I inhaled deeply as I drove down majestic Palm Drive away from campus. After a frustrating day in college classrooms, I thought of the country song that runs something along the lines of "The prettiest sight I ever saw was Texas in my rear view mirror." At the end of the parade of palms, I swung left onto El Camino Real. I headed north and away. Destination: Parkside High School.

The drive is an interesting one. El Camino acts as a benign(?) incision that allows a cross-sectional view of the area. First I cruised past Stanford Shopping Center, or "The Temple of Mammon" as I heard one local resident call it. The road runs straight as a ruler through Menlo Park, giving you glimpses of well-landscaped and manicured shopping complexes and boutiques. Even the large and usually generic Safeway/Payless building diptych is pleasing to the eye, and the parking lot is host to orderly rows of well-tended trees. The new Kepler's bookstore to the right is a stunning bit of dark modern architecture, although it more closely resembles a luxurious office building than a place to buy *Les Fleurs du Mal*.

Soon the shops and cafes give way to nothing but high walls on each side of the thoroughfare. I had crossed the Atherton town line. Atherton has zoning regulations that have prevented commercial development within its quiet boundaries. El Camino becomes almost suburban for a mile or so and for me there's a mysterious feel to this town that has walled itself away from the traffic and transients of El

Camino. Behind the walls, tree-lined avenues curve by some lovely and some extravagant homes sitting on larger plots of land than is usual in Palo Alto or Menlo Park.

Coming around a bend, the walls disappear and it was evident I was about to enter a very different town. I looked up to see a huge sign reading YUMI YOGURT, embellished with a garish female mouth and a pink tongue protruding alluringly onto the upper lip. Incorrigible English teacher reflexes pushed me immediately into illusionary thoughts of the billboard eyes in *The Great Gatsby*. I briefly contemplate the symbolic significance of such a mouth poised thusly at a city limit.

In the meantime, I have driven straight into the bustle of Redwood City. Car dealerships, auto repair shops, fast food joints, miscellaneous small businesses, and enormous franchises (Anderson's TV and STEREO) shoulder each other as they crowd the sides of the road. Few here seem concerned with green landscaping and nothing is hidden behind 8-foot walls. Redwood City seems to consider El Camino Real as its center, not as a force to be shunned. Life here is unabashedly busy.

Across from Food Villa, Sister's Beauty Salon, Los Pericos Mexican Food, and the London Boutique, I found Parkside High School. The weather-worn wooden entranceway announcing the school asserts itself at a corner of El Camino, but the school is set back behind stately redwoods and a couple of parking lots.

Parkside is either the oldest or one of the oldest high schools on the peninsula, depending on whom you ask. The school serves about 1,500 students and is approximately 57% minority, most of whom are Hispanic. The school has changed a great deal from the time when it was a "feeder-school" for Stanford, although the grand sequoias out front and the impressive moorish architecture lead your mind back to such an era. Redwood City is now host to predominantly low- and some middle-income families and has a large Chicano population. About 5 years ago, demographic shifts closed San Carlos High School, and those students and many of those teachers now make their academic home at Parkside. San Carlos is a middle to upper-middle class area, and this has created what is referred to as "an interesting mix" at the school. Bill Cresta, the teacher who is the protagonist of this paper (along with me, I suppose) is one of the teachers who came down "from the hill"—that is, from San Carlos High.

The first thing I saw on entering the main building of the school was a large formal painting facing the door. The painting was done by students at the school under direction of an art teacher some years ago. The painting depicts the meeting of Father Junipero Serra and Father Crespi near Redwood City on a trail that has since become, of course, El Camino Real. As I made my way to room 27, along dingy and battered rows of lockers and past a courtyard that has become a graveyard for chairs and desks, I felt that I had come a long way down that road.

III. Coverage = Rate x Time

> We haven't the time to take the time.
> EUGENE IONESCO (1963)

"Okay, let's wrap up *Apocalypse Now*."

Loudspeaker voices finished, students seated, and a few housekeeping items out of the way (such as announcing an upcoming field trip to "Henry V"), Bill Cresta wastes not a moment of time in launching into action. This is an Advanced Placement (AP) English class of 20 seniors (Bill also teaches another section of AP).

296 THE EDUCATIONAL IMAGINATION

Parkside is 57% minority, but I could identify only three or four in the class (one Asian student, and two or three Hispanic students) who were not "Anglo." I worried and wondered how many of these students would have attended San Carlos High School were it still open.

Bill and his students discuss the end of *Apocalypse Now* with vigor (they had seen the film in class that week). His energy is almost palpable; he moves quickly, bird-like; his head bobs as he speaks; his face is animated, and he often gestures with an index finger or with his hand to underscore a point. He never sits as he teaches, and he doesn't even engage in the classic "teacher's lean" against the front of his desk. He moves partway up one of the center aisles and works mainly from there, in front of some students and behind others, occasionally going back to the front and coming partway down another row. It's hard to imagine this man with his feet up, but I keep trying. (I hoped it would counter the exhaustion I felt just watching his output of energy.) There's a nervous, electrical quality to this man. And perhaps it was partly this quality that made me think he resembled Dick Van Dyke, only with not so long a face. I would guess his age at between 45 and 50, his hair is mostly gray, he wears glasses, and typically sports gray flannel pants and a button-down striped or check shirt (and perhaps a sweater). No tie.

Although animated, Bill isn't loud and he's not a performer. (When I asked Tito, the student in front of me, if all his teachers were like Mr. Cresta, he said, "Well, some are more outgoing and some are more quiet.") His energy seems to come from his passion for the subject matter and from his pressing sense of *how much there is* to read, to discuss, to know. It's almost as if he were himself a knowledge race against time.

Class moves, accordingly, at a startlingly quick pace. This is clearly a teacher who knows the direction of class before it begins.

Class isn't slowed down by tangential discussion. In fact, Bill habitually directs the students' comments more than I, as a teacher, would find desirable. He has a habit of playing "Match Game." For the uninitiated, this game show of the 1970s was hosted by Gene Rayburn and highlighted a panel of dim Hollywood stars. Gene would read a sentence to the contestants with a "blank" in it. The contestants would try to fill in the blank and match as many of the stars' answers as possible. Perhaps this comparison is unfair, but I found the students in Bill's class doing much the same thing. Bill rarely asked open-ended questions, and instead asked questions such as the following:

"He's a very—what? Yes, a shrewd man."
"Elizabethan staging is very different from ours because there's no—what? Good, no curtain."
"If you have God's grace, you have—what? Right, his love."
"When are we suspicious? When we feel we don't have—what?"
"What has the language of war done? Dove, or Hawk. There's no—what? Middle ground."

There are times when Bill will ask slightly more open-ended questions, but still I felt that the students' primary task was to "match" the answer that Bill has in mind. He once asked the class members to suppose that they were kings and that their nobles were acting up, challenging their power. What would they do? This question led to some creative and interesting responses (such as marry my relatives off to the nobles, convince the nobles it's a horrible life to be king, pit the nobles against each other). Bill listened carefully to each of these answers, but he grew increasingly restless and clearly there was a "right" answer he was looking for. "But you guys are forgetting one," Bill pushes. It's not long before Tito gets a "match", and says that the king could make another country into the "Bad Guy." In eventually coming to this conclusion the class had explored some other options, *but it took a bit of time*. Bill seems to be uncomfortable in such a situation in which perhaps the material could be covered more time efficiently. This explains his frequent use of word or phrase-prompts to elicit quick answers and keep things on track. I'll hand him one thing: he covers a lot of ground.

IV. The Importance of Momentum

> Every body continues in it state of rest, or uniform motion in a straight
> line, unless it is compelled to change that state by forces impressed on
> it. — Newton's first law of motion.

This is clearly a class which doesn't buckle under weighty statements. "This is Willard's existential moment," their teacher announces, as they discuss Willard's decision to kill the deranged Kurtz. "He sees the pain in the man—the split in him. The army man who will do anything to win the war, and the moral man who sees the horror of it." The students have already read *Heart of Darkness* and they seem familiar with the issues of the film. They seem to be keeping up with Bill who moves along compellingly, sweeping all comments and questions up with him as he goes, but there are moments when I wonder if the students are moving *with* him, or bobbing in his wake.

"What does *apocalypse* mean?" asks one student, after they have decided that Willard kills Kurtz in a sort of "act of mercy" (Bill's words). The class helps answer the question, as I wonder how far the students are climbing on the "abstraction ladder."

Bill sums up "Coppola's message" as "Let's understand this dark side. . . . Maybe then we can avoid it. . . . But there's also hope in the film. What is it? Melanie?" (Melanie, as perhaps half of the class, hasn't spoken up yet today.)

Melanie falters in a plaintive voice, "Uh, I don't know. . . . Oh yeah, he could just turn into another Kurtz but he doesn't."

Bill is quite satisfied with this answer and further illuminates it by pointing out the scene near the end where Willard throws his weapons down.

"Any other questions?" Bill asked, whirling the discussion of *Apocalypse* to its close. He allows no more than 2 seconds to pass before he asked, "Did you like the film?" The class murmurs an affirmation, but Bill has gone back to his desk and discussion has clearly come to an end.

There is only time to switch gears; he doesn't allow students enough time to become distracted and start interactions of their own. I think of the physics of bike-riding: momentum is everything; coming to a halt may mean falling over. (I also think of instructions given by my 11th grade English teacher who told the class that reading *faster* would keep your mind from wandering.)

Bill is already introducing the next activity with some relish. He tells the class that he wants them all to close their eyes and *think without using words* for 3 minutes, as he times them on his watch.

"When words come in, drive them out of your mind," he directs the students.

"I don't understand," a plaintive voice protests. Jim, a quick-thinking and capable student, turns around and glares at this girl with such a look of supercilious disgust, that I'm at a loss to describe it. Bill doesn't need to repeat instructions very often it seems; the students listen to him the first time and usually are clear about what is expected of them. Perhaps this isn't surprising in an AP class—not necessarily because of intelligence, but because these are students who understand the academic "system."

Bill merely repeats the "think without words" instruction in response to the girl. Even if she is still confused, I know she has been successfully hushed by a classmate's glare. They close their eyes and Bill instructs them to begin. The class is perfectly quiet and I am somewhat surprised that the students do not giggle or squirm with the novelty of the activity. They are concentrating good-naturedly. About 2 minutes of closed lids and furrowed brows pass before Bill says, "Okay, you can open your eyes."

To my great delight, one boy in the class quietly pipes up, "That wasn't 3 minutes."

"Well, people were getting kind of restless," explain Mr. Cresta. The truth of the matter is that I've rarely seen a *less* restless class than that class in those 2 minutes. In fact, I observed, at other times, members of this class in such a wide variety of enterprises such as letter-writing, message-passing, casual chatting, all while "class" was taking place. Once I watched Jim, in the front seat of a middle row, turn around with a piece of paper on which "SMILE" was written in large letters. The girl next to me, for whom it was meant, blushed and smiled momentarily, before she sank back into a self-conscious glumness. Bill rarely makes note of any of this natural entropy, but he felt during this exercise that people were getting "restless." I'd be willing to vouch that the only person in the room who was restless was Bill himself, and this moment illuminated something about him for me. He fears silence in the context of a classroom (not an unusual fear for a teacher), and he dislikes loss of momentum even when *he structures* that moment of repose. Three minutes, to Bill Cresta, is an eternity.

But it was perhaps the boy's comment that affected me even more. "That wasn't 3 minutes." It was said very matter-of-factly, not naggingly, or accusingly. Yet that one comment said so much to me. It said, "Mr. Cresta, here you made a big deal out of timing us for 3 minutes and everything, and then you stop us before the time is up. You can do that because you're the teacher, but we know that wasn't 3 minutes." It was the sheer bottom-line spontaneity of the comment that struck me. The boy sensed it wasn't 3 minutes and he said it as soon as he knew it. He didn't say it to challenge or to impress. I couldn't help but try to imagine this comment in a university classroom. What seems to happen between high school and college that makes older students play their cards so much closer to their chests? What happens to spontaneity and student willingness to say, "That wasn't 3 minutes" when it wasn't 3 minutes? What happens to that wonderful human system of checks and balances?

Bill now questions the students on their less-than-3-minutes of contemplation without words. Was it difficult? Yes, they murmur. What did you do? Zoey, a long-haired girl who sits in front of Tito, explained that she thought of emotions, that she thought of sadness.

"Did you need to put a name to it?" Bill asked.

"A little bit."

"Are you feeling sad?" he asks. She indicates no, and he quickly adds, "No, don't feel sad."

Another student, Karen, explained that she thought in pictures, like she was "watching a movie."

"Did anyone use anything besides pictures?" Bill asks.

"I thought in colors," someone says.

"Music," adds someone else.

Bill asks, "Did anyone do math?" It seems not.

Then Bill pulls together the meaning of the exercise. He talks about conceiving an idea, and asks, "Can we give birth to new things without language?" But instead of letting them answer, he passed out a handout entitled "Language, Thought and Reality." I was sorry to see such a terrific exercise come to such a sudden end. Attention turned to the handout and Bill goes over it. (Bill seems to have a handout for the class daily.)

The handout begins with a quotation from Ludwig Wittgenstein: "All I know is what I have words for." The second quotation "No human being is free to describe nature with strict objectivity, for he is a prisoner of his language," is attributed to Stuart Chase. A story follows involving Peace Corps volunteers who have some difficulty because the native population had no word for "garbage." In the middle of the page there sits a B.C. comic strip illustrating a difficulty with language. All of these parts are read through quickly by Bill (except the comic strip, which he must know they all read first) and without comment from the students. It is assumed that these young scholars can mine for their own significance and connection.

The next section on the two-page handout is a lone phrase "Some Thoughts on Watching Vaclev Havel Address Congress in Both Czech and English." Bill pauses briefly to ask the class, "By the way, did anyone see it last night? It was really marvelous . . ." No one had seen it, and Bill goes on, clearly animated by the subject matter and moved by the speech. I realize that the phrase on the worksheet was a reminder to him to bring up that example in class. I also realize that this worksheet is "hot-off-the-press," typed up on a Macintosh computer sometime between the night before and class; it is not a recycled prop from a previous year.

Tito gets up at this point, walks to the front of the room, gets a tissue from Bill's desk, and returns to his seat. No one pays much attention to this. There seems to be a structured casualness about this classroom.

The next paragraph on the handout is heavy with meaning, yet concisely and clearly written (by Bill). The connection to the 3-minute exercise is made clear, at least to me, in the following sentence: "Control or mastery of language can open up immense human potentials, and conversely, limitations in language can confine and restrict thought, imagination and creativity." Somewhat surprisingly, there is no further direct reference to the 3-minute exercise. Then Bill has written a brilliant transition paragraph to segue into the next activity:

> In our media study of *Apocalypse Now* and our literature study of *Heart of Darkness,* we have experienced both written language and a language primarily of visual images. (Think of the last 10-minute segment of *Apocalypse* when only four words are spoken.) Our language is becoming increasingly more a language of words *and* visual images, not just words alone.

> Watch the 10-minute segment from Stanley Kubrick's film *Full Metal
> Jacket*. On first viewing, pay particular attention to the use of language
> in the film. Consider the following questions . . .

After quickly warning students that this scene will contain "very, very disturbing language" and urging students to remember *Catcher in the Rye,* where they had to look
beyond "bad language" to get to the purpose behind the words, Bill turns on the
VCR (it's all set to go), the students adjust the blinds without being asked, and we all
watch an incredibly powerful and brutal scene from the beginning of *Full Metal
Jacket.* Discussion of what they see will be reserved for the next day, Friday.

I am quite impressed with this lesson plan. I admire the sheer organization
reflected here. The lesson was carefully planned to move logically from the closing
comments on *Apocalypse* to the 3-minute exercise, to contemplation on the power of
language, to another war film where language plays a crucial role. The handout is
not only well-written, clear, and concise, it also draws on examples from several
realms (from comics to *1984* to Vaclev Havel). The ideas here are positively meaty
and are food enough for philosophers, so there's no doubt they can challenge high
school students. These ideas have repercussions in all aspects of life. I also note the
benefits in Bill's strategy of setting students to a clear task before he shows them the
movie. They are instructed specifically to look at the use of language. They are
focused, and they know what direction their discussion of the film will take. The two
questions at the end of the handout focus them even further.

When the scene is over, students murmur as the lights come on, and one male
student chuckles as he repeats one of the obscene insults used by the sergeant in the
film. A girl turns on him in irritation. "It's not funny," she says. In very different
ways, it is clear that these two students have been engaged by the film.

Bill meanwhile hands out an excerpt from Spalding Gray's *Swimming to Cambodia,*
with three pages of questions attached. It is due Monday. The questions direct the
students to close analysis of the passage, asking about the use of particular words
and phrases, about tone, connotation, allusion, rhythm, repetition, voice. Skills of
close analysis certainly will come in handy on the AP exam. For Friday, students are
to answer the two questions about *Full Metal Jacket* and Bill says, "You may do these
individually or in groups." He adds a few more things they might think about as
they answer those questions.

Then Bill hands out *Henry IV* to the students and tells them they can begin any
time they want.

"How about next year?" asks Brett, from the back.

"Yeah, next year," laughs Bill good-naturedly, and class rolls on its remaining
momentum to its close.

The most striking thing about my experience in this first class was the sheer volume of material "covered" in a 50-minute period. There was no down time here. I
was also struck by the paradox I felt in this teacher. The classroom, with its chair-
desks facing front and all activity hinging on the teacher-authority, seemed to me
very traditional. On the other hand, the explicit obscene, violent, and racist language of *Full Metal Jacket* brought me home the nontraditional side of this classroom. The next day this was just as clear in the discussion of guns in the *Full Metal
Jacket* scene. Zoey had pointed out that the sergeant was taking the human sexual
impulse and turning it into a violent one in his language. Another student pipes in,
"And they are ordered to sleep with their weapon."

"What does your gun become then?" Bill asks the class, gesturing as if he were holding a rifle in front of him. A moment of embarrassed silence. "It's your penis, isn't it?"

Here was a teacher who saw value in modern American film, and who trusted his students enough to be able to handle subject matter usually considered "inappropriate" in school.

As well as being a teacher who is poised on the traditional/nontraditional line, Bill is also a teacher who walks the inevitable line between being the authority and being "one of the gang." The difficulty of treading this line is evidenced by the kind but flat-palmed and hesitant shoulder pats I saw him bestow on his students when he congratulated them or acknowledged them in some other way. It was also easy to see him struggle with his role when, on my last day of observation, he announced a reading quiz on *Henry IV* for Monday. A few students grumbled, and then one spoke up, "Did you know it's the senior ski trip this weekend?" He admitted that he didn't know, but as he turns toward the front of the room, he quickly says something about how they will still be responsible for the material. The student sense of injustice fills the room like silent smoke. Turning back to the class, Bill asks how many in the class are going. Approximately five students, the athletic-looking group who sits in the back left corner, raise their hands. Bill goes through a visible inner struggle.

"Okay," Bill says, "in the interests of your social education which has to happen as well as your academic education, I can switch the quiz to Wednesday. But it will be harder."

Now there is audible discontent from *other* members of the class. Bill immediately senses this and calls for a class vote. The Monday quiz wins. The group of five is still displeased, but they've received due process. At the end of class, Bill tries to reassure them further by announcing, "I promise you an easy quiz on Monday." In allowing his authority to be somewhat flexible, without ever really giving ground, Bill has managed to walk that fine line between being "us" and being "them." He defused a situation that could have embittered a powerful group of students in his classroom.

Bill Cresta clearly has high expectations for his students, both academically and behaviorally, and they seemed to rise to the occasion within the freedom he gives them. He avoids imposing severe discipline on them, with no fear of losing control. There was no punishment or even remark made when students neglected to bring a needed book or handout to class, and he wasn't overly concerned when students chatted quietly together while he was talking. On only two occasions did I see him react to this behavior. The first time, Brett was talking to his female neighbor as another student was answering a question. Bill said, "Brett, what did he say?"

"Nothing," said Brett, "I mean, I didn't hear it."

"He said an important thing. Why don't you say it again, Rick?"

No direct mention of Brett's inattention was made, but the message was adequately clear. The only other time I witnessed a reaction to talking during class was a simple, "Ladies" directed at two girls not even bothering to lower their voices. At times I got the impression that some of this in-class talking was related to the subject matter of the course, but that wasn't always the case. At any rate, this behavior didn't seem to be a disruptive or distracting one for the teacher or for the class as a whole, and instead merely gave me the impression of the structured casualness I spoke of earlier. My feeling is that Bill moves the class along too quickly for any of this peripheral activity to take any serious form. The momentum sweeps everyone up, if not into inspiration, at least into eventual silence.

V. You Are What You Teach, You Teach What You Are

> *Snake*
> *A snake came to my water-trough*
> *On a hot, hot day, and I in pajamas for the heat,*
> *To drink there.*
>
> *. . . The voice of my education said to me*
> *He must be killed*
> *For in Sicily the black, black snakes are innocent, the gold are venomous.*
>
> *And voices in me said, If you were a man*
> *You would take a stick and break him now, and finish him off.*
>
> *. . . I looked round, I put down my pitcher,*
> *I picked up a clumsy log*
> *And threw it at the water-trough with a clatter.*
>
> *. . . And immediately I regretted it.*
> *I thought how paltry, how vulgar, what a mean act!*
> *I despised myself and the voices of my accursed human education.*
>
> *And I thought of the albatross*
> *And I wish he could come back, my snake. . . .*
>
> D. H. LAWRENCE

A small American flag hangs in Bill Cresta's classroom, and seeing it the first day reminded me to attend to values present in his teaching. I didn't have to look far.

The first episode that brought values to mind was one in which he made reference to Vaclev Havel's address to the U.S. Congress. In this 1- or 2-minute interlude, he brought at least three values to bear in his classroom. The first was built into his question "By the way, did anybody see it last night?" This, backed up with other references I heard him make at other times to changes in the Eastern bloc, demonstrated the emphasis he puts on awareness of current events, or, awareness of a larger world than Parkside, or the Bay Area. He models this interest and spends time "keeping up." (How, oh how, I think to myself, does he have time to plan his classes so thoroughly, *and* watch Vaclev Havel, *and* find and photocopy three different movie reviews of *Henry V*?)

The second value he demonstrated here was an appreciation of American democracy. He spoke of how crotchety senators listened with tears in their eyes to Havel's speech about experiencing democracy for the first time in his life. He remarked how it made one realize "what a marvelous gift (democracy) is." The third value here is a value in what I might call the fullness of experience. Bill was telling his students how *moved* the senators and he himself were by this speech. This may not seem unusual, but I think students need to learn how to be *moved* by the world in new ways. That is how a curious mind is born. A student sees an adult absorbed or moved by a speech, or a poet, or a painting, and though the student may not understand at the time, he or she will begin to look at poems or paintings or listen to speeches in a new way—with closer attention to what it might potentially hold for them. Bill does what I feel is the most important job of a teacher: he conveys excitement about the world and its possibilities.

Bill touched on many other important values in my short 4 days of observation. Some I noticed because they were thrown out in a passing sentence. For example, when the field trip to *Henry V* was being discussed, Bill commented, "In the interest of the environment, let's take as few cars as possible." When making reference to Iago's character in *Othello* (a play the class read previously), he reminds the class how Iago asserts that Desdemona marrying an African is positively unnatural. "But we realize—what? That it's the most natural thing in the world." Here, too, values are implicit in his words.

In the discussion of *Henry IV*, "moderation" is a concept that Bill discusses at length. He speaks of Buddha's teaching and draws Buddha's "wheel" on the board. "When there is excess of some kind, the axis is on the side, not in the center," he says, drawing a lopsided wheel. "Buddha emphasized moderation." Bill lists rock music, food, alcohol, and drugs as possible vehicles to excess (Rock music? I thought). Then the class turns its attention to the excesses of characters in *Henry IV*: Hotspur, who is excessively aggressive; King Henry, who may be on a power trip; and our old friend Falstaff, who eats, drinks, and "wenches" immoderately.

The next day a handout addressed moderation again. The first paragraph reads:

> In a famous discussion about ethics and the attitudes necessary for an effective life, the Greek philosopher Aristotle saw virtue (goodness) as a mean or balance between possible extremes of behavior. For Aristotle and for the Greeks, the happy, productive person was one who experienced the wonderful variety life has to offer but avoided becoming obsessed with any one facet of life. The drug addict and the religious fanatic were equally "unbalanced."

Certainly these students could have gotten no better lesson on the virtue of temperance than they were getting in AP English class. And from four different sources: Buddha, Aristotle, Shakespeare, and, implicitly, their teacher Bill Cresta.

Something else struck me that is tied up in values. Bill does something in his classroom that I don't think I've ever seen a teacher do. He values his profession as an educator, and he communicates this to his students. There were a couple of examples of this. One was a very dramatic moment in the Friday discussion of *Full Metal Jacket*. Bill and the class had come up with an impressive list of purposes toward which the brutal Sergeant Hargrave had used language on his recruits. On the board, under *Purpose* they list:

1. Dehumanize/desensitize (to turn into fighting machine)
2. Erase individuality
3. Establish equality
4. Establish control

Under *Language Devices*, they list:

1. obscenity/vulgarity (but *not* profanity)
2. inflections/intensity
3. choral responses
4. renames men

5. acknowledge authority
6. stereotyping

(Bill notes in this lesson that the Marine Corps advertises for "A Few Good Men," you sign on the dotted line, and *then* you find out you are, as is portrayed in the film, "a worthless piece of amphibian shit.") As Bill pulls this discussion of *Full Metal Jacket* to a close, asking "is there anything we've left off the list?" Bill allows a rare pause in the classroom.

"You know," Bill says with some feeling, "As a teacher, I admire the lesson plan here (used by Sergeant Hargrave). I really admire the lesson plan." There is a hush and the air is tense for a moment with suspense. Bill's head bobs in his inner energy as he continues in a hushed dramatic voice, "Though it uses all the wrong things . . . all the wrong things. . . ."

I get a chill up my spine from the fullness of this message which has been built up from the class's examination of the phenomenal power of language. But before I have a chance to revel in the moment, Bill is off in the next activity.

Not only was the message powerful here on the "lesson plan" of the drill sergeant, but Bill used a sentence that struck me: "As a teacher, I admired the lesson plan . . ." I realized how rare it was for a high school teacher to so blatantly (and proudly?) point to his profession.

Other incidents made this come through even more clearly to me. His introduction to *Henry IV* went something like this: "Multicultural experience is an important concept in education nowadays. Those of us in education value multicultural experience because of its ability to place you in another world. Reading Shakespeare, and being transported to the Elizabethan world, should be considered no less a multicultural experience." Again, Bill here makes clear reference to himself as he is defined by being an *educator* ("Those of us in education"); he considers himself part of the profession, and he makes this clear to his students. His interest in the field was further displayed that day when they were discussing *Henry IV* and he announces with emphasis, "This is a great story about education."

As I thought about this, I realized that rarely, if ever, in my experience with high school teachers had I heard them validate themselves as professionals so explicitly *to their students*. Sure, teachers talk about their job, but when do they ever mention their *profession*? There are two questions raised by this observation. First, why are teachers so reluctant to present themselves as engaged in a concrete profession to their students? Is it because they would rather be seen as scholars? Is it because they themselves lack a feeling that they are part of that profession? Second, what effect might be brought about through Bill's presentation of himself as part of a professional group of educators? Perhaps those students will leave his classroom and then Parkside with a deeper respect for the teaching profession (not just because he is a fine teacher, but because he is part of a group of *educators* with similar concerns). Perhaps teachers need to do this more often—to present themselves as the professionals they are in front of their students. It models to the students how to take pride in your work, and it may be the beginning of increasing general respect for teachers. What you know about teachers is most often what you *remember* about teachers. Perhaps teachers must educate the public about their profession from the ground up.

I have often thought that the best teaching, especially teaching involving values, will drop, ignored, if the students have no respect for the teacher. Clearly these students respect Bill, as is evidenced by their general good behavior and receptiveness to class activities (such as the 3-minute exercise). Never did I see a student roll her eyes, or in any way cast derision this teacher's way. Students would engage him in conversation before and after class. The subject matter of these conversations was academic rather than personal. This isn't perhaps the teacher they'd come to talk to about their Saturday night, but he was liked and quietly admired.

VI. Unnatural Selection?

The special nature of a class like this cannot be ignored, and I don't intend to present this AP class as "typical." Instead, I observed knowing that these students would be academically capable and motivated, and that their teacher was "one of the best" at Parkside (the words of Fred Meyer, the English department head). I was aware that I was observing "the best face" of Parkside.

How did these students get into the AP section? For the most part, these seniors emerged from the honors "lane" at Parkside. (I suppose someone came up with "lane" because it's a softer word than "track.") According to Tito, most of the AP students were put in the honor lane in ninth grade. Technically, Bill says, any one can "get in" to the AP class if they really want to, but it was clear from his and from Tito's comments that that was rare. Most of the students in the class will actually take the AP exam, which might help them with college entrance or to gain some college credit. These students plan on college or junior college after graduation.

Parkside started "laning" students about 5 years ago (coincidentally, at about the same time San Carlos High was closed), but they are doing away with the "standard" and "regular" lanes next year. They will keep the honors track. The ethnic make-up of this AP class must be of concern to them, because it is so disproportional to the make-up of the school, but I got no indication that any changes were on the way. I assume the ninth-graders will continue to be funneled into the honors track and then onto AP English. It worries me to think what process of "natural selection" is going on.

Bill, at least, spreads his talents beyond the most advanced students. It is a habit of his to take on students at both ends of the spectrum, so he also teaches two "standard" classes of English. The timing did not work out for me to attend one of these other classes, but word has it (from a STEP student he supervises and from a past STEP (Stanford Teacher Education Program) administrator who knows him) that he is good with all levels of students.

There is a strange sort of isolation about this AP classroom though. Besides a scrawl next to me on the wall that announces "Satan Lives" or Tito's casual mention of school fights that have given rise to new restrictions, or an after-class discussion of severe bathroom vandalism, one might think these students and these teachers in a picture-perfect academic world.

VII. Teaching Toward Meaning

What impressed me the most about Bill's teaching style was his artful braiding together of three strands: present subject matter, past subject matter, and relevance to the real world. Bill does this with such natural skill that it must be teaching reflex. When discussing *Henry IV*, Bill relies heavily on comparison to *Othello* and *King Lear*. When discussing the intense popularity of Falstaff, and Shakespeare's killing off of this character so that he could move on, Bill makes reference to Woody Allen and his reluctance to keep on making his popular comedies. When he's trying to give his students a sense about the political world of Henry IV, he says, "Can you imagine if Redwood City had its own army, and could send it to lean on Belmont?" In reference to Prince Hal and his obligation to part company with his drinking buddies, Bill brings the concept home. "When you go off from high school and you come back years from now, you will have changed. You'll talk about the old days, the old things with your friends, but your conversation will eventually hit a wall. You might be into a career, they might be into family . . ." So Bill anchors new material both in making connections to familiar past material and in making meaningful connections to the students' lives.

In a similar way, on that same day Bill revealed what for me seemed a rare glimpse of his own life. He was discussing Shakespeare's concern with relationships between parent and child, and specifically, Prince Hal's relationship with his father. He stops here and slips into a personal tone to recall an incident from his own life. He tells the class how deferential he had always felt toward his own father. Then, 10 years ago, his father had a stroke, and Bill tells of how difficult it was to have to wheel around in a wheelchair this man he had always looked up to.

Literature *is* life, to Bill Cresta. And if his students are truly listening, it will come alive for them too.

VII. Conclusions

The natural laws of teaching are, like anything else, a matter of interpretation. I have done what I can here to point out some of the forces I observed at work in this particular classroom. Now that I've chosen and discussed some individual threads, I suppose it's time for me to step back and take a look at the whole fabric.

Bill Cresta is a fine teacher. I say that with confidence and without qualification. He is experienced, competent, and caring, and public education could use many, many more of him.

Bill has qualities that are indispensable to a teacher who's going to have staying power. First, he has a sense of humor. He can relax his students with a witty comment, and more importantly, he can laugh *with* his students. This ability can add years onto a teacher's life. Second, at least with this class, Bill doesn't have to waste any energy on a power struggle. The air of mutual respect he has created in the classroom allows students to feel adult freedom—no one is watching them like a hawk to catch them whispering or passing notes. They have some "space" in this class to move, to talk, and to study issues pertinent to *them*. Because of this, they have no need to test him, no need to assert themselves in troublesome ways. And because it's not an "us" versus "them" situation, the students feel free to invest themselves in the material.

It's clear that Bill does his best to be sensitive to students. When a quiet student answers a question, he is sure to give extra encouragement with a smile and a compliment. One student in the class, Michelle, was of particular interest to me. She had dyed reddish-black hair, wore a green leather jacket to class every day, and contributed little. It was clear this AP group did not make up her usual crowd (assuming she had one). She would come to class every day and slump into her desk, and then busy herself the whole class period, head down, over something that was seemingly unrelated to the subject matter (e.g., writing letters). One day she unexpectedly commented, however, when Bill had asked a question about superstition. "It's just like *Drugstore Cowboy,*" she said simply, head down. Bill responded immediately with a smile and came toward her, asking her to elaborate. She said, simply, that the movie showed a lot of superstition around drug rituals. Uncharacteristically, Bill allowed himself a tangent to try to engage her further. "Did you like the movie?" She nodded yes. It ended up that those were her last words for the day, but Bill had connected with her, if only for a moment, and he had made it clear that her contribution pleased him.

I also witnessed Bill encouraging students about assignments, improvement in their writing, and tests. He gave pep talks individually and to the class as a whole.

Lastly, Bill is a teacher with a clear sense of himself and of his purpose in the classroom. That he loves what he teaches is obvious in his energy and his smile. That he has clear purpose is obvious in his sense of organization.

My intent is not to soft-pedal, but even the criticisms I would level at some aspects of this classroom could be waved away. For example, I could criticize Bill's teacher-centeredness, where students can't even hear the comments of other students, so are unable to respond except to Bill himself. I could criticize his failure to allow students to take discussion in their own directions, his failure to give students adequate wait-time, and his failure to encourage participation from *all* students. (On average, I would say about two-thirds of the class contributes on a given day.)

But there are two things that make me hesitate in casting these critical shadows. First, on my last day of observation, Bill divided the class into small groups, and the following week they were going to work together on an aspect of *Henry IV* and then make a presentation to the class. It occurred to me that perhaps Bill makes up for his teacher-centeredness in other significant activities in which the teacher is eliminated. Perhaps it is in these other activities that Bill gives his students a chance to talk with each other. I would have to see a lot more to know.

The second reason I hesitated to criticize his teacher-centeredness is my awareness of an ambiguous trade-off between freedom of discussion and *coverage*. Some people might say coverage is less of a priority than direct student involvement and free discussion, but it's difficult for me to discount coverage in a course specifically designed to prepare students for a test in which coverage will be very important.

Fortunately, although Bill is the center of most of his classes, he isn't a boring monotone, and the subject matter he brings to bear, is, in my opinion, quite worthy of study. So although my own style would be to give the students more opportunity to think on their own, I must admit I enjoyed watching him teach. If he were a less talented teacher, I would criticize his teacher-centeredness more.

VIII. Final Thoughts

I would wager that Bill Cresta taught me more than he taught any of his students on the 4 days I spent in his classroom. He made me realize how much I miss being in the classroom, how much I miss teaching Shakespeare, how much I miss high school students. But perhaps the most important thing he showed me was how much college professors, as a group, could potentially learn from high school teachers *about being teachers.*

It struck me as a great irony that high school students go through all this agony to get "prepared" to apply and attend college, but then the college classrooms they enter will be a completely different animal than what most of the college freshmen encountered less than 1 year before. College teachers, in general, have a completely different way of operating with students, it seems; they are more removed, more blase. Bill Cresta made me wonder why. His energy, individual attention, organization, and use of a variety of materials and activities, made me, I must admit, slightly jealous of his students.

They, of course, don't yet know how lucky they are.

References

Ionesco, E. (1967). *Exit the king.* (Donald Watson, Trans.). New York: Grove.

Roethke, T. (1965). *On the poet and his craft.* Seattle: University of Washington Press.

Portrait of a Ceramics Class:

Control and Freedom in a Delicate Balance

LORNA CATFORD

The Story

It is May in a rather more than less wealthy California middle school. Before the buzz of the bell signals the start of Mr. Gebhart's 7th–8th grade ceramics class, life is well under way in this creative sanctum. This workspace crammed with tools of the trade and busy students hums with life, in striking contrast to the dreary gray angularity of the world outside this class room—where identical beige wings flank concrete walk-

ways. A delicate coating of clay dust clings indiscriminately to faded, dog-eared photographs of ceramics, spotted with fingerprints where umpteen students have traced
designs in their quest for inspiration, and to the instructor's laminated, hand-illus-
trated instructions for slab, pinch, coil, and modeling projects, pasted on available
wall space. Two birds building their nest in the ceiling chirp loudly to be heard above
the rock and roll issuing from the classroom's battered radio.

The students pay no attention. As they position themselves at 12 study tables,
their industry matches that of the birds. Some have taken their 18" coil pots from
the pottery-crowded counter and are already building their monuments higher, or
paddling or glazing them. Some have pulled plastic-wrapped clay shoes in various
stages of design from the unkempt student shelves that are trying to hide themselves behind huge, perpetually gaping, lavender doors decorated with enormous
silver stars and mud spots. Other students critique pieces on the overcrowded carts
by the kilns, where almost dry greenware, awaiting firing, balances precariously by
gorgeously glazed bowls, figures, boxes, and assorted items. Yet other students are
rummaging through the glazes, tools, slip, and sponges in the back of the room,
finding what they need and using it. At two back tables, seven students laugh and
talk, not working.

At first no teacher is visible. Then he can be discerned in his open-necked shirt
and clay-streaked pants, bending over one student's project discussing the aesthetic
quality of the glaze, then over another's to suggest how to solve the problem of reat-

taching pieces that fell off in the first firing. Two minutes after the bell has summoned the faithful, Mr. Gebhart stands up. He has already had individual consultation with five students.

"Bo, turn off the radio please, till everyone is working."

A boy from the nonworking table silences the music. Most of the students look up for a moment, then resume work. Some approach him with questions concerning evaluation of their work, further directions, or technical or aesthetic problems demanding solution. Mr. Gebhart attends briefly to them, but directs his attention to the back table where a girl is wrapping her scarf around Bo's head, talking.

"Penny, what are you working on?" She shrugs. "Don't just sit there and chat. You've had enough time to get started." Mr. Gebhart turns to somebody else. Penny pulls out a lacy clay shoe and starts smoothing out its high heel.

The radio is turned on. "Leave that off till everyone is working. I'll say when everyone is working." The radio is turned off. Students admonish one another to get to work. Fifteen minutes into the period Mr. Gebhart turns the music on. Another work day is in progress.

Every 2 weeks or so Mr. Gebhart introduces a new lesson. He asks the students to gather round, which they do, some perched on the front tables, one on crutches, balanced dangerously between two tables. This lesson involves sculpting a figure,

"doing something, not looking like it just died," from a small block of clay. Mr. Gebhart demonstrates the basic cuts and twists that produce a human form, telling students to attend to proportion, not detail. He shows them how to use their bodies to determine arm length. The students seem captivated by the emerging figure. Working quickly, Mr. Gebhart notes that the figure should be posed after its basic form is established, and then brings forth a seated figure, torso twisted, knee raised.

Having given basic directions, Mr. Gebhart shows the students illustrations in *Sports and Games in Art*—Bellows's boxers, Moore's abstractions, Greek wrestlers. He brings the pictures to life: "This one was probably made in clay first like you're doing." "We call this 'abstracted.' Just put in what you think is essential." "Notice how this conveys a feeling of movement." He throws his body forward to walk. "In art we create the same process by throwing the whole body off center."

Pointing to a Giacometti with slender legs. "What's the problem with this one if you were making it out of clay?" ("It wouldn't stand.") "How could you solve that problem?" With no hesitations solutions are offered: "put wire inside and clay around it," "a platform," "support."

Mr. Gebhart expands on the students' answers, showing further illustrations and reminding them to think about how they will present their figure. Then he recaps several tips: adapting ideas from existing art pieces, planning before starting, using one's body as a guide, adding details last.

During the 14-minute lecture, Mr. Gebhart has the students' attention. Barb, chin on hands, has her eyes riveted to him and the book, nodding to herself. Valerie is unobtrusively observing from behind some more assertive students. Even Bo and

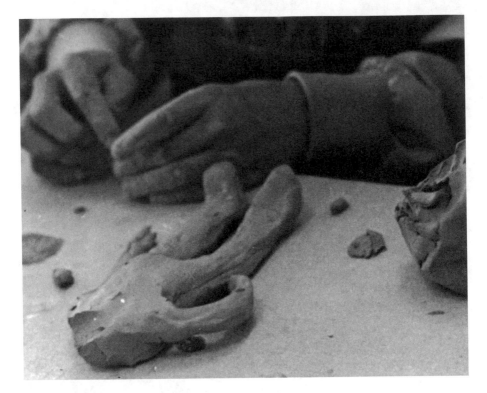

Penny watch. "Continue with your work," concludes Mr. Gebhart. The students disperse, and the day continues in the usual manner of individual instruction. Seven or eight different types of projects are underway.

Valerie holds her head down a lot. She has embarked on the new project, the figure in action, but has not progressed far. Its form is still reminiscent of the chunky rectangular slab from which it is fashioned. As Valerie smooths out a shoulder, a crack appears in the ankle. She puts it down and goes to find Mr. Gebhart. Bringing him to her table, she says, "I can't do it." "What can't you do? I see a guy there. You did that." "He doesn't have good shoulders." "What do you mean—not good shoulders?" "They're too big."

Pointing to their bodies, Mr. Gebhart describes the difference between the figure's shoulders and theirs. Valerie watches, nods. Barb, participating in the interchange, manipulates the figure, "It'll go in there. You can cut it off here . . . push it there." Valerie watches, hands clasped, while the others critique the piece and suggest what to do. Valerie comments that she is not sure how to shape it. Mr. Gebhart brings Valerie *Sports in Art,* but instead of looking in it she wrinkles her nose and says, of her figure, "It looks rejected." Mr. Gebhart suggests that she not be afraid to pick it up and view it from various angles. Valerie does this, holding it gingerly.

"Mind if I work on this side a bit?" asked Mr. Gebhart. He describes what he is doing as, in his hands, one leg becomes lifelike. Valerie notices the transformation. Then the crack deepens and the foot falls off. "Oh, don't worry. You can put it on later," remarks Mr. Gebhart nonchalantly. He hands the figure to Valerie, who

starts working on it. Mr. Gebhart leaves. He has spent 10 minutes with Valerie, more than with any other student at one time. "I think I'll take the feet off for now," she says, much braver, and she does.

Sue approaches Mr. Gebhart with a pot from another class. "Is this glaze beanpot brown?" When told it is, she asks how the striped effect was achieved, and after telling her and suggesting an alternate method, Mr. Gebhart asks her if she plans this for inside or outside her pot. Sue considers, and replies that if she uses blue and black she will stripe both, but if she uses browns, just the outside. "Well, think about that," says Mr. Gebhart, supporting her decision making, but not doing it for her.

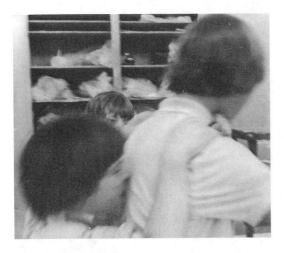

Later Sue explains what she decided, "Blue, because it's not as serious or gloomy as the brown." She points to two blue pots at the front of the room, on which the glaze has been applied so that the tops are lighter than the bottoms. "I like the light on the top. I'll do blue on the outside and something else inside to make it interesting."

Two students are rough-housing on the other side of the room. One has the other in a bear hold. "Okay. Cool it on the hugs!" Mr. Gebhart raises his voice so

they will hear him. With this warning, there are several smiles, and the students get back to work.

Fred, tiny for his age, is the only Japanese student in the class. A timid seventh-grader, he is in a special "Core" program for students with problems adjusting to junior high school. For several days it has been sweltering and Fred has worn a huge down parka. He works silently at the outside corner of a front table, perhaps the least frequented area of the room. His tablemate is another quiet boy, engrossed in his work.

Fred bends over his coil pot, patting the dry cracking clay. Mr. Gebhart comes and crouches next to him. "I want you to get a bowl of water and dip your hands in, and put it on your clay as you work, to keep it wet so it doesn't dry out." He straightens up and stands by the table until Fred has fetched the water.

Some time later Valerie's figure has developed a more shapely lean look. The feet have been attached. She leafs through the book for a few minutes and decides on a pose. When she starts bending the figure, cracks appear in the clay, so she asked Mr. Gebhart if he will bend it into position. This time he does not take such an active role in her problem solving. "Don't worry if it cracks," he says. He does not bend it, but shows her how to smooth it over, mentioning that his work cracks, too. Valerie nods in acknowledgment of his reassurance.

A piece of clay whizzes past Mr. Gebhart's head. "Who's throwing clay?" he asks, looking around the room. No response. He moves to a table of three boys. "Are you throwing clay?" One angelic-looking child slowly shakes his head, and utters a wide-eyed lie, "Oh, no." "Well from the trajectory it looks like its from the direction of this table," remarks the teacher. "If you are, you'll get a written assignment and cleanup duty." There is a murmur of denial from the boys. "I'm not accusing you. I just want to make sure you know the consequences." No more clay is thrown that day.

During the next few days Mr. Gebhart continues his versatile manner of teaching. He scans the room for students needing encouragement, intellectual challenge, or discipline. His manner of interaction seems endless: humor, stern words, touching, doing, watching, inquiring, reflecting on his own work, giving directions.

He gives one other 15-minute lecture in the 10 hours of class during which this story takes place. On this occasion he encourages the students to recall and describe the four basic techniques they have learned and to brainstorm possible applications of these techniques. After a brief lecture on art as problem solving, Mr. Gebhart informs the students that, in the past when he has given problems and steps for solving them, they have not had to create the problems themselves. Explaining that as artists, they, and he constantly need to invite challenging problems, he assigns the final project of the semester. The students are to spend a few days browsing through art books, interacting with the environment, allowing an idea to germinate, and then to present a plan for their final project. He acknowledges the value of frustration and negative reactions as containing seeds for problems to be solved. Although most students are attentive, the "social group" laugh and talk, not always facing the front of the room. Mr. Gebhart seems to ignore this, and talks to those who are lis-

tening. He fields a few questions, then tells the students to take out their work. The hum of music and industry resumes.

Jane, who has been absent for many days, admires Valerie's now smooth and fluid figure. "If I can get the leg back on, it'll be like the picture in a gymnastics magazine," says Valerie, working on the piece. Jane wants to know exactly what the assignment entails. The self-same Valerie who was too timid to touch her figure earlier not only describes the project with authority, but also reassures Jane that cracks

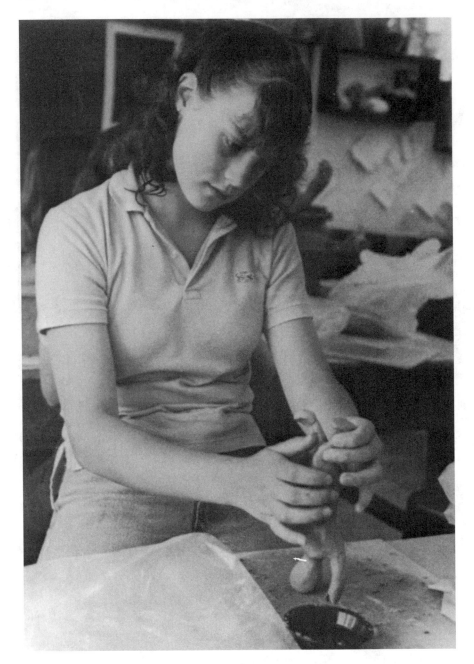

are not a problem, and that removing a limb can make it easier to work on the piece.

Five minutes before the end of class, Mr. Gebhart hovers by the radio, and when a song ends, turns it off. "We interrupt this program to announce cleanup." Groans

from some students; hurried last minute modifications; sponges grabbed to wipe tables. At the bell the class empties and the walkway comes to life.

Mr. Gebhart stretches, and begins unloading and restacking the kilns. The birds chirp and fly from nest to open door. The clay dust sparkles in the sunshine.

Analysis

The preceding story is factual. I saw and heard the events and words in it. Where thick description is used, ascription of motives or meaning is based on further observations, interviews, and a questionnaire completed by 26 students. My observations are shaped by 10 years' experience as a therapist, trained to perceive and interpret nuances of human interaction.

Mr. Gebhart is concerned about what he calls the "delicate balance between control and freedom" in his ceramics class. I saw him weaving the two into a rich educative experience in numerous ways, aided by his apparent sensitivity to students' needs. In this section I examine this balance in three areas: classroom management, curriculum, and teaching. In each area I try to understand the relationship between control and freedom in terms of the teacher's philosophy, student reactions, and educational theory. In the final section I discuss the relationship between Mr. Gebhart's teaching style and his personal style. Last, I suggest implications for teacher selection and training. The story enables readers to draw conclusions beyond those discussed here.

Classroom Management   Although there are many facets to classroom management, the term here refers to discipline. Beth Lyon, the school psychologist, describes Mr. Gebhart's class: "It looks as if everyone is running around being wild, but it takes structure to run a class like that. The kids and teacher know what the structure is, even if from outside it doesn't look like much." It is true that the movement, clutter, dust, and noise could suggest the unhappy stereotype of the "free art class." This is belied by the underlying self-direction of the students, and the quality of their aesthetic and intellectual judgments.

Mr. Gebhart realizes that the individualized way in which he runs his class invites students to test the limits of their freedom. However, he insists that developing skill and knowledge in art requires discipline and work, and that "control is the basis for everything else that goes on in this class."

He is comfortable with the discipline level in his class, which he has come to via the road of hard knocks. He recalls that the students would "walk all over" him when he started teaching, and was attempting authoritarian control. Describing this, he stated, "if you decide *now* they have to clean up their act, you create a battle you can't win." Herman Hesse (1968), in an essay on schooling, calls this sort of battle a "struggle between rule and spirit." After being trained in Cantor and Cantor's "assertive discipline" (a behavioral program with rewards and punishments for rule following or breaking), Mr. Gebhart developed a more effective way to maintain control. Rather than attempting to force compliance, thus ignoring the students' need for self-expression, he reminds them of the rules, respecting their ability to take responsibility for their actions. The exciting thing is that not only does he not have to work so hard, but also the students are less disruptive.

In the daily pseudo-battle concerning the radio, the students test Mr. Gebhart, who states the limits, and tells them how they can direct their energy so that they can have the music. Here, as in the clay-throwing incident, Mr. Gebhart attempts to structure the situation so that the rules are not oppressive—thus spirit finds an alternative mode of expression. He encourages an active rather than a passive response in his students—doing work rather than being quiet. Thus he allows a certain type of personal freedom in his social control. While the "social group," as Mr. Gebhart calls them, seem to take advantage of the freedom to talk and move around, they also tend to turn their attention to the task at hand at a few words from the teacher.

One student expressed a sentiment shared by several, that the freedom "makes it so that I don't just do my work to get it over with." Only one student, out of 26 answering a questionnaire, feels that Mr. Gebhart "hardly ever" has adequate control over the class, and only three state that they tend to "goof off" more in this class than others.

With minor variations in words and cast, the ritual dance of the forces of control and freedom, of rule and spirit, are enacted 5 days a week. The choreography is superb. There is a dynamic tension in which it turns out that the forces of freedom do indeed have a good amount of control, and vice versa.

It is clear that although the students appear to challenge the teacher's authority, the rules of the dance are such that the challenge is a token act of self-assertion. Penny's immediate return to work in response to Mr. Gebhart's statement suggests that she has an internal locus of self-control. (A Marxist educator might view this as compliance as the result of the system during the student's previous 7 years of schooling. Penny's—and others'—vitality suggests that this is not so.) Examination of the manner in which the teacher exerts control reveals that he is not forceful, but allows the students the freedom to create their own control.

Although the challenges happen, the majority of the students can be likened to the Greek Chorus, the actors in the background who call to our attention the "truth" of the situation. Their physical movement in the room and conversation are predominantly task-related (I noted several interchanges daily concerning techniques or aesthetic judgment, and few extraneous conversations), and the emotional color of their expression reflects elation, frustration, or pride about their work. In Dewey's (1938) terms, the external freedom is a means to intellectual freedom. Most students initiate work before the bell rings, and do not want to stop at cleanup time. I have a sense of time running away because of the students' involvement. As one student put it, "The problem with this class is it's over before you can start."

Most students are involved. Quality work is done. The formal rules of discipline and meta-rules of the dance are known by all. This suggests to me that Mr. Gebhart uses freedom and control effectively in his classroom management. The following words of Walt Whitman come to mind:

> *Of life immense in passion, pulse and power,*
> *Cheerful, for freest action formed under the laws divine.*

Curriculum   Mr. Gebhart's curriculum involves gaining control of terminology and materials. It consists of knowledge and application of five technical skills—pinch, slab, coil, modeling, and glazing. Is this not made clear by the instructions on the wall, and the mountains of students work? As is the case with classroom management, what might seem so at first does not necessarily reflect the extent of what is there.

True, Mr. Gebhart teaches skills according to "a recipe," and students are required to learn these skills. Making a coil pot requires the use of a specific technique, and its size requirement ensures that in completing it the students would be practiced in this. Mr. Gebhart notes the necessity of drill to become proficient, and describes this acquisition of technical control as "freeing, because once you have this, you can go on and do anything." Although technical control is necessary, too much "concern with technical skill can interfere with aesthetic expression and appreciation," he comments.

Susanne Langer (1957) describes the difference between a product and a creation. Although both involve technical mastery, a creation is an expressive form—its meaning goes beyond the limits of the materials and how they were shaped. Mr. Gebhart's aim is that his students learn to *create*. He states that his curriculum is designed to maximize the problems of creativity, which call on control of material and freedom of aesthetic expression and judgment for their solution.

Mr. Gebhart, therefore, does not just present his students with instructions on how to manipulate materials, but includes emphasis on ways of seeing and thinking. The lesson on figure sculpting includes recognition of existing art work, and appreciation of the motion and shape of the students' own bodies to suggest ideas. He encouraged them to plan before working, and to consider how to solve problems that might arise during the conceptualization and construction of their pieces. His creative problem solving reflects the *creative design* orientation of the Bauhaus (Eisner, 1972).

Watching him work with Valerie, I saw him attempt to increase her control over her material by explaining what to do and giving her the opportunity to practice. He increased her freedom by presenting an alternate way of viewing broken limbs— as an asset rather than a liability. Over the next few days, I noticed a marked difference in the quality of Valerie's figure, and the self-confidence with which she talked about it.

I saw a relationship here, of greater control yielding greater freedom, and vice versa. This is an example of Dewey's notion of the continuous interchange of intellectual and aesthetic components of an educative experience.

The curriculum also reflects Deweyan philosophy in its sequential organization of subject matter. Students progress from concern with technical skill to increased attention to artistic vision and judgments, both within each lesson and during the semester. Each lesson starts with a lecture–demonstration in which Mr. Gebhart presents "the watch-points, the crucial steps." As students gain control of a technique, say slab, he encourages them to select more complex applications—perhaps a mug first, then a mask with raised, textured, and cut-out areas, a square box with a fitted lid, a model of their shoe. The final project allows students, after they have gained control of basic skills, the freedom to create and solve an artistic problem (which also gives them an opportunity to show control over all that they have learned).

The comments and actions of a number of students suggested that Mr. Gebhart's curriculum actually affected them. Sue's reasoning concerning her glaze revealed aesthetic judgment and appreciation. When I asked two students if one made a coil pot smaller by using smaller coils, they raised their eyes and shook their heads (as if incredulous at my ignorance) and ably showed me how to score and smooth a coil, supporting and pushing in on the pot. Although there was no consensus on a specific assignment, 16 students noted that their most creative project involved freedom to make judgments about it: for example, "You had to think about what kind of creature you wanted to make, and what kind of details there'd be on it."

On the questionnaire I administered, a majority of students (over 13) said they usually are challenged to use their minds, express themselves freely, are encouraged to make independent decisions, discuss their work with others, put a lot of effort into the course, enjoy it, and find it worthwhile. Only six students indicated that they found the course especially easy, and only three indicated that they were not learning as much here as in other courses.

In contrast, students in several art classes offered by four other teachers in the school district did not show such *consistent* technical control, aesthetic and intellectual thought, or involvement in their work. For example, in one class of 28 students, the seven I questioned told me that the most important thing they had learned was to use their imagination and not to copy, but their work was relatively simple and trite. By comparison, Mr. Gebhart's curriculum weaves a fabric of control and freedom such that the students are doing much more than learning terminology and techniques. His students truly seem to be developing a creative eye.

> . . . esthetic cannot be sharply marked off from intellectual experience
> since the latter must bear an esthetic stamp to be itself complete.
>   JOHN DEWEY (1934)

Teaching   The structure of Mr. Gebhart's teaching strategy is an outgrowth of the curriculum. To help students gain initial control over the material, he introduces lessons with teacher-centered lecture-demonstrations. He is center stage, and the student audience is in his control as they gather round the center table.

Freedom, as it concerns the structure of Mr. Gebhart's methodology, is manifested in the individualized instruction that occurs most of the time (95% of the time I observed). Mr. Gebhart believes that the teacher should "plug in to where the students are at" (Dewey's notion of the experience of the student as the starting point for education), and that "everyone has aesthetic values and the ability to create in varying degrees." Thus, his task is to "make contact with each child daily" so that he might know what that student needs, and assist or push him or her toward success, given that particular student's capacities.

Structurally, Mr. Gebhart's methodology consists first of control—giving students technical and cognitive tools in whole-class instruction. Next, freedom to discover how to use these tools is assisted by individual instruction. However, there is another aspect to his methodology, in which there is not such a clear-cut delineation of control and freedom. This aspect is the psychological level, the manner in which he relates to his students.

Mr. Gebhart states, "I'm critical of my students. I expect everyone to participate and reach closure. . . . At this age level they don't reach closure. You need to structure the lesson or they won't do it." Hence, within the flexibility of individualized instruction, Mr. Gebhart's role is that of constantly exerting control, pushing students, challenging them to seriously attack the creative problems at hand. Like Dewey, he recognizes that the growth he is trying to develop in his students involves their being able to use intelligence to overcome difficulties. He does not aim to solve his students' problems for them. "Learning involves frustration. If you eliminate frustration, you eliminate learning."

Sometimes Mr. Gebhart extends support and simplifies a problem into small steps, as with Valerie, who had paralyzed herself with anxiety about her piece. Sometimes, as with Sue, a minor suggestion and acknowledgment of her decision making is all that is needed. Several times I observed Mr. Gebhart say firmly, "I want you to . . ." to students who were not progressing, and demand a specific amount or type of work.

He is not a soft teacher, not easy. But he is sensitive. Within Mr. Gebhart's control there is a sense of freedom because he attempts to lead out each student to whom he is or might be. There is not a mold that all students have to fit. He puts effort into knowing each student's personality, style, and needs. This shows in his appropriately differential treatment of the students. Penny could be set to work with a few words. Fred needed to be touched gently; a less aware teacher might simply have told him to put water on his clay, or to remove his parka.

Thus, in terms of the structure and philosophy of his lessons, Mr. Gebhart's methodology can be seen as the relationship of separable elements of control and freedom. In terms of the psychology of his methodology, Mr. Gebhart exerts control to give students the freedom to discover their capacities. This allows them to develop their own manifestation of control. Like Dewey, he wishes to educate his students for ongoing growth, "To get them ready to begin learning on their own. To get them to see how to create their own problems to solve."

> Come to the edge, he said.
> They said: We are afraid.
> Come to the edge, he said.
> They came.
> He pushed them . . . and they flew.
> GUILLAUME APOLLINAIRE (cited in Ferguson, 1981)

Reflections

I have presented a glimpse of Mr. Gebhart's ceramics class and examined the "delicate balance of control and freedom" in his classroom management, curriculum, and methodology. It was not appropriate to come up with a simple statement of the way in which Mr. Gebhart weaves these elements together. For one thing, "control" and "freedom" demand slightly different definitions and are in slightly different relationship in each of the three contexts considered. Also, Mr. Gebhart does not simply look for a middle ground on the continuum between control and freedom. A characteristic of his class is the dynamic interplay of these elements, whether it be in classroom management, curriculum, or methodology. The nature of this interplay, as well as Mr. Gebhart's philosophy, give his teaching a strong Deweyan flavor.

Three things remain to be discussed. These are considerations for the improvement of Mr. Gebhart's class, the influence of Mr. Gebhart's personal style on his teaching, and the implications of my observations.

Considerations for Improvement   In the *Analysis* I focus on the strengths of Mr. Gebhart's teaching because I view him as the most effective middle school art teacher in this school district. (I spent about 30 hours in the classes of all five middle school art teachers in the district.) His dynamic interweaving of control and freedom results in students with relatively sophisticated technical and critical skills in ceramics. There are, however, some areas in which consideration for improvement seems to be in order.

The ritualistic pseudo-challenge to authority occupies 10 to 15 minutes of class time daily. This ritual may not be necessary. Perhaps if an aide were used to manage organizational matters, Mr. Gebhart's time could more efficiently be used for teaching.

Individualized instruction necessarily limits time for whole-class lecture, idea sharing, and student critiques of one another's work. Mr. Gebhart has expressed frustration at the resultant loss of momentum and productive competition, and at having to repeat things 30 times. At this age (11 to 14) children are exceptionally critical of their art work (Lowenfeld, 1947). Some (Pasto, 1964; Burt, 1922) have referred to this stage of artistic development as "deterioration" or "repression." Regular aesthetic appraisal sessions might solve some of the problems mentioned in this paragraph.

From my observations I tentatively assumed that the students had considerable freedom in their choice of projects. Yet, in response to the question, "What, if anything, would you change in this class," nine out of 26 students stated their desire for more independent choice of work. Perhaps this is a reaction to Mr. Gebhart's insistence that they all learn the basic techniques, indication that there is little choice, or that they have not developed the ability to make that choice.

The students ranked this class virtually equal with Physical Education as the most enjoyable of six school subjects. However, they ranked it sixth in importance and fifth in amount learned. This does not reflect the philosophy Mr. Gebhart attempts to convey in his curriculum. Perhaps these ratings reflect the school system's and community's views. An attempt should be made to alter this attitude. It may be that the students perceive the freedom as indicative of low importance of art. Perhaps expanded work time, homework, or a tidier room would correct this impression. The low ranking of learning may reflect the lack of quantifiable measures of accomplishment in art.

These observations and ideas for change are suggested to improve what is already a comparatively effective class.

Personal Characteristics   In the *Analysis* I examined what Mr. Gebhart does and its effect in the classroom and on the students. I was struck by how much his personality seemed to shape his classroom management, curriculum and methodology. Five personality characteristics were salient: respect for and sensitivity to students, humor, and his tendency to be strong-minded and reflective.

Mr. Gebhart's respect for his students is evident in his tendency to ask them questions and to consider their responses. This is noticeable in his aesthetic criticism and implementation of assertive discipline. This is in contrast to some teachers who, according to the school psychologist, interpret the program as a punishment system. Mr. Gebhart also gives students the freedom to set up displays of student art work in the school. The "hidden curriculum" here is that their thoughts and feelings are of worth, and that they are responsible.

Mr. Gebhart's sensitivity to students has already been mentioned. Small actions, such as his interchange with Fred, eye contact, a hand on a shoulder, or asides to students about their lives show that he is attentive to their emotional as well as educational needs. He has the capacity to enter into a relationship with each student, recognizing that "other" in what, on occasion, seems to approach (in Martin Buber's terms) an I-Thou relationship.

Mr. Gebhart's humor is not that of a stand-up comic. Rather, he has a subtle whimsy with which he defuses potentially tense situations, as in the bear-hug incident. On another occasion, a student responded to an order with: "What are you? A dictator?" Without hesitation, Mr. Gebhart responded, "I'm training to be one. This is the first step." The girl laughed and the problem was solved.

What Mr. Gebhart says goes, whether it is an instruction for attaching an armature or an order to clean off a table. Mr. Gebhart is clearly the authority in his classroom. He has strong opinions, and can be demanding at times. This complements his gentler side, establishing a natural union of freedom and control in his manner.

His reflectiveness facilities this union. He notes that he constantly evaluates and revises his teaching. For example, he is currently rethinking how he might more efficiently teach technique without losing aesthetic appreciation in another class. His final assignment for the ceramics class was "an experiment" based on a conversation he and I had about creativity. Mr. Gebhart was anxious for feedback from me, and regrets the paucity of inservice training. He is flexible, and concerned with his growth as well as his students'.

Mr. Gebhart's personality colors how he creates his "delicate balance between control and freedom." The quality of his personal interaction with students and his considerable technical skill enable him to be an effective teacher. It is clear that *personal* qualities are an integral part of his effectiveness. What is the implication of this for teacher training?

Implications   The implication is obvious. Theory and technique are only part of the story. Personality characteristics of the teacher are the electricity that brings the parts to life and determines the quality and ultimate effectiveness of teaching.

Obvious though this may be, current selection and training of education students and teachers pays pitifully little attention to personal development. Test scores and statements of purpose get students into schools of education, where they are filled with theory and techniques and sent out to teach. If they are lucky, inservice training will equip them with more theories and techniques.

It has always struck me as odd that therapists are required to develop personal sensitivity as a tool to help people expand their vistas, and teachers are not. Both are involved in the professional task of educating people, of facilitating others' development. We remember our most influential teachers not primarily by what they did, but by who they were, how they inspired us. It is their qualities as human beings that profoundly affect us.

The idea of considering personal sensitivity as an important quality of the educator, and in the students' education, is not new. In high Athenian culture (around 400 B.C.) the ultimate aim of education was not simply acquisition of knowledge, but development of self-understanding and sensitivity. This concept of *paidea* has become lost. Myopic educators, unaware of important factors that do indeed shape educational experience, give students partial education and wonder at the low correlation between particular techniques and student achievement.

It is time for educators of educators to formally recognize what has been known since ancient Greece, what is known intuitively by every student, and what is neglected in our present educational system. The skill of a good teacher does not consist of only theory and technique. Sensitivity to self and others and ability to communicate and to inspire students are essential. If we are to have meaningful education, schools of education and inservice training programs must acknowledge this and radically alter their curriculums to recognize and cultivate teachers' internal educative qualities.

References

Buber, M. (1970). *I and thou.* (Walter Kaufmann, Trans.). New York: Charles Scribner's Sons.

Dewey, J. (1934). *Art as experience.* New York: G. P. Putnam's Sons.

Dewey, J. (1938). *Experience and education.* New York: Macmillan.

Eisner, E. (1972). *Educating artistic vision.* New York: Macmillan.

Ferguson, M. (1981). *The Aquarian conspiracy.* Los Angeles: J. P. Tarcher.

Hesse, H. (1968). *Beneath the wheel.* (Michael Roloff, Trans.). New York: Farrar, Straus & Giroux.

Langer, S. (1957). *Problems of art.* New York: Charles Scribner's Sons.

Lowenfeld, V. (1947). *The nature of creative activity.* New York: Harcourt, Brace & World.

An Educational Psychologist Goes to Medical School*

STUART J. COHEN

———————◆■◗■◆———————

The case is that of a 38 year-old male, employed as an associate professor in the Department of Internal Medicine at Indiana University School of Medicine. On August 13, 1980, he was admitted to the medical center as a sophomore with no evidence of a prior history of biochemistry, microbiology, gross anatomy, histology, or physiology. His chief complaint was the inability to understand how physicians make decisions about patient care when managing chronic illnesses.

A review of symptoms and his previous medical history were unremarkable. Because his insatiable medical curiosity is of recent onset, the recommended treatment is tincture of time. If his symptoms persist, consider obtaining a serum porcelain and a referral to psychiatry.

Today I will share with you my experience as a sophomore medical student. Because the meanings I derived are dependent on my background and the context in which the events were experienced, I will start by describing my background and my reasons for attending medical school.

I am an educational psychologist and serve as Director of Research in Education for the Department of Medicine. My undergraduate and master's degrees are in experimental psychology and my doctorate is in educational psychology. My science background is limited to having taken a few biology and chemistry courses in college along with neurology and physiological psychology in graduate school. I spent 9 years as a faculty member and later Department Chairman of an educational psychology department prior to coming to Indiana 4 years ago. Among my current responsibilities, I am an associate director for training of a National Diabetes Research and Training Center. In that role, I am involved in the training and evaluation of a variety of health professionals including house staff in internal medicine.

* Supported in part by the W. K. Kellogg Foundation

My observation of physicians' interactions with their diabetes patients has led me to question how physicians are trained to care for patients with chronic diseases.

Two years ago I was fortunate in being awarded a W. K. Kellogg National Fellowship. Each of the 40 Kellogg Fellows, representing a variety of disciplines, was given a 3-year award including a 25% released-time commitment from his or her own institution. One of the goals of my fellowship was to try to understand how physicians make decisions when caring for patients with chronic diseases. Toward that end, I proposed obtaining first-hand experience in the socialization process by which physicians are trained into making clinical decisions. The tolerance of the faculty at the medical school along with the blessings of the Chairman of Medicine afforded me that opportunity of attending medical school as a sophomore student. I chose the sophomore year because it was the introduction to clinical medicine and involved the first contact with patients.

I wanted to examine three major issues. My first concern was how students learned to make decisions about patient care. Included in this area were questions such as how were students socialized in problem identification. Related topics were how they learned to interact with patients and to view preventive and chronic diseases management.

My second major concern focused on the impact of stress on the social and personal development of medical students. How did they cope with the demands of an overwhelming schedule? How did they learn to handle experiences with death, disfigurement, and incurable diseases? A third and lower priority issue was evaluating the quality of instruction. I considered evaluating the quality of instruction of lesser concern because I didn't feel that such evaluation required full-time attendance in medical school. Despite my protestations, the director of the sophomore course, with whom I had worked previously, assumed that evaluating instruction was an occupational hazard of an educational psychologist and, therefore, would be a major function of my attendance.

On August 13, I left my office for the 5-minute walk to the large, turn-of-the-century lecture hall in the Emerson Building. I was clutching a white lined notepad, a copy of the locally produced medical history taking text and *Physical Diagnosis—The History and Examination of the Patient* by Prior and Silberstein (1977). The discomfort in the pit of my stomach increased as I entered a cavernous lecture hall and selected a seat that I hoped would be unobtrusively located in the middle of the left side, a third of the way into the auditorium. The hall began to fill with the 270 students who, despite the mixture of ages, shapes, and colors, seemed to be unified by their cut-off jeans and t-shirts. Only the lecturers and I wore neckties. So much for anonymity!

We were welcomed to the sophomore year and told how sophomore medicine was the bridge between the basic sciences and the clinical clerkships. Lectures would be organized by organ systems with emphasis on the pathophysiology of diseases and their clinical manifestations. Because one of the goals of the course was to gain proficiency in obtaining a medical history and performing a physical examination, we were handed a card (see lists p. 332 and p. 333) detailing a history on one side (Outline of the Medical History), and the physical on the other (Outline of the Physical Examination) and told to memorize it. The rest of the orientation lecture was devoted to a review of the syllabus, the procedures for purchasing medical instruments, and a discussion of grades and dress code when serving on the hospital wards.

OUTLINE OF THE MEDICAL HISTORY

I. Identifying Data:
   1. Date history taken
   2. Biographical data (patient's name, age, sex, race, marital status, occupation, hospital record number)
   3. Source and reliability of history
II. CHIEF COMPLAINT: briefly state the patient's primary complaint and indicate the duration
III. PRESENT ILLNESS: listen, ask open-ended questions, and finally specific questions to develop description of all symptoms in chronologic order considering:
   1. Onset—date and manner (gradual, sudden)
   2. Characteristics—quality, severity, location, temporal relationships (continuous, intermittent), aggravating and relieving factors, and associated symptoms
   3. Course (continuous, progressive, intermittent)
   4. Effects of therapy
IV. PAST MEDICAL HISTORY:
   1. General health and vigor
   2. Growth, development, and childhood diseases
   3. Immunizations
   4. Previous illnesses, injuries, and surgical procedures
   5. Allergies and drug reactions
   6. Toxins and/or industrial exposures
   7. Recent medications
V. REVIEW OF SYSTEMS:
   1. General: change in weight, weakness, fatigue, fever, state of nutrition, heat or cold intolerance
   2. Skin: eruptions, pruritus, color, texture, hair or nail changes, bleeding, or bruising tendency
   3. Head: headaches, dizziness, trauma
   4. Eyes: vision, diplopia, pain, inflammation
   5. Ears: hearing, pain, discharge, tinnitus, vertigo
   6. Nose and sinuses: epistaxis, obstruction, discharge, pain
   7. Mouth and throat: dental hygiene, bleeding gums, sore tongue or throat, hoarseness
   8. Neck: pain, stiffness, thyroid or lymph node enlargement
   9. Breasts: pain, masses, discharge
   10. Respiratory: chest pain, cough, sputum, hemoptysis, wheezing, asthma, dyspnea, tuberculosis or exposure, recent chest x-ray
   11. Cardiovascular: substernal pain or distress, exertional or nocturnal dyspnea, orthopnea, edema, palpitations, hypertension, heart murmurs, recent electrocardiogram
   12. Gastrointestinal: appetite, dysphagia, nausea, vomiting, food intolerances, eructation, hematemeses, heartburn, abdominal pain (discomfort,

aching, colic), jaundice, character of stools (form, color), melena, constipation, diarrhea, change in bowel habits, hemorrhoids
13. Genitourinary:
   a. Urinary—urgency, frequency, dysuria, hematuria, color of urine, difficulty starting the stream, incontinence, polyuria, nocturia, renal colic, stones or infection, recent urinalysis
   b. Female—menstrual history, post-menopausal bleeding, vaginal discharge, contraceptive history, obstetrical history, sexual history
   c. Male—scrotal pain or masses, hernias, genital lesions, discharge, sexual history
14. Back and extremities: joint pain, stiffness, swelling, limitation of motion, varicosities, edema, redness, phlebitis, claudication, cramps, resting pain
15. Neuropsychiatric system: syncope, alterations of consciousness, convulsions, mentation, memory disorders, orientation, tremor, incoordination, paresthesias, weakness, paralyses, affect, thought processes, behavior, degree of anxiety
VI. PERSONAL HISTORY:
   1. Personality patterns or adjustments, behavior during interview
   2. Marital and sexual history
   3. Social and economic status, education, occupation, standard of living, environment
   4. Habits: sleep, diet, exercise, drugs, tobacco, alcohol (note recent changes)
VII. FAMILY HISTORY:
   1. Summary of age and state of health or cause of death for immediate family
   2. Family members with similar symptoms and signs
   3. Presence of infections or chronic disease in family members

OUTLINE OF THE PHYSICAL EXAMINATION*

   I. Vital Signs: temperature, pulse, respiratory rate, blood pressure, weight, height (orthostatic hypotension).
  II. General Appearance: apparent health, developmental status, apparent physiologic age, habitus, nutrition, gross deformities, mental state and behavior, facies, posture.
 III. Skin: color, texture, moisture turgor, eruptions, abnormalities of hair and nails (pallor, pigmentation, cyanosis, clubbing, edema, spider nevi, petechiae).
  IV. Head: symmetry, deformities of cranium, face and scalp (tenderness, bruits).
   V. Eyes: visual acuity, visual fields, extraocular movements, conjunctiva, sclera, cornea, pupils including size, shape, equality and reaction, ophthalmoscopic exam including lens, media, disks, retinal vessels and macula, tonometry (pallor, jaundice, proptosis, ptosis).
  VI. Ears: hearing acuity, auricles, canals, tympanic membranes (mastoid tenderness, discharge).
 VII. Nose: nasal mucosa and passages, septum, turbinates, transillumination of sinuses (tenderness over sinuses).

*Selected abnormalities in parentheses

VIII. Mouth and Throat: breath, lips, buccal mucosa, salivary glands, gingiva, teeth, tongue, palate, tonsils, posterior pharynx, voice.

IX. Neck: range of motion, thyroid, trachea, lymph nodes, carotid pulses (venous distinction, abnormal arterial and venous pulsations, bruits, tracheal deviation).

X. Lymph Nodes: cervical, supraclavicular, axillary, epitrochlear and inguinal nodes (enlargement, consistency, tenderness, and mobility).

XI. Breasts: symmetry (nodules including size, consistency, tenderness, mobility, dimpling, nipple charge, and lymph nodes).

XII. Thorax and Lungs: configuration, symmetry, expansion, type of respiration, excursion of diaphragms, fremitus, resonance, breath sounds (retraction, labored breathing, prolonged expiration, cough, sputum, adventitious sounds including rales, wheezes, rhonchi, and rubs).

XIII. Cardiovascular System: precordial activity, apical impulse, size, rate, rhythm, heart sounds, abdominal aorta, peripheral arterial pulses including carotid, radial, femoral, posterior tibial, and dorsalis pedis pulsations (thrills, murmurs, friction rubs, bruits, central venous distention, abnormal venous pulsations).

XIV. Abdomen: contour, bowel sounds, abdominal wall tone, palpable organs, including liver, spleen, kidney, bladder, and uterus, liver span (scars, dilated veins, tenderness, rigidity, masses, distention, ascites, pulsations, bruits).

XV. Back and Extremities: symmetry, range of motion, joints, peripheral arterial pulses, color, temperature, (curvatures of spine, costovertebral angle tenderness, joint deformities, muscle tenderness, edema, ulcers, varicosities).

XVI. Neurological Exam: cranial nerves, station, gait, coordination sensory, and motor systems, muscle stretch reflexes (paresthesias, weakness, muscle atrophy, fasiculations, spasticity, abnormal reflexes, tremors).

XVII. Genitalia:
1. Female: external genitalia, vagina, cervix, cytology smear, fundus, adnexae, rectovaginal exam (vaginal discharge, tenderness).
2. Male: penis, scrotal contents (urethral discharge, hernias).

XVIII. Rectum: sphincter tone, prostate, test for occult blood (hemorrhoids, fissures, masses).

XIX. Personality Status: affect, intellectual functions, thought content and processes in motor behavior. Consider patterns of adjustment, ability to handle life crises and behavior during the interview.

SUMMARY AND INTERPRETATION

1. Summary of Important Data
2. Initial Problem List
3. Initial Management Plans (for each problem)
4. Signature and Date of Completion

From that day in August until 4 May 1981, I attended medical school. Although I was officially an auditor, I participated in most of the activities including sitting for a number of exams. Mornings were spent attending lectures. Classes were large because there is only one medical school in the state. A lecture could contain as many as 270 students, although the usual number was much less.

With the exception of one half-day free, afternoons were devoted to either physical diagnosis, specialty physical diagnosis (e.g., ophthalmology), pathology, or radiology. Physical diagnosis was usually taught by fellows or junior faculty to groups of four or five students. My preceptor was an endocrinology fellow. We saw patients on the wards of a medical center hospital that served the indigent of Indianapolis and Marion County. Each week we would learn about and often practice on each other some component of the physical exam. We would then go on the wards and, with the aid of the preceptor, examine patients who presented interesting or pertinent findings. Weekly we had to conduct a history and physical on a new patient, and submit the results in writing to our preceptor for evaluation.

The specialty physical diagnosis rotations ranged from activities such as using lifelike simulators for learning venepuncture and spinal taps, to conduct a gynecologic examination on paid instructors. The radiology rotation involved learning how to read various x-rays and scans. The radiologist would first describe a particular technique and then break the class of 30 into small groups of five stations where radiographs and a set of questions would be located. Each group attempted to answer the questions that would be reviewed at the end of class. Few students knew one another. This was not surprising considering the size of the medical school class and the fact that many students had spent their first year learning the basic sciences at any one of eight regional campuses located around the state. The first question involved an x-ray of a chest into which a catheter had been inserted. The question asked to name the point of insertion of the catheter and the location of the tip. With no previous instruction in anatomy, I was unwilling to venture a guess. Perhaps, because of my age or the fact that I wore a suit, the eyes of my fellow students all turned to me awaiting my answer. I did not know the correct answer but was sure that it wasn't "into the shoulder and out the chest." I pleaded ignorance but did concur with the suggestion that the catheter was probably inserted into the subclavian vein and the tip was located in the superior vena cava.

I did not attend the pathology lab because I needed at least two afternoons a week to perform many of my regular tasks for which I still had responsibility. Fortunately, my colleagues and secretary assumed many of my chores, so that 80% of my weekly effort could be devoted to medical school.

Throughout the year I did not seek to identify my special status, nor did I make an effort to conceal my identity to the other medical students or to instructors. If questions arose, I would explain that I was a special student and, although a faculty member in the Department of Medicine, I was auditing sophomore medicine, because my training was in educational psychology.

In order to more systematically examine my experiences, I usually kept two sets of notes. To the right of the margin, I would record at breakneck speed the information being disseminated. To the left of the margin, I would comment on unusual events or remarks. For example, I noted that it wasn't until the middle of October that any lecturer mentioned the cost of a diagnostic test. I also tallied the sexist remarks made by lecturers. In my sample, sexist remarks were made approximately four times more frequently by surgeons than internists.

Occasionally, I would record students' comments and my own thoughts. An example of the former occurred after a particularly confusing radiology class. One of my classmates lamented that radiology was pushing her to a career in psychiatry. I often recorded my own reaction to exasperating events. When lecturers were attempting to establish their claim in the *Guiness Book of World Records* with new standards for speeded speech and showing slides in microseconds, I would record the appropriate expletive while resisting the urge to leap up on the stage, grab the microphone, and yell "STOP."

Although my system for observation might appall an ethnographer, it seemed manageable and appropriate for my objectives. I wanted to devote most of my energy toward experiencing life as a medical student. I did not want to consume my time detailing the experiences of myself or others.

On a typical day, I arrived at my office about a half hour before class to review my checklist of tasks for the day and to leave messages asking favors of my secretary and colleagues. I attended lectures from eight until noon. I then returned to my office in 3 to 5 minutes, depending on the weather and the status of my running injuries. While eating lunch, I would attempt to complete a diabetes center task before dashing off for my one o'clock rotation. Most of the rotations finished by five and I returned to the office for an hour or so before going home. Evenings were usually spent studying. Ideally, I would try to stay ahead of the next day's assignment. More realistically, I was usually trying to keep from falling further behind. Depending on my state of fatigue, I studied from 4 to 6 hours a night. Contributing to my burden was my limited background in the basic sciences. In case anybody questions the necessity of the basis sciences for medical training, let me offer myself as evidence of their merit. The deficits that I faced were overwhelming. I would often sit with an anatomy and a physiology book opened in order to begin to comprehend the medical text assignments. Medical texts like *Harrison's Principles of Internal Medicine* (Isselbacher, Adams, & Braunwald, 1980), although difficult for most sophomore students, were impossible for me. Little did I dream that I would do such things as spend an entire weekend trying to teach myself steroid biochemistry, and at the end of Sunday night, realize that I probably knew little more than I did when I began.

As you can sense, my year was challenging and frequently frustrating, but not without its rewards. I hope I am able to convey some of the richness and intensity of my experience. I will focus on three major issues that prompted my quest:

1. How are medical students taught to think about patient care?
2. What stresses occur when going to medical school and what, if anything, is done to help students cope with them?
3. What is the quality of instruction in lectures, laboratories, and at the bedside? What might be done to remedy deficiencies?

Thinking About Patient Care   Medical students in general, and sophomores in particular, are not taught to think. Sophomores have profound deficits in their medical knowledge. The faculty attempts to remedy this situation by inundating students with information. It was not uncommon for me to record a dozen pages of single-spaced notes during a 50-minute lecture. Knowledge-level questions predominate on examinations. Thus, success in medical school often depends not on your ability to reason, but on your willingness to memorize vast amounts of information. Cramming inordinately large bits of information that are rarely meaningfully organized produces a steep forgetting curve. Therefore, it is not surprising that a month or two after studying a particular area, students could be paralyzed by a remark such as "Cohen, what are the names and functions of the ligaments of the knee?"

The heavy emphasis in lectures and examinations on rote learning coupled with little effort to help students synthesize the material or allow them adequate time to do so is a source of numerous conflicts. The fundamental fact of life facing any sophomore medical students is that you cannot become a competent physician if you are not advanced to your junior year. Consequently, any test, quiz, or experience that might jeopardize the chances of becoming a junior medical student is viewed as career-threatening. On the other hand, faculty believe that the goal of medical school is to train people to become competent physicians. Predicated on this assumption, instructors assume that the more a student is taught about a particular organ or disease—usually the one in which the subspecialist has expertise—the more competent a physician he or she will become. Thus, the goals of the students and those of the faculty are frequently incongruent. Faculty are distressed by questions about "what's going to be covered" on an examination, whereas students are frustrated by lectures that overwhelm them with information. Like most novices, students have difficulty seeing the forest for the trees. Because medical students are bright, they employ a number of survival strategies such as purchasing class notes, relying on upperclasspeople for information about examinations, and cutting classes that they do not feel aid in preparing for tests. Unquestionably, these survival strategies displease faculty and help promote adversarial relationships.

Just as thinking becomes subordinate to memorizing, so too the focus on patient care is transmuted into an emphasis on diseases and physiological measures. "Let's examine the diabetic with a BUN of 70" would not sound like an unusual comment a preceptor would make to students on the wards. What would sound strange would be a statement such as "Let's talk to the man with diabetes whose kidney failure is jeopardizing his career and his family relationships." Although it is undeniably important that students learn to diagnose and manage diseases, it is also imperative that they not lose sight of the human context in which their knowledge and skill will be applied.

One of the most important goals of sophomore medicine is to become proficient in obtaining a patient history and performing a physical examination. Many students are uncomfortable about their initial interactions with patients. Although they usually take pride in wearing white jackets and carrying a stethoscope, they are often anxious about asking intimate questions and fumbling through a physical, especially with patients who are dying or are in severe pain. If students question why they should obtain a sexual history for a patient who is hospitalized for a fractured leg, they are told that they have to learn to ask these questions so they may as well start now. Students soon discover that they are there not to serve the patients, but rather it is the patients who are there to serve them as teaching material. Even though I understood this problem, I was astounded at how readily I become desensitized to viewing patients as instruments for my own learning. My reaction to performing a physical examination on an obese woman who had had a radical mastectomy of her left breast was not one of revulsion or of pity, but rather one of relief—relief as how easy her cardiac examination would be because I could readily listen to her heart. Thus, even if you are sensitized to the potential influence of your environment, it can still affect you.

Just how profoundly we can be shaped by our environment became evident to me as a result of another experience with a patient. Most sophomore students are given

2 or more hours to complete a history and physical before they even begin to record and present their findings. Medical residents and faculty attendings take much less time. In fact, the time taken usually decreases as one increases in training. Students are taught to ask open-ended questions and to encourage the patients to talk; yet, these behaviors decrease as physicians advance in training. I now understand why this is so. One day my preceptor for physical diagnosis told us that we were each to perform a history and physical examination on a patient we had not seen before and to write up the results and turn them in within an hour. I was in trouble! My write-ups required at least 20 minutes and usually much longer because I often had to look up the medical terminology for parts of the anatomy. I would have at most 40 minutes for conducting the history and physical. Under the time pressure, I controlled the entire conversation restricting the patient's discussions only to what I considered as the pertinent aspects of the chief complaint. Needless to say, my write-up was incomplete and included numerous abbreviations.

I was astounded by my behavior with that patient. Intensive training in interpersonal communications would not have altered how I behaved. Given the time constraint, I dispensed with small talk, barely retaining a semblance of amenity. I omitted my usual preventive medicine questions about seat-belt usage and my chronic disease questions such as problems in complying with his therapeutic regimen. The focus of my thinking was on the patient's physical signs and symptoms and the physiological reasons for them.

In light of my experience, it is easy to see how medical students learn to think about problems (i.e., diagnoses) in the context of biomedical measures. This same context is then applied for selecting and evaluating the merit of a therapeutic intervention. Although biomedical measures are essential, they are not the only criteria for identifying problems and for choosing among alternative therapeutic strategies or solutions.

The focus of sophomore medicine is on the pathophysiology of disease rather than disease management. Discussions about therapy were infrequent, but were always limited to the biomedical consequences of therapy. I once attempted to discuss the importance of psychosocial criteria for evaluating medical therapies. My hematology/oncology small-group section had a lecture on the management of lymphomas. The instructor used 5-year survival as a criterion for choosing among therapies. He stated that treatments were equivalent if they did not produce differences in 5-year survival. I suggested that "quality of life" measures would aid decision making. I mentioned research done at the National Cancer Institute that used both survival and quality of life measures such as return to social functioning in deciding between irradiation and amputation in the management of soft tissue sarcomas. The results indicated that the 5-year survivals were equivalent. However, the quality of life measures showed considerable differences. When the tumor was located below the knee, those with surgical management suffered greater depression and longer delay in returning to work than those who had radiologic management. The results were quite different when the tumor was located in the thigh. People who had hemipelvectomy, an obviously disfiguring operation, actually had less depression and earlier return to social function than did those treated by radiation. Evidently, irradiation destroyed sexual function, which people viewed as far more disfiguring than loss of a limb. I am sad to report that after presenting my argument for the consideration of psychosocial values, my discourse was viewed by both the instructor and many of my peers as a needless diversion. I was probably preventing the coverage of material that would be included on an examination.

In summary, medical students are not taught to think about patient care. They learn to memorize organ systems and disease states.

Stress and Personal Development   As I mentioned previously, one of my major concerns was understanding the stresses experienced by medical students and determining what, if anything, is done to help cope with them. Two important conflicts seemed inevitable. The first was the conflict between a student's desire to be an autonomous and productive member of society and the enforced dependence of medical school requirements and procedures. The second dilemma arose from the desire for personal growth and the expression of social needs, which often conflicted with academic demands.

The majority of sophomore students are in their mid-20s with most having gone directly from college to medical school. They are preparing for an autonomous career that is greatly respected by our society. What they experience as students is a state of prolonged dependency. There are no electives in the sophomore year. Your life is preplanned and your only choice is the degree of compulsivity for following assignments.

On the wards, you are at the bottom of the totem pole. Everyone else knows more about medicine and hospital procedure than you do. When the staff physician says, "Jump," your only thought is "How high." Although many senior students, house staff, and attending physicians try to help you through the "rites of passage," some house staff and attendants delight in flaunting their medical knowledge and publicly interrogating students. For example, one lecturer used an electric pointer to select students to answer his questions. Although I did not approve of this technique as a motivational strategy, it did serve to demonstrate that my sympathetic nervous system was functioning. I found such public interrogation particularly frustrating. I knew that I could embarrass most inquisitors with questions about diabetic microangiopathy that they would be unable to answer. However, retribution was unthinkable. Learning to cope with prolonged dependency was a necessary survival skill and one that seemed to decrease with age.

The time and energy required for becoming a physician are enormous and have impact on personal development and social relationships. Spending 8 hours in class and having 4 to 6 hours of reading each night leaves little time for social activity. Academic demands strain existing relationships and retard the development of new ones. Prototypical of this conflict was the request by students to cancel one of the daily neurology quizzes in order to watch Indiana in the finals of the National Collegiate Athletic Association basketball game. The quiz was retained with the response "Physicians have to make difficult decisions."

Although most students struggle to become physicians, little is done to help them in the coping process. They are never asked to explore their feelings about experiences such as seeing a cadaver, caring for a dying patient, examining a quadriplegic, or seeing children with severe congenital anomalies. Although counseling services are available for those experiencing adjustment problems, the stigma attached to seeking help precludes countless others who are wrestling with doubts about their career decision and themselves.

Social maturity and an interest in health policies that would affect their lives and those of their patients were uncommon among the medical students. Admittedly, most 23-year-olds are neither worldly nor politically aware. Yet, I was surprised at the embarrassed giggling and boorish behavior of some of these future physicians. I had the opportunity of examining the final grades for sophomore medicine. I looked up the results of the handful of students who I thought characterized my ideal of a physician as being caring, thoughtful, sagacious, and socially mature. I also examined the scores of those who, because of their immaturity or lack of perspective, I had difficulty envisioning as physicians. Not surprisingly, there was little relationship between my evaluations and their grades. In sum, the message seems to be that the medical school takes some responsibility for a student's intellectual growth but that personal growth is a student's own responsibility.

Quality of Instruction   It had been 11 years since I completed my doctoral studies. In the interim, I attended lectures and workshops at professional meetings and at grand rounds in medicine. Nevertheless, being thrust again into the role of a student took considerable readjustment. My survival as a sophomore was, in large part, dependent on the quality of instruction I received. In evaluating that instruction I will focus first on what was taught and then on how it was taught.

As I mentioned previously, the emphasis was on the pathophysiology of disease. Little is said about therapy and even less said about psychosocial factors such as stress. Although there are studies that indicate that stress can elevate both blood pressure (Shapiro, Schwartz, & Ferguson, 1977) and blood glucose (Hauser & Pollets, 1979), nontraditional issues were ignored or downplayed. During a break after a lecture on asthma, I asked the pulmonary professor if stress could be a precipitating factor in an asthmatic attack. His response implied that my question was equivalent to an inquiry about the moon's being made of green cheese.

Another content area virtually ignored was preventive medicine. Little attention was given to either the risk factors for diseases or their prevention. Even in the discussions of chronic disease, in which the prevention of complications from the disease is the ideal, the management of complications received equal if not greater emphasis than did their prevention. When presenting our history and physical exams, I was the only student who ever inquired if the patient wore a seat belt. Trauma, much of which is caused by automobile accidents, is the major cause of death for people under the age of 40. Therefore, inquiring about seat belt usage assesses a major risk factor. Similarly, I was the only person to ask patients with chronic diseases about problems encountered in trying to comply with their medical regimens. Because many patients misunderstand their regimens and/or believe that the benefits of adherence do not outweigh the barriers, I would ask patients what medicine they took, for what purpose, how frequently, what mnemonic they used to remember to take their medication, and whether they thought the medicine was helping them. Needless to say, I was the only sophomore medical student to ask patients these questions. Although preventive medicine and patient compliance are real health issues, they were overlooked in the training of physicians at our medical school.

Perhaps the most persistent and pervasive issue for sophomore medicine was information overload. Students were inundated with material during lectures. They had lengthy and difficult reading assignments, and precious little time for synthesizing the material. Although the gap between a sophomore medical student and a competent physician is great, it cannot be closed appreciably in just 1 year. The failure to remember this fact is a source of frustration for both faculty and students.

Most of the sections of the sophomore course were organized by organ systems. They were taught by subspecialists who were so far advanced in their level of expertise that they forgot what it was like to be a novice. We know from the work of deGroot (1965) and Chase and Simon (1973) that experts and novices do not share the same worldview. Experts may keep in mind fewer pieces of information than novices because experts are able to sort through, analyze, and rule out what is irrelevant. Unfortunately, novices don't see the big picture that would allow them to be more efficient as well as accurate. This inefficiency is clearly seen when a medical students takes 2 hours to do a history and physical, which a competent physician could do better in much less time.

Because sophomore medical students do not think like competent physicians or even like residents or senior medical students (Mazzuca, Cohen, & Clark, 1981), their current level of development needs to be considered more carefully in the design and implementation of the curriculum. As an aid to the process, a feedback system for instructors and course directors needs to be developed. Although there are hundreds of student evaluation systems extant, the one I am proposing is intended to reduce some of the information overload by highlighting "fat" in the curriculum. A sample of sophomore students and a sample of the generalist faculty should evaluate every examination question (i.e., de facto objectives) by responding to the following two questions: First, does this question ask something that is important for a practicing physician to know? Second, does this question ask something that is important for a sophomore medical student to know? A response of "yes" to the first and "no" to the second question can identify information that may be deferred to a later stage of training.

I would like to focus now on the "how" of instruction and examine the three basic instructional settings: lectures, skill laboratories, and bedside instruction. In all three areas the quality of instruction varied from superlative to abominable, depending on the section leader and the instructors. On the whole, the instruction was as good if not better than the instruction I had as a graduate student taking courses in departments of psychology and of education. Much of the quality of the sophomore course was due to dedicated section heads and the conscientiousness of the course director. Certainly, there were weaknesses. Although my discussion is devoted to what can be done to remedy deficiencies, I don't wish to leave the impression that all was not well.

The lectures and sections that received the highest praise from the students were well-organized within and across lectures and, without spoon-feeding, geared material appropriately for sophomores. Those lectures and sections that caused the most complaints were those in which the lectures were poorly organized and contained too much information. Often an excessive number of slides were used, including many that were overly detailed. In addition, coordination among lecturers was lacking. Illustrative of the worst was one excruciating pathology lecture. The first 45 minutes were spent in elaborate descriptions without visuals. In the last 5 minutes, the lecturer flashed about 20 slides to illustrate everything previously described.

Lecturers need to focus on the three or four of the most important points and to organize their material so that these points are highlighted and integrated.

Educational psychologists and other medical educators can help in this effort. There were occasions in which I was almost willing to establish arbitrary rules for the number of slides that could be shown per hour or the maximum amount of information that could be put on a slide. However, I trust that the advice of an educational consultant would suffice to arrange the details in each particular setting.

Related to the problem of information overload is the dilemma students face in trying to synthesize and apply what they learn. One technique ideally suited to facilitate synthesis is the use of patient vignettes or small-case simulations of patient problems. These devices take advantage of literature on adult learning which suggests that adults learn the most and retain best when learning about problems that they actually face or will face. As most basic science professors will attest, medical students are more highly motivated when the information about which they are learning is related to patients. Appropriately designed patient management problems with feedback can help students draw on their knowledge to select, analyze, and evaluate information (Elstein, Shulman, & Sprafka, 1978). In essence, it helps them begin to think like clinicians and not become repositories of clinical information, devoid of the context in which it will be applied.

Some of the principles that apply for improving lectures also apply for the teaching of psychomotor skills, such as conducting a physical or reading a CAT scan. Again, the quality of instruction varied dramatically. The best skill instruction had the following components. First, a framework was given for the skills being taught. Second, the appropriate behavior was demonstrated either live or by an audiovisual model. Third, students practiced the skill, and lastly, they were given feedback on their practice. Unfortunately, these conditions were not always met. For example, the ophthalmology instruction consisted primarily of lectures about ophthalmology with numerous slides of retinopathy and little opportunity for practicing fundoscopic examinations. You may not be too surprised to know that when I first practiced using an ophthalmoscope on a family member, I managed to hold it incorrectly and blinded myself. Fortunately, that did not happen at the bedside.

Patient simulators can be invaluable for learning motor skills. Most medical schools have some patient simulators such as Ginny for the gynecologic exam, or Resusci-Anni for learning cardiopulmonary resuscitation. These devices can enhance diagnostic acumen and minimize awkwardness when working with patients.

There are a number of excellent audiovisual aids available for learning how to perform a physical examination. The videocassettes produced by Dr. Barbara Bates at Rochester are very helpful in learning the components of the physical examination and how to orchestrate them. My only criticism of such models is that the patients are health models, examined under ideal conditions. For example, in one of Dr. Bates' tapes, the cardiac examination was conducted on a normal weight man. My first cardiac exam was performed on an obese woman. In turning her on her left side, as is done on the film in order to hear mitral sounds more clearly, her right breast whipped across her chest, knocking my stethoscope off her body. Such mishaps are never illustrated by the audiovisual models.

A common problem students have in skill acquisition is smoothly coordinating separately learned skills. One helpful technique for facilitating fluid performance is covert rehearsal. I taught my peers to rehearse mentally their physical examination prior to performing them. A potential disadvantage of covert rehearsal is the possibility of becoming locked into a routine. I usually did the cardiac exam after completing the pulmonary exam and before assessing the abdomen. One day I had just begun the cardiac exam and was listening very carefully for a low grade murmur, when I heard a loud thump, ka-thump, thump, ka-thump. No, it was not a grade six murmur. Postural drainage of the lungs was initiated on a patient in the next bed. Obviously, I needed to proceed with something that didn't require the use of a stethoscope.

The most effective of the special diagnostic skills labs was given by the Department of Obstetrics and Gynecology. Performing a pelvic examination can be anxiety-provoking for many medical students. After a week of lectures, reading, films, and frank discussions about obstetrics and gynecology, students in groups of four attended the special diagnosis instruction. We again reviewed the films of breast and pelvic examinations with an instructor present to answer any questions. The instructor explained that with her guidance we would conduct an exam on women who were trained to help medical students perform a thorough pelvic exam without hurting or embarrassing a patient. The patient-instructors praised appropriate performance and helped students improve deficiencies. This unit of instruction was universally acclaimed.

The last type of instruction takes place at the bedside. Because medicine is an apprenticeship system, bedside learning can be very valuable. At the same time, bedside instruction can be difficult for patients. Our physical diagnosis preceptor was able to ensure the dignity of the patient while at the same time making bedside instruction worthwhile. Our preceptor would ask a patient the following, "I have some young doctors with me who would like to have the opportunity of listening to your heart if you are feeling up to it." In this way the patient was not compelled to comply, and recognized that he or she would be contributing to the education of inexperienced physicians. Some preceptors showed little respect for the rights or the feelings of patients by holding discussion, replete with medical terminology, in front of the patient. All too often, I watched patients become anxious during these discussions. Because bedside teaching serves as an important model of patient care, it is imperative that preceptors respect patients' feelings.

Bedside instruction also demonstrated the influence of expectations on perception. Our preceptor would ask us to examine a particular system, and then compare our findings with his. I was amazed at the number of times I would, having missed a murmur or other physical finding the first time, notice it on reexamination. It appears that the more you know about medicine, the more you expect a certain constellation of findings. These expectations help sharpen detection. Thus, although the patient may afford the same information to an expert and a novice, the latter is less likely to ascertain it.

In summary, both the content and process of instruction can be improved. Information overload may be reduced if test questions are evaluated in terms of their relevance for sophomore medical students and for practicing physicians. Skill learning can be improved if students are given an adequate context, models, practice, and feedback. Bedside instruction provides the opportunity for modeling thorough, thoughtful, and humane patient care that will be imprinted on fledgling physicians.

Postscript   I would like to make a final point about my own "rites of passage." Although I had been on the faculty of my medical school for 2½ years, it was only after my year as a medical student that I was encouraged by the faculty to round with them when they saw patients. Also, for the first time, I was asked to discuss the medical curriculum at the meeting of the Executive Committee of the Department of Medicine. In addition, I was invited by the Dean to serve on the School of Medicine Education Committee. Although these events could be coincidental, attending medical school may have been the precipitating factor.

References

Burk, C. (1922). *Mental and scholastic tests.* London: P. S. King and Son.

Chase, W. G., & Simon, H. A. (1973). Perception in chess. *Cognitive Psychology, 4* 55–81.

de Groot, A. D. (1965). *Thought and choice in chess.* The Hague: Mouton.

Elstein, A. S., Shulman, L. S., & Sprafka, S. A. (1978). *Medical problem solving: An analysis of clinical reasoning.* Cambridge, MA: Harvard University Press.

Hauser, S. T., & Pollets, D. (1979). Psychological aspects of diabetes mellitus: A critical review. *Diabetes Care 2*(2), 227–232.

Isselbacher, K. J., Adams, R. D., & Braunwald, E. (Eds.). (1980). *Harrison's principles of internal medicine.* New York: McGraw-Hill.

Mazzuca, S. A., Cohen, S. J., & Clark, C. M., Jr. (1981). Assessing clinical knowledge across five years of medical training. *Journal of Medical Education, 56,* 83–90.

Pasto, T. (1964). *The space-time experience in art.* New York: A. S. Barnes.

Prior, J. A., & Silberstein, J. S. (1977). *Physical diagnosis: The history and examination of the patient.* St. Louis: Mosby.

Shapiro, A. P., Schwartz, G. E., & Ferguson, D. C. E. (1977). Behavioral methods in the treatment of hypertension: A review of their clinical status. *Annals of Internal Medicine, 86,* 626–636.

12

❧

A Criticism of an
Educational Criticism

Believing, with Max Weber, that man is an animal suspended in
webs of significance, he himself has spun, I take culture to be those
webs, and the analysis of it to be therefore not an experimental science in search of law but an interpretative one in search of meaning.

CLIFFORD GEERTZ

Chapter 11 presented five examples of educational criticism. Each of the
criticisms was undertaken by an individual who was interested in finding
out about some aspect of the educational world. In Barone's case, it was an
art program that had been cited as outstanding. What was it that made this
program excellent? What dynamics were involved? In Porro's case, it was an
effort to understand the qualities of educational life for a low-achieving
sophomore student. What was the school experience like for the student?
How did he cope with the demands his teachers made on him? In Catford's
case, it was an effort to understand how a middle school art teacher functioned in the classroom. What was it that he taught? How did he engage
middle school students in art? What was the quality of his classroom? In
Burchenel's case, the classroom was devoted to the teaching of English at
the high school level. And for Cohen the object of study was the second year
of medical school as seen through the eyes of an educational psychologist
attempting to understand how medical education proceeded for students a
year into the program.

The Features of Meta-Criticism

This chapter examines one of those educational criticisms: to do what might be called a *meta-criticism*, a criticism of criticism. How does the author proceed? What is the nature of the language that is used? What metaphors and categories are provided in the piece? What insights does it yield? How does the author support her conclusions? How does the reader "verify" what he or she has read? These and other questions can be asked of an educational criticism. Which particular questions are appropriate to raise of course depends on the kind of criticism that has been written. In the field of literature, there are schools of criticism: structuralism, Marxist criticism, the Chicago school of criticism, formalist criticism, as well as others. In educational inquiry, literary writing in general and educational criticism in particular are neither old enough nor sufficiently well-developed to have such schools. In any case, my own interests are not in the development of schools of critics or criticism, but in the creation of material that will help educators improve the quality of educational life for students and teachers. Educational criticism is a general approach to that end. Thus the aim of this chapter is to understand how one such critic went about her task.

Before going into Porro's criticism, the piece that will be used for this critique, there are a few observations worth making about all the criticisms found in the previous chapter. First, each critic has his or her own style of writing. In each criticism a sense of the author's voice comes through. Unlike many of the conventional research articles published in educational research journals where format is standardized—consisting of the problem, subjects, method, findings, discussion, and implications—or schema for writing are prescribed, and unlike the attempts to neutralize the writer behind the words one reads, educational critics exploit their own sensibilities and their own unique perceptions. They invoke their own voices to give life to their writing. Each educational criticism has its own signature. What one seeks in educational criticism is not fealty to a common format for voiceless writing, but quite the opposite. One hopes that the refined vision and skilled writing that mark the competent educational critic will be exploited in order to share with the reader the fact that a person, not an impersonal machine, wrote that criticism.

It is often claimed that such an approach to research or evaluation is ineluctably subjective and therefore undependable. I wonder how one can ever have objectivity without a subject who perceives and interprets the meaning of the object of attention. Furthermore, the efforts to eliminate through convention the subjectivities that must inevitably enter into any interpretation of reality seem to be less candid than an up-front recognition that a human being is providing his or her best effort to describe, interpret, and appraise some aspect of the world in which he or she lives. The credibility of the observations, whether written or verbal, is a function of the coherence they possess and the extent to which the observations are helpful in illuminating the situations they seek to describe.

The statement that credibility can be a function of applying the observations of an educational critic to situations like, but not identical to, those described by the critic is intended to convey the notion that the believability of a set of observations is influenced by the congruence between what a critic has to say and what one remembers about situations relevant to those the critic has described. Our memory is replete with images of school practice. These images are data for "verifying" the critic's observations. Hence, when a critic observes that "schools have few soft surfaces," we can check out this observation by reflecting on our past. The images of the past, even though they contain many features of classrooms and schools, might still leave us unaware of this particular quality of classrooms and schools until a critic's observations bring them to consciousness. In short, through the criticism we, in a sense, learn what we already "knew" but were not aware of.

A second feature or characteristic of the criticisms in the previous chapter is that all were created without the use of a formalized observation schedule. None of the critics who visited the classroom came armed with a standardized check-off form on which frequencies were recorded. What each critic did bring to the class or school was an immensely more complex set of categories and criteria, schema and frameworks, sensibilities and interests. These, however, were already in the critics' cortexes. They approached the task of observation with a highly differentiated network that enabled them to "capture" and interpret what they had experienced. The task was not only one of picking up cues—or perhaps more aptly, clues—but also of construing patterns that ultimately made for a coherent view of the situation they studied.

The achievement of such coherence and the formation of such patterns hardly ever occurs independent of writing or speaking. It is virtually impossible to carry the kind of intellectual load that these criticisms represent as fully formed bodies of meaning outside their inscription in words or images of one kind or another. The act of expression is not simply a means for conveying what is already formed, it is also a means for shaping thought and for editing it once expressed. The act of writing and speaking is, I am saying, a necessary means for construing the patterns we might dimly perceive in the situations we observe. In each of the foregoing criticisms, a creative construction of the situation observed occurred. What we read is no mere recording of events, no chronology of facts, no photographic replica of a scene. It is a human construction.

A third feature of the foregoing criticisms is that each displays a different way of organizing the writing. Several individuals in the field of education have urged me to provide a standard format for writing (as well as for observing) classrooms. I have resisted. I do not wish to circumscribe the ways in which critics go about their work. There is but one ultimate criterion for appraising a critic's work: does it shed light on the situation it describes, interprets, and evaluates? *How* a critic chooses to achieve that end is, in principle, an open issue. In Porro's case poetry is used, with three views of schooling conceptualized, and telling quotations from the major actors of the drama inserted into the body of the text. Catford uses photographs, Barone a literary style of writing, and so forth.

There are, to be sure, complexities engendered when such openness in approach is not only permitted but encouraged. Different forms of reporting (*reporting* is much too passive a word) need to be read using somewhat different kinds of skills. The demands on the reader are likely to be more diverse and at times more complex where personal style is given an opportunity to flourish. Yet, that price is one I believe worth paying if it helps us free ourselves from a standardized and often homogenized approach to the study of educational practice. In the foregoing criticisms, each writer made his or her own thumbprint quite visible. Let's look at how one critic did this.

Playing the School System—A Meta-Criticism

"Playing the School System: The Low-Achiever's Game." Consider first the title. Porro creates through this title a foretaste of the message that the piece as a whole is designed to convey. The metaphor is that schooling is a game, that there are players who play the game, and that there are differences in the way in which different classes of students engage in that game. In this case the focus is on the low achiever.

What she has done in the title is not only to create an image of schooling as an "unreal" type of sport, but also by implication she reveals that the rules are different for students who achieve differently within the school.

What immediately follows the game metaphor is a very serious verse. What comes to the reader after the game-playing metaphor has been read is a statement about the meaning of adolescence, about the relationship of adolescence to death, about spending one's life waiting to be in another place and in another space. The verse is enigmatic; it provides a tone that creates a sense of intrigue and suspense. The title with its game-playing metaphor is polar to the couplet that follows it.

In the first paragraph of the criticism Porro provides some facts and creates some credibility. She tells us that this criticism was part of her graduate study at Stanford University; she informs us what the general aim of her work was; she conveys to us the fact that she is not a newcomer to schools, having worked for 9 years as an elementary school teacher. She creates a sense of trust by her candor in explaining that despite her 9 years of classroom experience the public high school was "new territory" for her. This candid acknowledgment of the newness of the setting reassures us that we are dealing with neither a cocky professor nor a self-assured graduate student intent on telling us how American schools should be run. The tone is one of appropriate modesty.

Paragraph 2 takes us immediately into the setting. We are introduced to the low-achieving student Porro is to shadow. What she does not yet say, but might have said, is that her task was to attend school with Bob for a full 2-week period: 5 full days, a week's break and then another 5-day period, and that Bob had volunteered to be shadowed. This information, had it been included, would have filled out for the reader the procedures used in her work.

Porro's first paragraph not only takes us into the scene without preamble, but she also tells us something about the sense of affiliation that these low-achieving students have, and about the camaraderie they share. She comments about these and then supports her observations by using a direct quotation from one of the students. The quotation adds credibility to her initial impression.

The third paragraph introduces a paradox. The school labels these students low achieving, apparently expecting that their days in school are numbered—*terminal students*, they are called. But Porro points out that although these students' academic achievement is low, they are remarkably higher achievers in meeting their own goals. Their own goals, "to get through high school by doing the least amount of academic work necessary to pass their courses", are attained with skill and intelligence.

In the third paragraph, not only is the paradox of contrasting views of achievement noted, but Porro also creates a picture of Bob. She describes his appearance, his comportment, and reveals an obvious admiration for him. We get the sense—perhaps too early—that Porro's view of Bob is a sympathetic one. We also get the sense—perhaps too strongly—that Porro is not altogether sympathetic with the system that Bob has so skillfully learned to play.

The first subhead of Porro's educational criticism provides the reader a focus. Porro's criticism will attend to educational life outside the classroom before moving into the classroom. Her first sentence, "High school is played in two main areas—outside on the patios and lawns, and inside the classrooms," divides the world of schooling neatly for us. First, we will find out about life on the lawns and patios, then we will proceed into the classrooms.

What comes through in Paragraph 5 is impressive categorization of the ways in which students decide which classes to cut. Porro's presentation of these options conveys to us several things. First, they indicate that the students who are regarded as low achievers are sufficiently analytic to consider complex alternatives; they are not really "dumb," despite the implicit labels the school seems to assign to them. Second, we are impressed that Porro has sufficient rapport to be able to secure such a candid response from adolescents asked such a direct question. Candor and the array of options they provide give the reader a sense that what he or she is reading is not shallow but that it is displaying an important aspect of schooling for a group of high school students. The boxed inserts that Porro includes throughout the piece encapsulate observations that support the message that the body of the criticism is designed to convey.

In Paragraph 6, the section on the outside game is concluded with a message about the irrationality, from the student's perspective, of the school's rules about suspension. "It's stupid to kick you out of school when you do something wrong. We don't want to be here anyway. . . ." Their logic seems impeccable. To support their observation, Porro shows us how Bob was able to convert suspension into a socially and financially productive experience. Such observations have credibility and give the reader pause: is there a better way to think about how schools might handle "behavior problems"?

The overall message of the criticism thus far is to point up the paradox that exists between the students' needs and aims and those of the school. We are shown how the low-achieving students cope with expectations to which they do not subscribe. It points out the sophistication of their reasoning—at least with respect to their own goals—and how bureaucratized rules can, on inspection, appear less than fully rational.

In doing this, Porro has also authenticated her observation by sharing with us intimacies that the students shared with her. We consequently get the sense that we are learning things that are not self-evident. Porro thus seems to be a credible observer and writer. But so far we have not entered the classroom.

Paragraph 7 brings us inside the school. We now move into the insider's game.

In Paragraphs 7, 8, and 9, Porro gives us factual information regarding the number and duration of classes teachers teach (seven periods of 45 minutes each) and conveys the sense of impersonality that generally pervades these classes. Evidence is provided: "A map of Vietnam, a poster of San Francisco, and a picture of a girl dancing." We get the feeling that the environment is shaped by a collection of ad hoc choices regarding room decoration.

In contrast to this impersonality, the students provide the color and vitality that makes a place a school. What one grasps through Porro's seemingly casual observation is the camaraderie and informality, the spirit of sharing that the students create.

The urgency of getting through the school day is conveyed in Paragraph 10 by the direct quotation of students asking how much time is left. Porro creates a view of school from the perspective of the student. She uses direct quotations to do so.

Now it is clear that her view of the students' view of schooling is, in the last analysis, *her* perception of the students' views. Perception is selective, and Porro has chosen. Yet, the criticism that she has written is replete with quotations, observations of subtle but significant events (the sharing of lollipops, candy bars, etc.) that create credibility. We get the sense that what she describes has occurred and what she concludes is supported by the situations as they unfold. Her conclusions are structurally corroborated even though one might argue that another educational critic might have focused on other phenomena. That may very well be the case, but even if it were, it would not diminish the quality of what Porro has written.

In Paragraph 12, the subhead "Pretend School" moves the reader into the classroom. This subhead, like the title of the educational criticism itself, embodies some of the major points Porro wishes to make. *Pretending* is a form of play, and playing is what Porro has told us a part of schooling is about.

The primary message of Paragraphs 12, 13, 14, and 15 is one that adumbrates one of the major conclusions of the study: there is between teacher and student a tacit agreement to help each other to get through the school day without severely imposing on each other's comfort. In developing this idea, Porro does not, for example, cast Mr. Arnold in the guise of a "bad guy" and the student as the "good guy." Mr. Arnold, she tells us, *is* a good storyteller; he *is* entertaining. He seems to understand what students will be receptive to and what "they'll turn off to."

Yet, he does not seem to challenge the low-achieving student with whom he works. He takes their status as a given, almost as a natural condition. Even though we might be sympathetic to him and to his needs as a teacher, we cannot help wondering whether his accommodating attitude is contributing to their underachieving status. Is this an example of a self-fulfilling prophecy? His readiness to accommodate to the students' apparent lackadaisical attitude might be one of the factors that contributes to the situation with which he must deal.

In Paragraph 19 we move into Bob's general science class. The same syndrome found in Mr. Arnold's mythology class continues. Mr. Cleary, Bob's general science teacher, does not expect much from the low-achieving student, and these students do not violate his expectations. He expects little and they provide little.

What happens here, however, from the standpoint of educational criticism is fortuitous. A visiting scholar who happens to be a professor of science education visits Mr. Cleary's class, observing and talking with Porro about his observations. What is significant here is that not only are the teacher's expectations low, but that Mr. Cleary pays inadequate attention to the substantive aspect of the biological content that he is attempting to teach. He focuses on marginal material, and engages in excursions into anecdotes but does not infuse these excursions with material designed to illuminate the central scientific points that are really important. In a word, the teacher consumes the students' time with diversion *from*, rather than *into* the scientific substance of biology.

At this point it is necessary to comment about the ability to critique curriculum content in the context of instruction. It is not likely that Porro, who for 9 years was an elementary school teacher, would have been able to appreciate what Dr. Pinot was able to see. He is a specialist in science education. She is not. His knowledge of biology and science education allows him to observe and appreciate what others who do not have expertise are unlikely to see. Educational critics who do not possess subject-matter expertise are not in a good position to appraise or even to recognize the content being taught (or not being taught) in a given field. To be able to critique competently the substantive aspects of biology, one needs biological expertise. To be able to appraise the quality of an art course, one needs expertise in art, and so forth.

Yet, not to have such expertise *does not* mean that no useful criticism can be developed. Porro's own critique of secondary school classes, a level of practice in schooling with which she is unfamiliar as a teacher and a subject matter that she does not know as an expert, did not prohibit her from making extremely interesting analyses of what she was able to see. As I have already indicated, we should expect that different critics will see somewhat different situations in any complex array of occurrences. Dr. Pinot might very well have missed what Porro did not.

In Paragraphs 21 and 22 we learn why, from Mr. Cleary's point of view, he proceeds the way he does in his teaching. Mr. Cleary believes that his students' major problem is one of low self-esteem, and he wants to help the students improve the way in which they regard themselves. Mr. Cleary has good intentions. Yet, he seems unable to recognize that positive self-esteem is also related to the reality of human performance; one is not likely to feel positive about one's self if one continually fails at the tasks one undertakes. Mr. Cleary's science teaching is not likely to help students deal effectively with scientific ideas.

In Paragraphs 24, 25, and 26 we are introduced to another of Bob's teachers, Ms. Morton. Here we find, as is true of the other examples of *pretend* school, a continuation of low expectations and small intellectual stimulation. Health instruction is supplied through the use of films.

Films can be an extremely useful vehicle for stimulating thinking and generating interesting discussion and debate. A film can act as a catalyst to help teachers reach ambitious educational goals. But in Bob's Health class we get the sense that films are used to provide a kind of baby-sitting service. Films, videotapes, and slides were used in over half of the Health classes Porro attended. The level of use might give us some concern, but what is really troublesome is the way in which they are used. No discussion, debate, or analysis follow their use. Instead, lectures are given, worksheets are completed. In spite of the fact that the teenage consumption of alcohol is a problem of national scope and that is certainly present at Claremont High, no attention is paid to it in Health.

As one reads about these "pretend classes," something like a somnambulistic episode seems to be present: sleepwalkers pass each other in the night, but never touch each other either intellectually or emotionally. There is compliance with routine. The class goes through the motions of educational activity but is not really engaged in an educational process. What one begins to appreciate is that one is observing a kind of machine that works; relatively few problems are created, and those that are, are handled through routine procedures. No one in the descriptions and analyses we have read thus far comes off as having an evil intent or a malicious motive.

High Standards Classrooms signals a shift in category. When we come on it, we wonder what it means. We don't wonder for long, because in Paragraph 27 Porro tells us that the high standards classroom refers to those in which teachers base their curriculum and instruction on what they believe students *should* be able to do, especially if these pupils are to succeed in college. Claremont High is a school in a community that has high expectations for its students. Many of its students go on to attend highly selective colleges and universities. Hence, preparation for such colleges and universities is an important educational priority within the community.

How does Bob fare in the high standards classroom in which he is enrolled? Not well—but not disastrously either. Although Bob received a negative evaluation on the midterm, he received a B on the Abnormal Psychology unit afterward. Porro's message: Bob has developed a keen understanding of what he must do to get through with a minimum of effort.

Porro's comments on the high standards classroom are focused more on the general character of curriculum and instruction than on Bob's particular reaction to this particular classroom. What we might infer is that Mr. Kelly, the teacher of the class, treats the class according to his image of what a college course would demand. Mr. Kelly's classes are largely lectures, and lectures delivered slowly enough for students to copy the material delivered verbatim. They are expected to take notes. They are expected to pass the test in order to pass the course. They are expected to perform in a manner consistent with college student behavior. What does Porro make of this? Why is this not "real school," her title of the section that follows? Probably because even though the teachers have high standards, the students were, apparently—we are not really told and the situation is not clearly described—not genuinely engaged in this course. They are complying with the teacher's expectations because Mr. Kelly is hard to outfox; he "knows how kids are these days." Even, it seems, in classrooms with high-achieving students, something significantly less than "real" education can occur. It is clear here, also, that Porro has a particular image of what counts as real education and that she uses the image to evaluate what she has seen.

It is sometimes suggested that educational critics should state their educational values at the outset. The purpose behind such recommendations is to inform the reader of educational criticism what values the critic holds so that the reader can understand how a classroom or school was interpreted and appraised by that critic. Although I have no objection to such an approach to writing, there are certain difficulties that it creates. First, how many of us can state our educational philosophies in a paragraph or two, or even in a few pages? Can we lay out in writing as a preamble to a piece of educational criticism a statement of what we believe? Will such a statement be so general that it will be difficult to use to anticipate how we would regard particular events and practices? Second, are not the varieties of educational excellence multiple, and is it not likely that no one statement of philosophy will do justice to all that we might value? I take a leaf from the fine arts. I value different painters and different styles and paintings for different reasons. I like the paintings of de Chirico because of the surrealistic mood he creates through the juxtaposition of objects one normally would not expect to see together—giant artichokes and clocks, trains, and sleeping figures. I find his use of color offbeat, yet well-related to the scenes he paints. Yet I like Monet for very different reasons: his color is scintillating. It vibrates with life and creates an atmospheric quality that is opposite to what de Chirico creates. I like the work of Barnett Newman for still other reasons. Is there a single philosophy of art that could be used to enable others to predict that I prefer the work of Mark Rothko to that of Morris Louis, and that I am less enthusiastic about the work of Paul Jenkins? I doubt it.

We learn of Porro's educational values *through* her educational criticism. Her philosophic preamble, as it were, is embedded in the statements she makes about Bob, Mr. Kelly, Mr. Arnold, and the other teachers and places she comments on. I believe that in "real life" it is precisely in this way we come to learn about someone's values. We do not ask for a preamble, a manifesto, a statement "up front"; and even if we were to get one of these, it would be used only to see if the actual behavior of the individual were consistent with what he or she told us. It is in the ongoing course of human activity that the operational values an individual or institution possesses are expressed.

Yet, after having said that, I should repeat what I said earlier: I have no objection to someone who wishes to put up front a statement of his or her educational values. What I do object to is the requirement or expectation that those values be so stated.

Paragraph 31 brings us to the third type of class that Porro has identified as operating within Claremont High—"real school." She tells us what she means by "real school," but her use of a phrase "a fair amount of time" is not particularly helpful. In real classes teachers gear their instruction to the academic level at which their students actually are; they use a mode of instruction that is tutorial or personal in character; and they provide activities for students that require them to be active rather than passive receivers of lectures delivered by the teacher. These characteristics are provided by Porro up front; they define the categories of classes about which she will write and are helpful to us as we read on.

Porro then attempts to differentiate between what it is that makes for real school as contrasted with pretend school. In this she is identifying characteristics on the basis of her observations and using those characteristics to create categories. These categories could then, in turn, be used to determine if other schools have similar types of classes. Do such classes exist at the middle and elementary school levels? What are the effects of such classes on students? Do students of different abilities react differently to such classes? And so forth. The formulation of concepts—images that differentiate one type of object or situation from another—is the necessary condition for theory development. The categories that Porro formulates for Claremont High could have an important use in the study of classes in other schools.

What, in addition to the features that have already been described, accounts for "real school"? For Ms. Golden's math class it is that she sets clear expectations for students: they know what is expected. But Porro is quick to point out that high expectations are not enough. Another factor, and perhaps a crucial one, is that Ms. Golden cares about the students with whom she works. Porro makes this clear in her description of how Ms. Golden talks to students, but lest there be any doubt, she quotes Bob as saying in response to why he produces for Ms. Golden, "because she deserves it." What Porro does is to support her interpretation and conclusion with direct quotations from students. She quotes their casual comments and gives examples to back up what she has said. All such devices help increase the credibility of her criticism. In addition, she is analytic about her observations: "I realize that she [Ms. Golden] treated them individually and related to them on two different levels—as their teacher and their friend." She then proceeds to give the reader some examples filled with quotations to illustrate that distinction.

Woodworking II is the second class, according to Porro, that is an example of "real school." (I wonder if two out of six classes of real school is about average for high school classes.) Here the feature that makes for real school is the active engagement of students in the work to be done. Woodworking, like auto shop and similar courses, does often require a level of active physical participation that is absent from many academic classes. Also contributing to the real-school character of Woodworking II is the respect students have for Mr. Teicher: "He's a real good teacher. He knows what he's doing." "He can fix anything. And he jokes around a lot." The image we get is of a teacher who is in control, competent enough to have an informal relationship with his students and able to demonstrate his skills to students. He thus gains their respect.

For my taste, this segment of Porro's criticism is thin. The entire class is treated in two paragraphs, and even though the description of this class is only a part of a larger body of work, it would have been helpful to have found out more about how this class functions, what students are learning, and why. Classes such as woodworking, auto shop, cooking, and even the fine arts are often regarded as frills, as courses with no intellectual challenge. Yet these classes might be among the most "real," the most *educationally* meaningful in which the student is enrolled.

Paragraph 40 brings us to the final section of Porro's educational criticism. Here she devotes her attention to the question "What does it mean?" Porro's talk here is one of further interpretation and evaluation. What does she have to say?

In this section she distills observations that were made only partially in the previous material. Bob, though not working, is winning the game he is playing—he is passing his courses and in doing so is not exceptional. Although the school is running smoothly, much of what goes on is not particularly educational for students. There are some significant educational experiences provided by some teachers in some classes, but these, according to Porro, are due to the exceptional quality of the teachers as people, not because of the structure of the school. In the end, it seems, Porro focuses on the particularity of individual teachers to account for the quality of what occurs at Claremont High.

I wonder if such an interpretation is a bit too glib. Does it not underestimate the potential influence of the educational leadership in the school? Cannot the principal and department heads, the community, and the other teachers have a significant role to play in moving the school from one place on an educational continuum to another? Is Porro not inadvertently assigning too much responsibility to the individual teacher and, by implication, suggesting that educational leadership can account for too little? Or am I perhaps expecting too much from context and leadership? I don't think so. If we can *only* rely on the talents, sensibilities, and commitments of individual teachers, the quality of education will be determined largely at the point of selection. Who chooses to go into teaching as a career, and who schools of education permit to enter the profession, will be the crucial decision points. Clearly, those decision points are important. The optimization of whatever it is that a faculty possesses in the way of talent, sensibility, and commitment is what educational leadership is about. Porro says precious little about this aspect of Claremont High.

Porro explains Bob's behavior on the basis of his inadequate academic skills, the paucity of really effective teachers he encounters at Claremont, and that for him school is boring. She speculates that being able to choose is something that is very important to Bob and that school is compulsory—Bob has not been chosen and he "doesn't like to be told what to do, so he rebels in any way he can." Yet he does work for Ms. Golden and for Mr. Teicher. He is willing to work in classes in which the teacher cares, where they have clear expectations, and where they are skilled. The ability to choose as an explanation for Bob's behavior goes only so far.

Near the end of her criticism in Paragraphs 46 and 47, Porro speculates further that Bob's actions may be modeled after the game that she believes to be ubiquitous among adults he observes. "It is quite possible," Porro observes, "that Bob is mimicking the approach to life we unconsciously teach through our actions. How do we play the game?" Here she is commenting not simply about Bob's behavior but on our culture. She then proceeds to relate our preoccupation with making the grade, with success, and—perhaps most of all—putting off real life today for a brighter day tomorrow—to the kind of game that Bob has learned to play so well. Her comments begin to develop a more general theme, a theme that runs deeper than the analysis of the high school experience. One senses in this section of the criticism a focus on the meaning of life. We are reminded of the verse with which Porro opened the piece:

> So much of adolescence is an ill-defined dying,
> an intolerable waiting
> a longing for another place and time,
> another condition.

We have returned, it seems, to the place from which we began. She provides both a description of the state of affairs and an interpretation. Through Becker's excerpt from the *Denial of Death,* she urges us to pursue a meaningful life.

Porro concludes her educational criticism on a note of optimism. There are times during the school day when Bob rises to the occasion of real school. What is needed is to go beyond the warm friendly relations between student and teacher, which are so generally a part of life a Claremont, to something that is genuinely educational. Although Porro has shed significant light on the experience of schooling for Bob and his peers, she does not say much about how the construction of such an environment can occur. But having a better fix on the problem is, after all, one of the important steps toward the achievement of such an end.

The Uses of Educational Criticism

The importance of attending to the processes of schooling as a basis for understanding what needs change is made clear by the foregoing educational criticism. Most efforts to evaluate schooling focus on the students' level of performance. Tests are administered to students—often having little relevance to what they had been taught—then performance is noted, and a mean derived from individual scores and recommendations is made, often for improving test performance. The National Commission on Educational Excellence recommends a longer school year and more time in the classroom. Is more time in the classroom appropriate for Bob and his peers? Why—it escapes my logic—if schools are huge mediocrities for students, should the situation for them be educationally better if they spend more time there? Some critics of schooling in America recommend more discipline and more homework, harder courses, and more clear-cut expectations. Only the last of these appears to have any relationship to performance and satisfaction with school in Bob's case.

Part of the reason why such nostrums are suggested is that they are comparatively easy to administer and to monitor. It is easy to find out if the school district is requiring its students to be in school 215 days in contrast to, say, 180. It is not so easy to determine if it is helping to improve the teaching practices of its professional staff. The kind of problems that exist for the students at Claremont High will not be resolved by requiring more homework, more time in school, or higher standards. Such prescriptions are much too superficial and much too simplistic. What needs significant change, and what is excellent in schools, can be known best when an observer is able to see the way in which schooling unfolds. It requires the connoisseurship to see what is significant but subtle, to appreciate the muted cues, the achievements that do not shout from the quarterback, the hidden lessons that are being taught. Porro's own sensitivity and, I am sure, her 9 years of experience as a teacher enabled her to hear the melodies of the classroom played in the lower registers of experience. Her writing skills and her conceptual ability made it possible for her to share those observations with us.

Can we generalize from what she has to say? Not in a formal sense. Claremont is not a random selection. Her observations were not random. There is no statistical measure of the reliability either of her observations or her interpretations. Yet we can learn in at least two ways about things that can help us in the future. First, we can use what she has disclosed to reflect on our own experience. To what extent does what she has written square with what we already know? Second, we can, if we are able, go to Claremont High and see for ourselves if what she has said is occurring. For the vast majority of readers, this is an undertaking that will not be possible. What is possible? There are other schools like Claremont High. Do they also display the features Porro has described? What her educational criticism provides is a guide to the perception of schools that we can have access to in our own locale. She provides a guide for making our own perception more perceptive and efficient. What is generalized from the study are anticipatory schemata for the perception of other situations. This method and these consequences are the stuff of ordinary life. It is how, in fact, we most characteristically go about dealing with the world. All we are doing here is refining such processes, bringing them to consciousness, and using them to understand and improve the processes of schooling.

13

Summing Up Some of the Major Points

I'd rather learn from one bird how to sing
than teach ten thousand stars how not to dance
e. e. cummings

In the preceding pages I have tried to describe major views of education and to identify some of the problems and issues that pervade educational planning and evaluation. In many respects, the ideas I have expressed fly in the face of those that now dominate our thinking about education and evaluation. For this I make no apology. So many of the assumptions that we have used have, in my view, been inappropriate for the problems with which teachers and others concerned with planning school programs must deal. Rather than to continue to pursue, virtually exclusively, goals and methods that have borne so little in relation to the effort, it has seemed to me useful to try to broaden the base from which educational inquiry can be undertaken. One aim of this book is to help establish that base and to contribute to its legitimation by indicating how qualitative forms of educational inquiry might be undertaken. In this final chapter, I would like to identify and discuss some of the major ideas found in the pages of this book that have given direction to my thinking.

The metaphors and images of schooling and teaching that we acquire have profound consequences for our educational values and for our views of how schooling should occur.

All of us, through the process of acculturation and professional socialization, acquire a language and a set of images that define our views of education and schooling. These images do not enter our cortex announcing their priorities. They do not herald a position or proclaim a set of virtues. Rather, they are a part of the atmosphere. When we talk about learners rather than children, competencies rather than understanding, behavior rather than experience, entry skills rather than development, instruction rather than teaching, responses rather than action, we make salient certain images: our language promotes a view, a way of looking at things, as well as a content to be observed. This language, I am arguing, derives from a set of images, of what schools should be, of how children should be taught, and of how the consequences of schooling should be identified. Language serves to reinforce and legitimize those images. Because differences between, say, terms such as *instruction* and *teaching* are subtle, we often use a new word without recognizing that the new word is capable of creating a new world.

The process of professional socialization is particularly influential in this regard. When prospective teachers and graduate students are trained (educated?), they are in a vulnerable position. Their careers are at stake. The selection of reading lists used in courses, the student's dependency on his or her professor's positive regard, the language that pervades the culture of the professional school or department, the need to use the right jargon on essays and exams: all of these factors create a powerful culture for socialization into the profession. The images are easily instilled: it is an overstatement to say that the student's professional life depends on it, but not much of an overstatement. Doing well means at least in part being able to use— indeed, to believe in—the images, concepts, and language of the culture within which one works as a student.

In arguing the importance of images and metaphors in shaping our conception of schooling and teaching, I am not suggesting that we would be better off imageless. All of us need some conception of education, schooling, teaching, and the student's role in order to deal with the professional world, just as we need some conception of honesty, truth, virtue, and affection to deal with our world in general. Images are the bedrock on which we build our theoretical palaces. They are indispensable. What I do argue is that the critical analysis of these images is seldom undertaken, and because they enter our minds unannounced we are in a poor position to treat them with the kind of scrutiny they deserve. What so often happens is that when our views are challenged by those holding different ones, instead of examining our own we tend to attack theirs, thereby avoiding the critical examination of what we believe by investing our energies in demolishing other views. The moral here is not to rid ourselves but rather to recognize what these structures are. This will help us guard against the unwitting internalization of subtle but powerful concepts that pervade the pages of professional journals in education, public debate about schooling, and other forms of persuasion and socialization.

*The dominant image of schooling in America has been the factory and the domi-
nant image of teaching and learning the assembly line. These images misconceive
and underestimate the complexities of teaching and neglect the differences between
education and training.*

In the preceding pages, I have argued that both image and language
play a crucial role in shaping our conception of schooling and that the
images and the language that they yield are necessary for conceptualization
to occur. Imageless thought is empty.

At the same time, the images we hold—whether of education, society,
democracy, or the good life—deserve analysis and critical appraisal. All
images are not created equal. The images of schooling, teaching, and learning often reflect a factory view of schooling and an assembly-line conception
of teaching and learning. Consider, for example, our interest in control, in
the productivity of schooling, in the creation of measurable products, in the
specification of standards against which products can be judged, in the
supervision of the teaching force, in the growing breach between labor
(teachers) and management (administrators), in the talk about quality assurance and quality control, in contract learning, in payment by results, in performance contracting, in the hiring of probationary teachers on the one
hand and superintendents on the other. What happens is that such terms
become ubiquitous, their conceptual implications are taken for granted,
they become a part of our way of educational life without the benefit of critical analysis. The consequences of such concepts and the images they imply
are, in my view, devastating. They breed the illusion of a level of precision
in practice that is likely to be achieved only by reducing education to training. The assembly-line mentality that was so persuasively described by
Callahan in his study of the scientific management movement in education
between 1913 and 1930 is still with us. Such an image of education requires
that schools be organized to prescribe, control, and predict the consequences of their actions, that those consequences be immediate and empirically manifest, and that they be measurable. In such a school, the exploitation of the adventitious, the cultivation of surprise, and the use of ingenuity
are regarded as "noise." They disturb routine and require that formula be
replaced with judgment. For, as everybody "knows," judgment is not to be
trusted.

There are several motives for the use of industrial metaphors in educational discourse. First, the use of such metaphors implies technical acumen
on the part of the user. It affords educationists with a technical language
that suggests systematization and rationality. When one is working in complex organizations that do not lend themselves well to systematic control
and long-range planning or prediction, the illusion of control and prediction can be secured by using language from domains where control and
prediction are possible. Eventually, the use of such language changes the

aims of the enterprise. Aims that do not lend themselves to the precision or criteria that the users of such language value are deemphasized. If none of the old aims will do, new ones are created. The curriculum specialist's position gets converted to that of a program manager. The education of school administrators increasingly takes place in the business school. Education becomes converted from a process into a commodity, something one gets and then sells.

For the lay public, the use of industrial metaphors is reassuring. Schooling is, after all, serious business. It is not surprising that business procedures should be regarded as more effective than discussions about mind, culture, wisdom, imagination, sensibility, and the like. Such terms and the images they convey have no business in an enterprise concerned with the really serious business of getting ahead in the world.

Rationality has been conceived of as scientific in nature, and cognition has been reduced to knowing in words; as a result, alternative views of knowledge and mind have been omitted in the preparation of teachers, administrators, and educational researchers.

The use of industrial metaphors in educational discourse is itself reflected in the ways that both laypeople and professional educators conceive of human rationality. This conception is one that is scientific in the context of verification rather than scientific in the context of discovery. *To know* has come to mean to be able to state some form of proposition and to be able to verify the truth of that proposition through scientific criteria.

Consider, for example, the term *cognition*. Cognition to a great many educators is contrasted with affect: cognition refers to thinking and thinking means linguistically mediated thought. Hence, unless one can utter in discursive terms what one believes one knows, one does not know. Given such a view of thought and rationality, human performance and experience that take form in nondiscursive modes of conception and expression are regarded as nonrational, somehow less a function of human intelligence and clearly having little to do with knowing or understanding.

This is perhaps nowhere better exemplified than in the use of the Scholastic Aptitude Test and the Graduate Record Examination, both of which focus on the use of discursive language and mathematical reasoning. Each of these areas depends on the student's ability to apply rules to the tasks that constitute the tests. The intelligence needed to create poetry, music, or visual art simply does not count.

This view of human rationality is not only reflected on those widely used tests; it is also reflected in elementary and secondary curricula. At the elementary and secondary levels, the primacy of scientific rationality is evidenced in the subject areas that are given priority, in the forms of human performance regarded as most important, in the amount of time devoted to particular fields of study, and in the requirements for graduation from secondary schools. Approximately 90% of all high school districts require some work in the sciences as a condition for graduation. Only about 10% require any work in the arts in order to graduate.

This limited view of human rationality permeates programs in teacher education, school administration, and educational research as well. Part of the impact results from an overt emphasis on the importance of systematic planning, on the use of operationally defined goals, and on the need for scientifically valid methods and criteria for determining educational effectiveness. The tacit ideal is that of the hard sciences, the methods used in the laboratory, and criteria that can be quantified and hence made "objective." The other part is due to the absence of other views of mind, knowledge, and intelligence, views that have a long and distinguished intellectual history but virtually are never considered in the curricular conversation.

I speak here of the views that argue the importance of tacit forms of knowing, of nondiscursive knowledge, of the expressive power of qualitative symbols, and those of Dewey as expressed in *Art as Experience*, one of his books that goes unread by American educators. When one view of mind, knowledge, and intelligence dominates, a self-fulfilling prophecy emerges. School programs emphasize certain modes of expression and certain subject matter fields. Educational evaluation uses modes of assessment consistent with the assumptions in fields that are emphasized, and "the most able" students are then rewarded by criteria that do not afford equal opportunity to students whose aptitudes reside in areas that are neither attended to in school programs nor adequately assessed. We legitimize our own view of what counts without serious consideration of alternative or complementary views.

The model of natural sciences on which much educational research is based is probably inappropriate for most of the problems and aims of teaching, learning, and curriculum development.

One might be more sanguine about the promise of conventional forms of educational research if past efforts had been more productive in guiding practice. The fact of the matter is that there is precious little practice in education that is data-based. When research does guide practice it is often because the values embedded in the research are consistent with the values of the practitioner. In such cases, the practitioner uses the research to legitimize what he or she already believes.

Some argue, of course, that the reason practitioners do not base their practices on research is that they do not read it. Although it is true that most teachers and school administrators do not read educational research, one can only wonder about the relationship between the effort and the return. There is typically little in research that can be used to direct practice; for example, the descriptions of the methods used in experimental research are minimal, dependent measures almost always underestimate the range of outcomes with which teachers are concerned, and one is almost always forced to violate the limits of scientific generalization in applying research findings to one's own teaching circumstance. Even those who do experimental educational research in teaching seldom use the results of such research to influence their own teaching.

If research conclusions as they are now presented in the pages of educational research journals do little more than advance the careers of educational researchers, what function do they have in guiding practice at the elementary and secondary levels? Educational research provides not so much conclusions or recipes for practice as it does analytical models for thinking about practice. I believe the models that are most readily used are those that are consistent with the educational views one already holds. Rogerians are seldom converted to a Skinnerian world on the basis of data.

In emphasizing the impracticality of conventional forms of educational research, I may have risked overstating the case. There are *some* educational practices that are based on research findings—computer-assisted instruction, behavior modification techniques, the Distar Reading Program, are examples—but compared with the world of educational practice, research-directed practices are rare. When they do occur, it is because they are highly focused and control-oriented. When it comes to educational aims that focus on the cultivation of productive idiosyncrasy, the development of imaginative thought, the acquisition of the skills of critical thinking, the invention of new modes of expression, educational research has not been notably productive. The character of the context has imposed itself too prominently. The contingencies are too salient when people are allowed to exercise free will. In such contexts, rules cannot replace judgment; procedures cannot be substituted for intelligence. The natural science model may not after all prove to be the most helpful means for improving the quality of educational practice or for understanding what occurs in human affairs. Our most difficult task might reside in determining when in our concerns and aspirations such a model of inquiry is appropriate and when other forms of inquiry are more felicitous.

The canons of behavioral science have too often determined what shall be studied and what shall be regarded as important in education.

The point here is straightforward. When an enterprise tacitly or explicitly establishes certain criteria for respectable intellectual work, problems are defined that can be treated by the methods that can meet those criteria. In educational research, this has meant that problems that do not lend themselves to methods regarded as empirically rigorous are neglected or, even worse, dismissed as pseudoproblems or inherently meaningless ones. The paradigm case of such occurrences is in doctoral programs in which students are expected to do some types of inquiry but not others, with the true experiment being the most rigorous ideal. Students who see other lights, who wish to march to other drummers, are often subtly persuaded that they will be seriously out of step, that nonscientific modes of inquiry (with the exception of philosophy and history) are not really acceptable ways to do a doctoral dissertation. Furthermore, in many schools there is still precious little offered in the way of courses on nonscientific research methods that would prepare students for such inquiry. In most schools of education, research is defined by methods taught in courses on statistics and research design—which almost always means quantitatively oriented inquiry.

When one adds to this the fact that most research journals—access to which determines many young assistant professors' chances for promotion—define research in the ways that research methods courses conceive of research, the significance of method in circumscribing the problems into which one can inquire is magnified even further.

The influence of canonized research methods does not stop here. Not only do such methods define what is amenable to study, they also often result in misleading conclusions about teaching and learning in school. That this should occur is ironic, because scientific research procedures are intended to yield objective, unbiased, factual conclusions. Consider, for example, research on class size. According to a great many research studies, class size has no bearing on what students learn. But when one looks to the indices of learning that were used in such studies, it turns out that learning is defined as achievement measured on standardized achievement tests. No attention is devoted to what children learn that tests don't measure.

What happens is that our view of learning is shaped by what we can measure, because what we can measure defines what we regard as learning. Because what is not measured is not considered, the conclusions we draw from what we do measure may seriously bias our perception and understanding. The bias in this respect is not a function of the logic of the inquiry but rather a function of what the criteria used in the inquiry exclude. We come to regard the ear of the elephant, if not as the whole, as its most critical feature.

The procedures and criteria used to evaluate students, teachers, and school administrators have profound effects on the content and form of schooling.

By and large, tests and testing procedures are not developed to influence the content and form of schooling. The major commonly held reason for their use is to determine how well students and teachers are doing in their respective roles. One uses tests to find out if students are learning, if teachers are effective, if school administrators are providing adequate leadership and guidance. Tests are used for these purposes, but their ancillary consequences are even more important. Because test performance is used as an index of educational quality, being able to do well on tests becomes a critical concern for students and teachers alike. As this concern grows, educational programs become increasingly focused on those content areas and forms of teaching that are related to test performance. The curricula of the school and the priorities that both students and teachers come to hold are influenced by what they think will influence test performance. Because tests test what psychometricians can measure, the canons of measurement indirectly influence what is taught in schools and what priorities will be established among those fields that are taught. Consider again the Scholastic Aptitude Test. This test is given to approximately two million students each year. It has two major parts: one verbal and the other mathematical. Scoring well on this test is important for admission to many colleges and universities. Students who want to score well believe—whether true or not—that the more courses they take in mathematics the more likely they will receive high scores on the mathematical section of the SAT. Thus, students often feel compelled to forgo courses in which they may have a genuine interest in favor of courses in mathematics that may improve their chances for admission to the college of their choice.

The influence of testing on school curricula is also felt at the lower levels of schooling, at the kindergarten and primary levels, where the quality of education is judged in terms of student reading scores and at the intermediate level where tests in mathematics and language arts become the public criteria of educational quality as test scores find their way onto the pages of local newspapers. Few teachers can withstand the almost certain public pressure for high scores on district- and state-mandated tests, even if the teachers wanted to pursue educational values that those tests did not assess. The social significance of the means used to measure student performance through testing is profound. I do not believe that major changes can be made in the content and aims of educational practice in schools without significantly broadening the criteria and methods used to assess educational effectiveness. The formalized rites of passage provided by tests are likely to constrain any effort to put into practice a really broad view of human development, despite our aspirations to the contrary.

Operationalism and measurement have focused so heavily on behavior that the quality of the student's experience has been generally ignored or seriously neglected.

The employment of empirical procedures that lend themselves to operational definitions, definitions that can be measured, has been one of the tenets of the social sciences. In education this has meant that overt behavior is to be the primary referent for determining the success or failure of a new teaching method, curriculum, or form of school organization. The measured variable referenced in what students do is critical for achieving objective description. The quantified variable can provide a score to the third or the fourth decimal place. Scores have attractive features; they can be added, subtracted, averaged, multiplied, and divided. They can be subjected to sophisticated forms of statistical analysis on the most up-to-date computers. Statistical conclusions can be derived that provide a compelling illusion of precision and objectivity, a value-free image of pristine description, untouched by personal judgment, bias, or human failing. Furthermore, the tests that often yield such data are prepackaged, almost hermetically sealed, before the students open them, and they are identical for all students taking the test. It is almost as if we did not want to touch or get to know the student; the aim is to remain distant, dispassionate, aloof, unbiased.

This attitude, often erroneously regarded as a mark of scientific objectivity, leads us away from understanding the quality of life the student is experiencing. Because our focus is on behavior, our aim is to shape that behavior and our success is achieved when that behavior is displayed. But what of the student's experience? How does he feel about what he is doing? Is what she is learning becoming a part of her worldview? Are the major lessons he is learning those that are being taught? To answer these questions, we must of course look beyond behavior. We must make inferences from behavior about experience. We must seek an empathetic understanding of the kind of lives children lead in school. But this means that we must make judgments, that we must attend to what is not easily standardized, and that we must get to know students as people. These are not relationships to which operationalism and quantification lend themselves. And when we add to this our penchant for efficient forms of standardization, all in the name of impartiality, we risk seriously misreading what students are learning in school. Beethoven's Fourth Symphony is not, after all, the incidence of D minor occurring in its four movements. It is not even the notes taken in their entirety on the score. Beethoven's Fourth Symphony is first and last music, sound, and experience. Rank forms of reductionism miss the point, and I fear that in our efforts to be "objective" and operational we too often miss the most telling points of school experience. Our penchant for standardization hampers our ability to perceive what is truly unique about students, and our preoccupation with measured behavior distracts us from appreciating and understanding what students experience in school and what they genuinely learn after all the test taking has been completed.

In urging that attention be devoted to the quality of life students experience in school, I am not suggesting that attention to performance be neglected. There has been in some schools at some periods in our educational history so much romantic attention to the students' feelings that the development of various forms of competence was seriously neglected. The neglect of competence and the failure to foster it appropriately can be a major source of emotional difficulty for children. Yet, our focus today is not in that direction. Our infatuation with performance objectives, criterion-referenced testing, competency-based education, and the so-called basics lends itself to standardization, operationalism, and behaviorism as the virtually exclusive concern of schooling. Such a focus is, I believe far too narrow and not in the best interests of students, teachers, or the society within which students live. Empathy, playfulness, surprise, ingenuity, curiosity, and individuality must count for something in schools that aim to contribute to a social democracy.

The history of the curriculum field has been dominated by the aspiration to tech-nologize schooling and to reduce the need for artistry in teaching.

Except for notable exceptions during the progressive era and during the free school period of the 1960s, the pervasive orientation among curriculum theorists and school administrators has been an effort to develop a scientifically based technology of curriculum and teaching. This aspiration was first articulated during the scientific management movement I have already alluded to. But it also was central in the writing of those who attempted to ground educational practice in scientifically based knowledge derived from educational research. The optimum aim of such inquiry was to yield laws that would do for educational practitioners what the work of Boyle, Einstein, and Bohr did for physical scientists. It was aimed at eliminating the chancy and undependable, and replacing them with rule, procedure, and method. What is the best method for teaching reading? What is the best method for instruction in mathematics? What is the optimal ratio of students to teacher in the classroom? How can we formulate aims that are so clear that anyone who can see can determine whether they have been achieved? How can we study the community to discover what our educational needs really are?

In the curriculum field, per se, this orientation culminated in the aspiration to develop teacherproof curriculum materials. Nothing was to be left to chance. The intelligence of the teacher was not something one trusted. Ideally, the teacher was to serve as a handmaiden to the materials that were produced by a set of methods that approximated those used in the manufacture of cars, washing machines, and television sets. If such procedures worked so well in these industries, why would they not work in schools, particularly in the design of curriculum and in the process of teaching? Examine our metaphors: they are right out of the computer sciences and the assembly line. Somehow, if curriculum planning could be systematized and teaching appropriately monitored, the complexities of large schools and school systems might be managed more efficiently. The whole affair would be simplified, everyone concerned would know just where we want to go and how to get there: nothing would be left to chance.

For teaching, the tack has been the same: what we need is precision teaching; we must diagnose and prescribe; above all we must individualize instruction. Never mind that these concepts have seldom been analyzed, they possess an aura of conceptual rigor. Particularly when the pressure is on, the vicissitudes of art and artistry can hardly be tolerated.

What is ironic is that most administrators, I believe, would regard most of what they do as resting on judgment rather than rule, as more a matter of art than a matter of science. Getting a feel for an organization, developing a sense of where your support rests, looking for openings in which you can move, bringing coherence and spirit to the central staff, keeping your finger on the pulse of the community, enjoying the playing of school politics: these are some of the features that dramatize the lives of school administrators. Indeed, they are crucial for survival.

The same holds for teachers; at its best, theirs is largely an artistic act. This is not to say that neither teachers nor administrators can use concepts grounded in scientifically based research. It is to say that concepts and generalizations must always be interpreted and that judgments that exceed the information provided by the generalizations must always be made if they are to be used in classrooms. Yet, despite practitioner's recognition of the arts of the eclectic, to use Schwab's phrase, those arts seldom get examined in the research literature. Indeed, they are often regarded with derision, something to be excised rather than cultivated, appreciated, or emulated. If scientific research on teaching provided more to practitioners than it does at present, its potential might appear more promising and the assumptions on which it is based more robust. This is not the case. Perhaps it is time that other assumptions about teaching and curriculum planning be entertained, not as a substitute perhaps, but surely as a complement to what we have been doing over the last 75 years.

Knowing, like teaching, requires the organism to be active and to construct meaningful patterns out of experience. At base, such patterns are artistic constructions, a means through which the human creates a conception of reality.

People, Aristotle once observed, by nature seek to know. To construct a meaningful world requires that we conceptualize patterns of the environment, recognize the rules that are both tacit and explicit in our social life, and feel sufficiently free to play and to take risks so that conceptual invention can occur. The creation of these patterns means in part the construction of structures that hang together, that are coherent, that express both order and interest and enable us to make sense of the world. This sense making is, I believe, an artistic act. We function as the architects of our own enlightenment; we build our own conceptual edifices and we want them to be beautiful as well as serviceable.

How telling that in our vernacular we talk about a *sense* of justice, making *sense* of things, having a *sense* for what is fitting and proper. Pattern is an inescapable quality of the organization of thought. Logic in action preceded logic as rule. The former made the latter possible, not vice versa. But patterning is not limited to propositions; it is a part of practical action and of activities aimed at the creation of art, per se. For schooling, or more properly for a theory of education, the notion that the human organism is stimulus-seeking and pattern-forming is crucial. What it implies is that all forms of learning, and some more than others, are at their best creative acts. The organism must always act, even to make simple distinction among sensory qualities. For the more complex forms of conception, more complex distinctions and patterns are necessary. But to make such patterns well requires an environment supportive of exploratory thought that encourages children to entertain ideas in a spirit of tentativeness. It is an environment that recognizes the desirability for children to have opportunities to create and play with patterns that enable them to appreciate the structure of ideas and to enjoy the process through which those structures are formed. In short, the aesthetic of both process and form must become a consciously sought virtue in schooling if schooling is to be converted from an academic experience into an intellectual one.

Teaching that is not hamstrung by rule-governed routine also requires the creation of patterns of thought by a teacher orchestrating an educational environment. Such a mode of thought is of course not required when teaching is like working on an assembly line. But to move teaching in such a direction is to deny students the opportunities to see creative intelligence at work. The classroom should be what it is trying to foster.

Practical judgment based on ineffable forms of understanding should not be regarded as irrational. Such judgment might reflect the highest forms of human rationality.

Universities have a tendency to make those who have high degrees of practical knowledge feel uncomfortable if they cannot provide reasons for action. In the academy, knowing how is nowhere near as honorable as knowing why. To know means, whether one can act appropriately or not, to be able to state in words what one knows.

Yet the tasks of teaching are far more demanding than discursive knowledge can explain. Indeed, if our activities as teachers and school administrators needed to be justified in relation to data-based, scientifically validated knowledge, most of educational practice would come to a standstill. We know, as Polanyi has pointed out, more than we can say.

The foregoing remarks should not be taken as a prolegomenon for mindless teaching or for curriculum development unenlightened by theory. In any case, neither is possible: mind requires conception to operate just as conception requires mind to exist. What the foregoing remarks do emphasize is that the process of knowing often uses qualities that are ineffable, that these qualities exist in both profusion and interaction, and that they must be "read" quickly and acted on swiftly if the information they yield is to be educationally useful. One example of how such knowledge is used is found in the activities of the stand-up comedian. To be sure, a comedian is not necessarily a teacher and a teacher is not necessarily a comedian, but an examination of the overlap between the two will be instructive.

For the stand-up comedian to function effectively, he must be able to "read" the qualities emanating from an audience. These qualities change as he proceeds with this act. The tone of the laughter, the tempo of his own words, the timing from line to line: all of these must be grasped immediately. Indeed, it is almost as though acting becomes second nature: no time to formulate hypotheses, no time to consult and compare theory, no time to seek substantiating evidence or data, and certainly no time to administer tests to determine the level of interest. Out of the flux of interacting the comedian must blend his own; a line 1 second late falls flat. And the configurations change. Automaticity and reflectivity must go hand in hand. The act must reach a crescendo and finally, when the audience has nearly had enough, be brought to closure.

The exercise of intelligence involved in such action is apparent in Arsenio Hall, Lily Tomlin, Roseanne Arnold, Joan Rivers, or Richard Pryor, yet no comedian could give a theoretical account of why what he or she does "works." We appreciate the comedians' skill, we recognize their artistry, but we do not expect from them psychological explanations that account for their effectiveness.

Because such explanations are not forthcoming, should we regard such activity as irrational or arational? Should we regard it as outside the realm of intelligence? I think not. What we are seeing when we see artists work—on the stage, in the studio, in the concert hall, and in a classroom—is not the absence of rationality and intelligence but the ultimate manifestations of its realization. Such individuals work with the creation and organization of qualities, the actor with the qualities of speech and gesture, the musician with those of sound, the painter with color, line, and form, and the teacher with words, timing, and the creation of educational environments. What all of these artists have in common is the aspiration to confer a unique, personal order on the materials with which they work. And most work in contexts that are in a state of continual flux. No recipe will do. No routine will be adequate, even if routines must be acquired as a part of one's repertoire. The point here is that much of what we know and the basis for much of our actions rest on inexpressible forms of consciousness that recognize the feel of things and sense the qualities that lead to closure and consummation. When we see such abilities displayed in public, whether on the stage or in the classroom, we should give them their due. The achievement of art is not, after all, a menial accomplishment.

The process of curriculum development, like the process of doing quantitative empirical educational research, appears much neater and much more predictable in textbook versions of curriculum development and research than it is in practice.

Philosophers of science characteristically distinguish in their writing between the context of discovery and the context of verification. In the context of verification, the rules of inference and logic are applied to determine the veracity and consistency of statements about the world. The context of discovery, however, is another matter. How ideas are generated, how insights are formed, and how fresh conceptions emerge into consciousness are not now adequately understood. And so, too, in writing about curriculum development and in reporting the results of empirical quantitative research, the illusion is created that the "rational" procedures outlined for describing curricula are the ways, in fact, that curricula are, can be, or ought to be created. It is not that the vicissitudes of curriculum development are denied; it is simply that they go unmentioned. As a result, the

372   ◆   THE EDUCATIONAL IMAGINATION

novice may get the impression that curriculum development typically proceeds or ought to proceed with the neatness with which it is described in
textbooks. This is misleading on several counts. First, it gives the inexperienced reader an oversimplified image of a process. Second, such descriptions tacitly imply that if one does not proceed along the lines suggested in
the textbook, something is wrong. One isn't doing one's job well. Third,
such presentations make curriculum development seem essentially like a
technical task. Once the objectives are formulated, the task is simply to follow a set of steps to achieve them. Such an image fails to help students of
education know how messy program planning really is and how much flexibility, ingenuity, and tolerance for ambiguity are needed to do it well. But
perhaps most importantly, such a rendering of what is a complex, fluid
process serves to sustain a limited conception of rationality and tends to
underestimate the qualities of playfulness, humor, and artistry needed to do
really excellent work in the curriculum field. It is important for students of
education to understand that what is finally published is a sanitized version
of the reality that preceded it, a reality that in many ways is often far more
interesting than its written description.

*The aspiration to create teacherproof materials rests on a mistake. Teachers need
materials that stimulate their ingenuity rather than materials to which they are to be
subservient.*

There is a temptation in the development of curriculum materials to try
to create materials that will replace the need for teachers to exercise judgment. The aim is to design materials that are so robust that they can withstand even the most incompetent teaching. The reason for this aspiration is
clear: if such materials can be created, then one can control the educational
process from a distance; one can build an error-free program. Having done
this, one need not rely on the frailties of human judgment; decision on the
part of the teacher can be minimized. Routine can replace reason.

Such an aspiration operates, of course, in the creation of the assembly
line. The ultimate manifestation of such an orientation to development is to
have the worker become an extension of the machine he or she uses.
Personal identity and idiosyncratic thought are replaced by something
more impersonal and more predictable.

Because some curriculum developers want the materials they develop to
be effective, they seek to make them as errorless as possible. All one needs
to do is follow the directions right on the package. The aspiration to construct such teacherproof materials is, in Illich's terms, the aspiration to create anticonvivial tools, tools that eventually define and determine what a
person should do. Although the assembly line is a paradigm case of an anticonvivial tool, such tools abound in cultures with high technology. In the
long run, such tools restrict rather than expand choice.

Convivial tools—the telephone, for example—expand one's options, can
be used without extensive training, do not restrict what messages one can

convey, and do not impose time constraints on their use. Convivial curriculum materials can have similar characteristics. They can provide a structure within which a teacher can operate, but they still can provide options; indeed, they can stimulate ingenuity.

Although different teachers may require different amounts of detail in the curriculum materials they use, the ultimate aim of such materials is to minimize the teacher's dependency on them, to offer to the teacher materials that will foster a sense of competence both in pedagogical matters and in the content to which pedagogy is directed. In short, one function of well-designed curriculum materials is to free the teacher to teach, with ingenuity, flexibility, and confidence.

Now such an aspiration, such a conception of teaching and the materials that teachers use, seems to some to be a utopian dream. Teachers, some say, do not as a group have the intelligence to use such materials, most do not want to change or learn, and the creation of such materials requires a level of sophistication that teachers do not possess. And on and on.

I believe that most people want to make their lives more interesting and that we seek events, ideas, and materials that help us achieve a more interesting life. The view that teachers are largely dullard is, in my opinion, false. It is simplistic and leads to a control-oriented conception of curriculum and an assembly-line view of the tasks of teaching. And even on the assembly line the results fall far short of their goals.

The creation of curriculum materials cannot be separated from our conceptions of what teaching is and what the teacher's role is to be. If the teacher is to be a functionary in a system that is standardized, a system that is intended to yield common outcomes for all students, then the aim of standardized materials in form, content, and use is consistent. Although there may be some educational services that lend themselves to such a view, its pervasive use diminishes the very qualities that educational programs, as distinct from training programs, can foster.

Differences among both educators and laypeople regarding particular educational issues and practices are often based on more fundamental, deep-seated differences regarding the functions and aims of schooling.

Differences of option about the virtues of particular educational practices are often the hubs of intense educational controversy. Should students be placed in tracks according to achievement? Should children be given letter grades in elementary school? Should curriculum content include controversial issues? Should common minimum standards exist for students at each grade level? Should elementary schools assign homework to students regularly? Should teachers be encouraged to take children on field trips? These are some of the questions for which a great deal of disagreement exists. Yet the differences among laypeople and educators alike with respect to these questions are not limited to the particular questions posed. If one digs a bit deeper, one finds far more fundamental differences in the ways in which the contesting parties conceive of the school's function—indeed, in how they conceive of education itself.

The existence of disagreement about educational practices should not be conceived of as a liability. It would be a serious liability indeed if a subject so important as education were not a matter of concern and dispute. The resolution of these views, even a temporary one, can be treated on two levels: through accommodation and compromise and through encouraging the contending parties to penetrate more deeply into the values that animate the controversy. It is here that the school administrator has a truly educational function to perform. That function is one of helping community members understand the implications of their educational values, to appreciate the alternatives, and to anticipate the second- and third-order consequences of the practices they are considering. Clearly, at some point in the debate, a state of readiness exists; the community or a portion of it is interested in an educational issue. Before positions get crystallized, before the prospect of a public reversal of a position makes it impossible for positions to be altered, the school administrator can help initiate the kind of dialogue that might educationally enlighten a community about an educational policy.

The major orientations to education that underlie disputed policies in schooling have been identified in Chapter 3. Although these views do not exhaust the possible positions groups might take, the five views described provide a framework through which the value base underlying the symptomatic issues might be identified and discussed.

The factors that influence schooling may have their source far from the school or school district.

Because schools are social institutions—that is, institutions created by the society for the achievement of socially defined purposes—they are influenced by the forces that pervade that society. Some of these forces operate in close proximity to the school: the availability of excellent teachers; the support, both moral and financial, that the professional staff enjoys from the community the school serves; and the quality of the physical resources with which teachers and students work are a few examples. But other factors also shape the direction and priority of the school, and some of these are subtle. The development of a pill to control conception, for example, has had an enormous influence on what schools will offer students in the way of school programs. The influence is not direct, but it is extremely potent nevertheless, because with fewer children in school, there is less money made available to schools by the state. With less money, school boards must cut back on expenditures. Because most of the money a school district expends goes into salaries, when funds are cut salaries must be cut, and this means the loss of programs.

I use the birth control pill as one example of an important source of influence on schooling, an influence that is several times removed from schooling itself, yet has had significant consequences.

Other influences such as national testing programs, college admission criteria, and federal funding made available for some fields but not others also have important effects on the climate within which schools operate. This climate makes it possible for certain priorities to emerge and for certain groups to exercise influence. Sputniks I and II put the capstone on a growing sentiment during the first half of the 1950s that American public schools were too soft. With Sputnik, those holding this view had the leverage they needed to drive home the message and to have it supported by increasing amount of federal funding for curriculum development and teacher training in mathematics and the sciences. Thus, what occurred halfway around the globe influenced what happened in our educational backyard in the United States.

What such examples illustrate is that educational practices and educational priorities are not the sole consequence of the aspirations of either educators or those in the communities that educators serve. Schools are a part of a large cultural ecosystem. They respond to that system in ways that are not always obvious. If those interested in educational change are to be successful, aspects of that system—though they be far removed from the school—may need to be altered. In sum, the alteration of constraints and other forms of influence at several levels removed from the school may be the most effective way to change what goes on in schools. A direct attack on an immediate school program might not be the most effective way of dealing with the problem.

To identify these distant constraints calls for a holistic, ecological view of schooling. One must be in a position to see the system as one whose boundaries extend beyond the contours of the school district. Furthermore, one must have the conceptual ability to identify and analyze the relevant forces. Politics, the so-called architectonic science, is one potentially useful frame of reference for such an analysis. But whether the framework is that of political science, sociology, and social psychology, economics, or cultural anthropology, analytic skills are not sufficient. One must know what is educationally significant in order to give direction to analysis, and one must be able to exercise the arts of political action if analysis is to lead to more than an academic understanding of a state of affairs; the point of analysis is to lead to the creation of the conditions that will allow the educational process to thrive.

Educational slogans serve to replace educational thought and enable school practitioners to avoid dealing with the persistent problems of practice.

The problems that beset schooling are not due to the behavior of any single group. I have already argued that, by and large, those working in universities tend to have marginal interest in the improvement of educational practice, per se. Similarly, educational practitioners, particularly those serving in administrative positions, have a tendency to avoid the tough educational problems by grasping the slogans that parade through the field of education year after year. Consider, for example, the back-to-basics movement. Throughout the United States, communities (or vocal segments thereof) are urging a return to "basics." School leaders are all too willing to oblige. Because of the mass media proclaim that schools are slipping in their effectiveness, that test scores are dropping, that Bonehead English is oversubscribed in colleges and universities, the time appears ripe to return to the basics. But what are the basics anyway? Are they the same for all students? If they are the skills of reading, writing, and arithmetic—the three R's—does it matter at all *what* is read or written? Does imagination count in writing? Does any book or magazine article count equally in demonstrating the ability to read? At what level does competency in mathematics exceed what is basic? Alas, such questions seldom get asked. Instead, slogans replace analyses, and school practitioners too often lead the race toward an ideal that has not had the barest form of analysis or critical scrutiny.

This example is not an isolated case; *individualization* is another one. What counts as a form of individualization? Does individualization refer to the rate at which students move toward the achievement of common objectives? Does it require that goals be differentiated, as well? Does individualization refer to the differentiation of teaching methods for different students, to the differentiation of the response modes that students can use to demonstrate what they have learned, to the forms of presentation by which they encounter new concepts? If one looks at the field, one finds hardly a soul who is against individualization, but when one presses for a clarification of what the term means, too often a superficial understanding of the term's possibilities is revealed.

Similar conditions exist with respect to terms such as *educational standards, flexible scheduling, peer tutoring, learning by discovery, the inquiry method*, and the like. The virtues of such slogans for the practitioners—particularly for those in administrative positions—is that they provide a public image of up-to-date educational practice. In addition, they confer on the educational practitioner who uses them in the presence of laypeople an aura of technical sophistication. Such a consequence of technical language is not unusual: medicine is another prime example of an area where language is so used. And technical language has, of course, its virtues; properly used, it increases precision in discourse. But in education, such language is all too often pseudotechnical; it covers up or substitutes for the kind of rigorous thought that educational problems require.

The school is the basic unit of educational excellence.

By and large the most "natural" unit in schooling is the school. The school both physically and psychologically defines the environment of teachers and students. It is the school that establishes the structure within which teachers and students must function and that establishes a territory distinct from the rest of life. The school possesses a physical character that no other aspect of education can achieve: a school district is too large and a classroom is an integrated part of the physical structure of the school. The school stands out as an entity; it is something that secures allegiance and provides students with an identity.

But beyond the physical characteristics of the school and their impact on our perception, the school defines a set of social parameters, as well. The structure of classrooms, the rules, time schedules, and the psychological climate create the milieu within which the purposes of schooling are realized.

For the school to function as an organization, some modus vivendi must be established, some balance must be secured among the forces that animate it. As in a living organism, the parts exist in a transactional state, and changes in one part must be compatible with the rest of the structure or the changes must be so potent as to change the rest of the organizational structure. If the structure of the school as a whole is resistant to change, as is true of many schools, then it is likely that the change agent will itself be changed rather than the school.

Consider, for example, the life-style of beginning teachers. Beginning teachers often enter the school with strong aspirations acquired during their professional training or on their own. Most new teachers soon realize that their aspirations must be significantly changed to fit the school. For some teachers, the compromise is such a difficult ethical problem that they choose to leave teaching rather than alter their core educational values. After a few years of teaching, those who choose to remain adapt to the institutional press and eliminate the sharp corners of professional idiosyncrasy. They become a well-rounded lot, a more homogeneous and adaptive group that does what it must to survive.

Because the press of the institution is so significant, the problem of bringing about change within classrooms cannot be isolated from the school's constraints on and incentives for change. In this regard, the principal of the school is of central importance. In general, the principal sets the tone for the school and provides the formal positive and negative sanctions, even when a well-regulated evaluation system is not in force. His or her expectations for punctuality, record-keeping, student performance levels, educational priorities, and the like are communicated in both formal and informal ways. Other factors, including timetables, the allocation of fiscal resources, and the allocation of space, further define both what counts in school and what is possible. Given these conditions, attention to the macrostructure of the school becomes crucial for those interested in raising the quality of the educational experience for students. It is difficult for a teacher to sustain a mode of teaching or to achieve educational aims that are contradicted daily by the culture in which he or she works. Such a teacher must almost always adapt to or leave the school; only in rare cases can a teacher alter the macrostructure. So what I am arguing is that the professional life-style of the teacher is significantly shaped by the characteristics and structure of the living organism we call a school. In a rational model of schooling, the form of the school organizationally as well as physically follows the function it is intended to perform. In the real world, it is more often the case that the function of the school is defined by the forms we create to manage it.

The current emphasis in schools on verbal and mathematical reasoning seriously biases our conception of human intelligence and significantly impedes the development of socially valuable interests and aptitudes.

The coin of the realm in schooling is words and numbers, so much so as to constitute a form of educational inequity for students whose aptitudes are in realms other than verbal or mathematical. Consider the impact of testing on the educational mobility of students. Virtually all achievement tests given to students in elementary and secondary schools by school districts or state education agencies assess verbal or mathematical performance. Students whose aptitudes are verbal or mathematical or who have opportunities out of school to learn in these areas of human performance are advantaged. The game being played, as it were, is consistent with their background or capacities.

But what of those students whose aptitudes lie outside of these realms: the dancer, the poet, the painter, the filmmaker, the composer? As things now stand, their aptitudes never enter the equation for calculating intellectual ability. To clarify this problem, consider what would happen if current practice were reversed. Instead of verbal and mathematical criteria, suppose that a student were admitted to college on the basis of the quality of his or her drawings, musical performance, dance, or films. Suppose that written skills did not count, nor did mathematical skills. How equitable would that be?

This is not a plea to substitute nonverbal and nonmathematical forms of performance for the forms now used but rather to broaden both the curricular options and criteria that affect students' lives.

A part of the reason such skills are now emphasized, I believe, is that they lend themselves to forms of testing that appear objective. For example, Educational Testing Service, which once tested the writing skills of students by having them write compositions and having readers judge their quality, has now devised a "writing test" in which students respond to multiple-choice questions that can be machine-scored. Because the multiple-choice test correlates highly with the scores assigned by judges to written compositions, the latter is an efficient way to learn about the former. Yet one cannot help but wonder what readers were attending to when they were judging compositions that were actually written: insight, imagination, sensitive use of language, ability to use metaphor, inventiveness, significance of the substance of the topic?

We see once again that our technique defines our ends; rather than being servant, it becomes master. What we can efficiently do that meets one model of objectivity sets the ceiling on what we believe we ought to do. This goes so far as to determine who is gifted. In California, for example, students who have a measured IQ of 130 or more are classified as "mentally gifted minors" and the school is entitled to additional state funds. What about the artistically gifted minor?

The cost of such a parochial view of the human mind is borne not only by the students who must experience the inequity of denied opportunity but also by the society that may never reap the benefits that such children could provide to the culture at large. The time for changing this situation is long past.

What often goes unnoticed by both secondary school faculty and those working in colleges and universities is the impact of testing on the curriculum of both institutions. The impact is essentially a conservative one. Because universities use high school test scores to predict success in college and because those scores are derived primarily from performances on written and mathematical tasks, the predictive ability of the scores increases as the tasks in college increasingly approximate the skills tested. The same holds true for high school grades. If one seeks to make good predictions, one can do this by designing programs and using criteria that share common assumptions and require similar skills. Either the secondary school program must approximate that of the university, or the university program that of the secondary school. Given the aspiration to predict, a conservative circle emerges. The greater the competition for admission to universities, the more conservative the secondary school program becomes for those who seek such admission.

When one adds to this the fact that many university admission committees discount grades in art, music, theater, and other creative forms in calculating grade-point average, the liability to the student who wants to take secondary school courses related to his or her interests—if those interests are in the arts—is quite clear.

The school must be a growth environment for the teacher if it is to be an optimal growth environment for the student.

Very little attention has been devoted in educational planning to the impact the school has on the professional staff who work there year after year. Somehow we expect the central problem in planning educational programs to be that of designing an environment or a set of learning opportunities that will foster the growth of the student, almost independent of the effects those conditions may have on teachers and school administrators. I want to suggest that neglecting the needs of the professional staff of schools is one of the surest ways to decrease the quality of the educational service provided to students. Teachers, like everybody else, somehow adapt to or change the environment in which they function. When change is not possible, adaptation occurs. For many teachers and school administrators, such adaptation has resulted in the development of routine repertoires and stock responses that they have learned to use to cope with the demands made on them. Rather than having an environment that stimulates, they function in an environment that affords them few new challenges. They want to do well in the eyes of their students, and many have developed the kinds of routines that will enable this to occur. But life in the fullest sense is that lived outside of school; it is reserved for weekends, vacation periods, and sabbaticals. Growth occurs outside rather than inside the place where teachers spend most of their waking hours.

For many teachers, especially midcareer teachers, this has begun to pose a problem of the first order. Opportunities for professional advancement are not as plentiful as they used to be, because of the decline in school enrollment. Because of budget cuts, sabbatical leaves are more difficult to secure. The public's desire to judge the school's quality by the measured performance of students exacerbates these pressures. For many teachers unionization has been one way of coping with these problems, but increases in pay will never adequately compensate for an inadequate professional life space. What will it require of school programs to provide the conditions for teachers and school administrators to have time for reflection, for experimentation, for adequate planning, for consultation with new colleagues? Would the achievement level of students decrease if teachers were given 3 or 4 hours each week to meet for purposes of educational planning or individualized work?

The specific forms that such planning might take may differ from school to school, but the need to work in an environment that allows—indeed puts a premium on—the teachers' and administrators' professional growth will not.

One of the things I have learned in talking to school administrators is that a great many of them moved into school administration to escape the constraints and the routine of the classroom. What they were seeking was not so much power or money but a more interesting professional life, a wider field in which to play. The creation of an expanded professional life space, the development of an environment that is educational for teachers and administrators as well as students, is, I believe, one of the most seriously neglected needs in education.

Schools teach both more and less than educators realize.

In Chapter 4, I pointed out that each school offers children three curricula: the explicit curriculum that is public and advertised, the implicit curriculum that teaches because of the kind of culture that a school is, and the null curriculum, those voids in educational programs that withhold from students ideas and skills that they might otherwise use. The utilities distinguishing among these types of curricula are several. First, it allows one to raise questions about what children are learning that would never be identified if one were to focus only on the intended goals of the explicit curriculum. We tend in the planning of school programs to act as though what schools explicitly teach constitutes the whole of what students learn. Yet what schools teach by virtue of their structure, their expectations, their timetables, and their rules might in fact have a much greater impact on what students learn.

Second, by distinguishing among these three types of curricula we are in a position to evaluate the consequences of each. A school might offer an exhilarating course on critical thought about social problems and yet might, in its general culture, be promulgating a type of intellectual dependency that contradicts the values and skills the course attempts to foster. Consider, for example, the use of student hall guards in secondary schools. In some schools, such guards are on duty at every intersection in the building. Monitoring these halls guards are teachers, one assigned to each floor or section of the school. Monitoring these teachers is a vice-principal who from time to time makes rounds to be sure that the teachers are on duty; the teachers in turn monitor the hall guards, who in turn ask each student who walks through the halls after classes have begun to see his or her hall pass. What we have is a hierarchical system, all in the service of control. One might wonder what such a system teaches students who are enrolled in courses dealing with critical thought about social problems.

Third, these distinctions remind curriculum planners to look beyond what is not traditionally offered in school programs in order to identify areas of human understanding that have been neglected. A great deal is offered to students in school that is not a function of choice but rather a function of tradition. Much of what we teach, we teach because it has always been taught. The concept of the null curriculum reminds curriculum planners to ask about what has been neglected. For example, which forms of knowing have been omitted and what is their significance? What are the potential consequences of curricular neglect? I am not suggesting that the program of the school can teach everything or that it can be all things to all people. I am suggesting that content inclusion–content exclusion decisions are among the most important decisions curriculum planners can make. These decisions, as far as possible, should be made with appropriate consideration to what one rejects as well as to what one accepts for inclusion in school programs. What we don't teach might be just as important as what we do.

The complexities and significant qualities of educational life can be made vivid through a method used to describe, interpret, and evaluate other cultural forms. This method is one of criticism; in education it can be regarded as educational criticism.

One of the central focuses of this book concerns the influence that testing has on the ways in which we conceive of the effectiveness of schooling, curricular content, and educational aims. Since the turn of the century, testing has rested on fundamental beliefs about how we come to know; our use of testing as means of educational evaluation is itself rooted in the episte-

mology of science. Knowledge about educational practice and its consequences is to be derived by applying methods of social science to the study
of education. The more closely those methods approximate those used in
the laboratory, the more positive we can be about their conclusions.

Although I certainly do not advocate abandoning scientific methods to
study educational phenomena. I have argued in this book that those methods in no way exhaust the means through which educational phenomena
can be studied. This book has attempted to provide not an alternative but
rather a complementary approach. The approach that my students and I
have been using at Stanford University is called educational criticism. It
depends on the observation and appreciation of the events of materials that
constitute educational life. The object of such attention is to perceive those
qualities that are educationally significant.

The appreciation of such phenomena requires, I have argued, the application of educational connoisseurship. But connoisseurship is a private
event, and, to be made public, some externalization of what one appreciates
must occur. It is there that criticism operates. The aim of criticism is to
reeducate one's perception of the phenomena to which one attends.
Criticism is a written or spoken statement about something. Educational
criticism is about educationally important matters. Because criticism is in
large measure—although not exclusively—an artistic creation (the critic
must render the qualities he or has perceived in a form capable of eliciting
in part, an empathetic understanding), the skills the critic needs are significantly artistic in character. The critic needs to perceive what is subtle and
complex, must appreciate the connotative meaning as well as the denotative
meaning of events, and must be able to make those meanings vivid through
the language he or she uses to communicate. The major aim of such activity
is not primarily to discover laws but rather to illuminate, to provide those
concerned with education with the kind of understanding that will enhance
their own teaching or professional deliberations. In this sense, educational
criticism leads to a more complex and particularistic view of an educational
situation. It aims not at the reduction of complexities but at their illumination in order that the factors and qualities that make situations unique as
well as general can be understood. With such understanding I believe that
both educators and laypeople are more likely to be able to exercise intelligence about the matters of concern to them.

That such an approach to educational evaluation has not been salient in
the literature is obvious to anyone familiar with it. Our conception of
research, our conception of knowledge, and our conception of evidence
have derived from other premises. The time has come, I believe, to look to
other views, not as a rejection of old ones, but for the promise that a fresh
perspective can provide. Educational criticism represents one place on
which to stand.

Schools are robust institutions that are difficult to change; hence, successful change is more likely as one recognizes and addresses the variety of interacting factors affecting the way schools function.

School reform efforts have typically focused on single-shot panaceas: flexible scheduling, educational accountability, curriculum reform, authentic assessment, site-based management, voucher programs. None of these single-shot efforts have had or are likely to have a major impact on the character of schools. Schools possess a tradition that virtually all who inhabit them understand. Teaching is one of the few professions in which professional socialization begins at age 6. Most children spend more time with their teacher than they do with their parents. The role of teaching and the life of schooling is learned early in life.

To create schools that genuinely educate, policymakers must pay attention to the deep aims of the enterprise, to the structure that schools possess, to the curriculum that they offer, to the quality of teaching that occurs, and to the forms of evaluation and assessment that are employed to understand its consequences. In short, an array of interacting factors must be taken into account in both planning and assessing the consequences of schooling. Once they enter the school, single factors are gradually eroded by virtue of their inability to change the context in which they are to operate. Inductive forms of learning, for example, become eroded as teachers recognize that they will be held accountable for outcomes that do not require the time-consuming character of inductive methods. The desire to integrate among curricula erode as teachers find it increasingly difficult to find time to collaborate; the ways in which schools are structured makes discretionary space limited for teachers. And so it goes. What we need to recognize is that schools are like ecological systems. We need to consider the entire balance of the institution and this will mean attending not only to what goes on inside of schools but also to what goes on outside of schools. The public needs to understand better than it does at present what matters in education. It needs opportunities to reflect on its deepest aspirations and to explore some of the visions of our deepest thinkers concerning the possibilities of education. We ought not to be limited by existing conceptions of what schools ought to be. What they have been is surely not good enough for our children.

We also need to address the constraints that other agencies in the society impose on our schools. The criteria used by universities for purposes of admission have a profound effect on which subjects in the secondary school become privileged. This, in turn, influences the priorities that operate at the middle and lower school level. Secondary schools ought not, in my view, be primarily in the business of preparing for college. As long as secondary school teachers, school boards, and communities regard schooling primarily as a vehicle to get some place else, the possibilities of the present will be lost to an out-of-reach future. We simply need a different perspective on why we do the things we do rather than a perspective that justifies the aims of schooling in something called "preparation."

Thus, the last major point I wish to emphasize here is the need for an ecological orientation to school reform, one that does justice to the complexities of the enterprise. It is the mark of a sophisticated educator to understand this complexity and to avoid the panaceas, nostrums, oversimplifications, and slogans that are often found in the public press. We need to provide responsible leadership that embraces the possibilities of education and is willing to explore the alternative routes that can be traveled to achieve them. If this book has made those possibilities more vivid and if it has provided a sense of what it may take to realize them in our schools, the effort will have been worth it.

Index